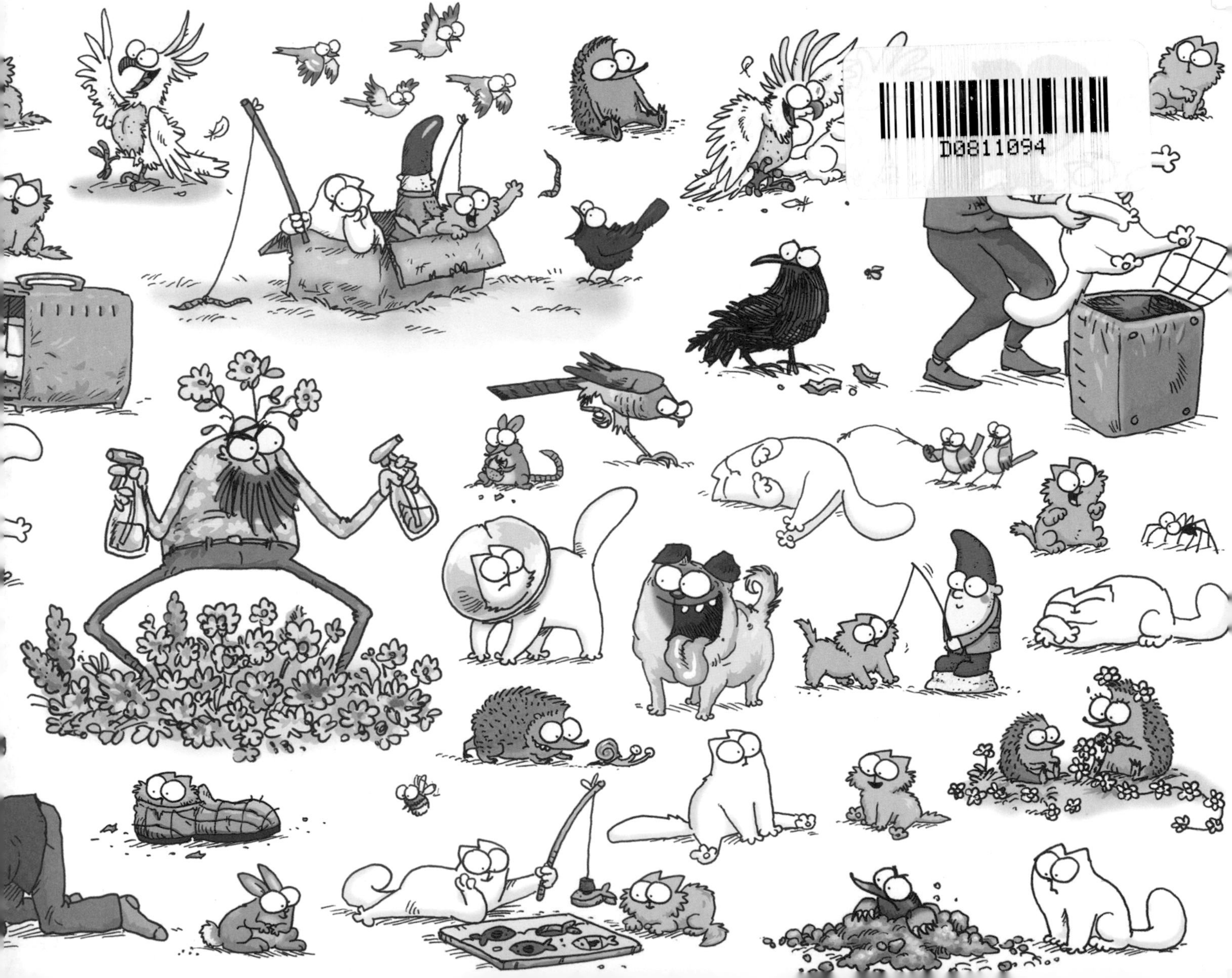

Simon's Cat ©

Simon's Cat©

Off to the Vet

by

Simon Tofield

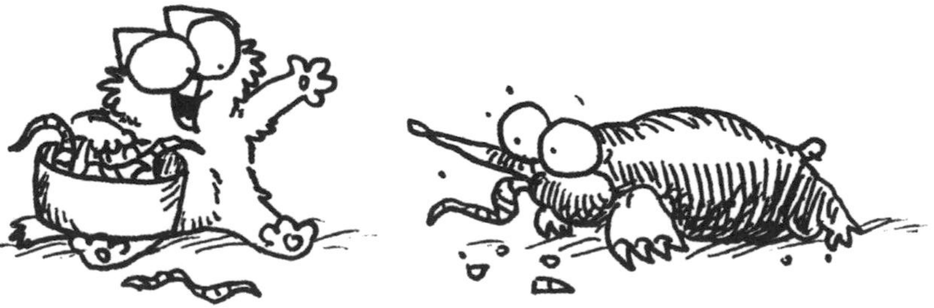

CANONGATE
Edinburgh · London

Published in Great Britain in 2015 by Canongate Books Ltd, 14 High Street, Edinburgh EH1 1TE

www.canongate.tv

1

British Library Cataloguing-in-Publication Data
A catalogue record for this book is available on
request from the British Library

ISBN 978 1 78211 587 8

Typeset by Simon's Cat

Printed and bound in Slovenia by GPS

For my little James

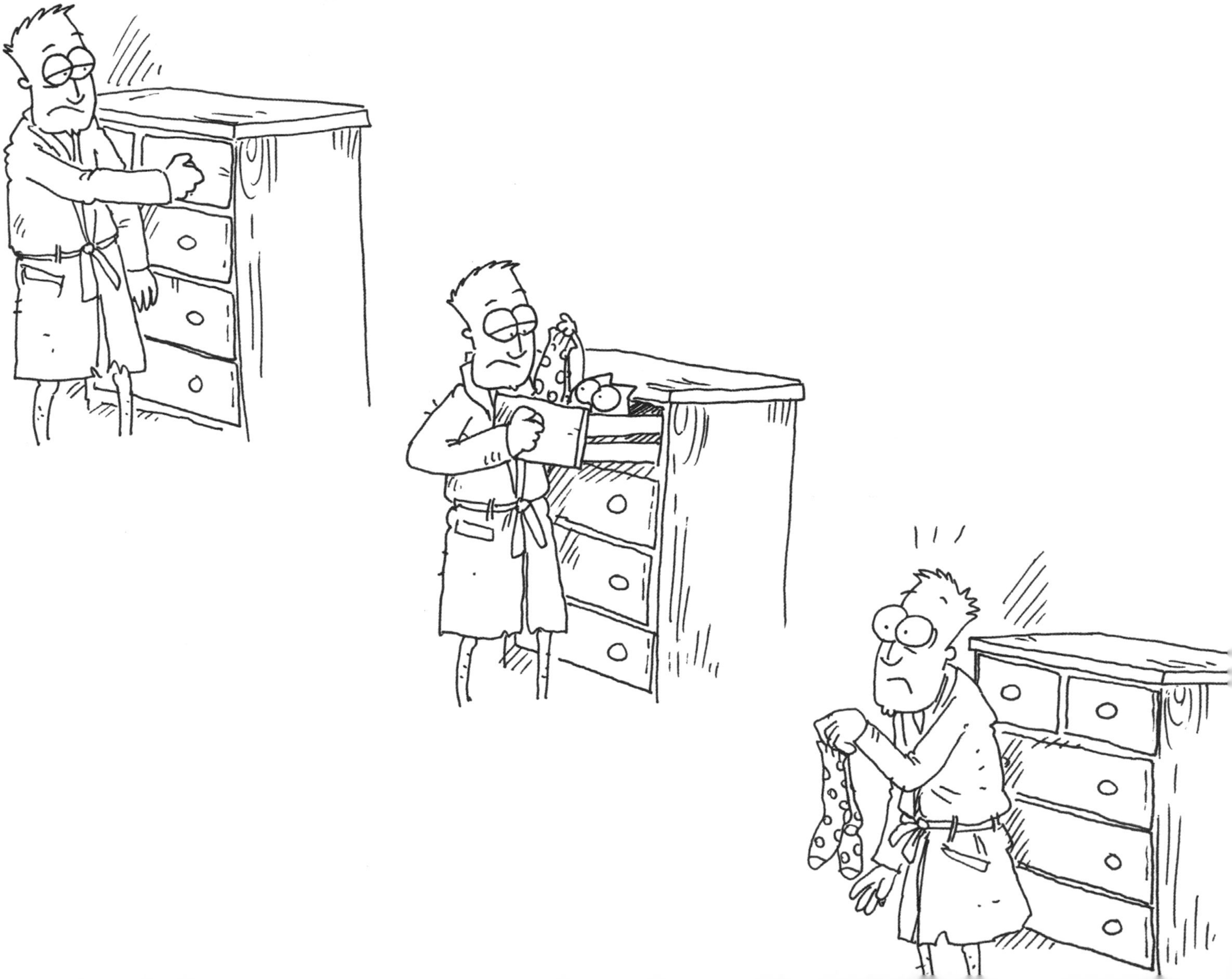

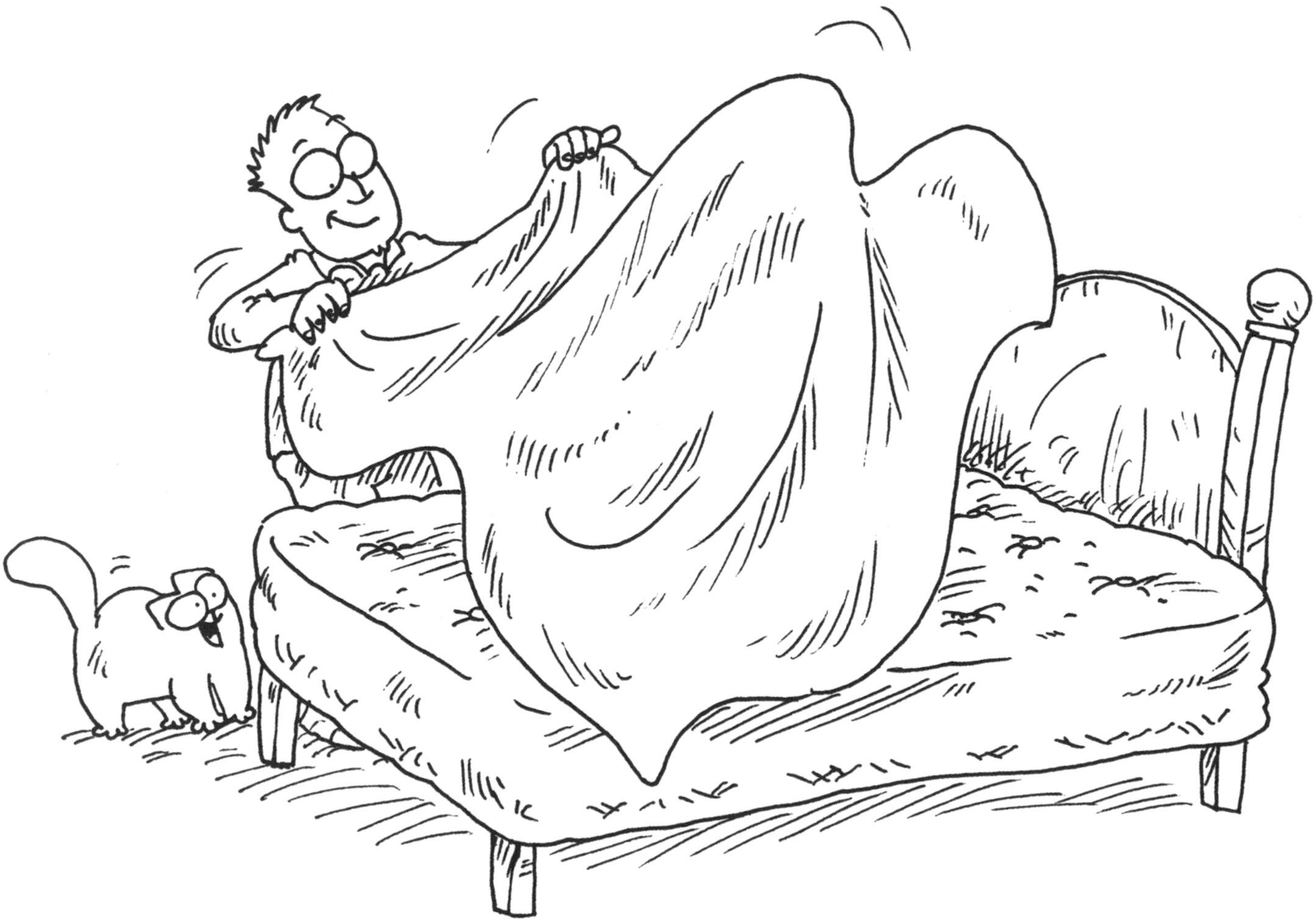

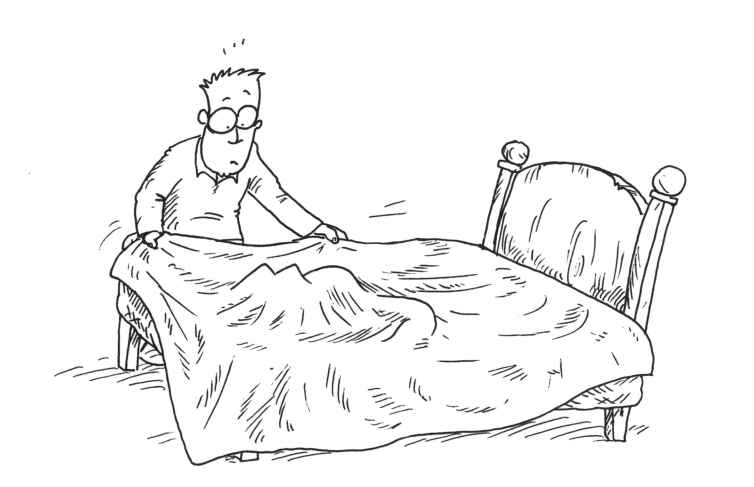

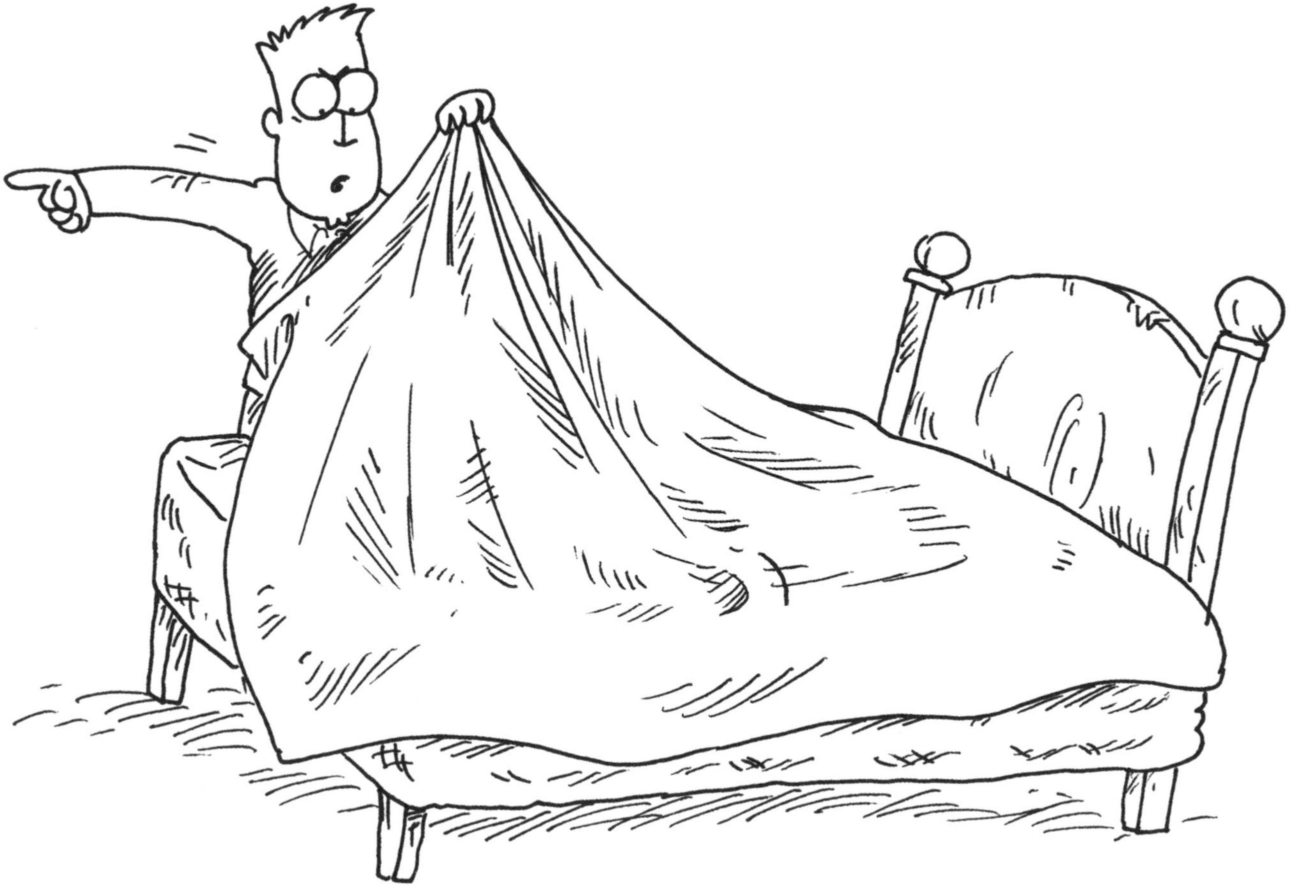

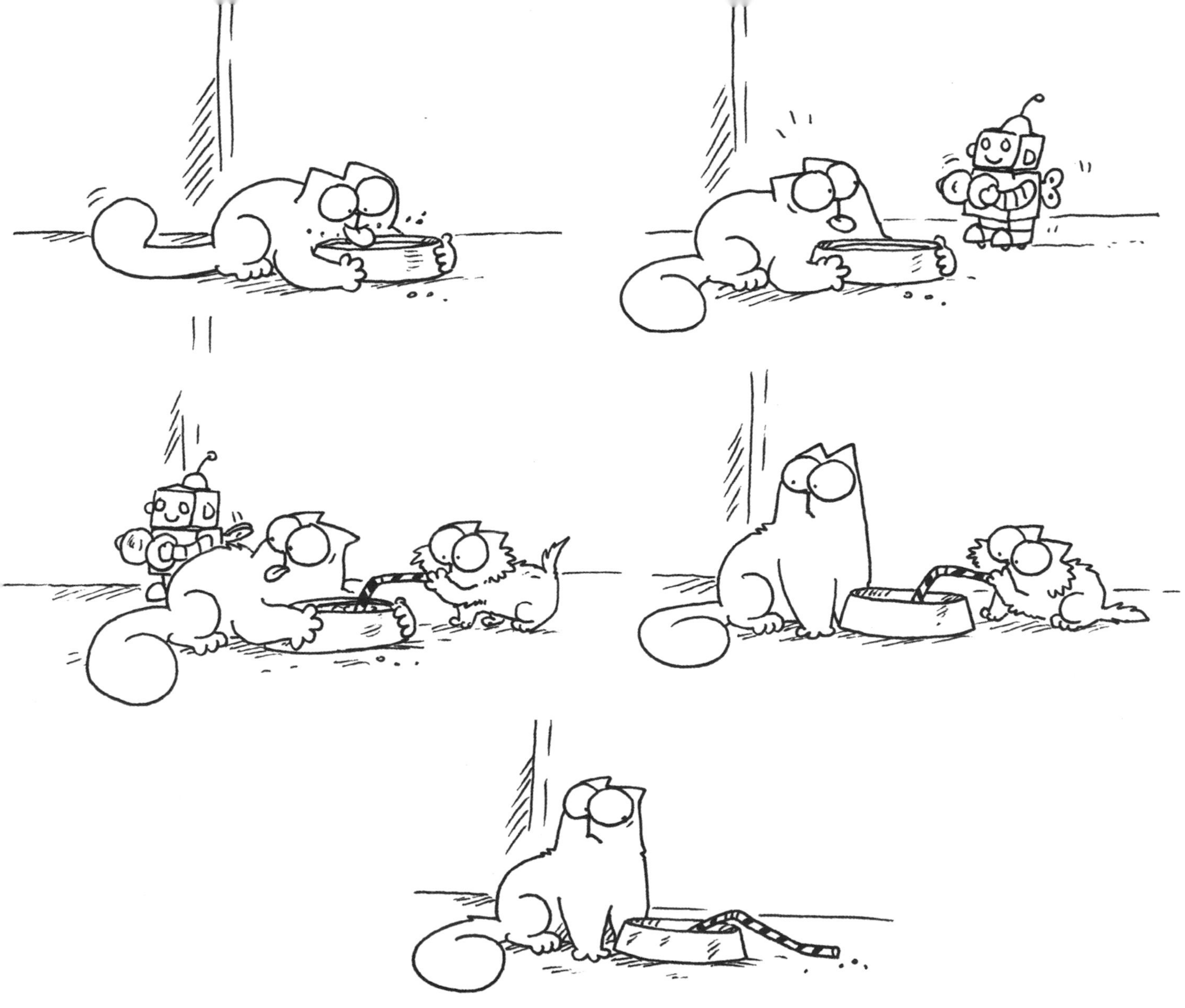

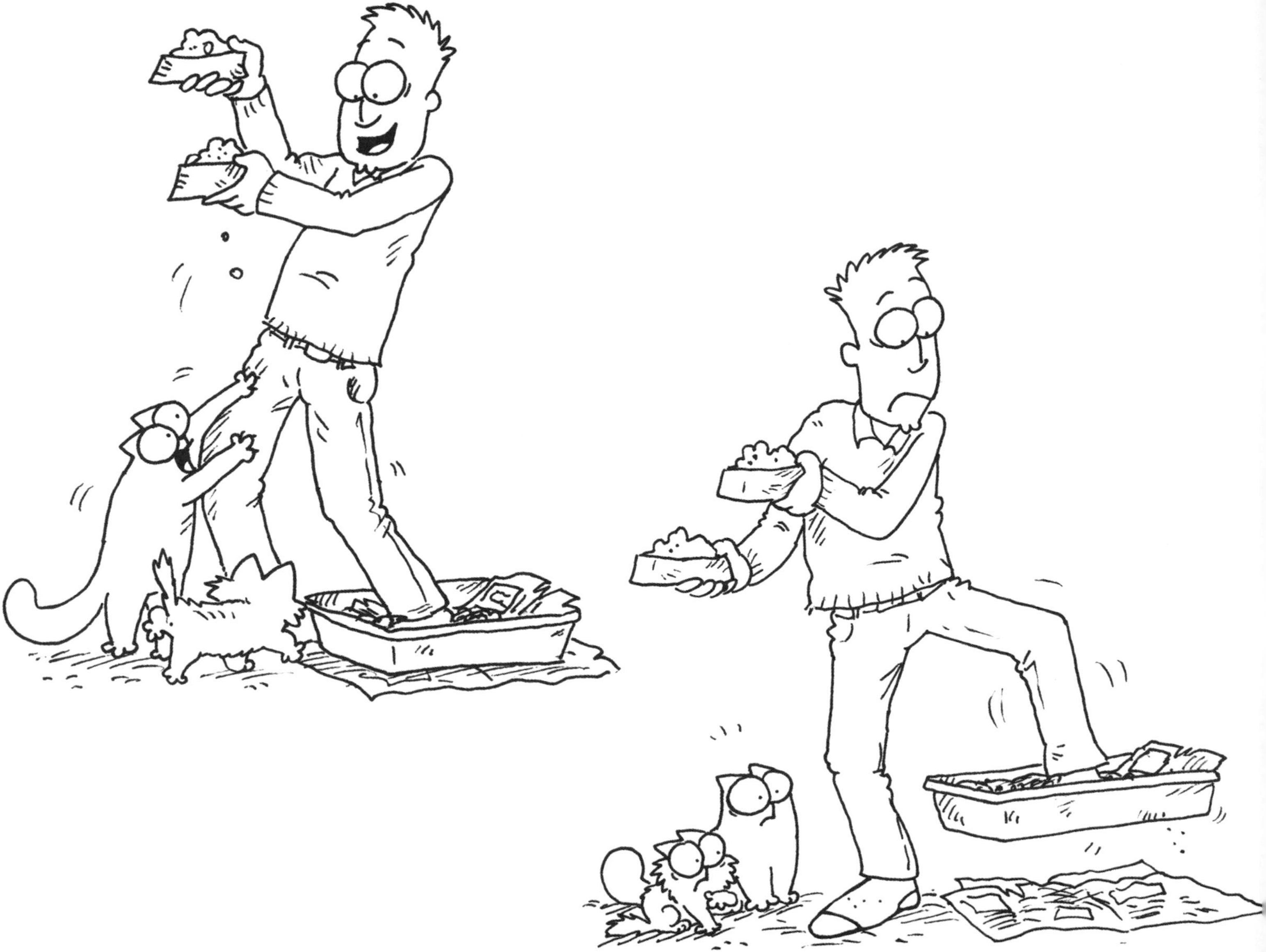

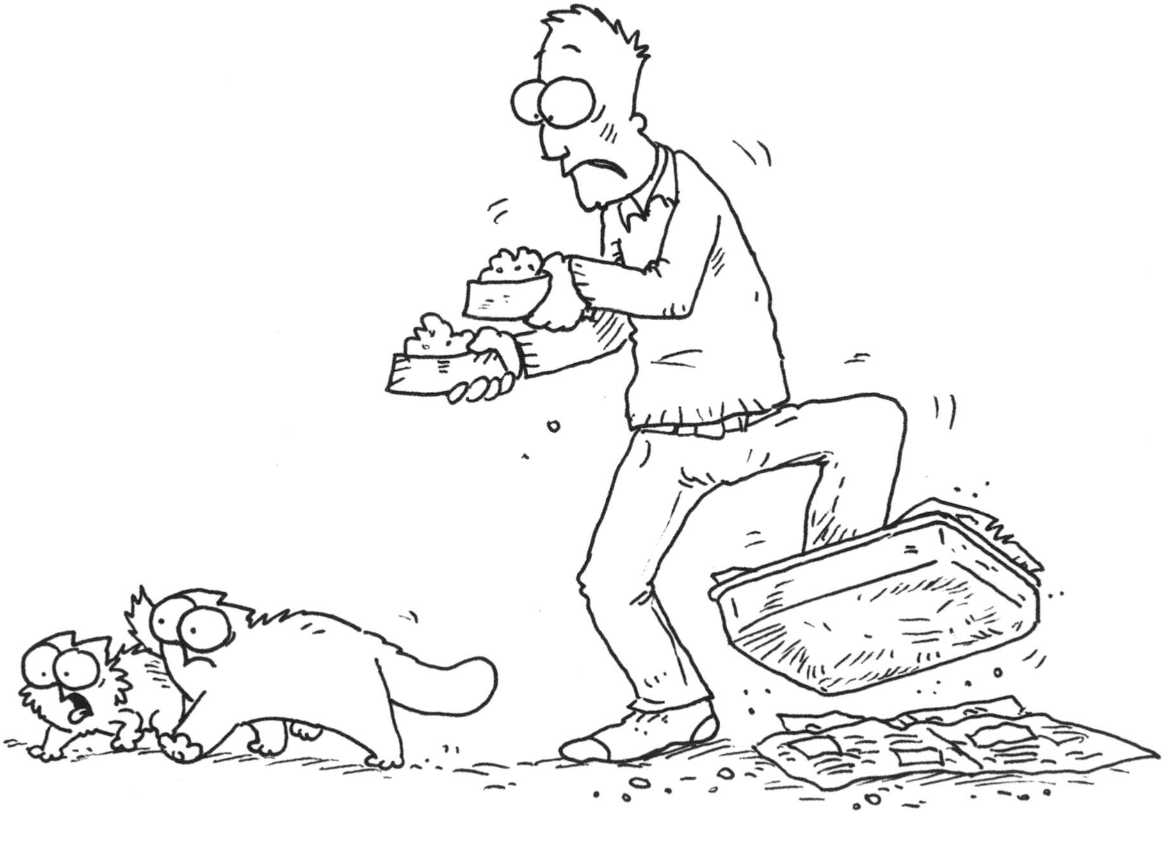

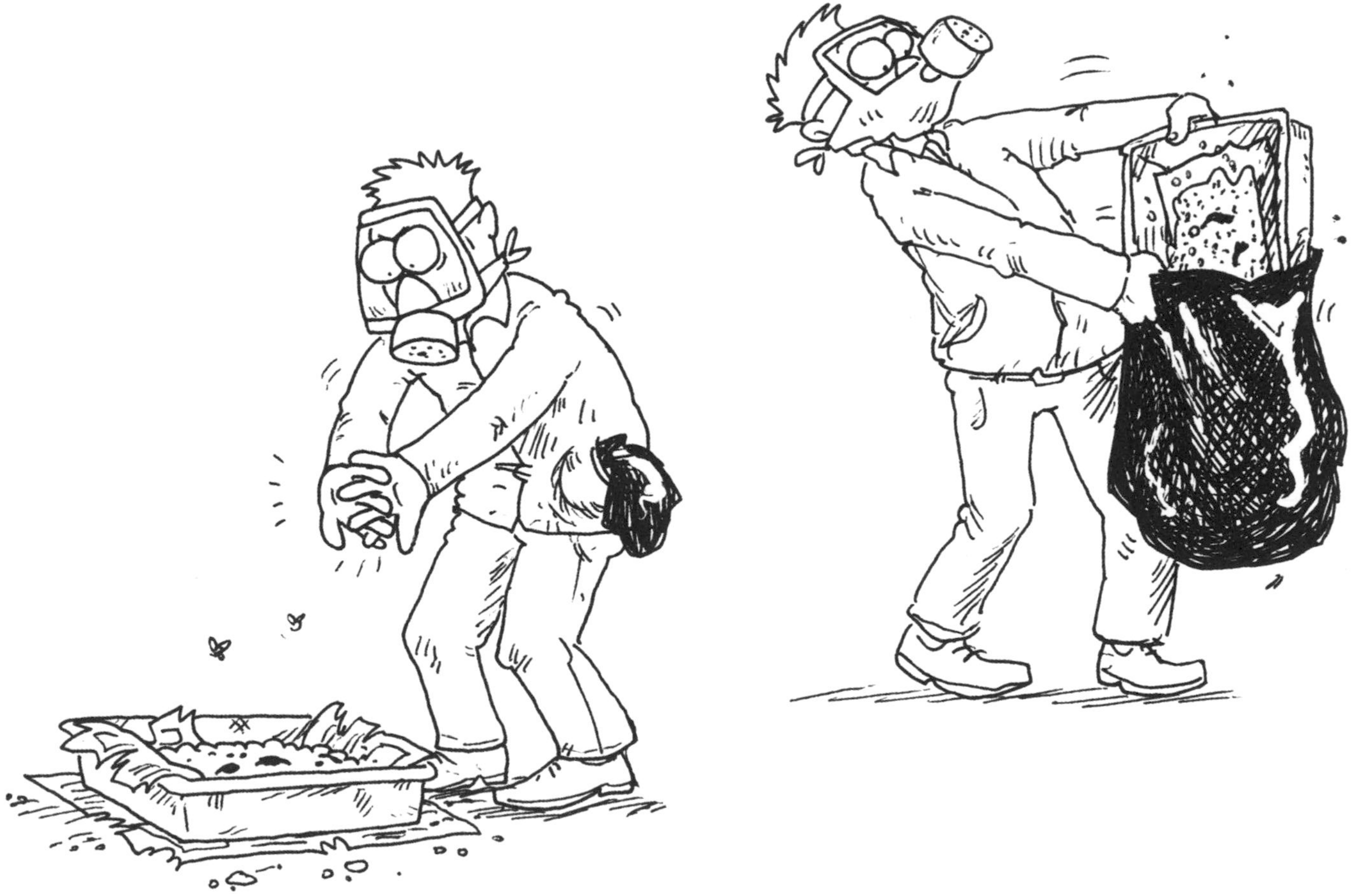

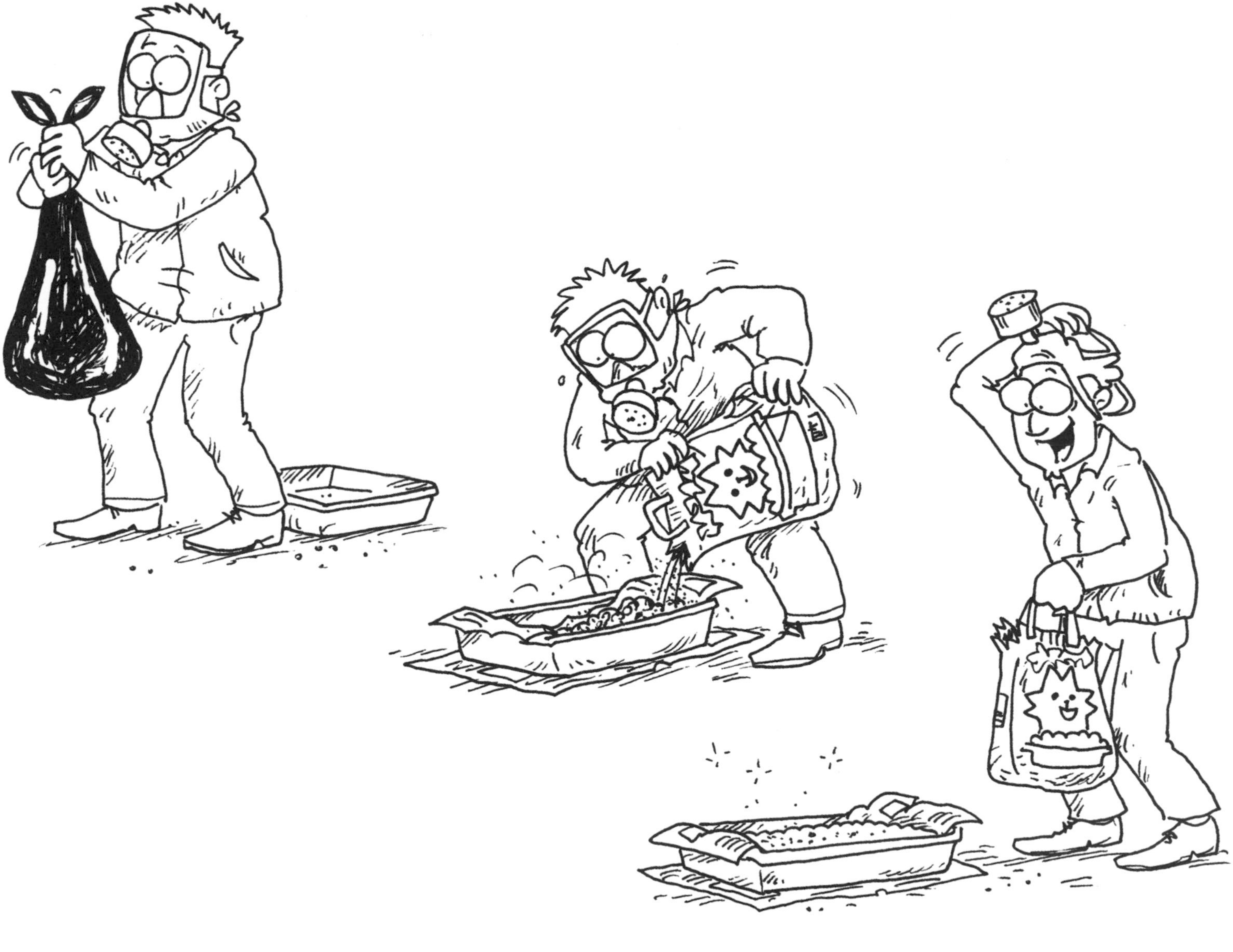

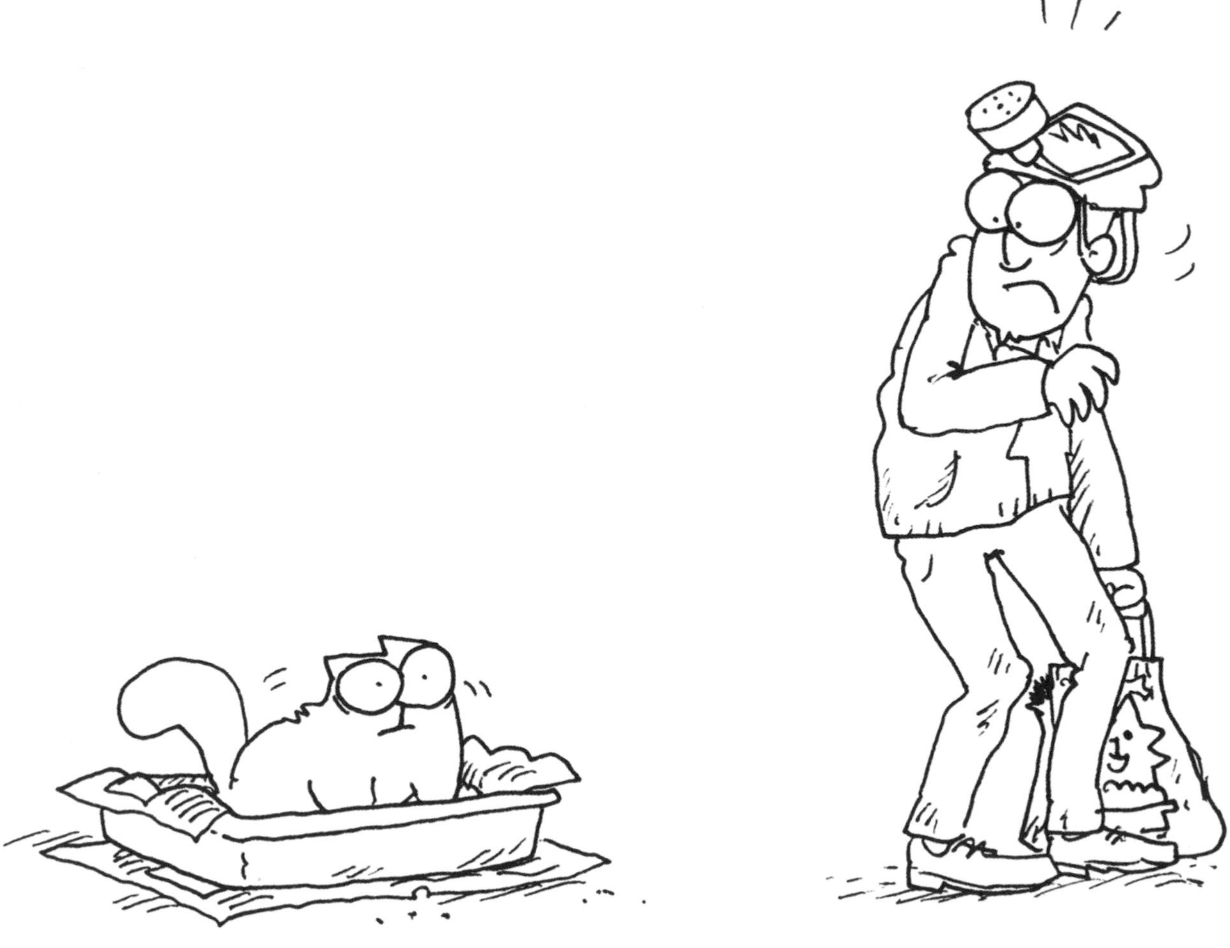

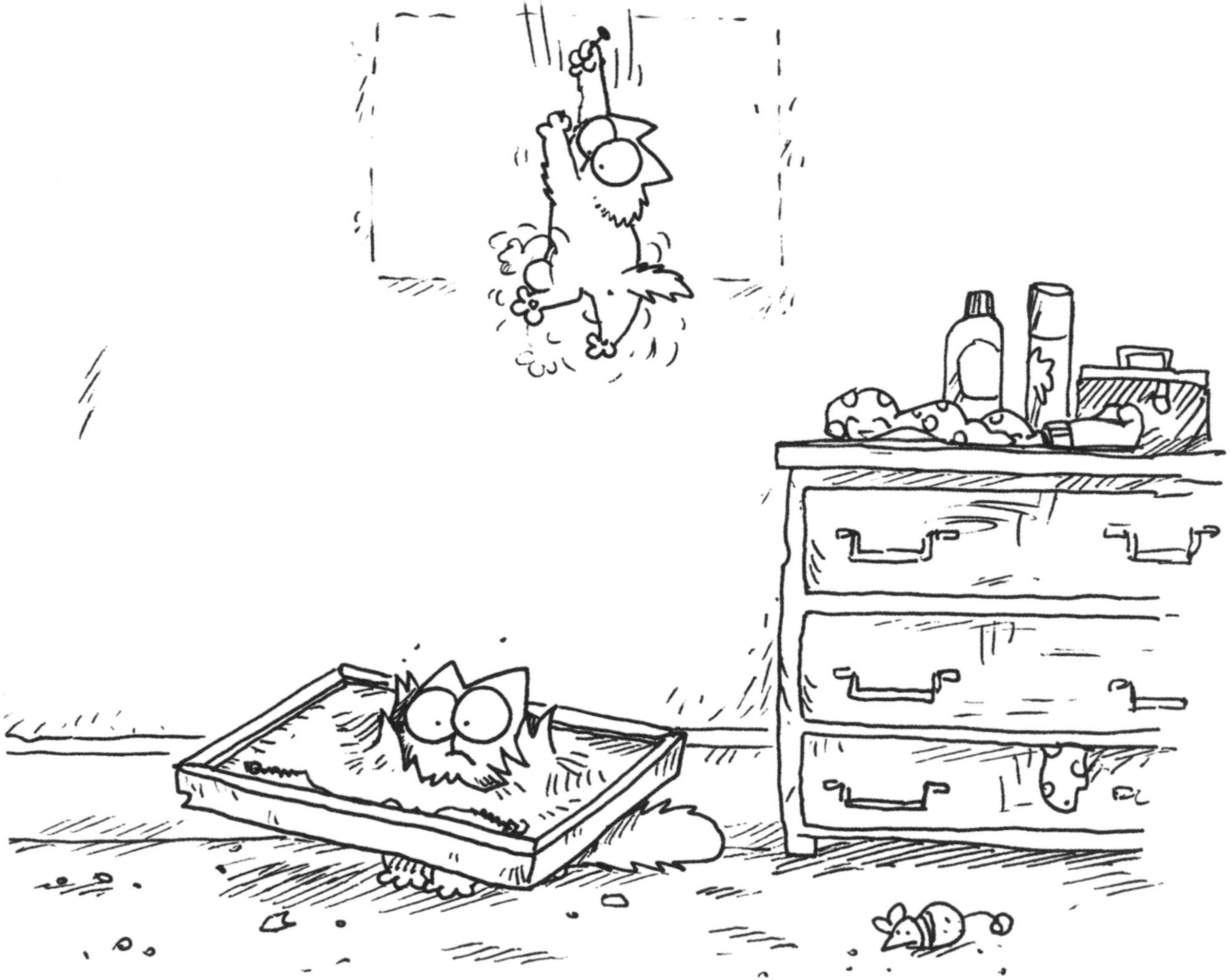

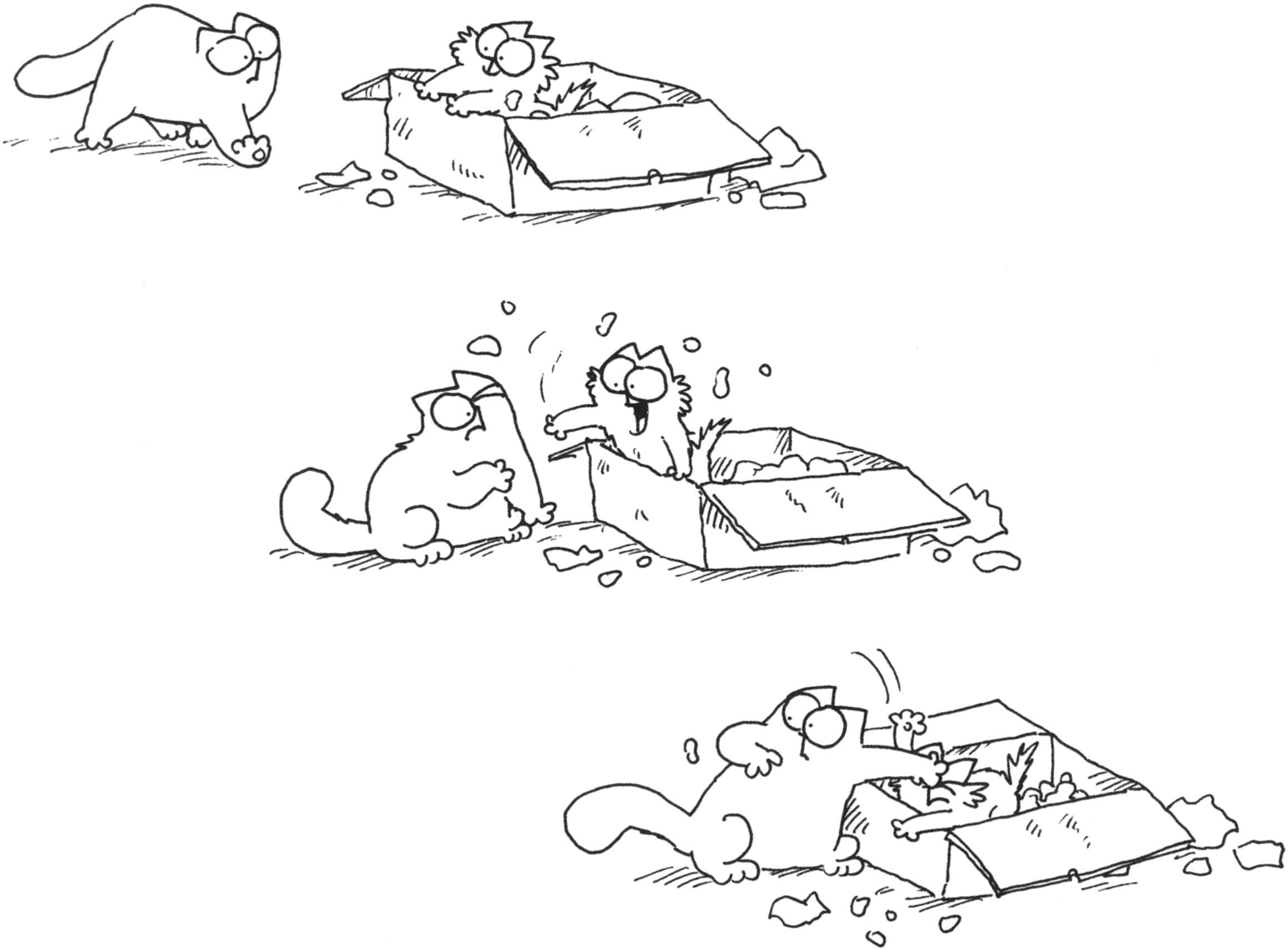

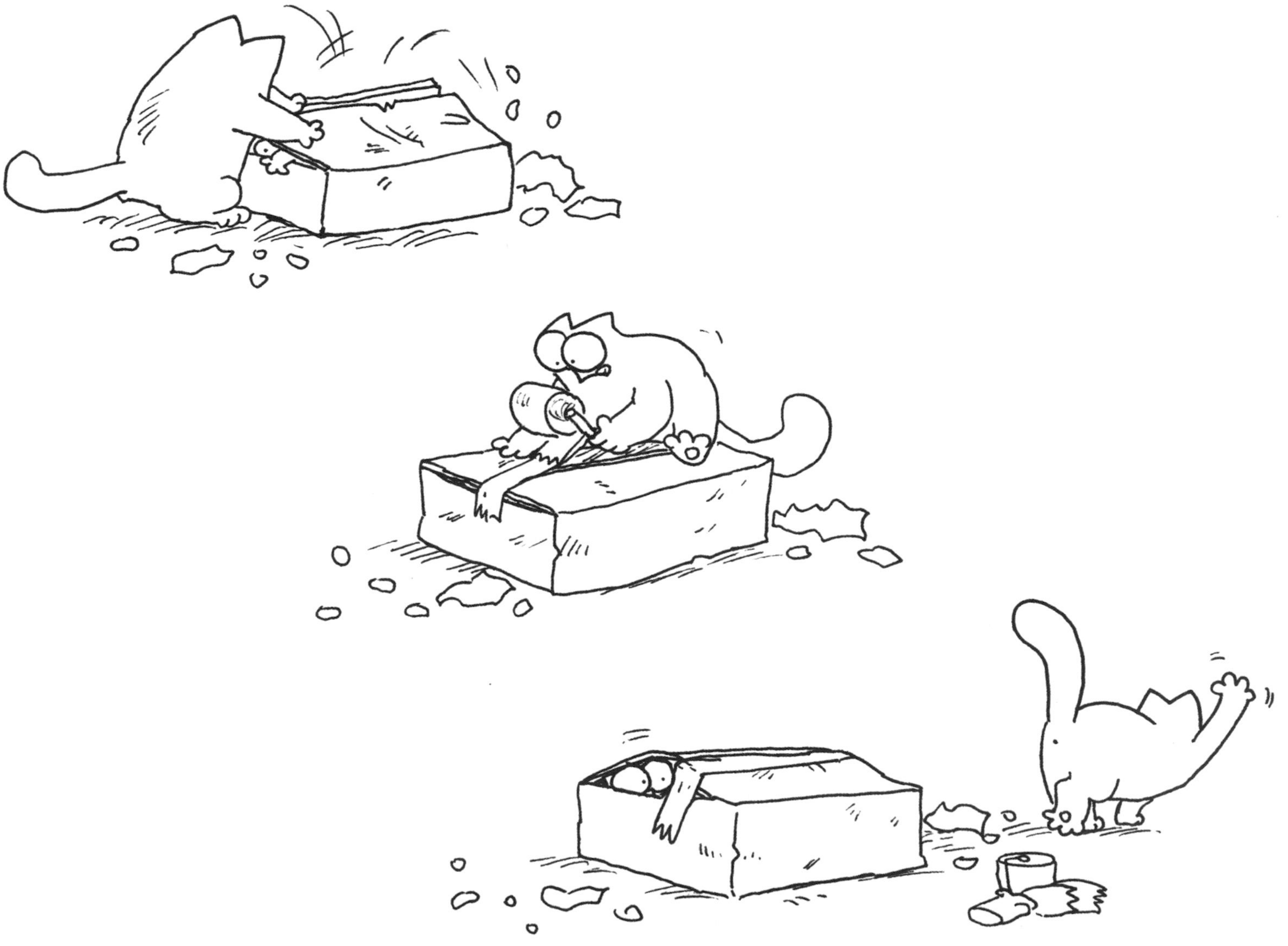

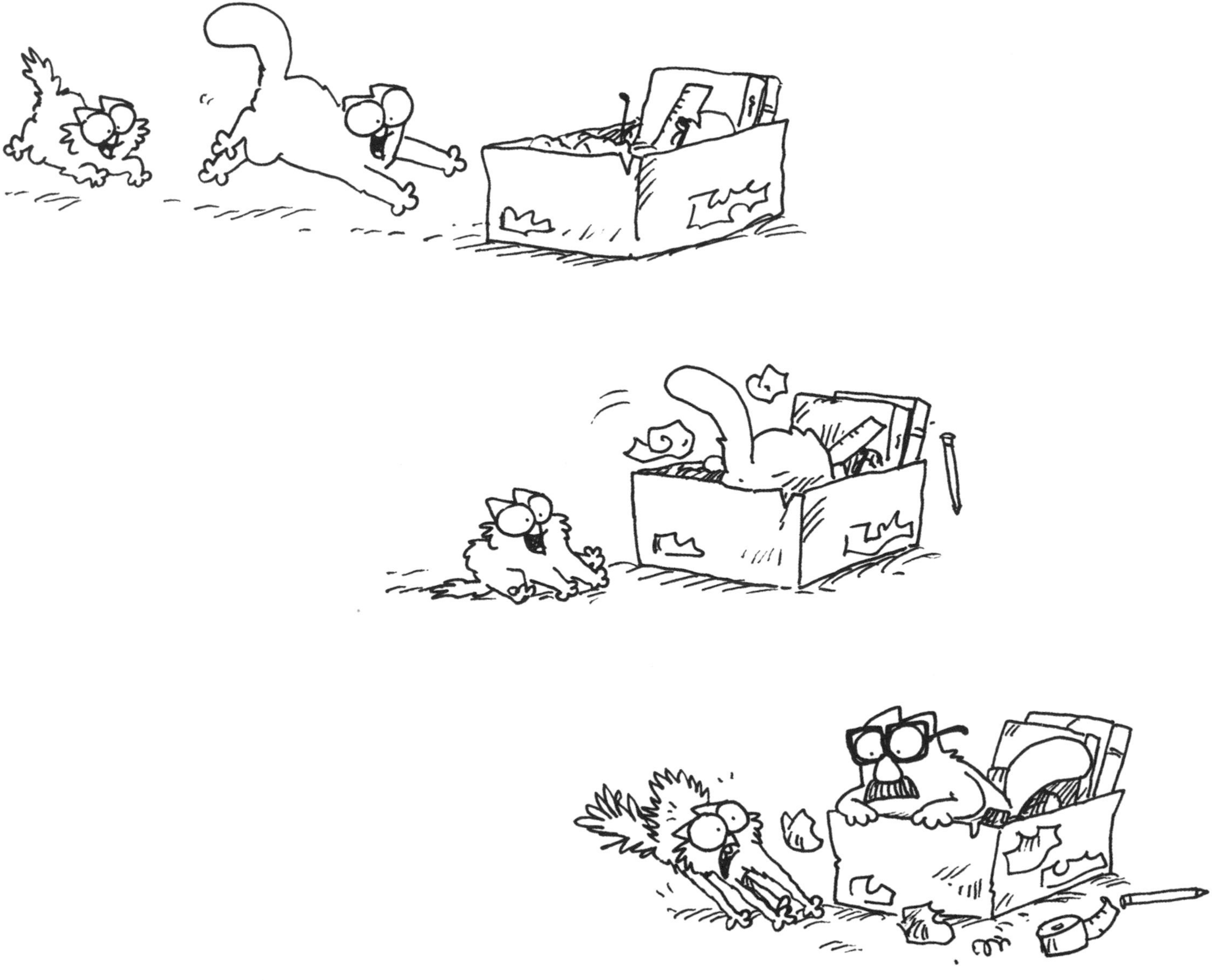

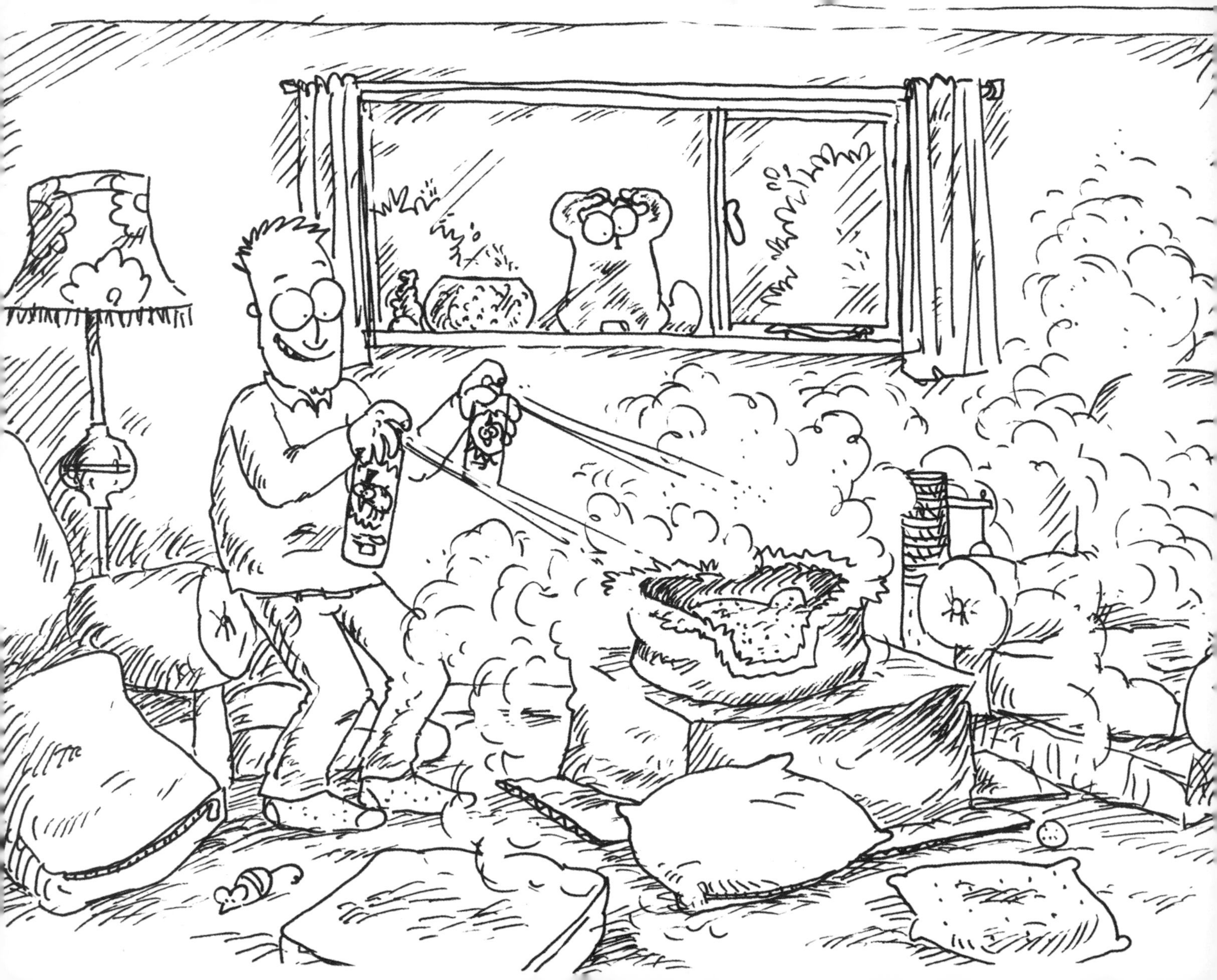

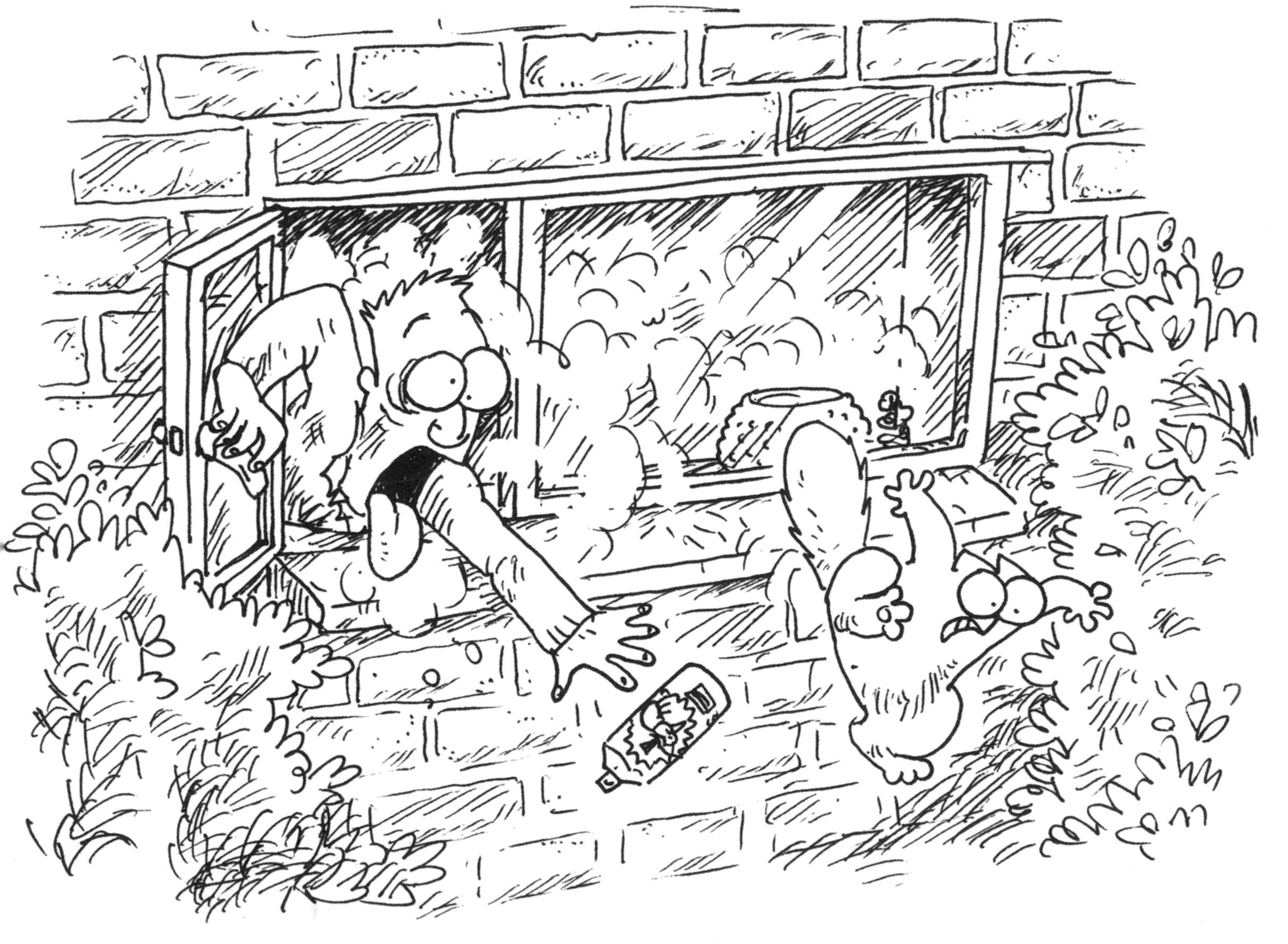

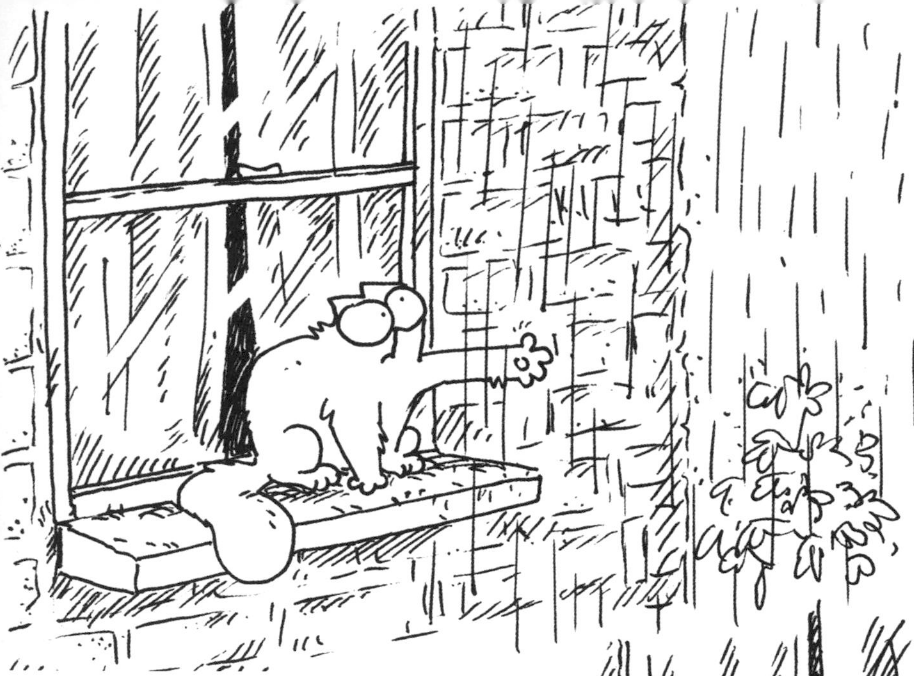

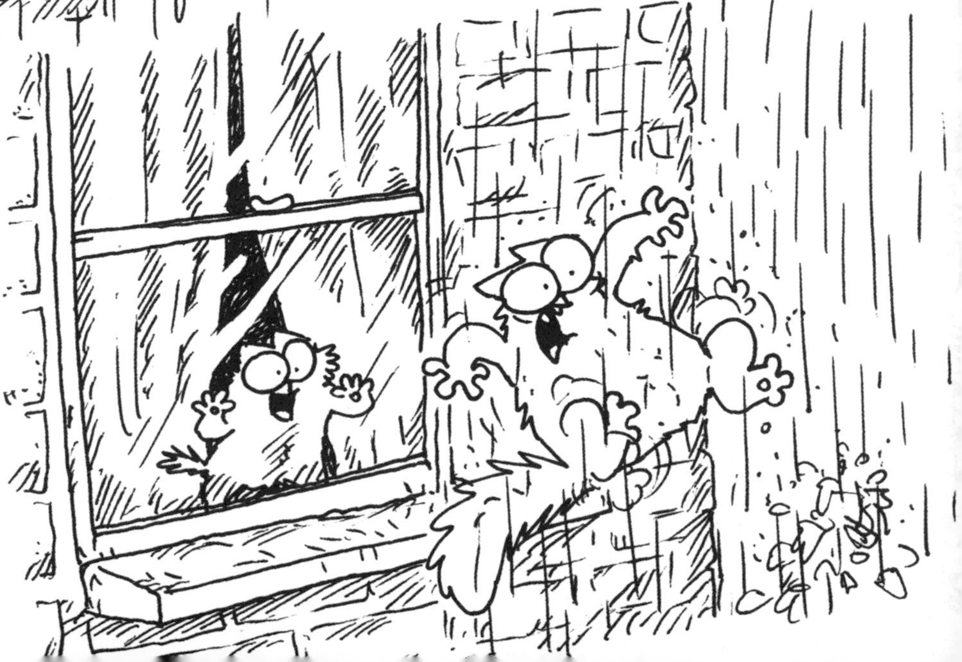

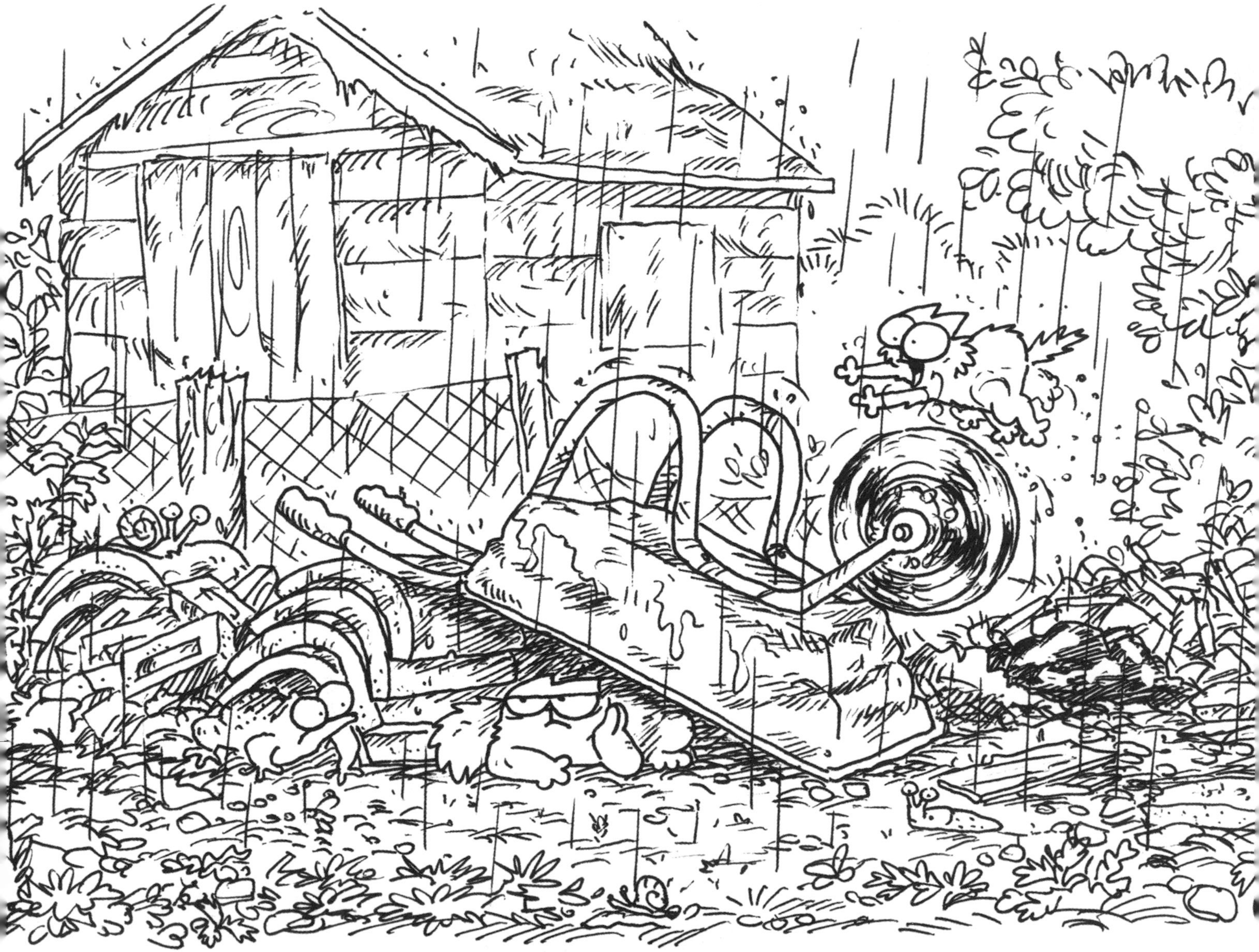

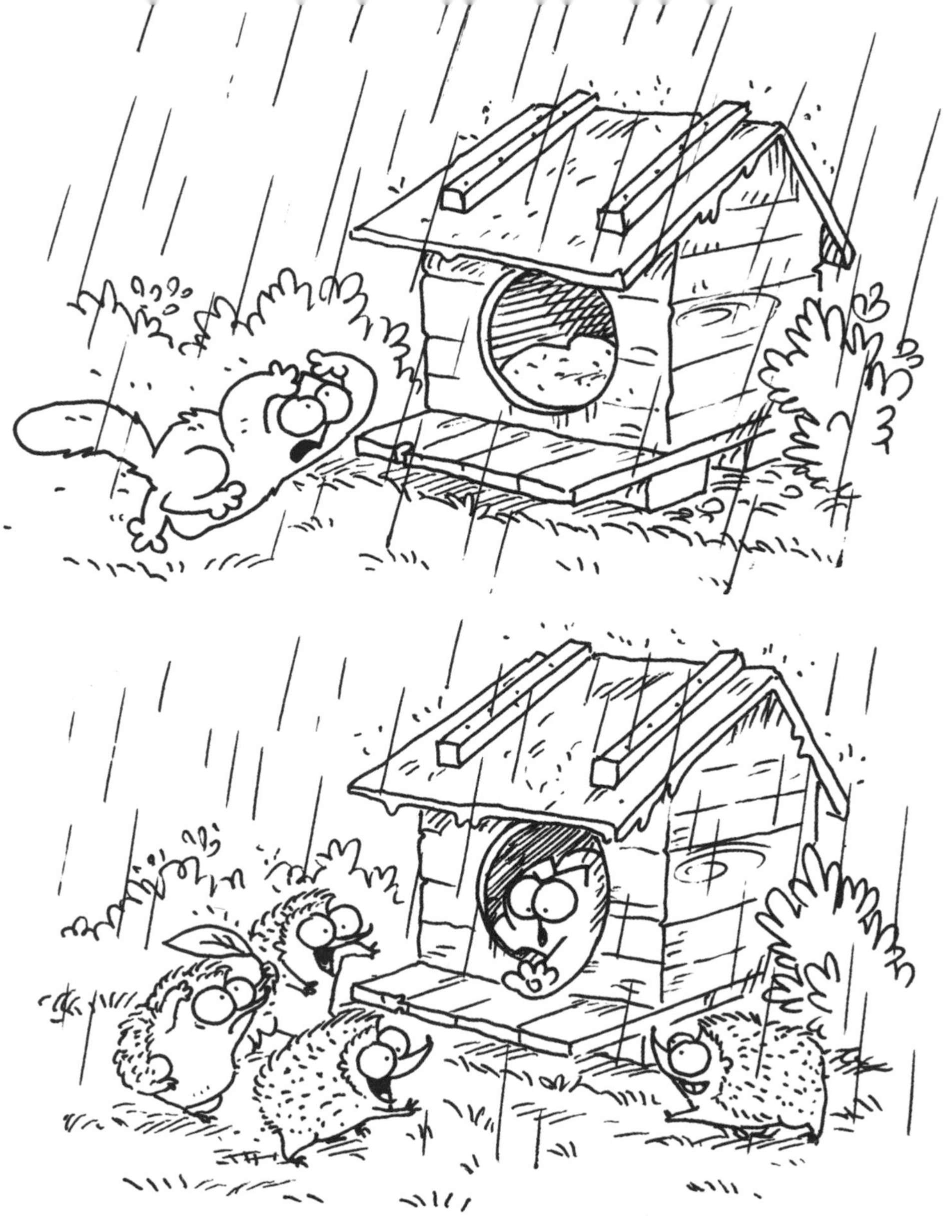

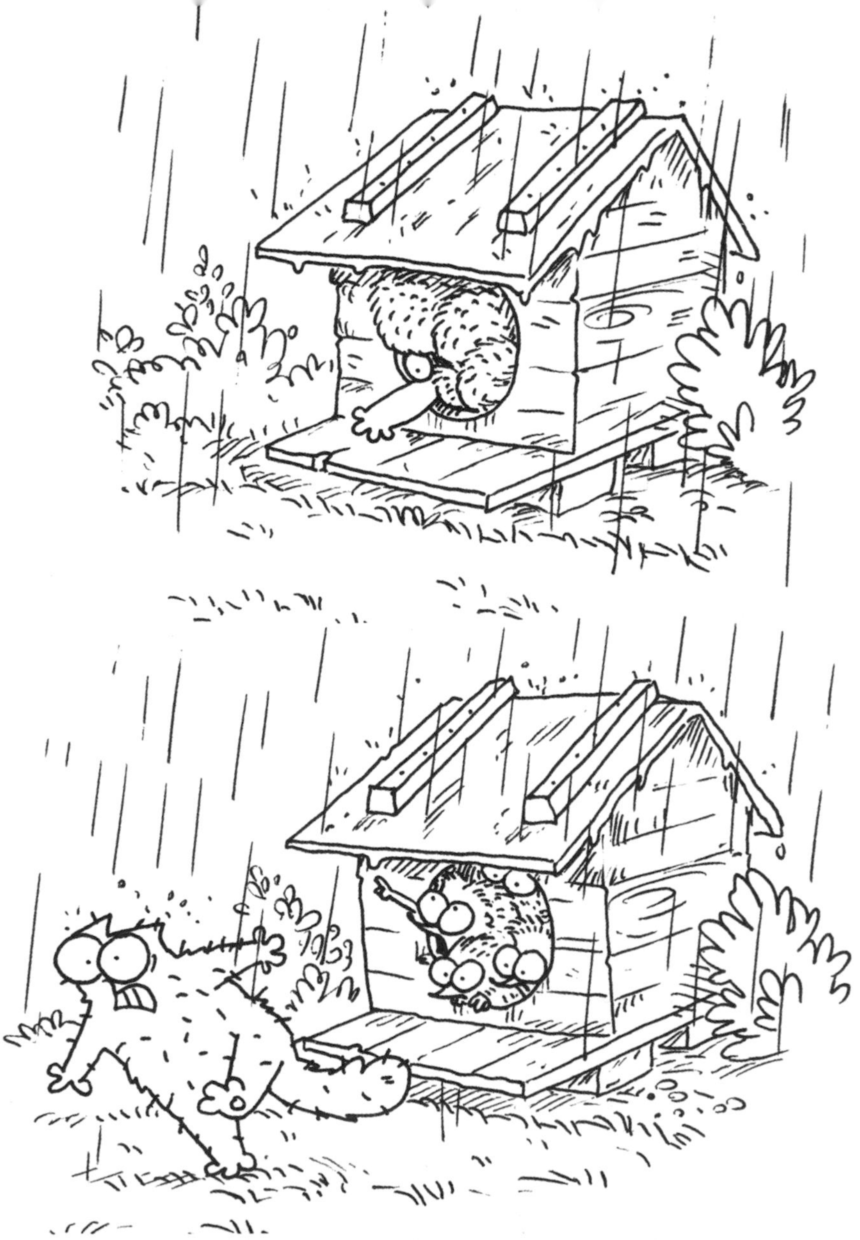

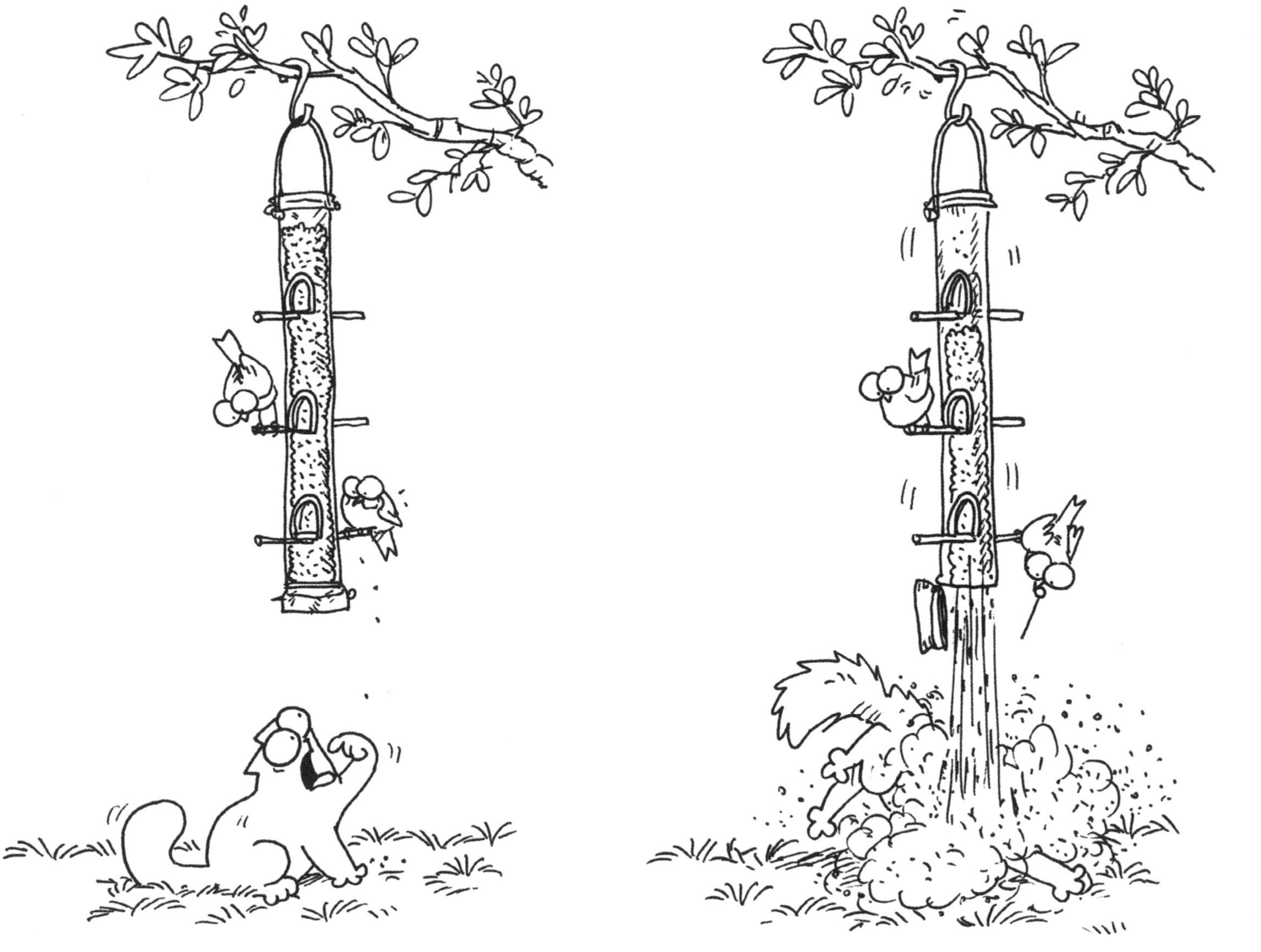

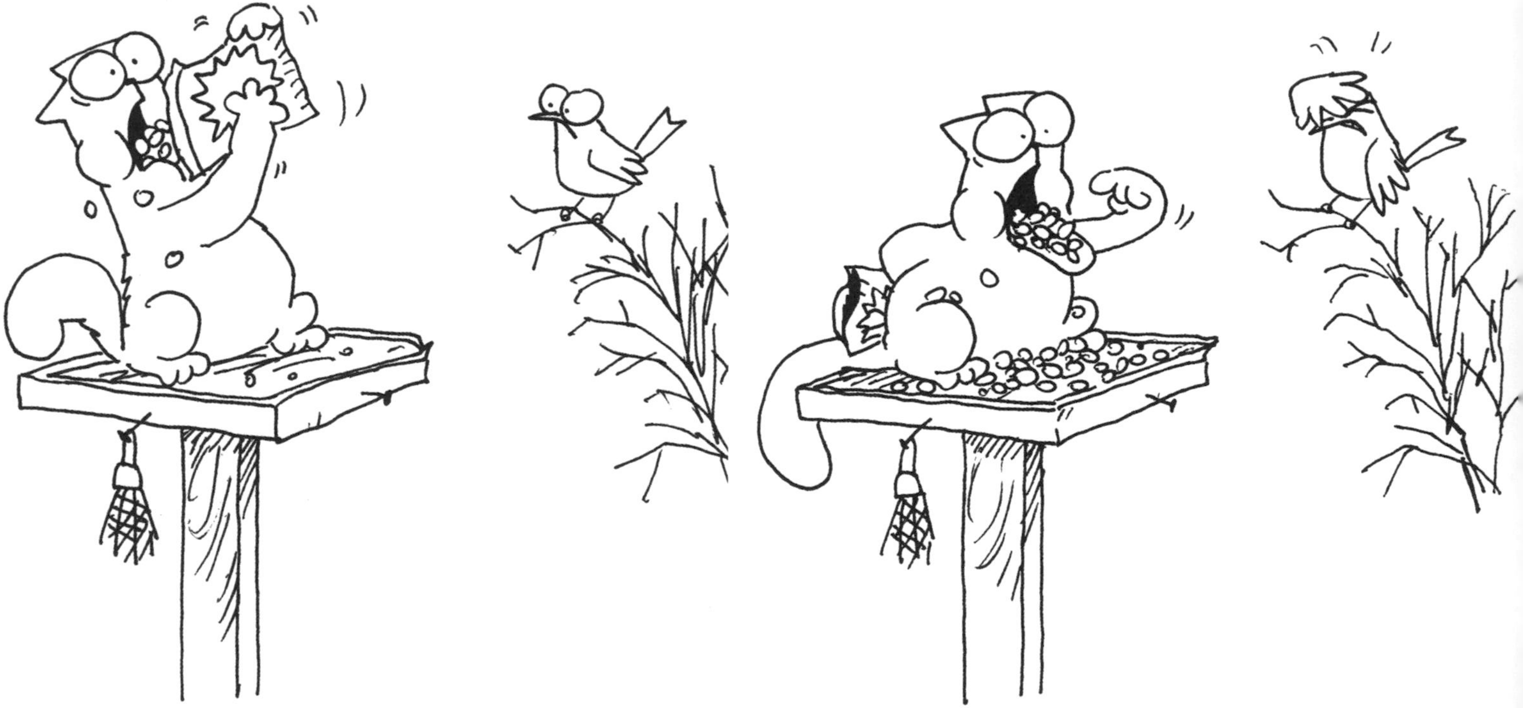

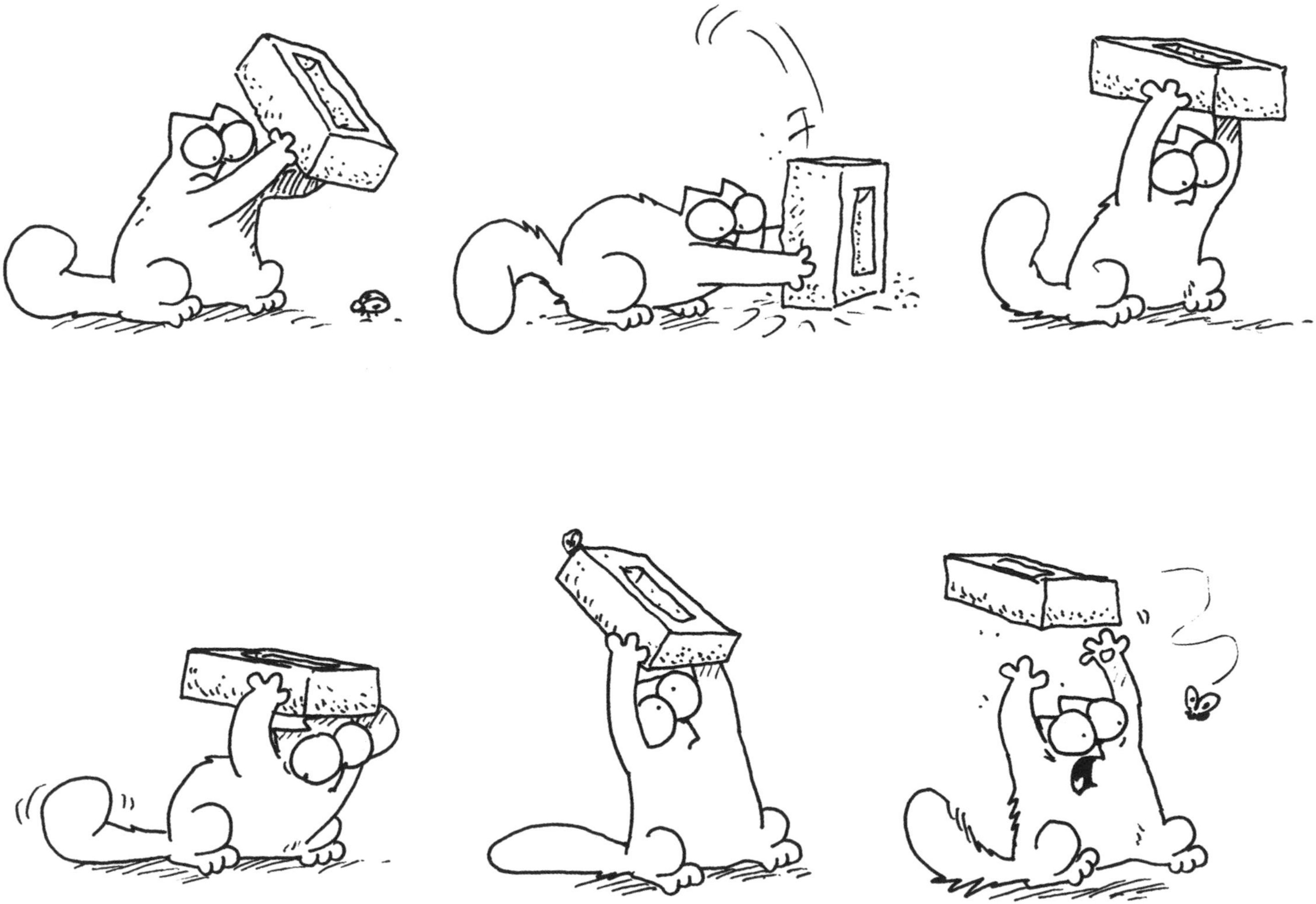

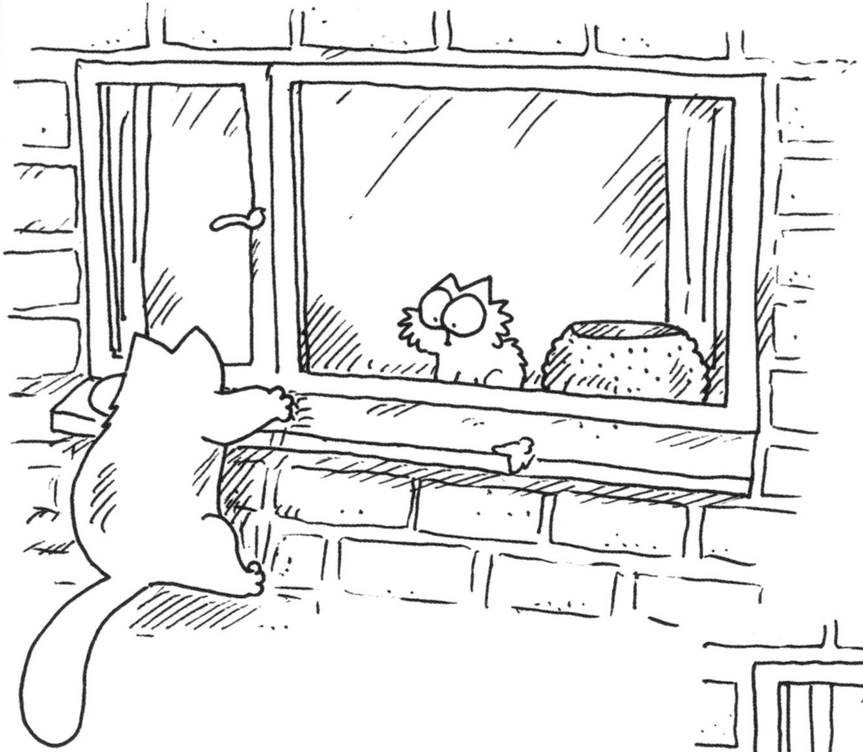
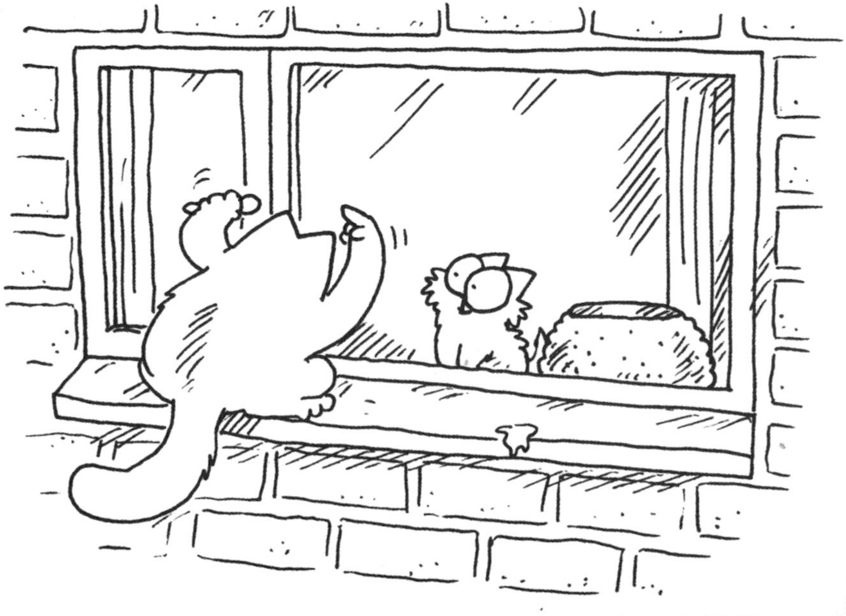

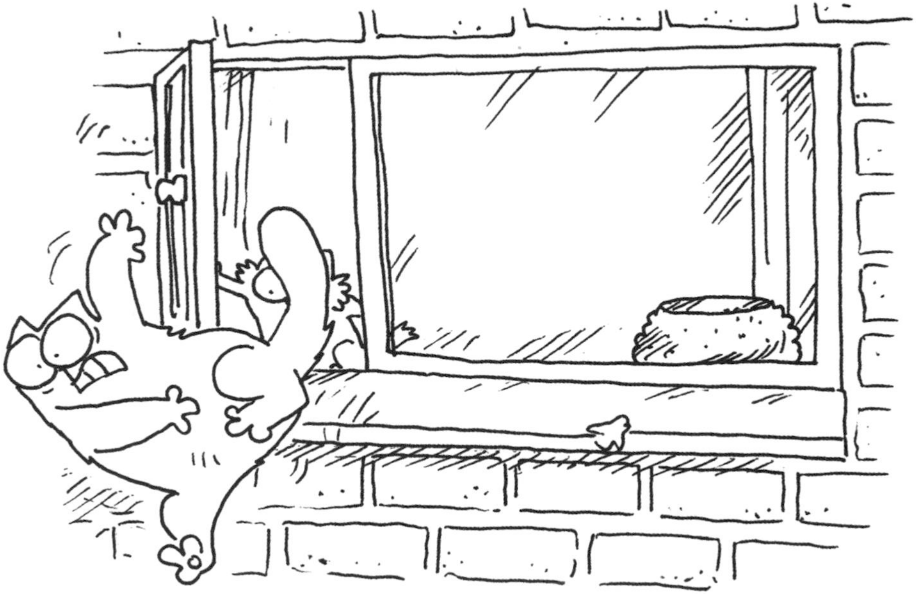

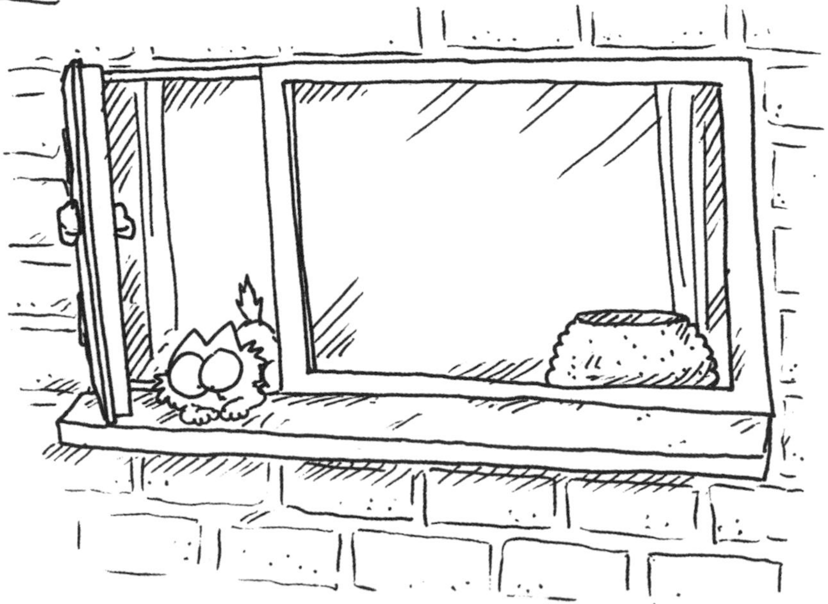

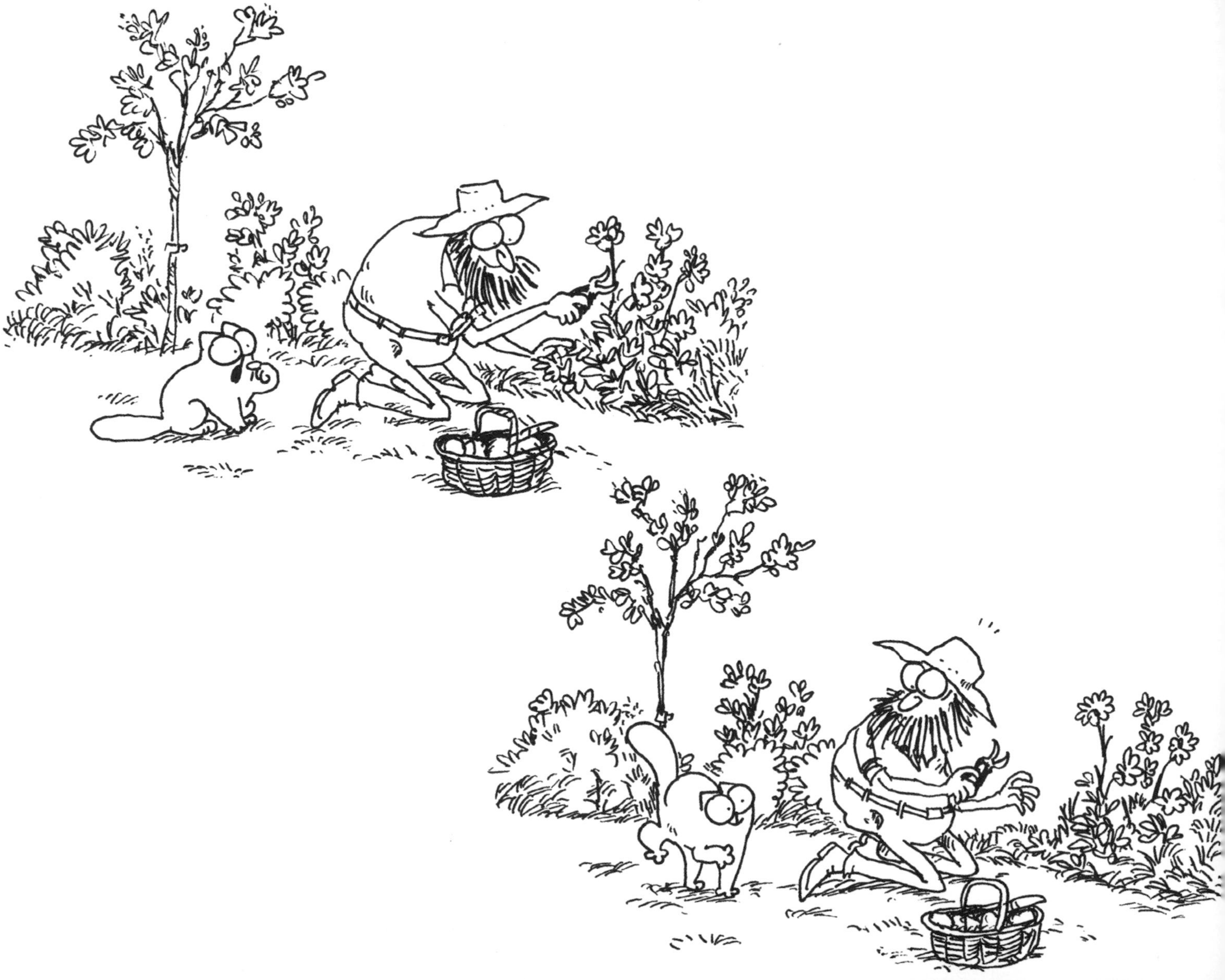

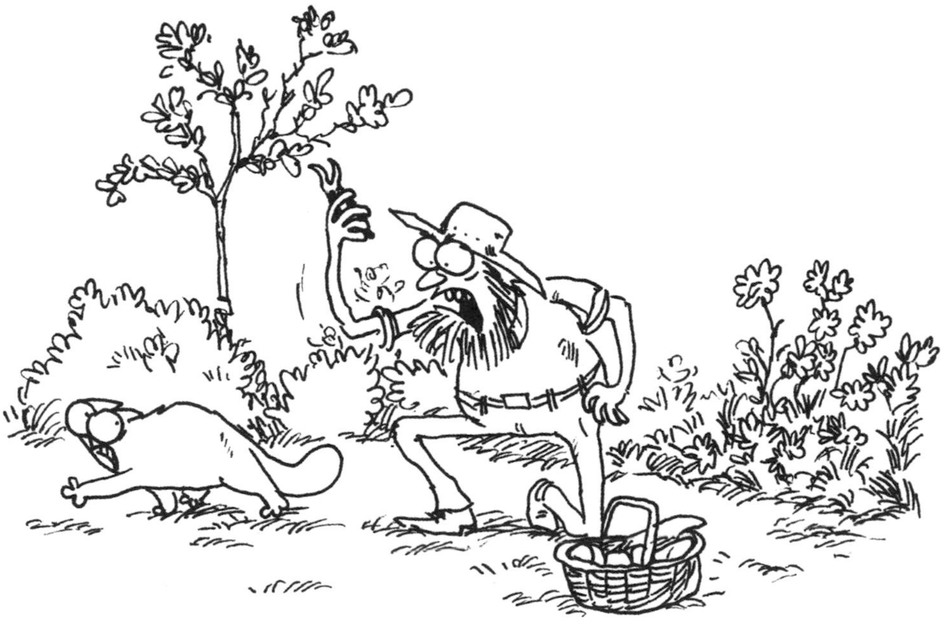

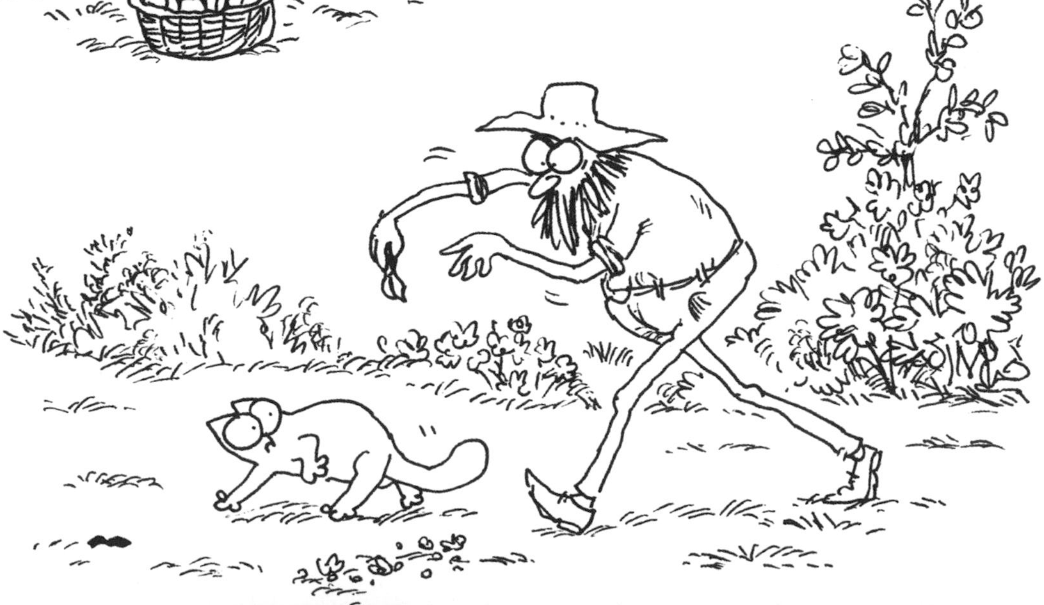

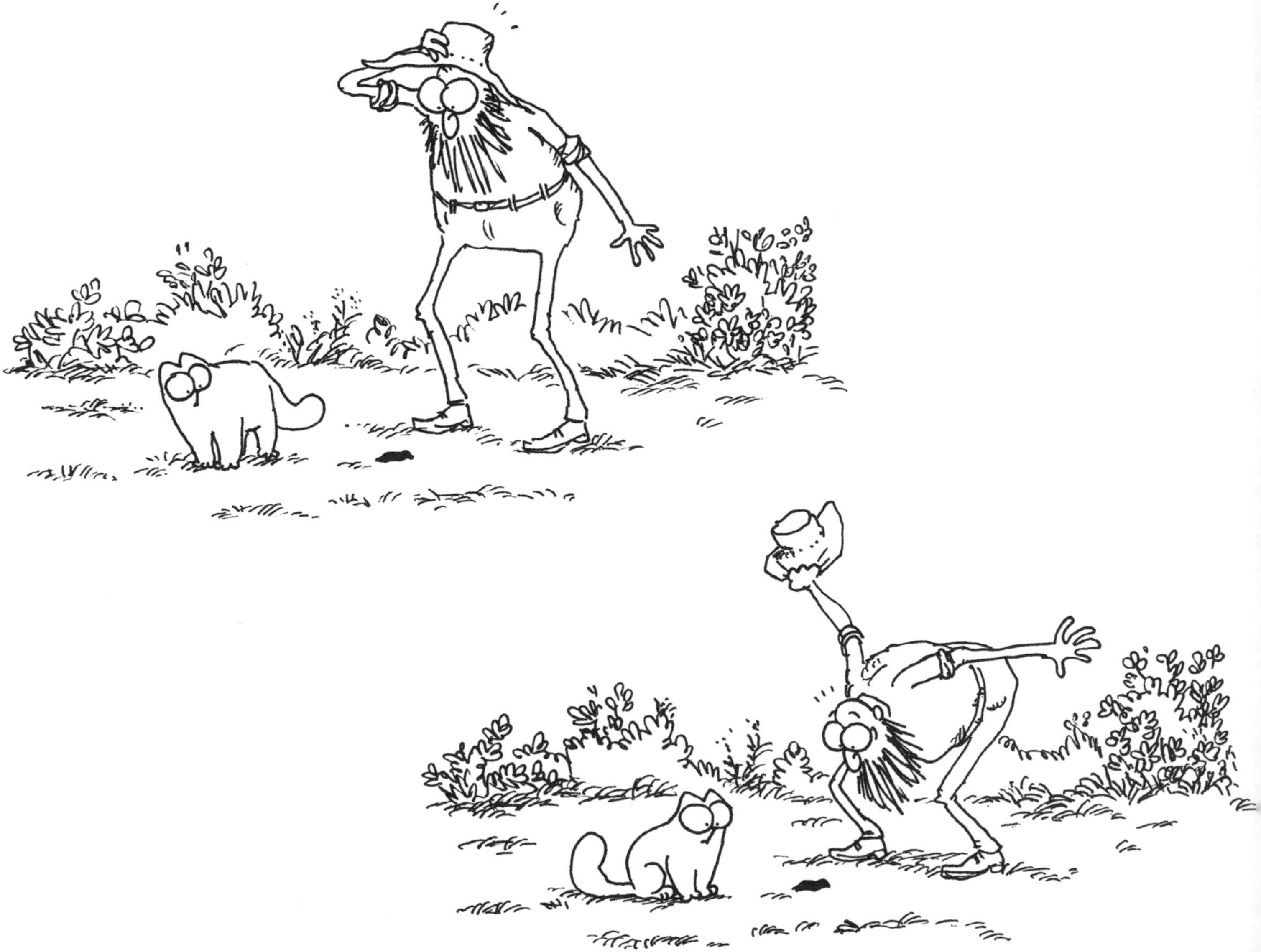

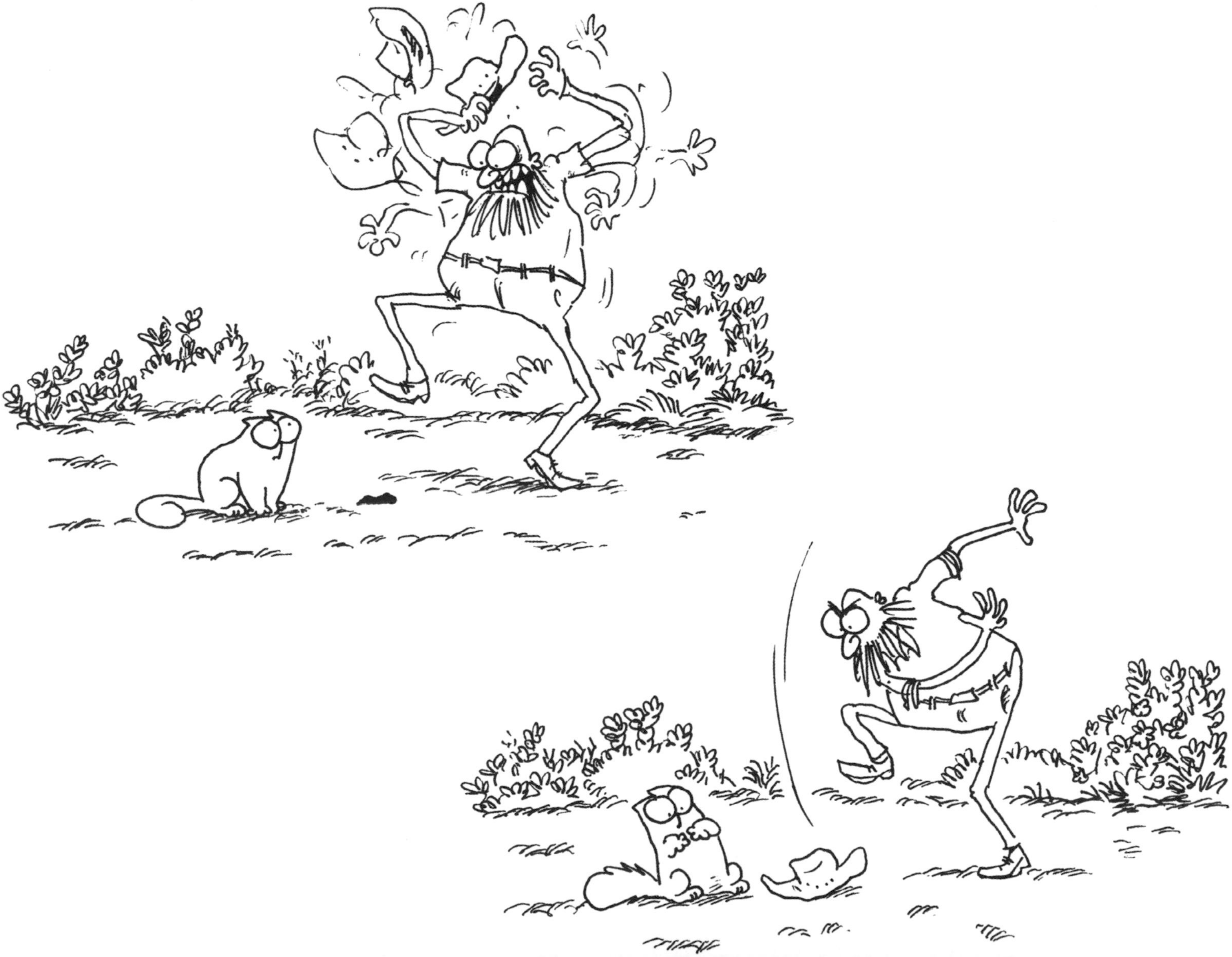

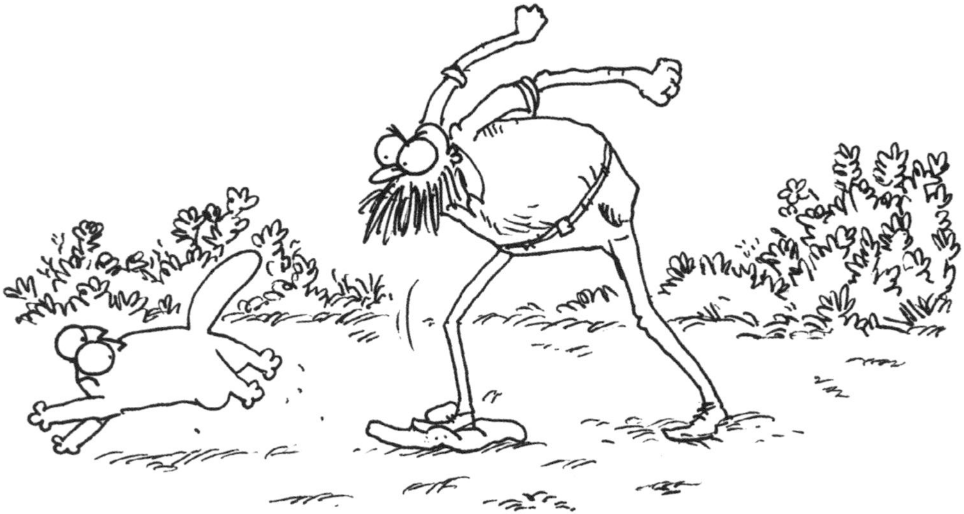

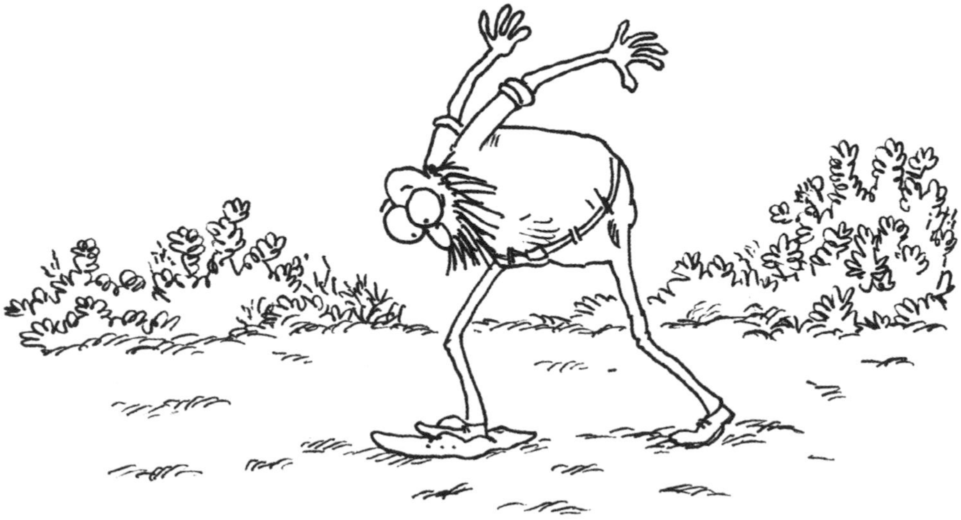

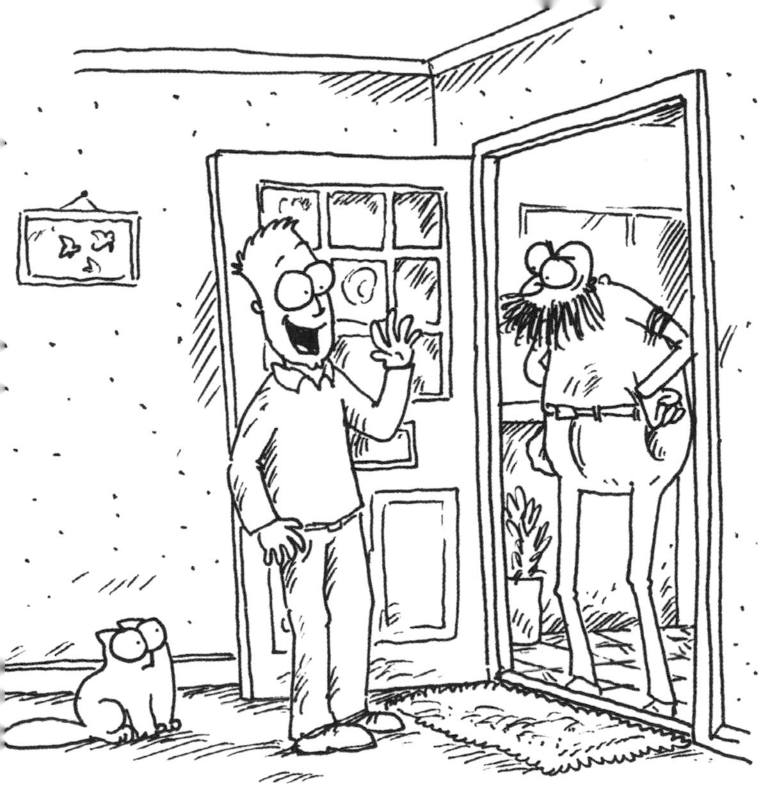

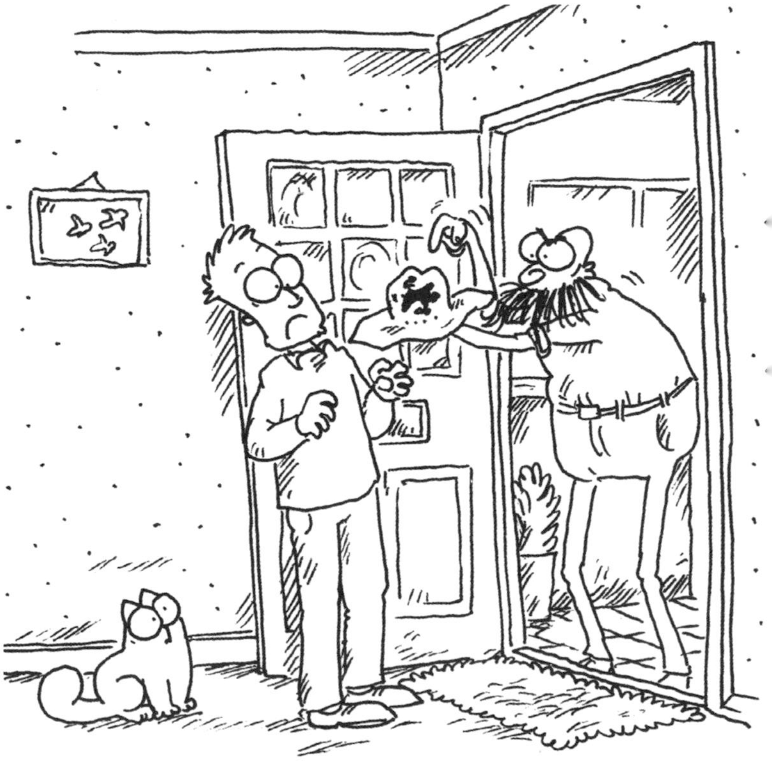

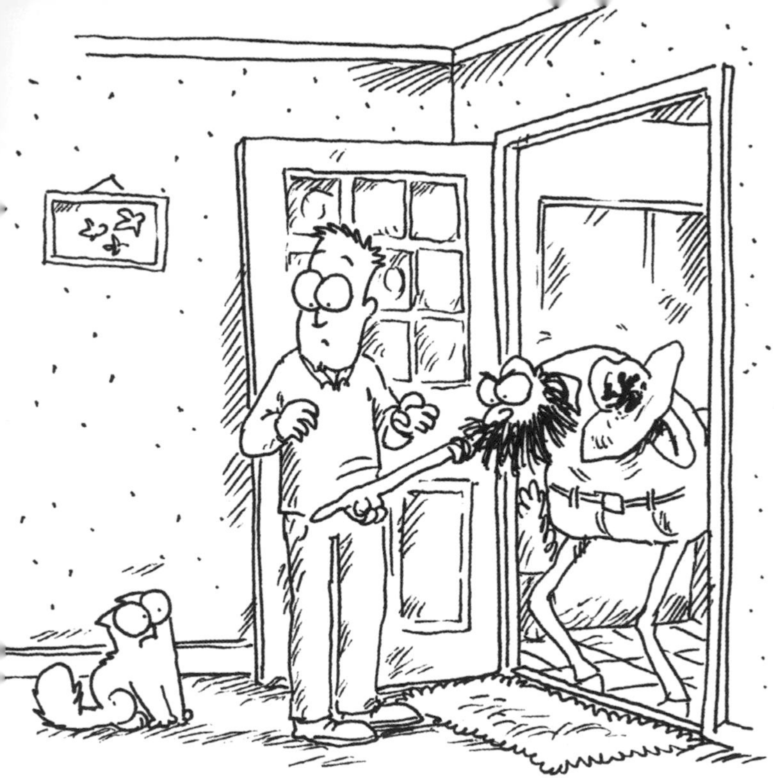

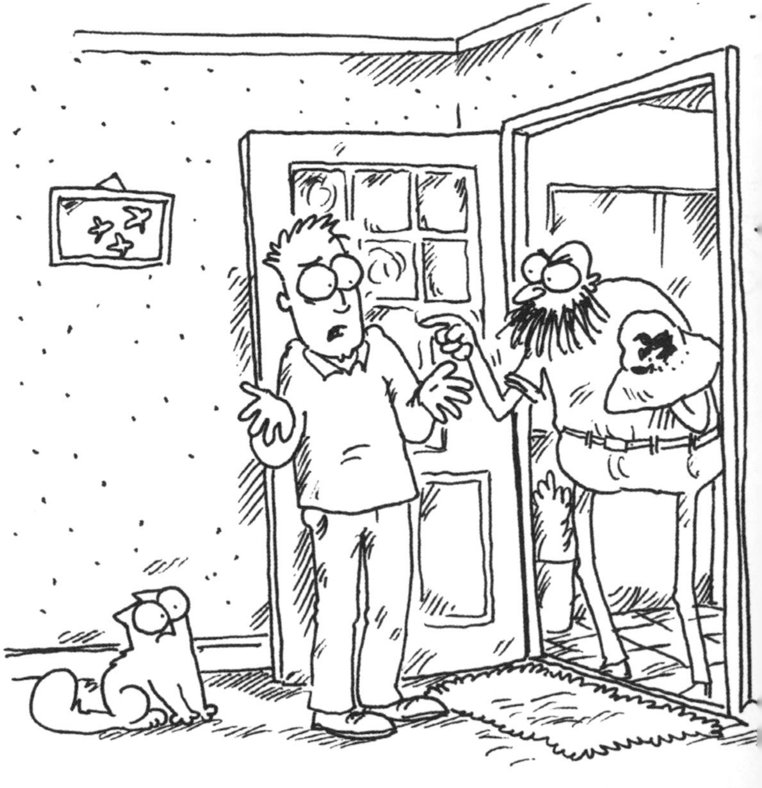

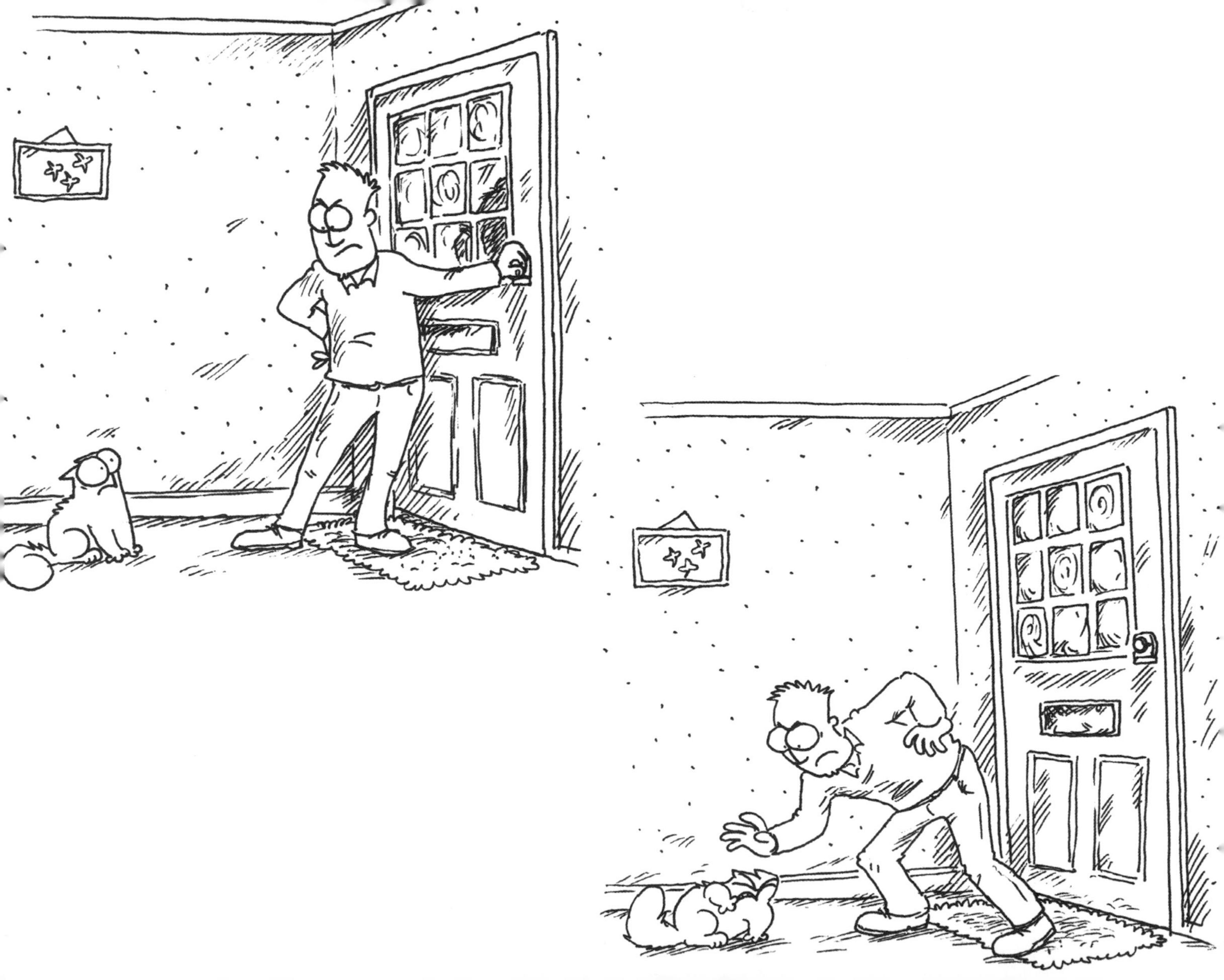

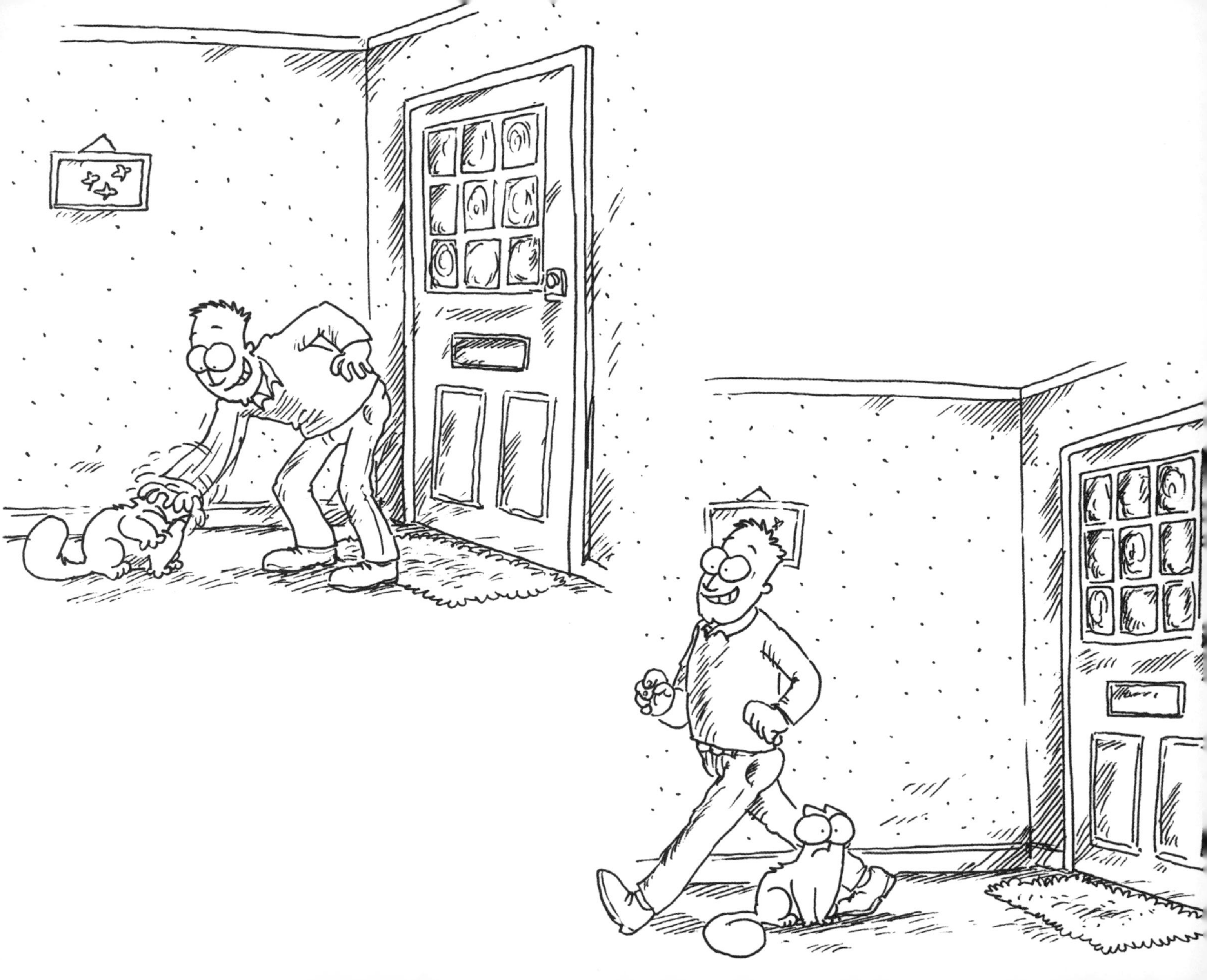

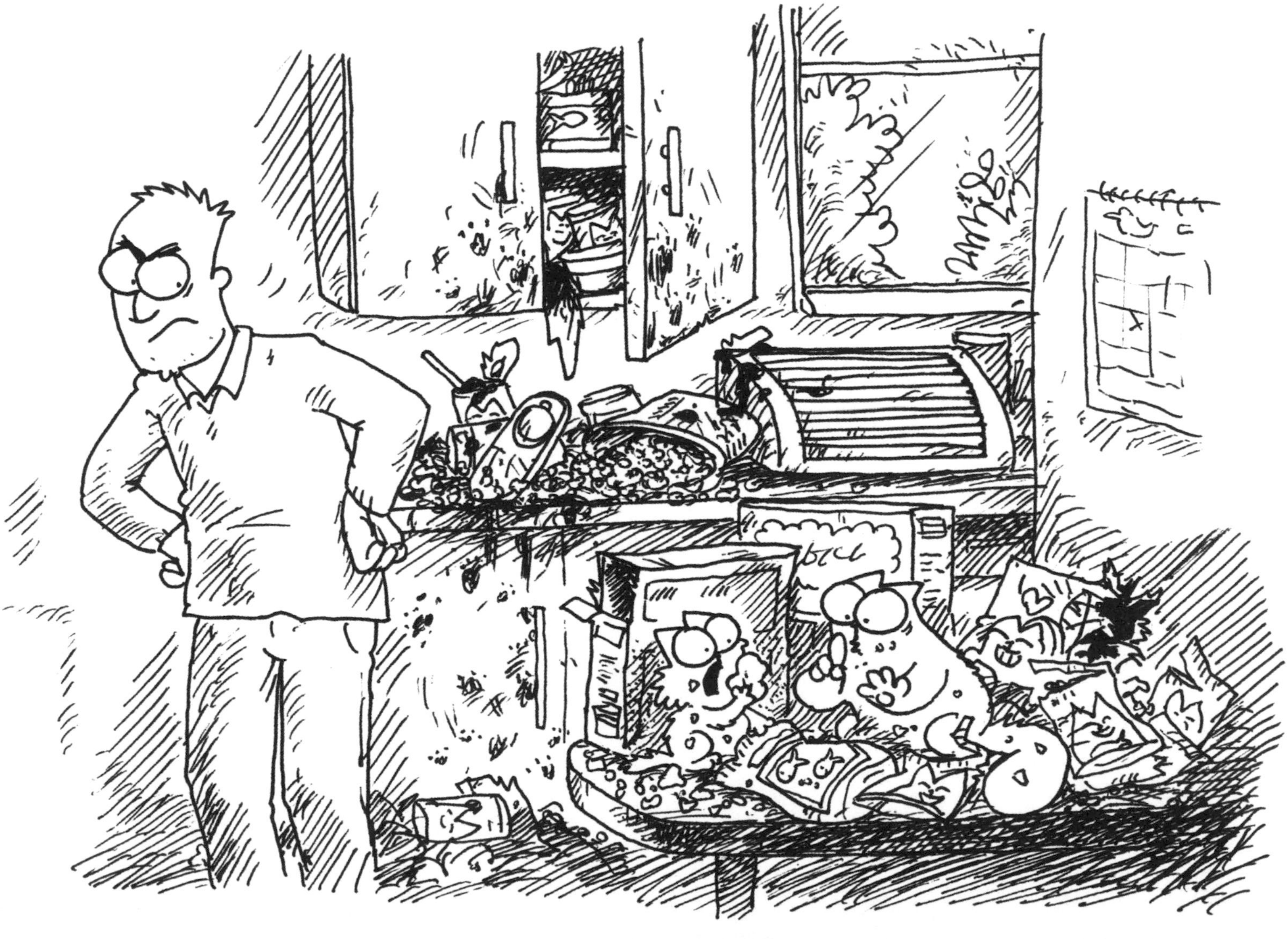

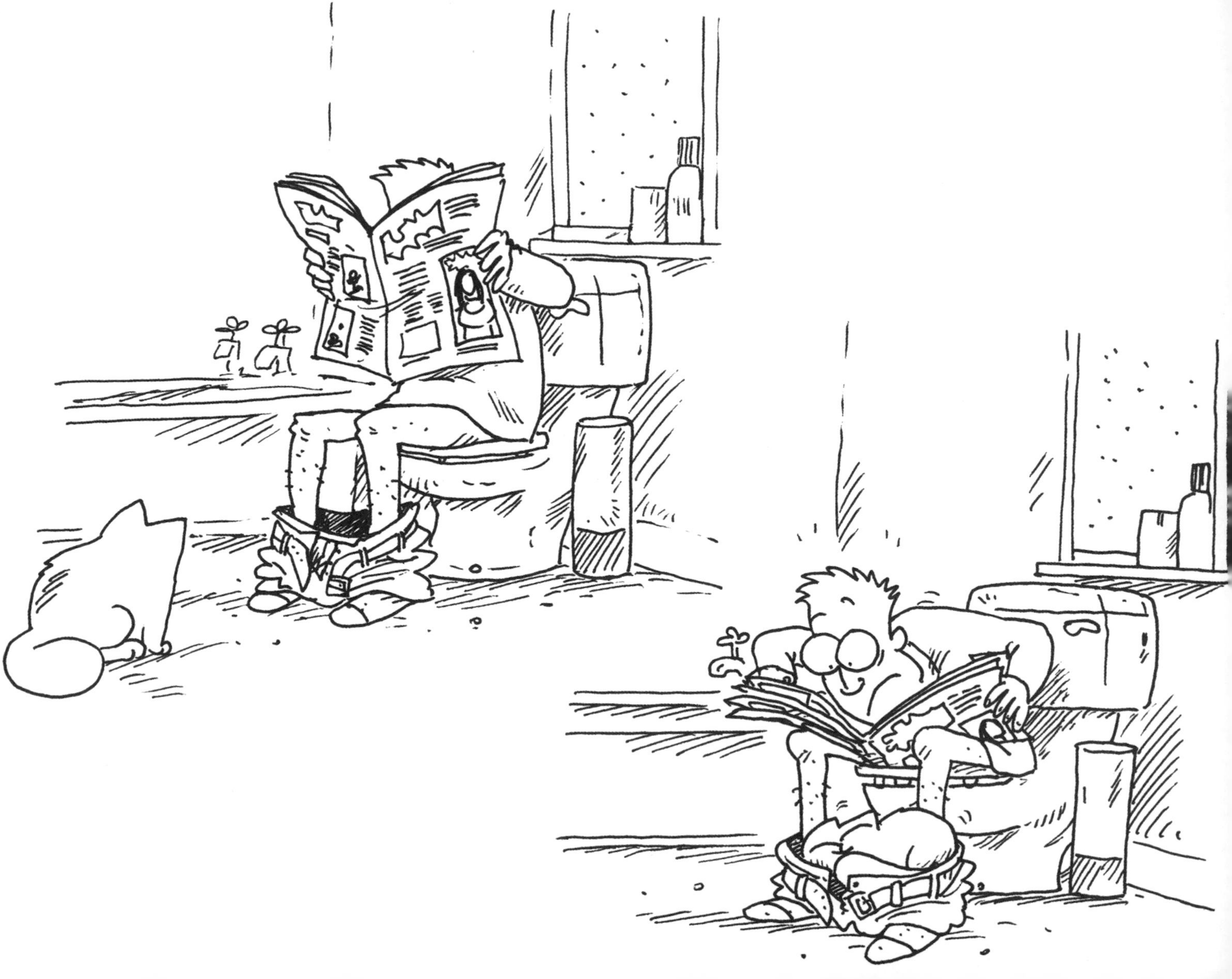

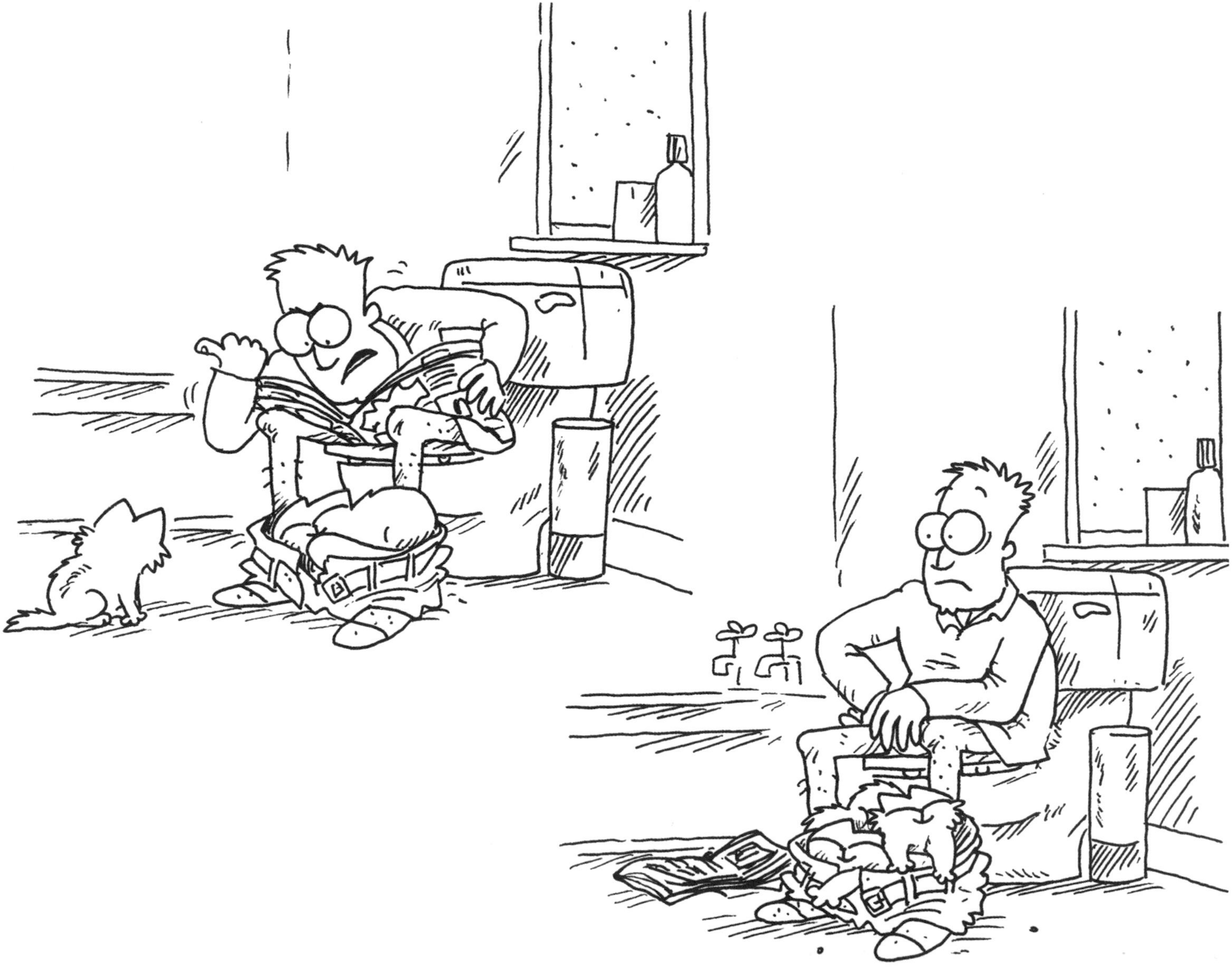

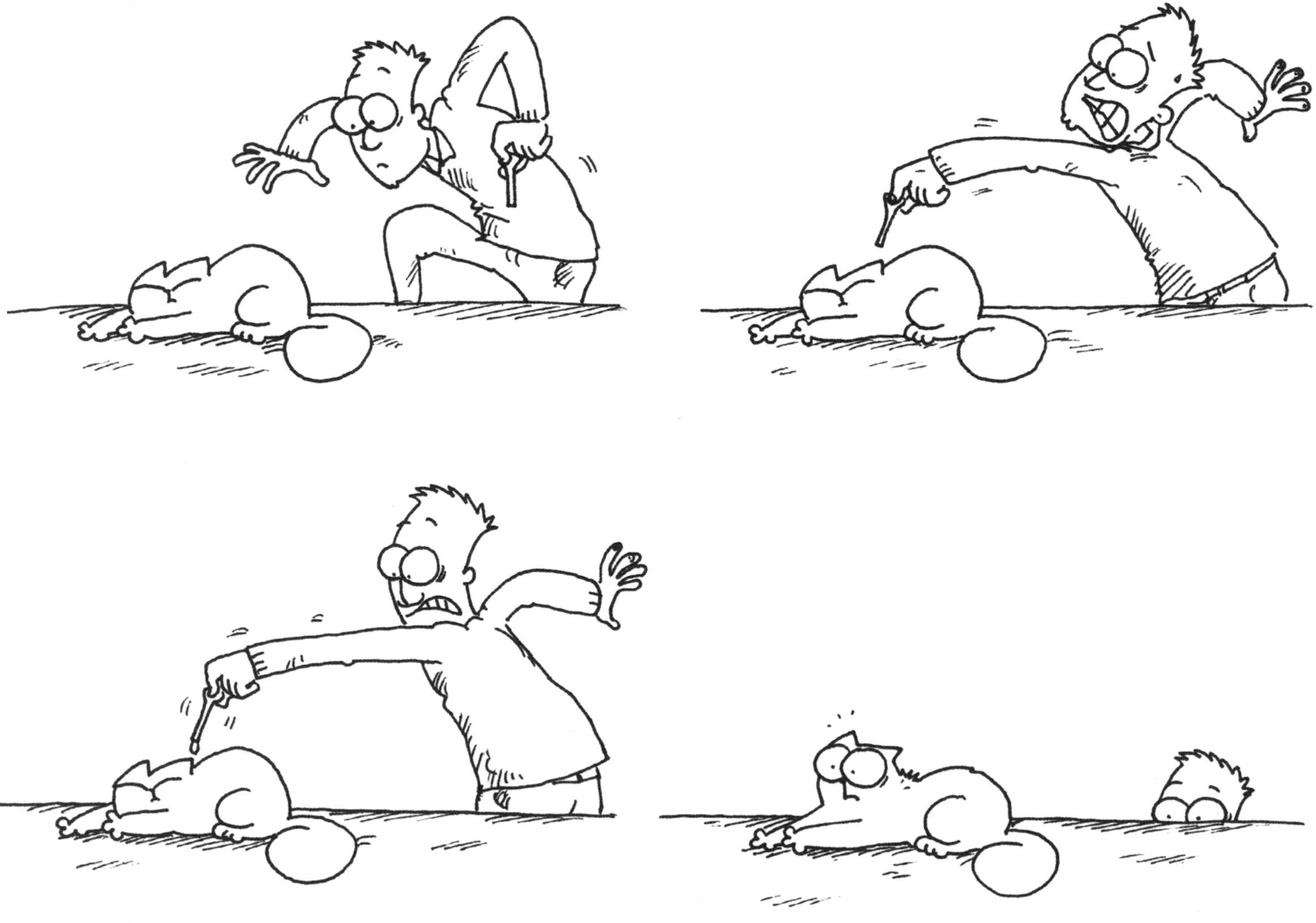

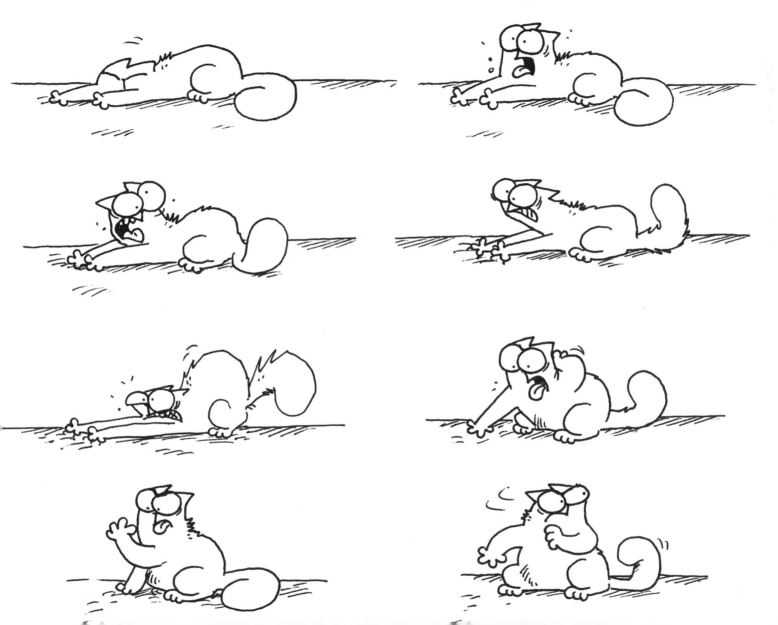

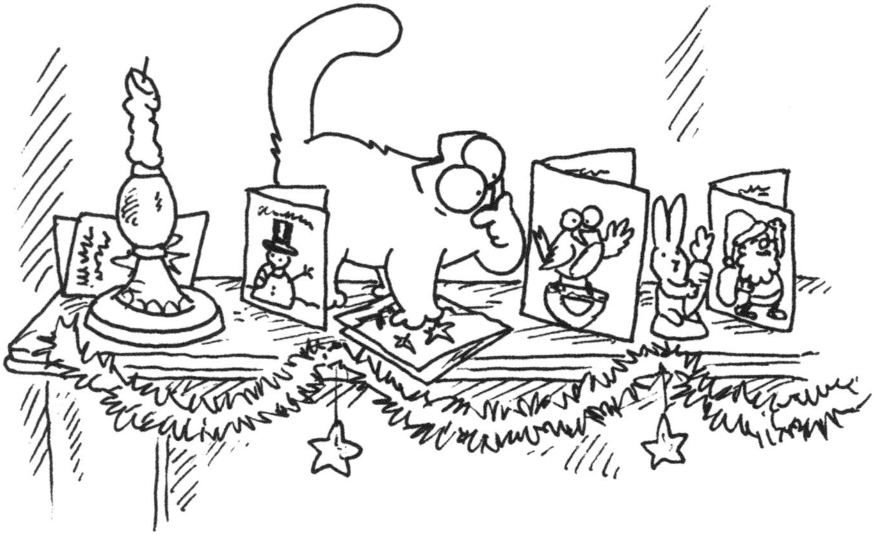

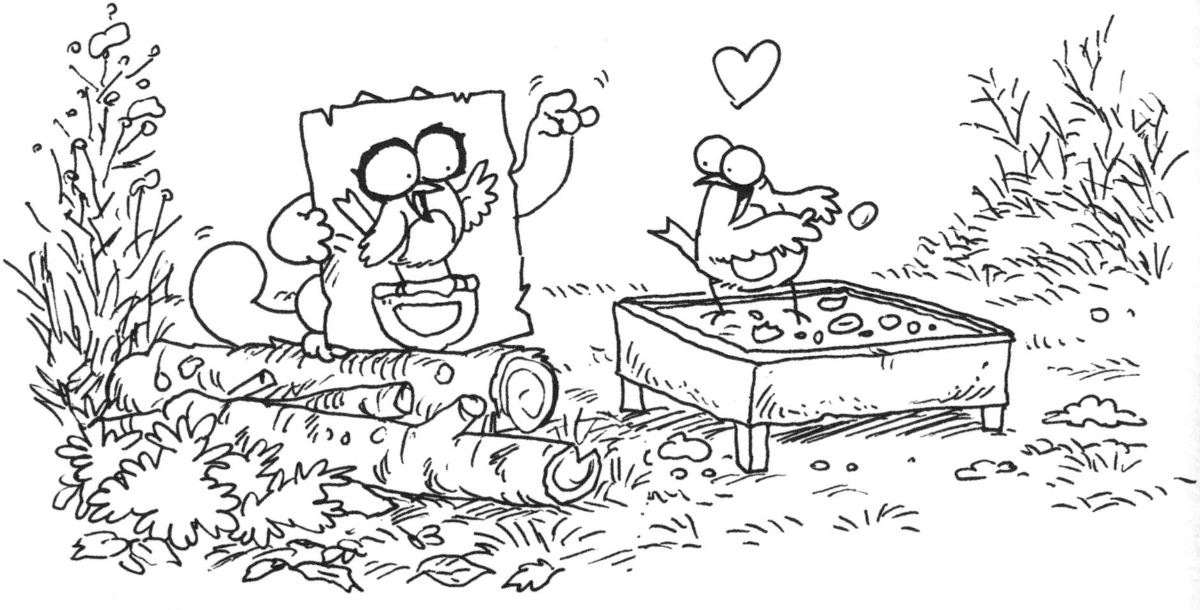

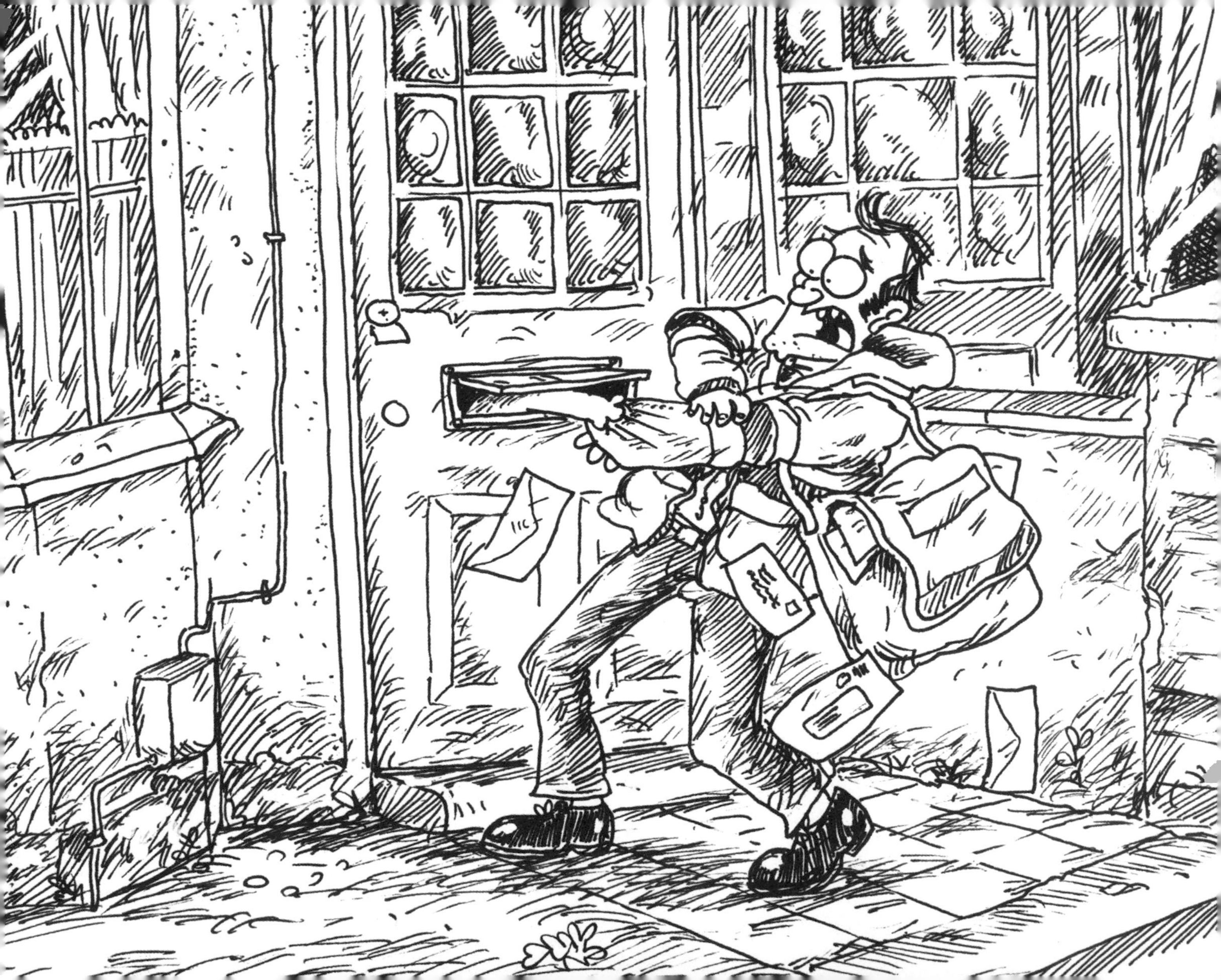

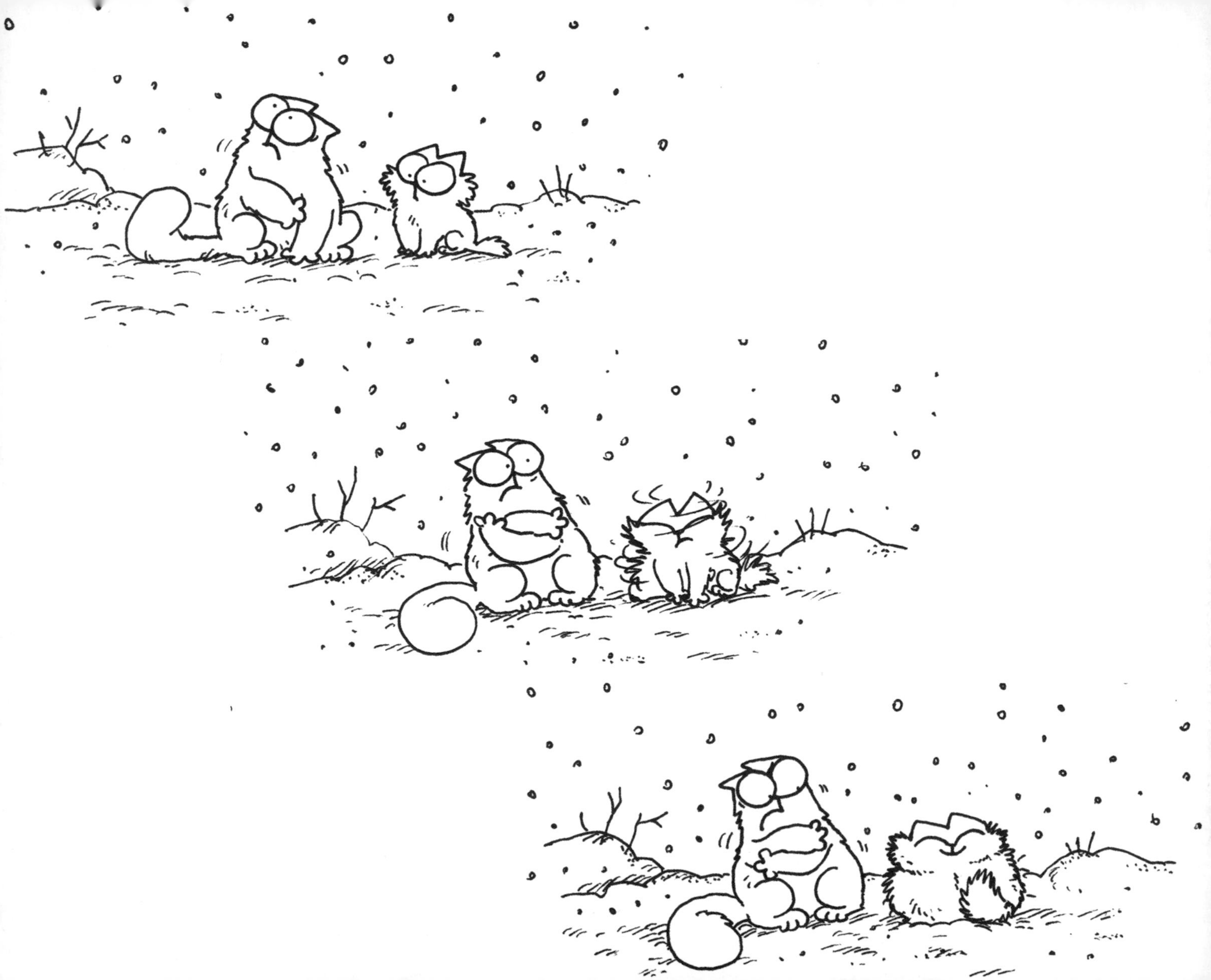

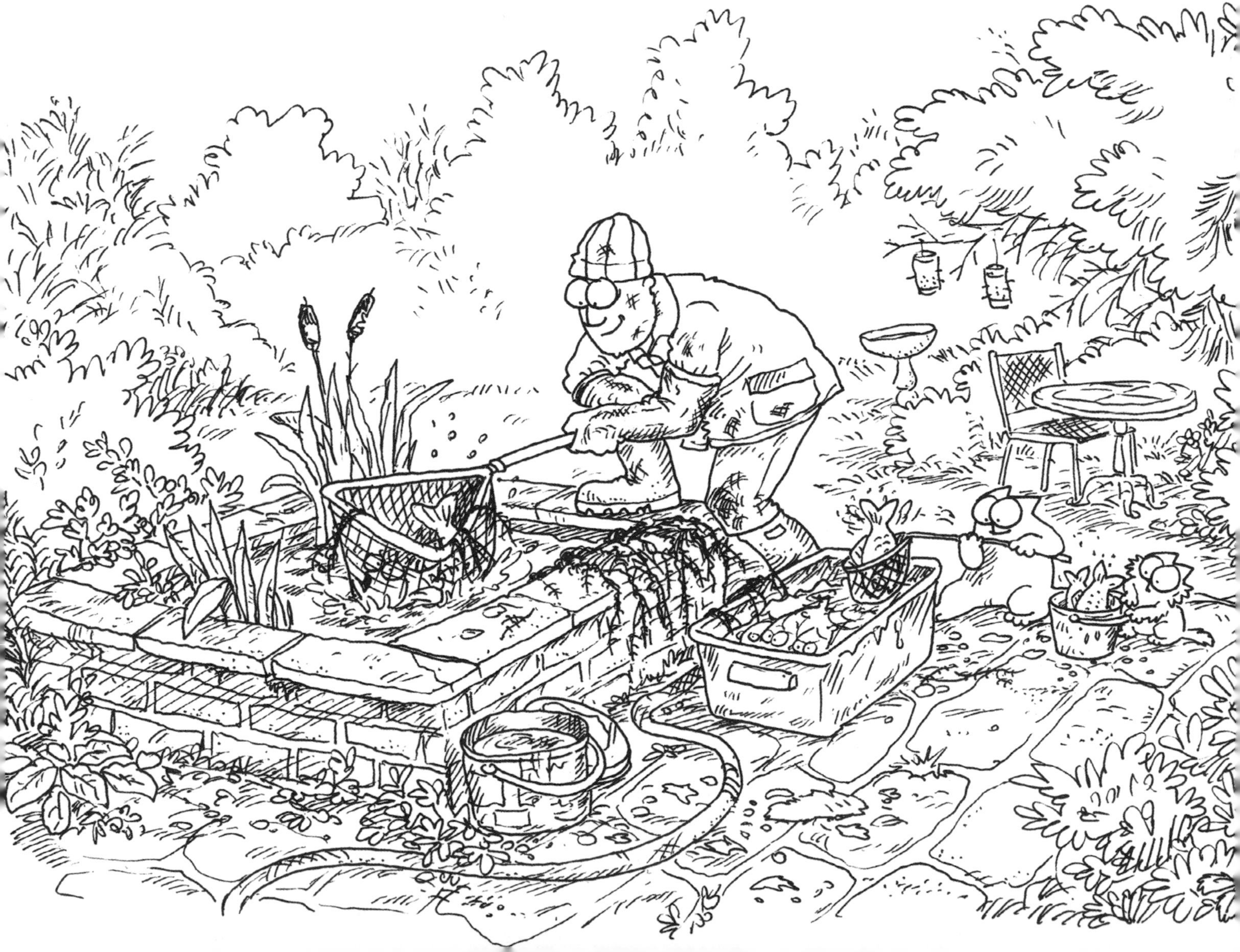

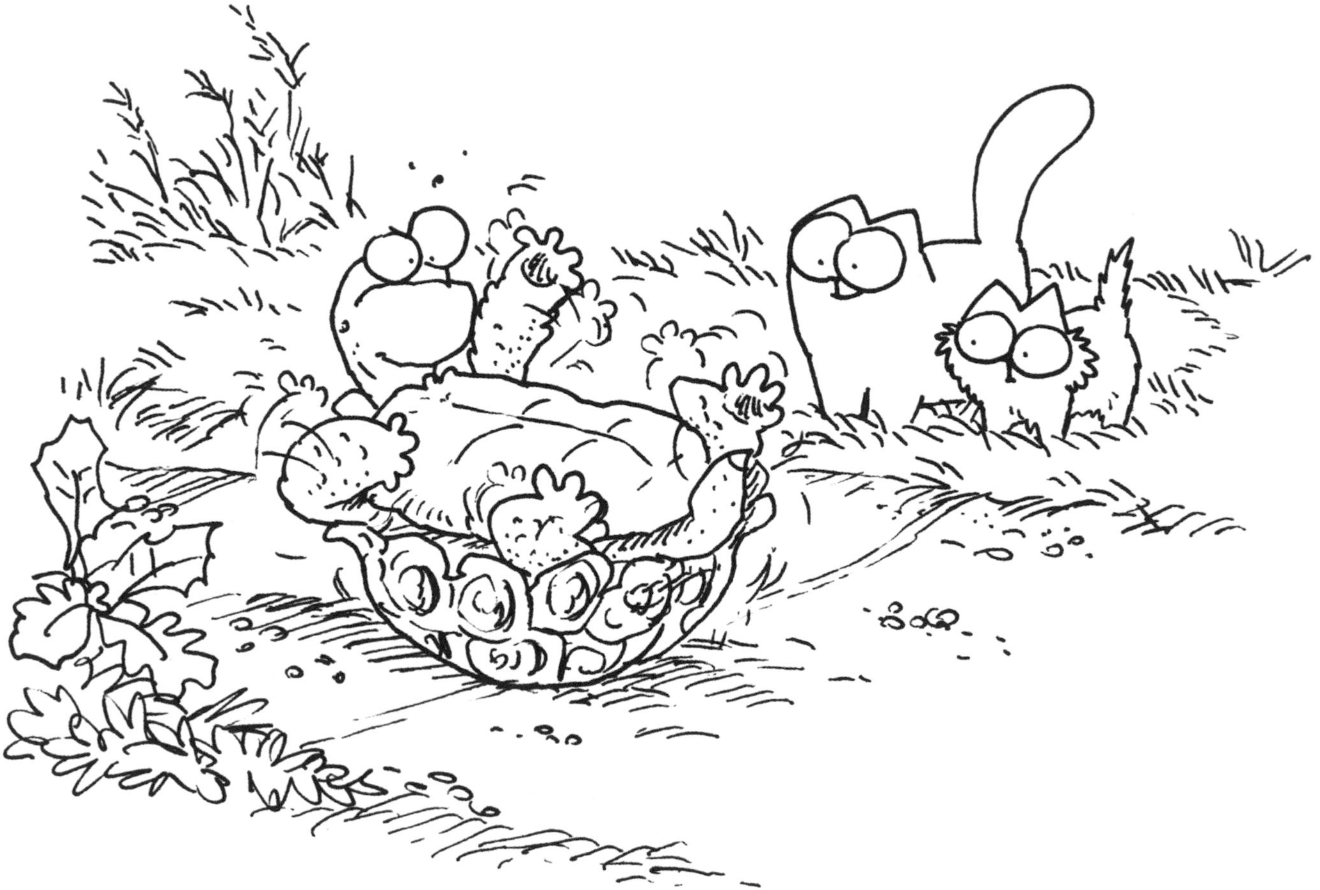

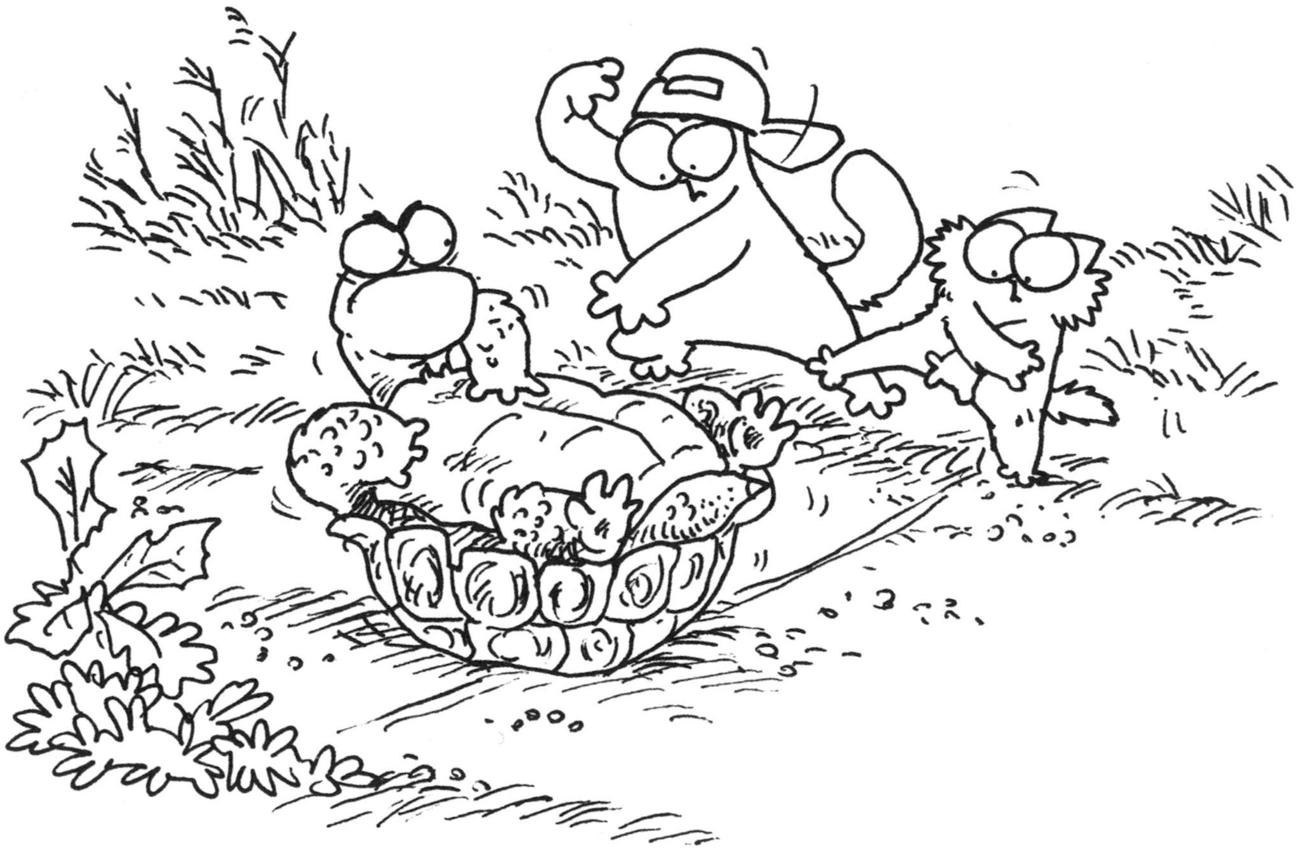

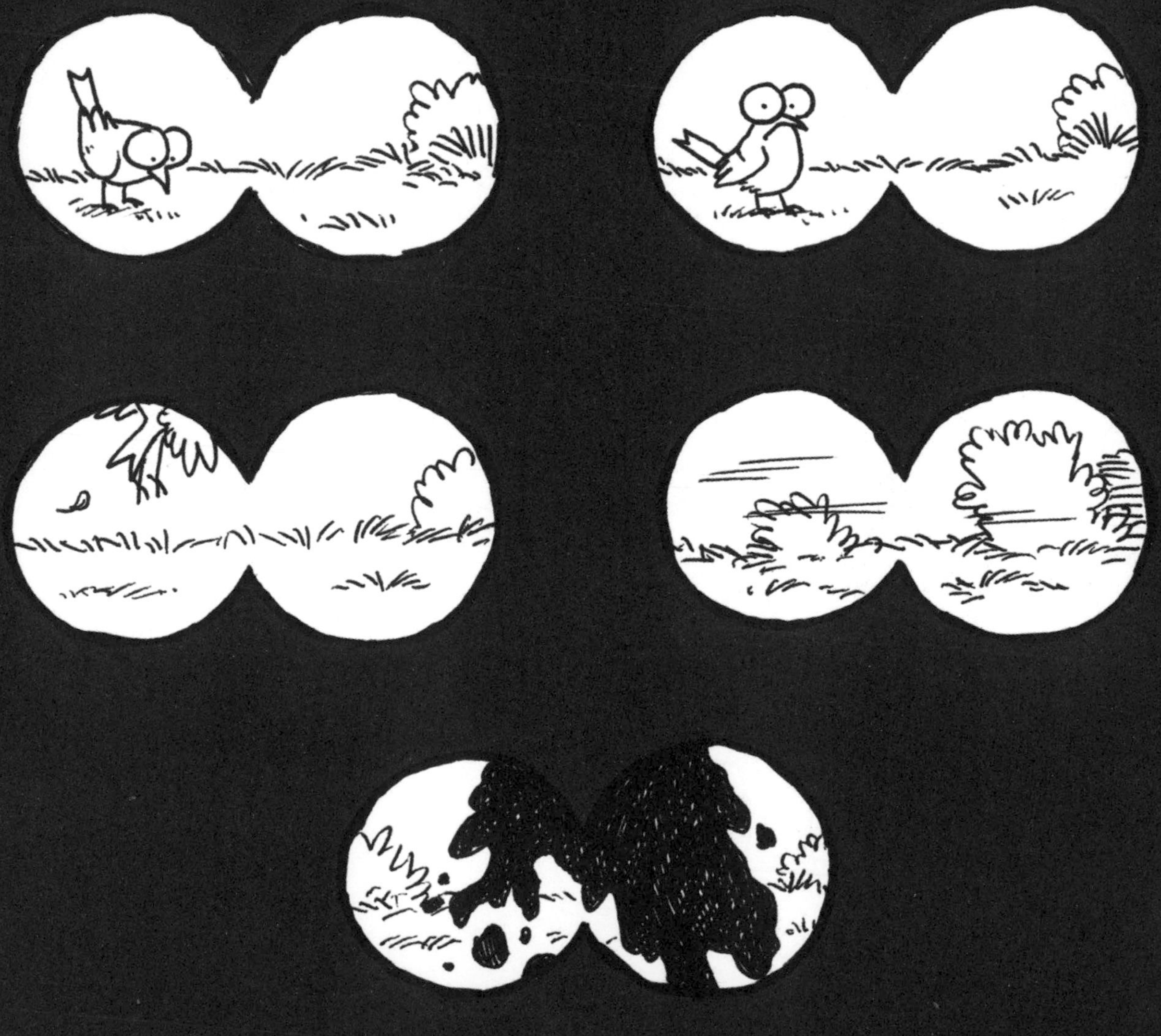

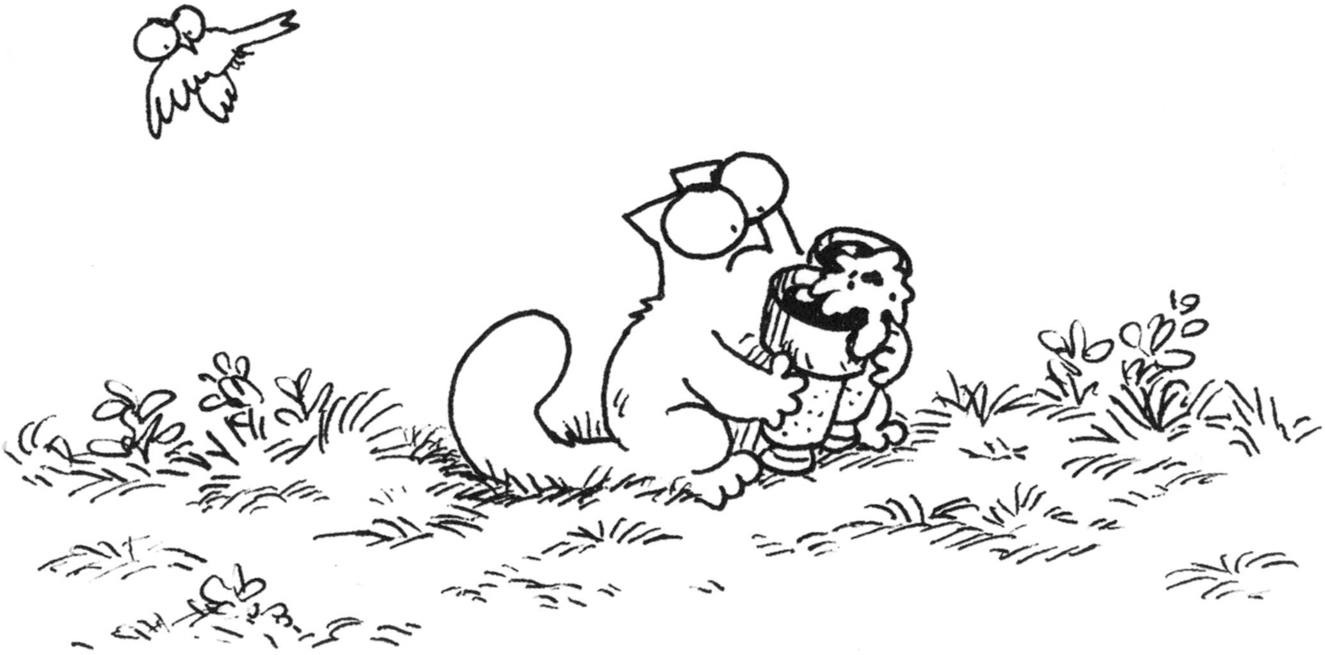

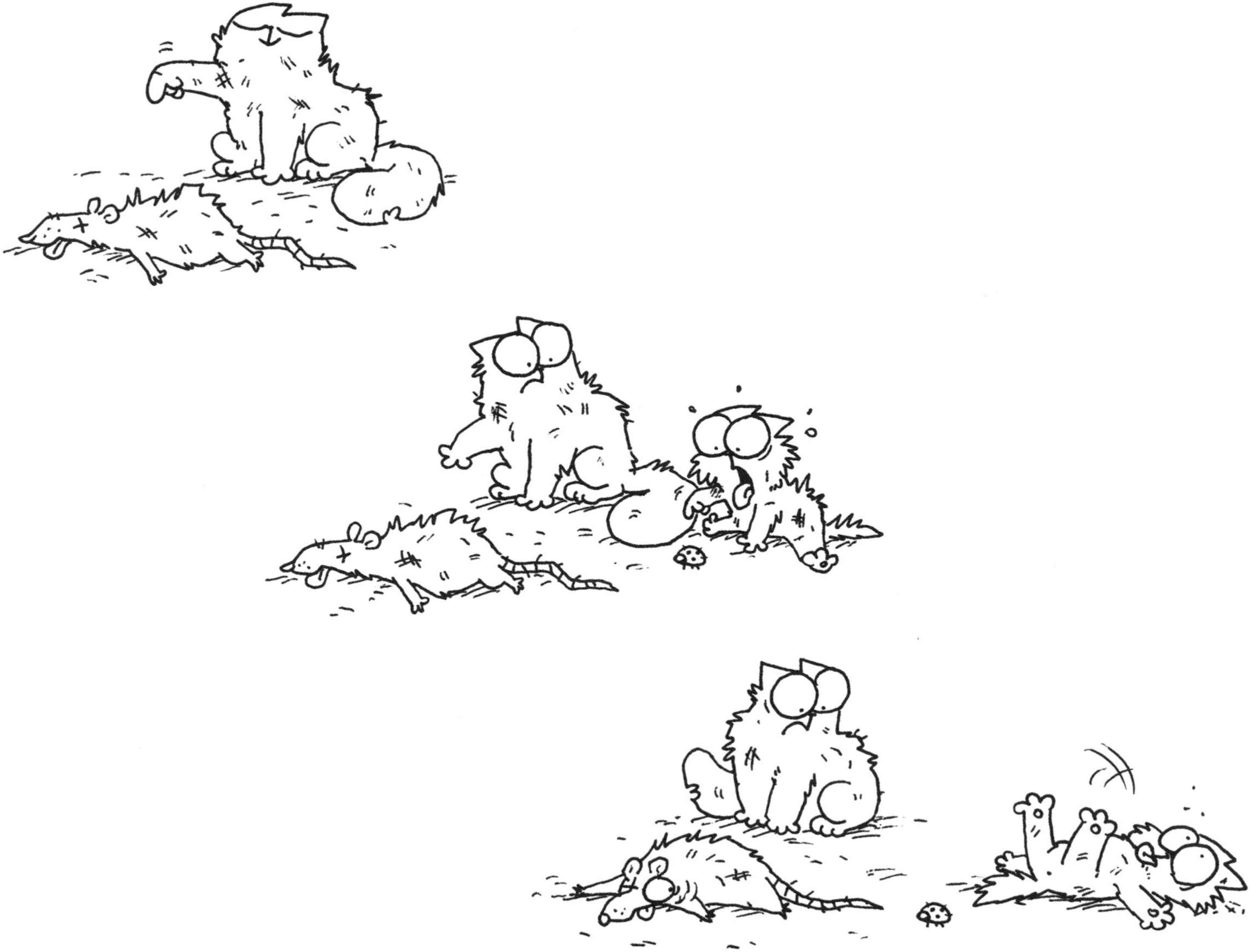

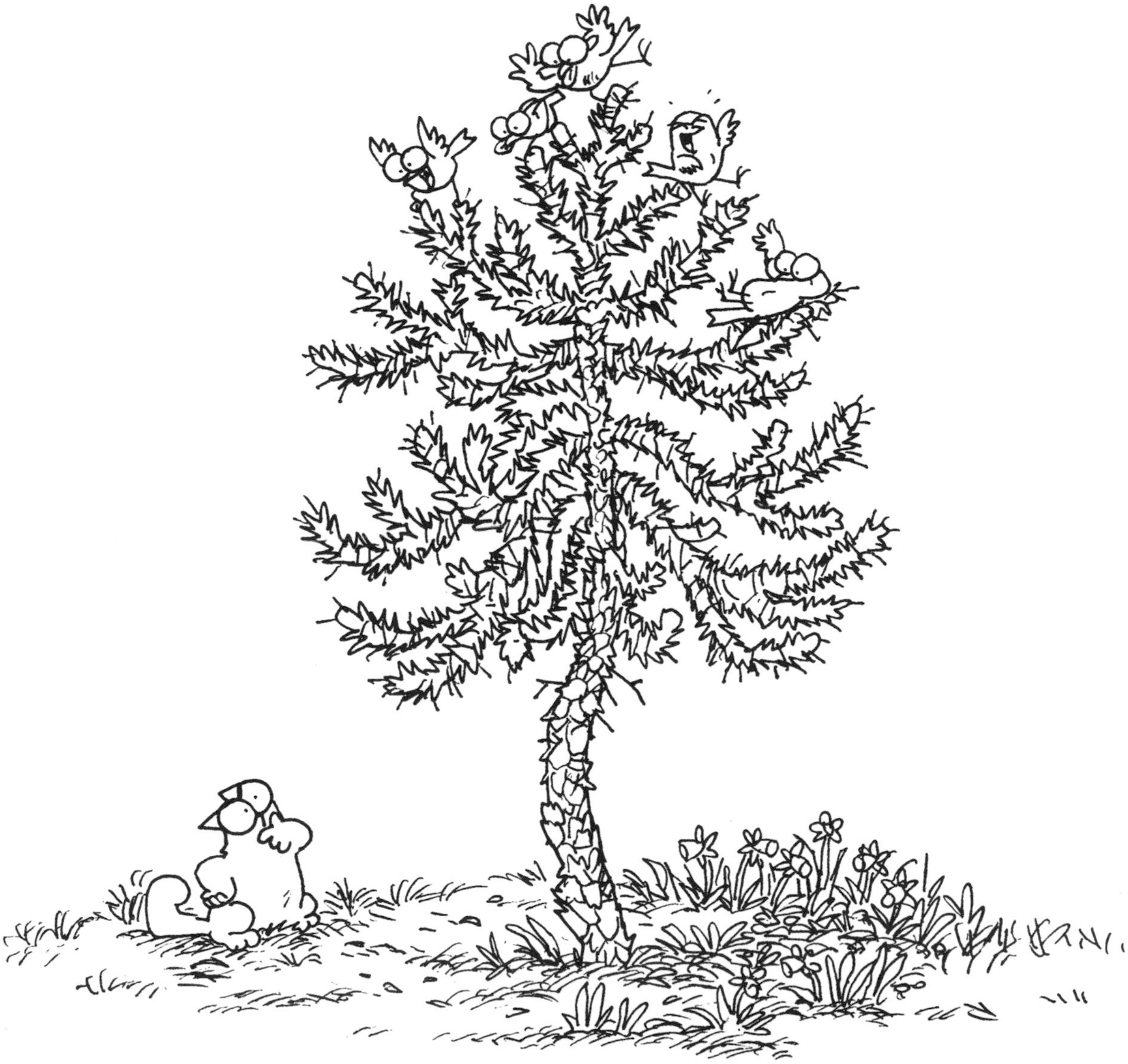

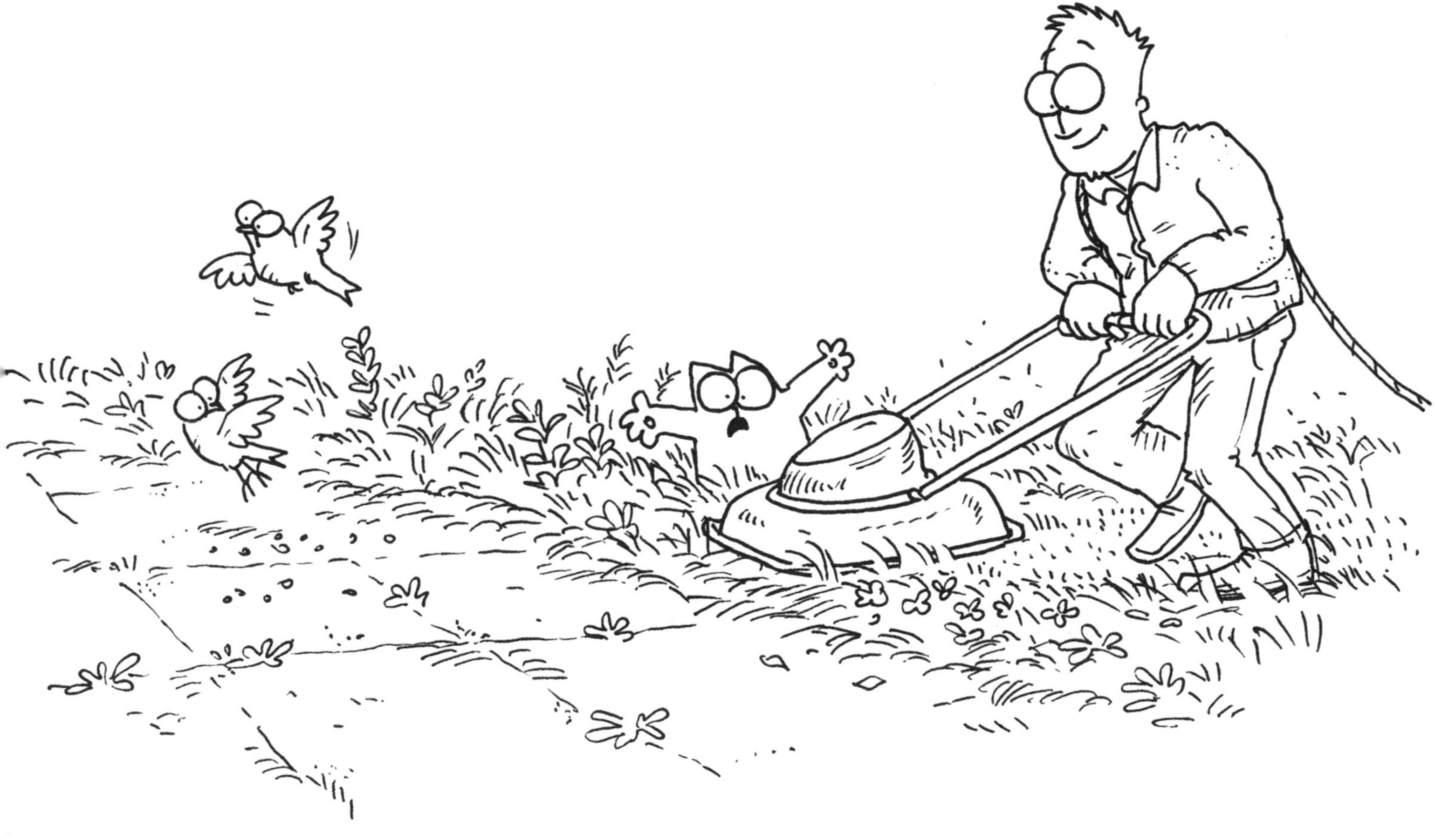

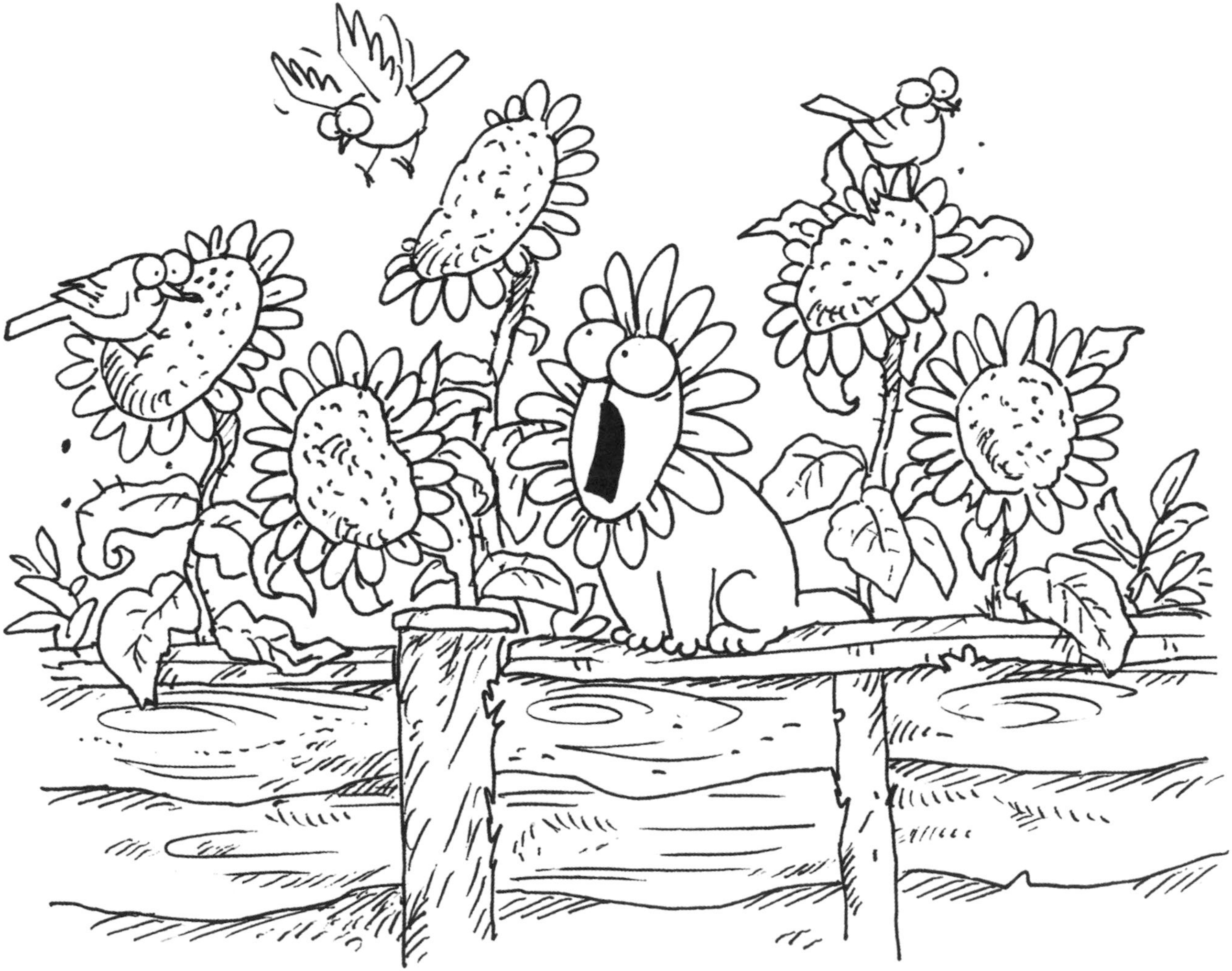

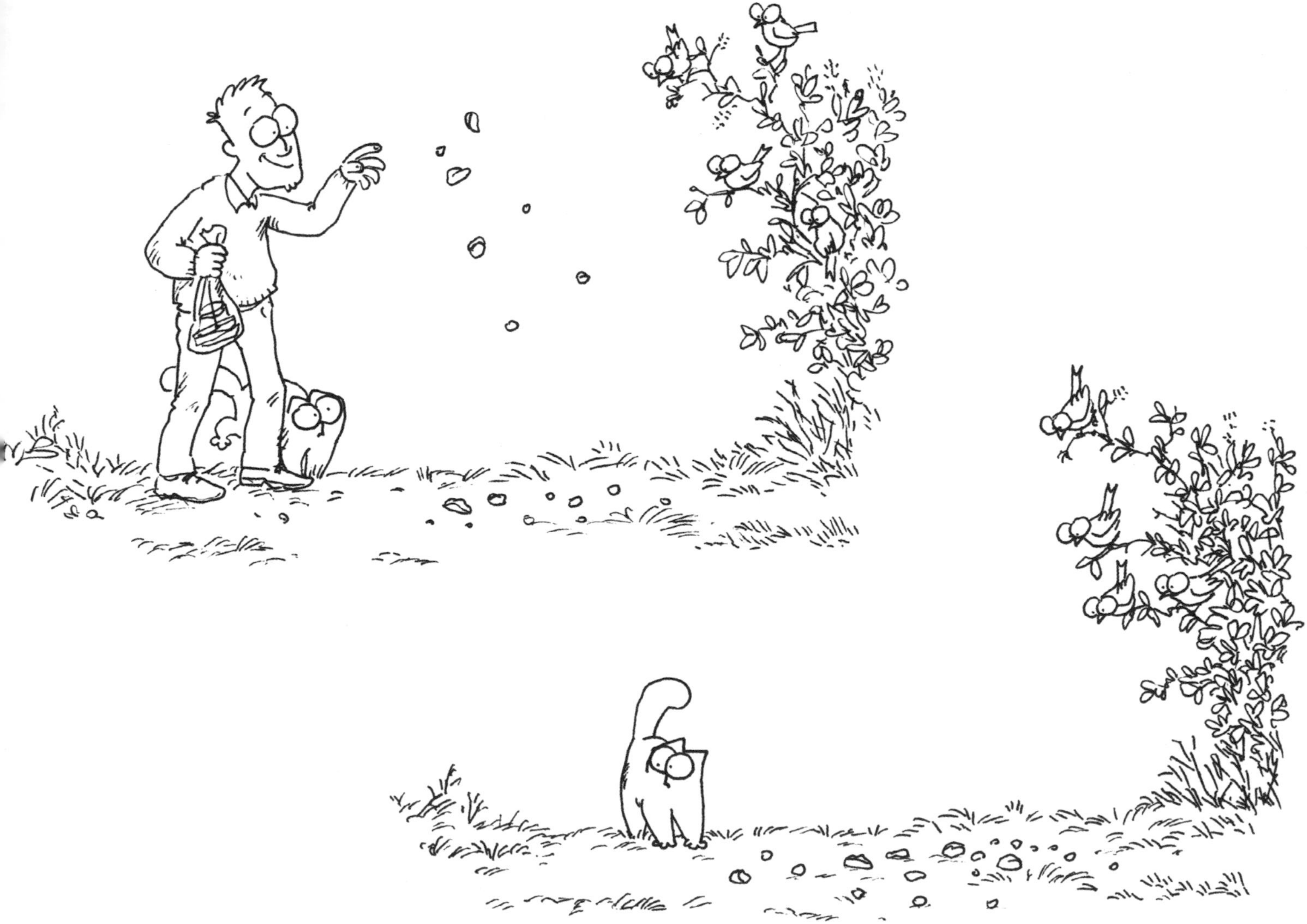

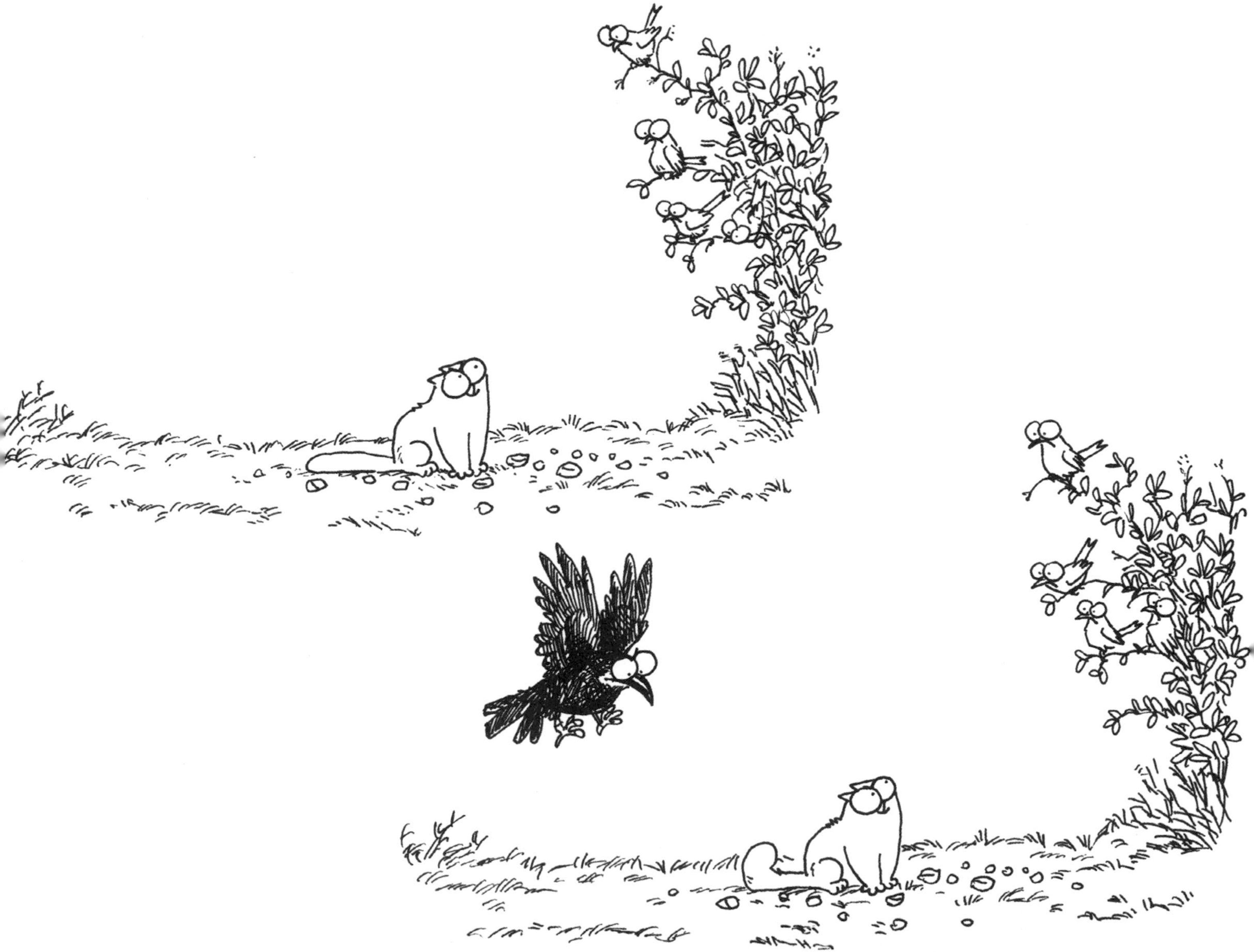

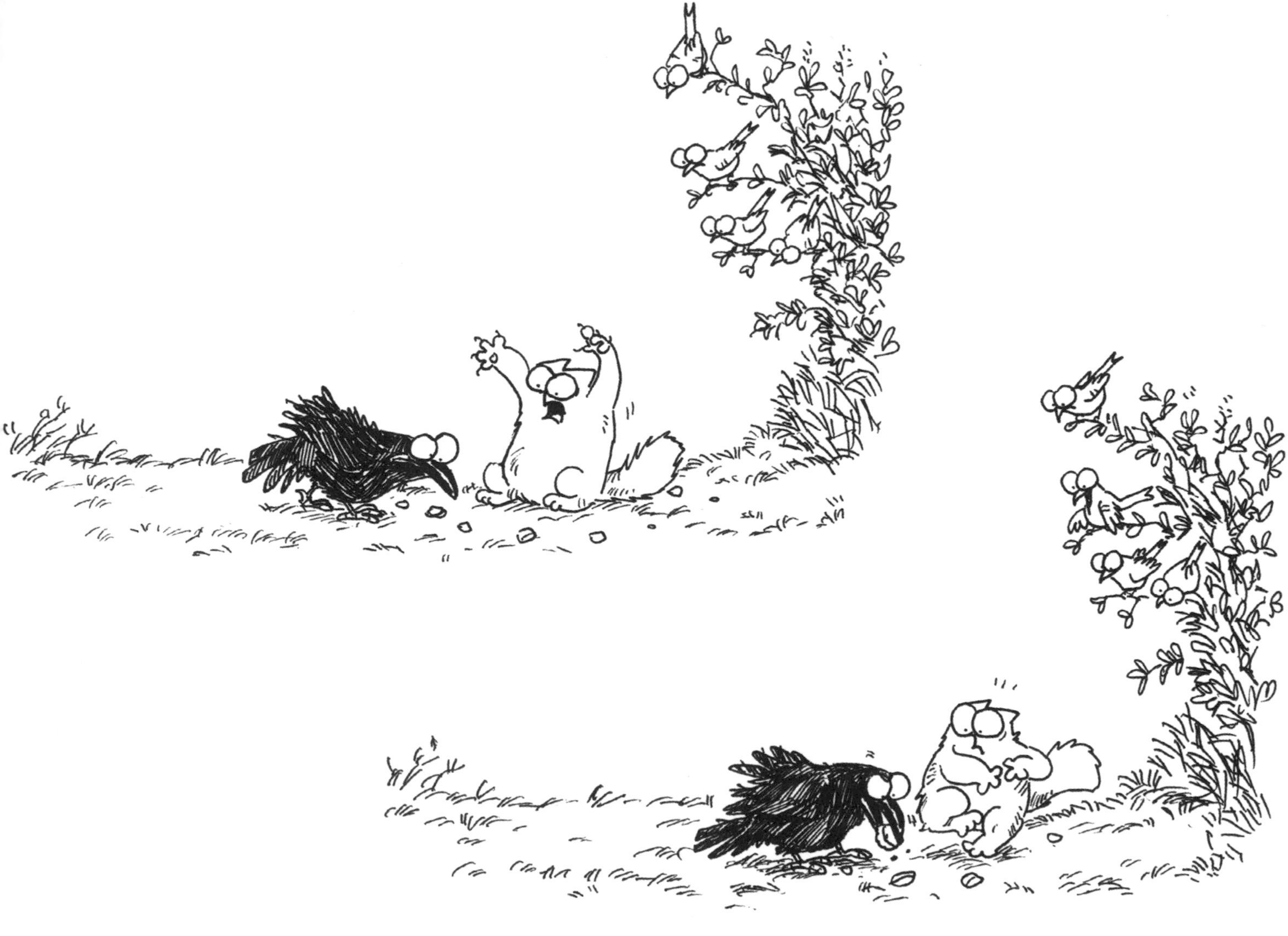

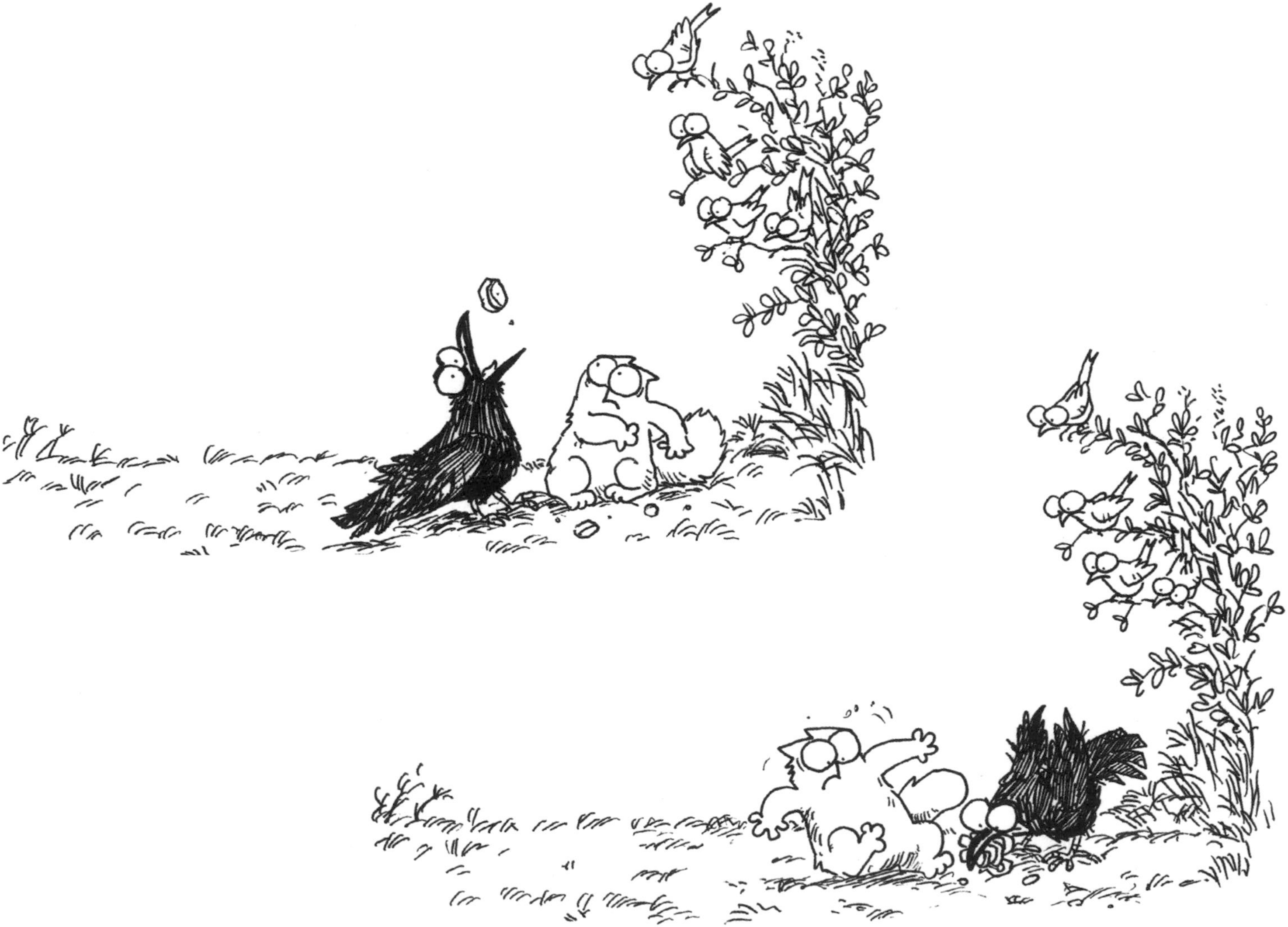

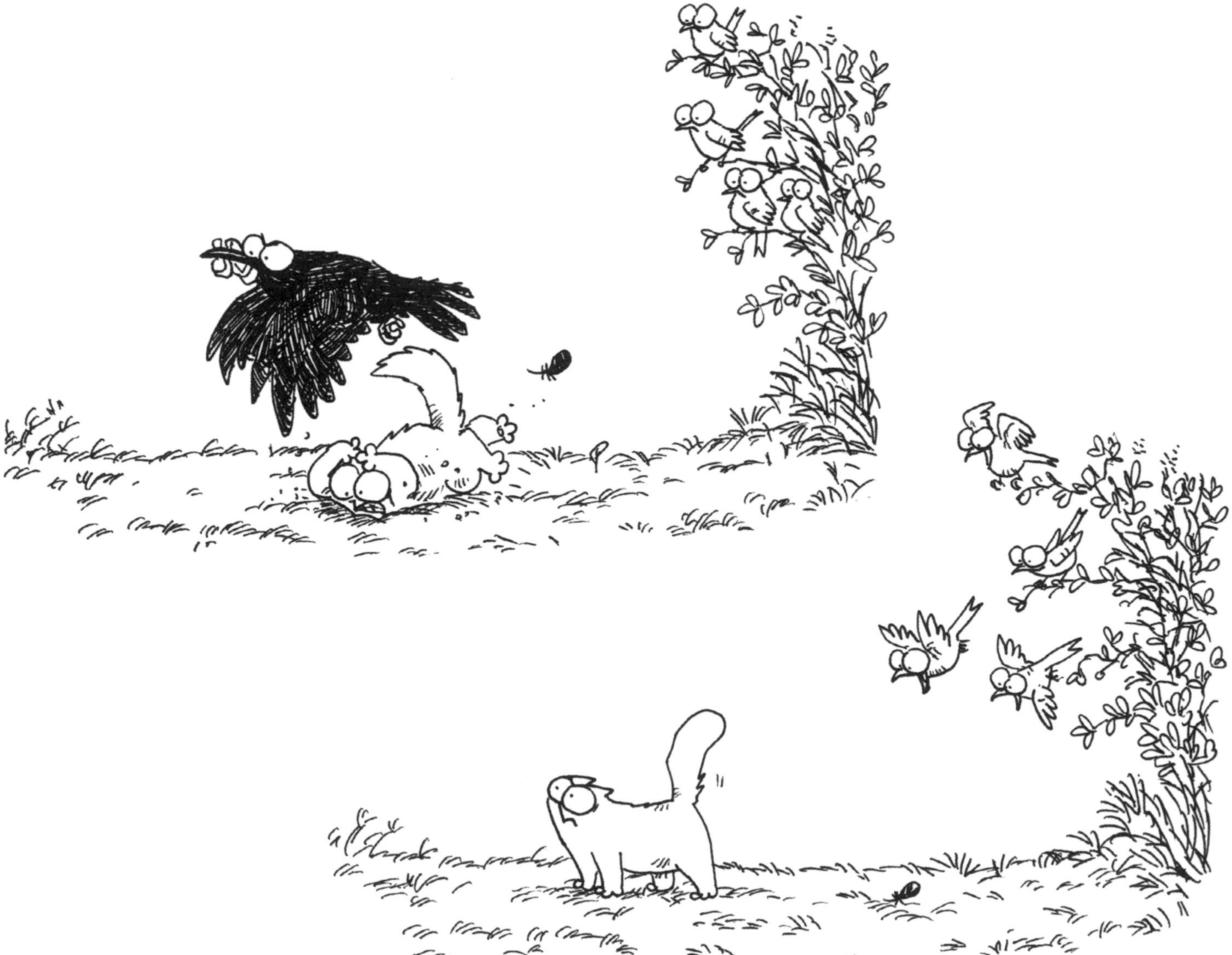

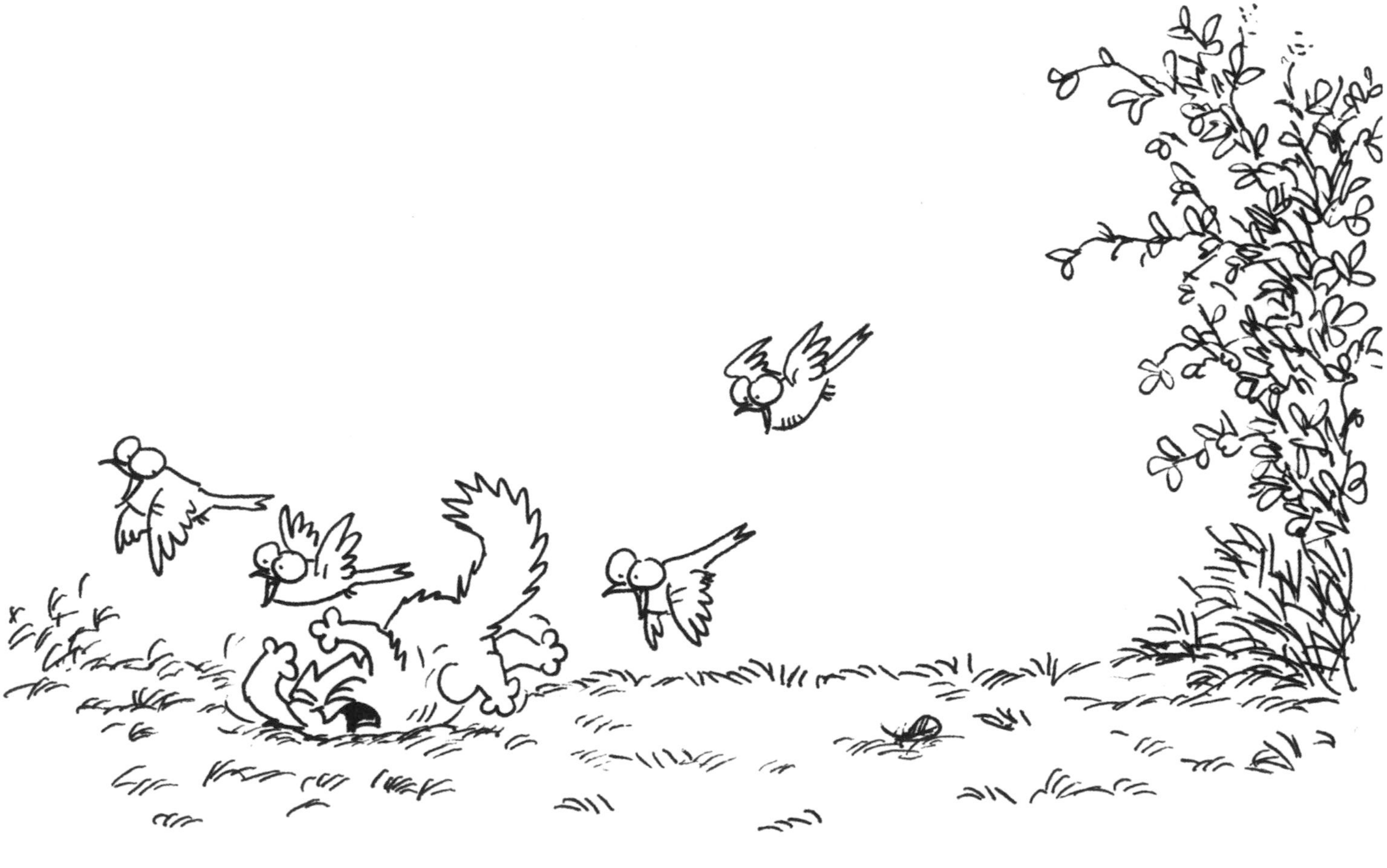

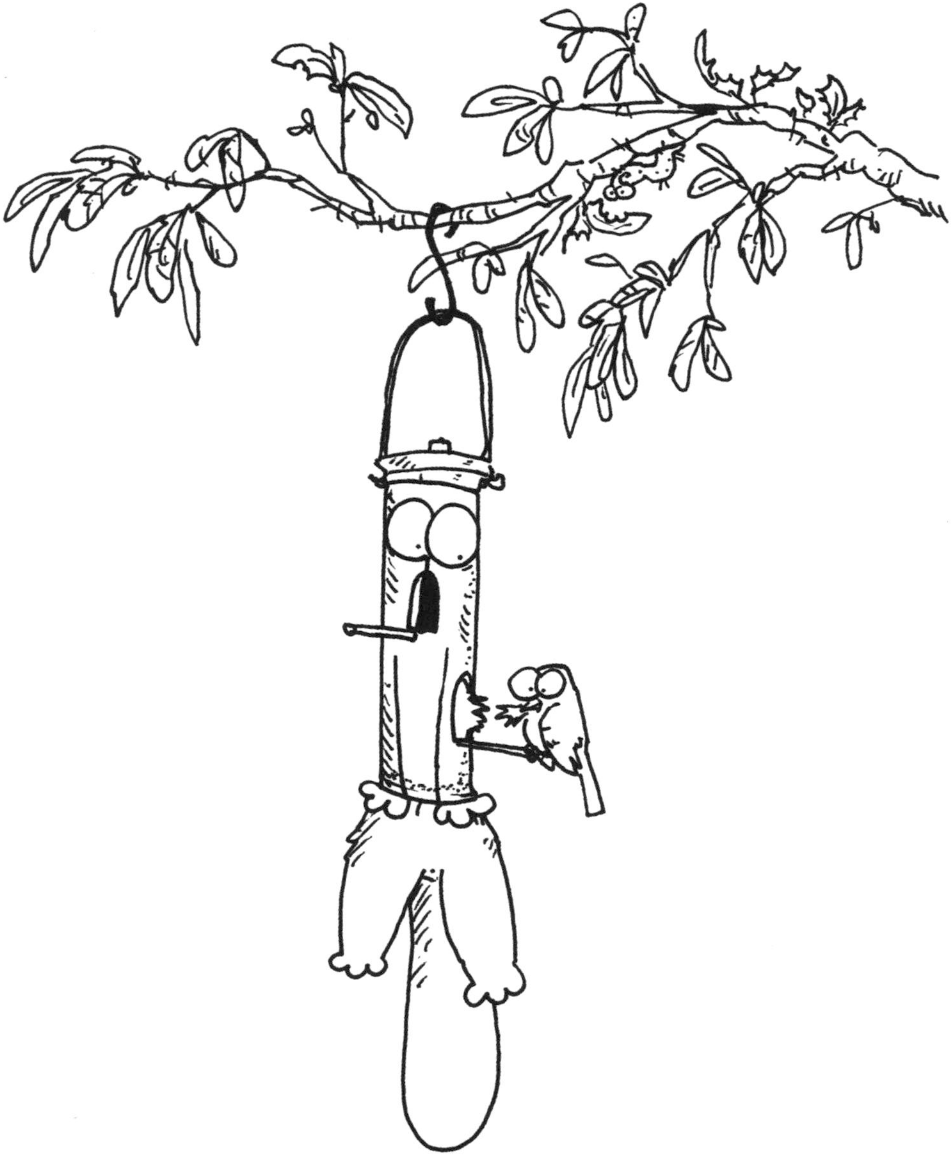

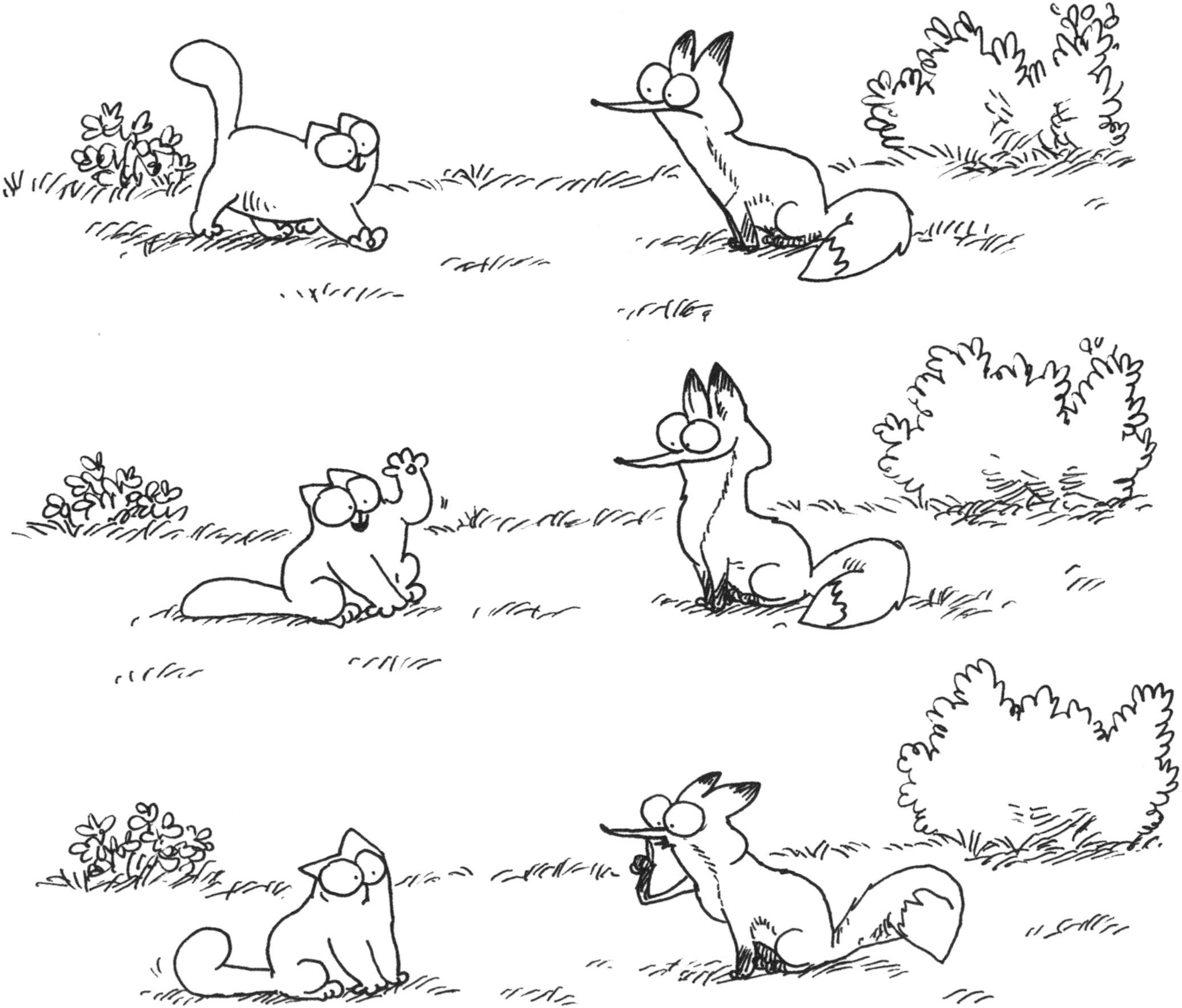

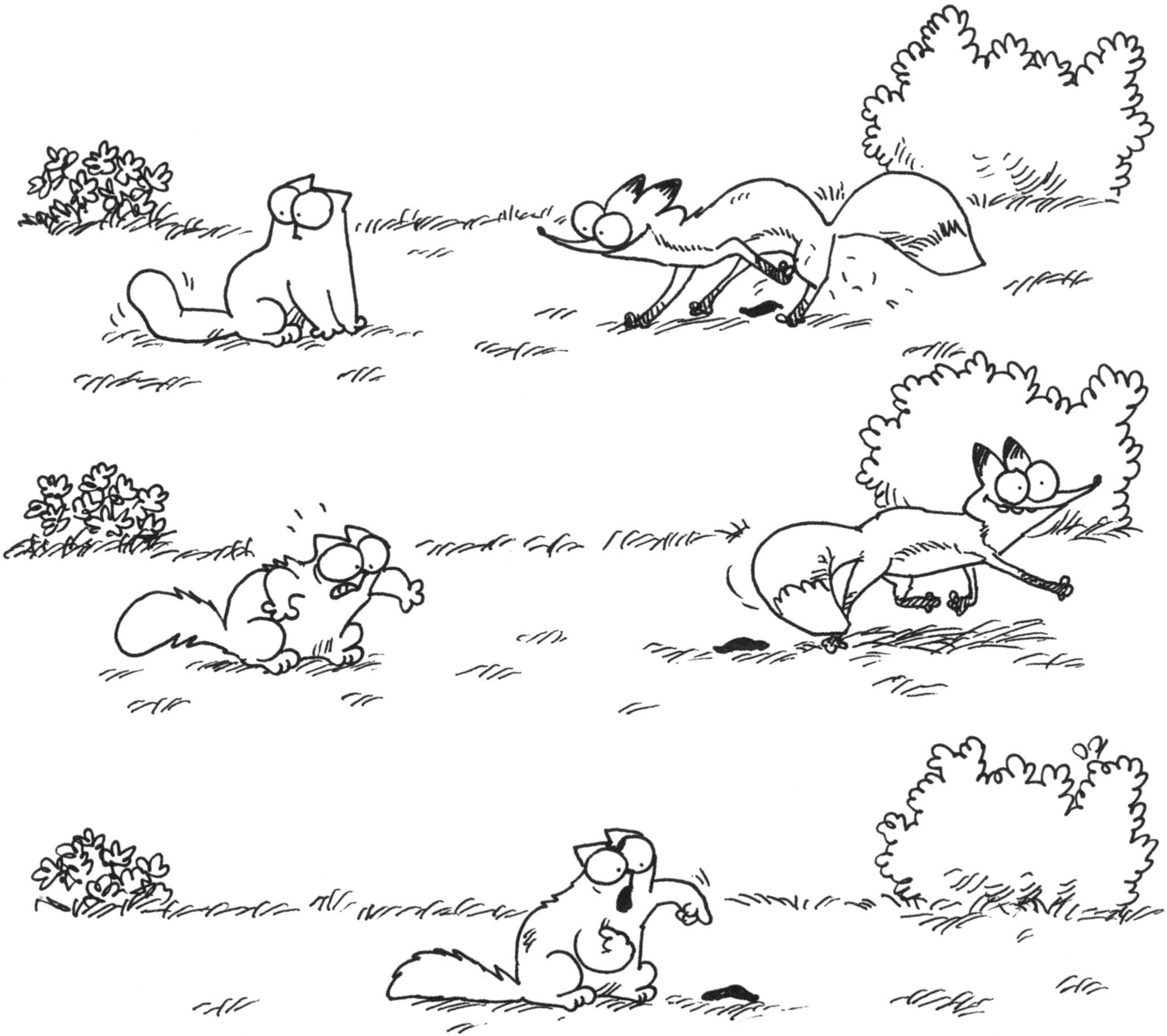

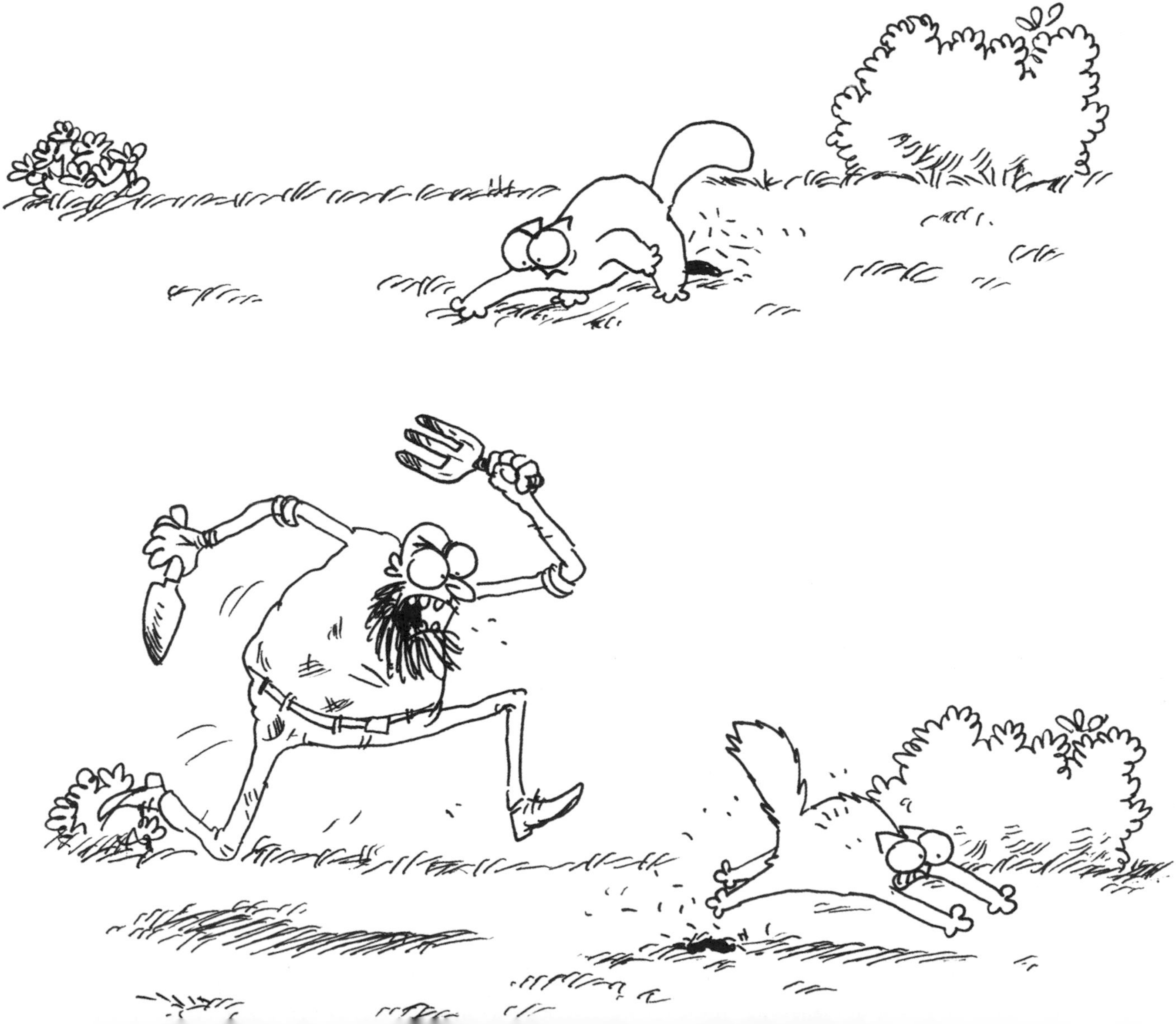

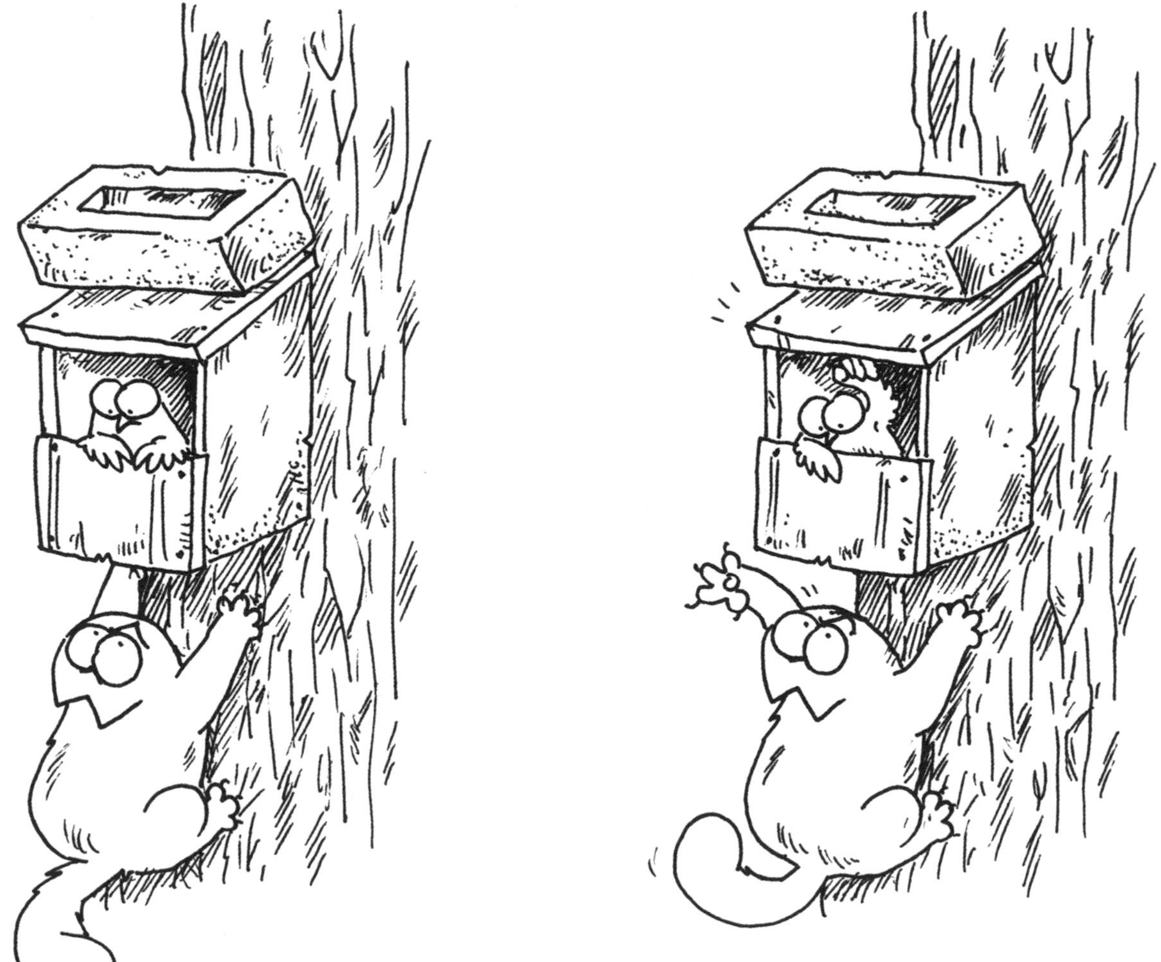

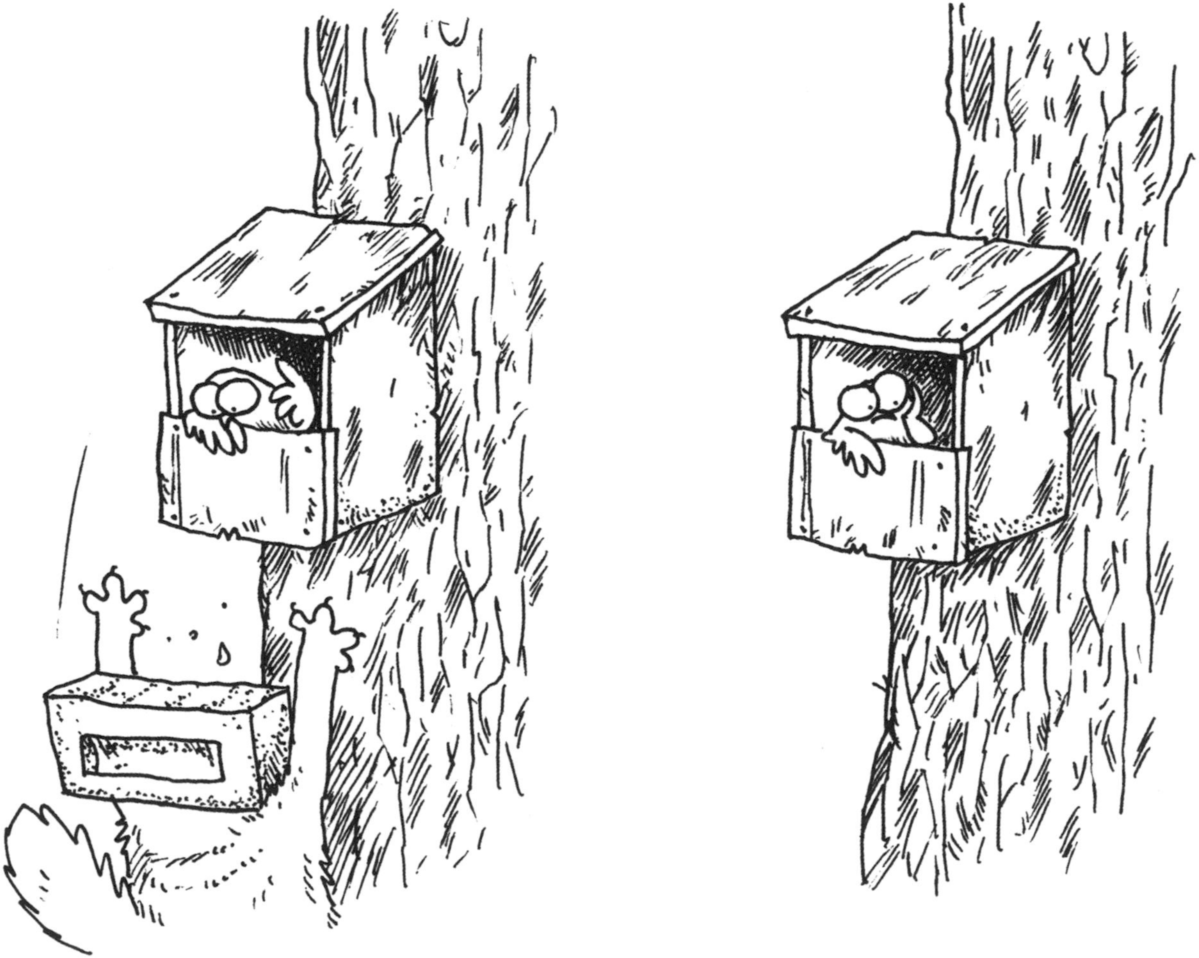

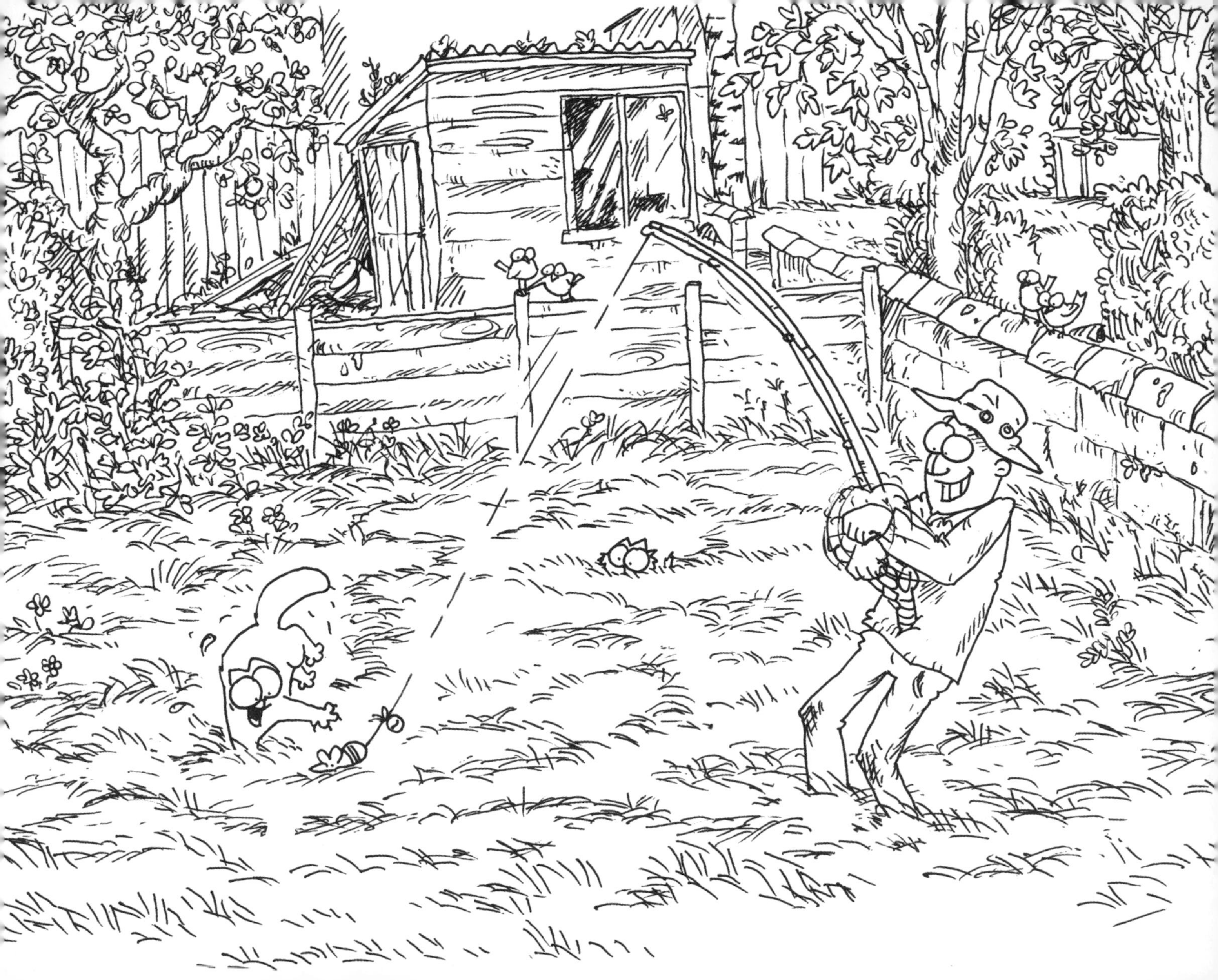

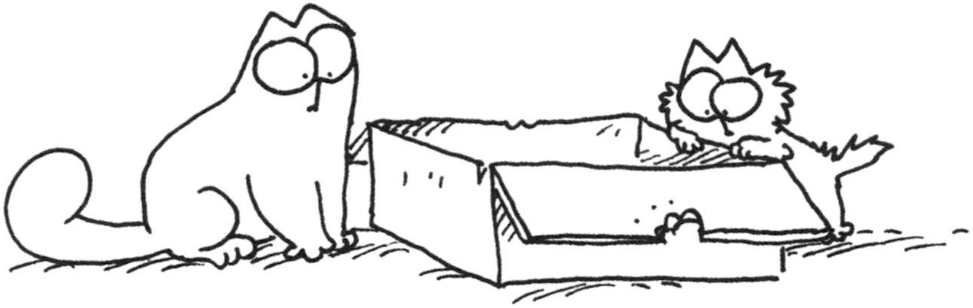

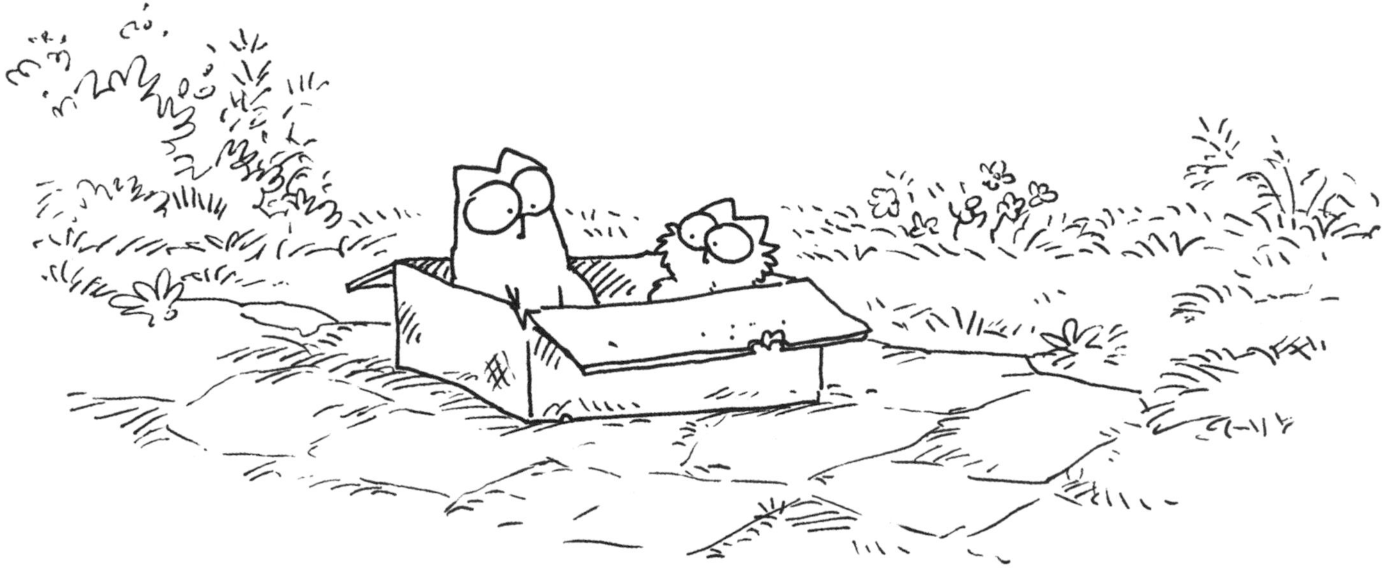

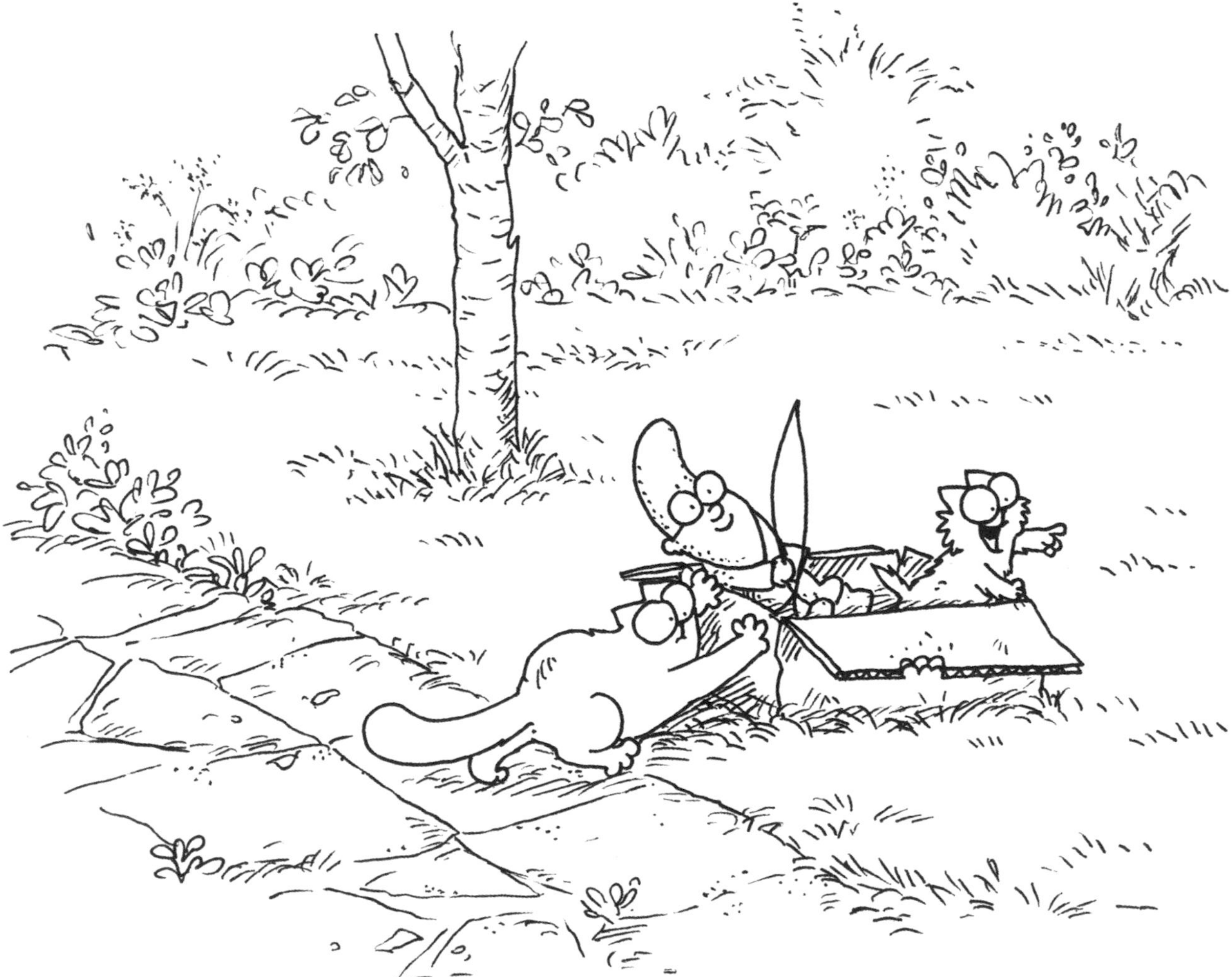

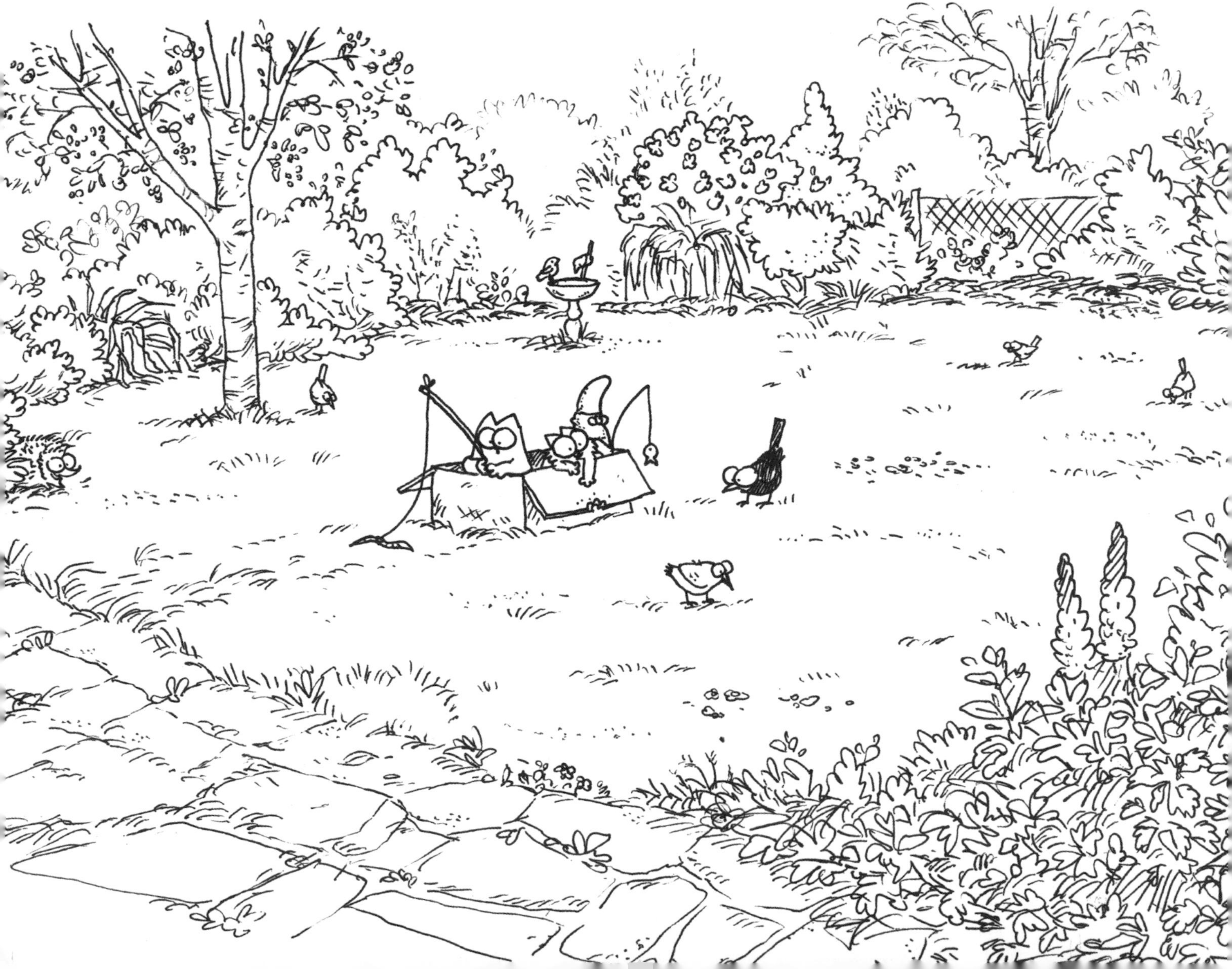

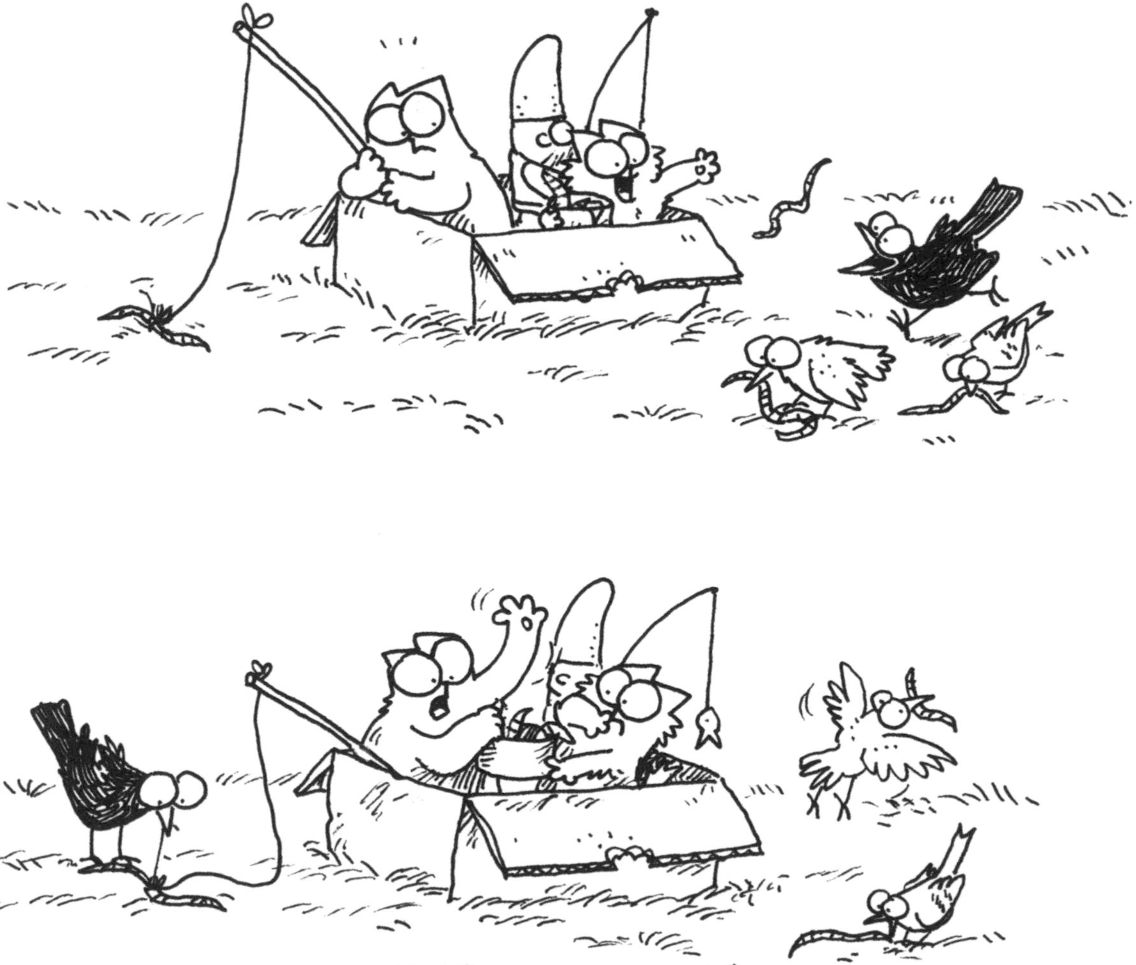

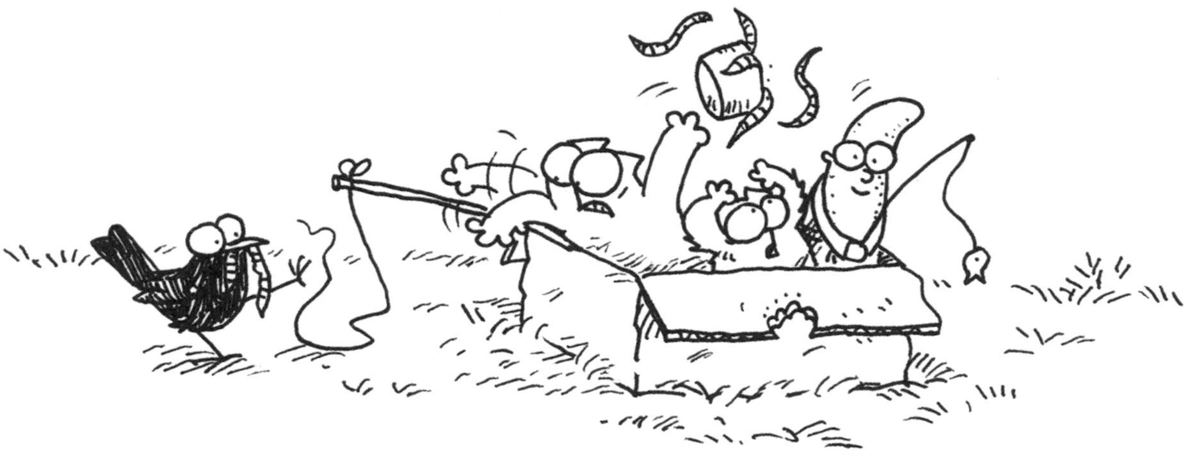

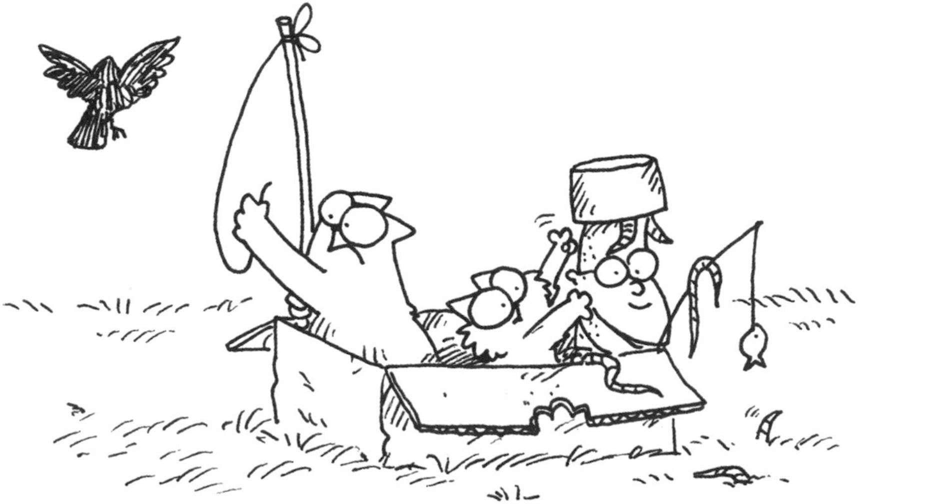

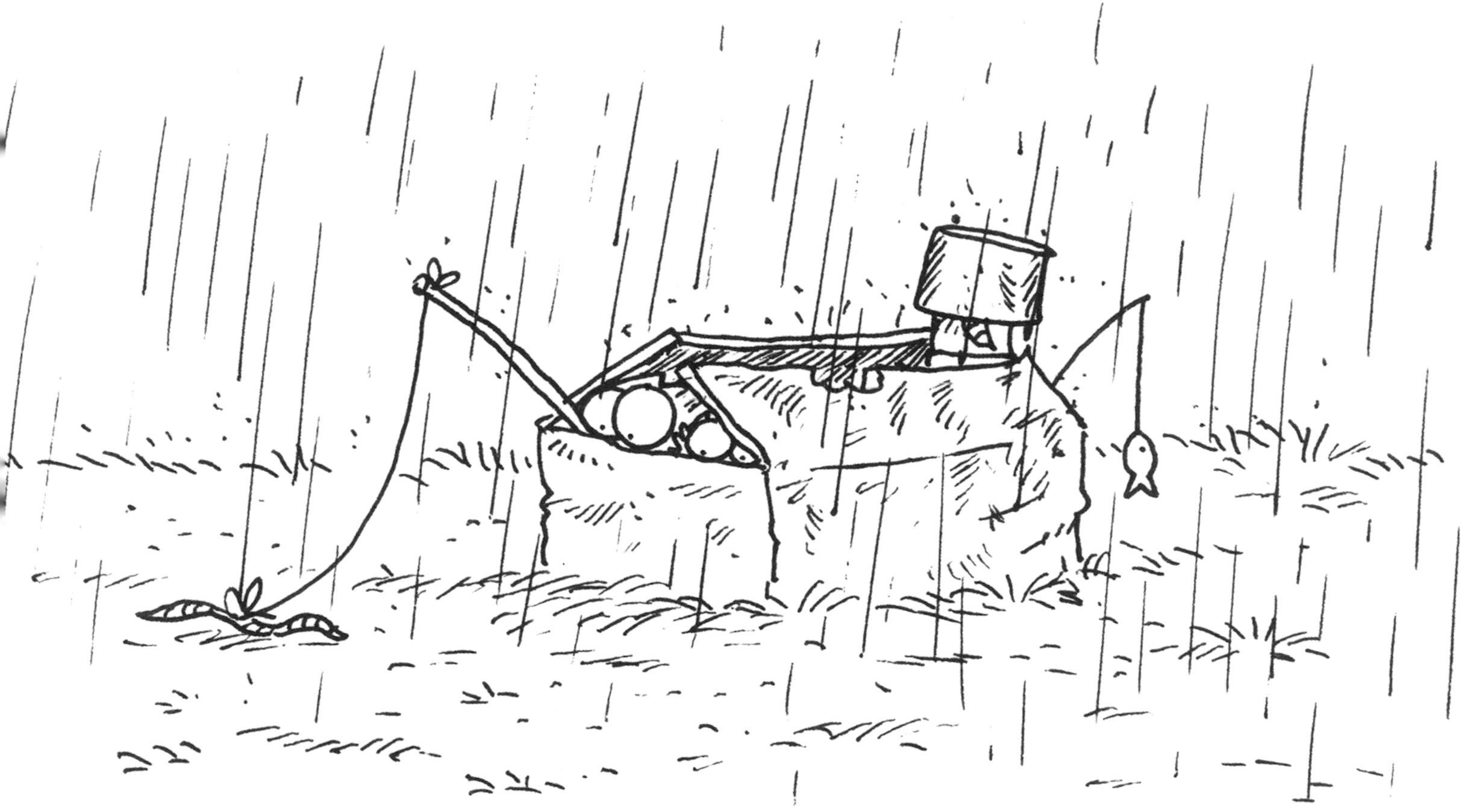

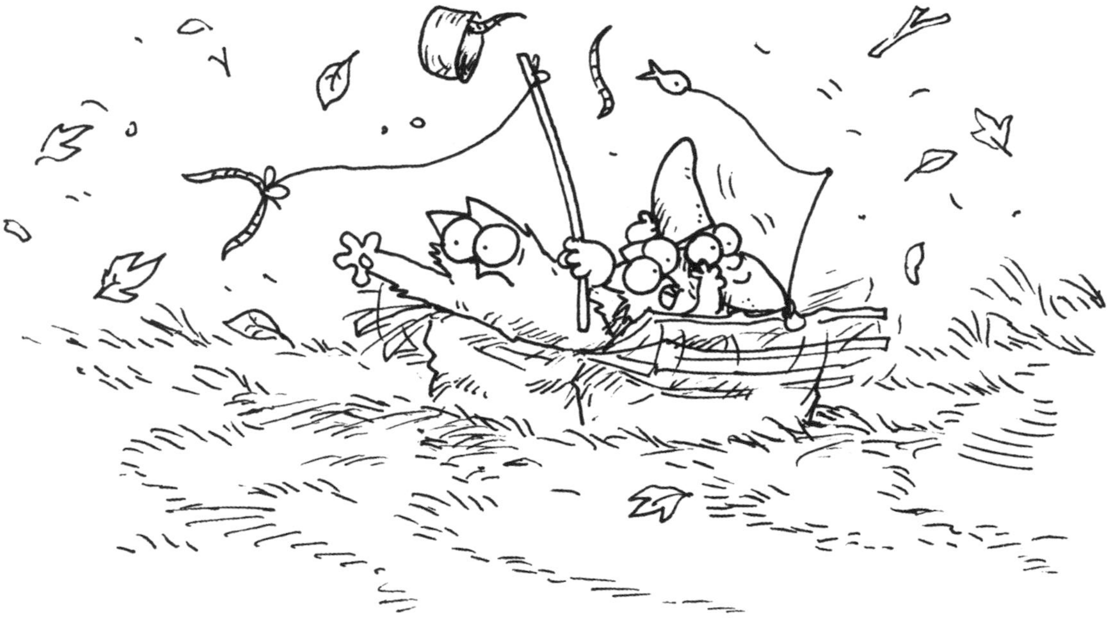

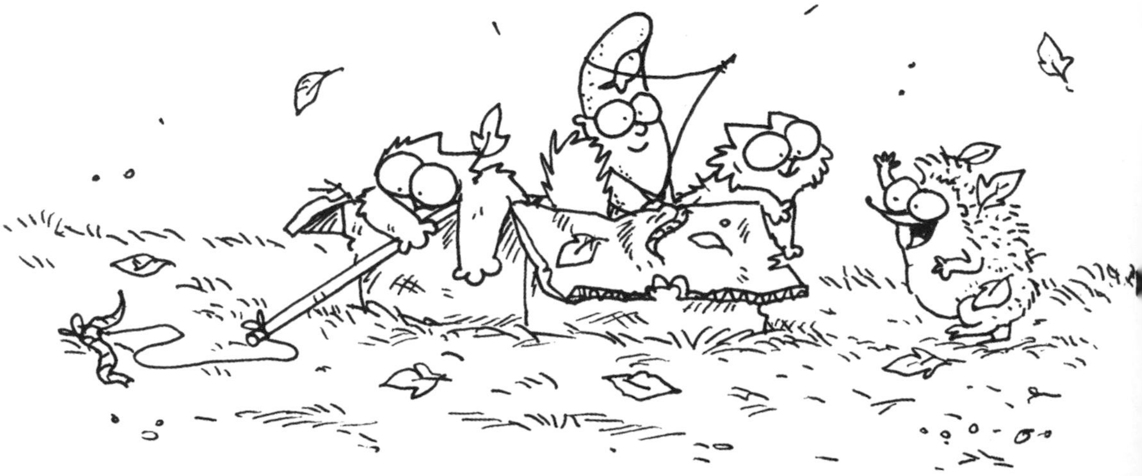

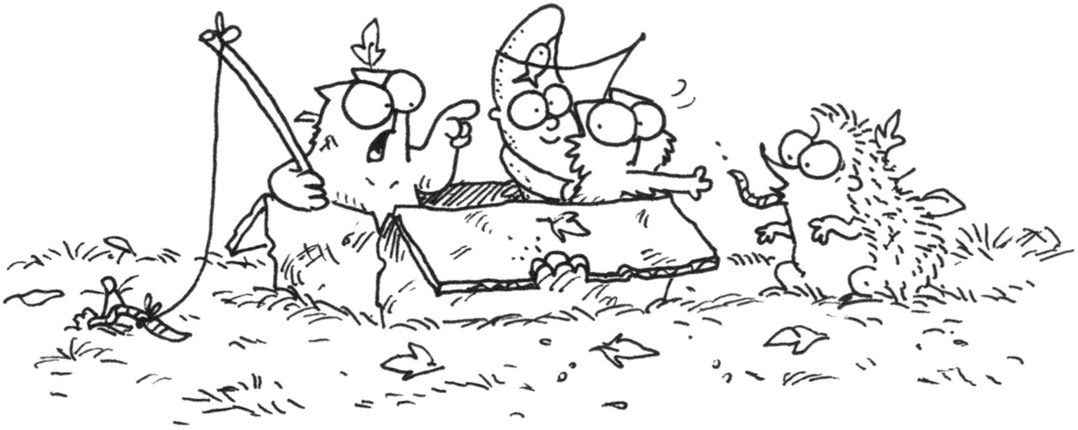

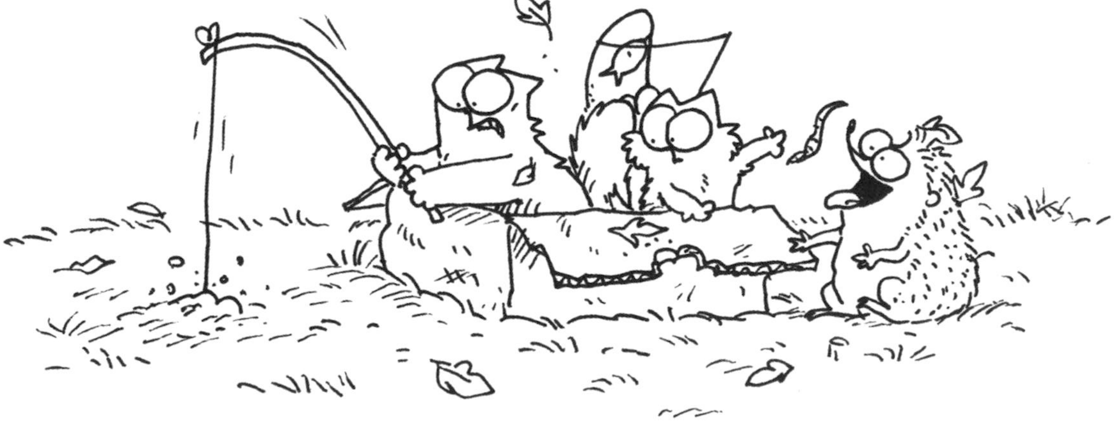

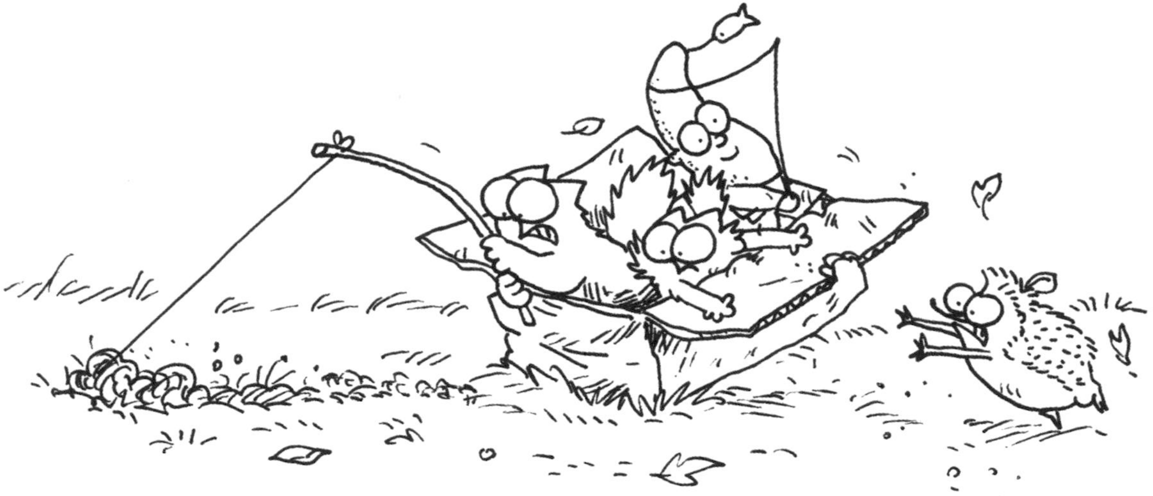
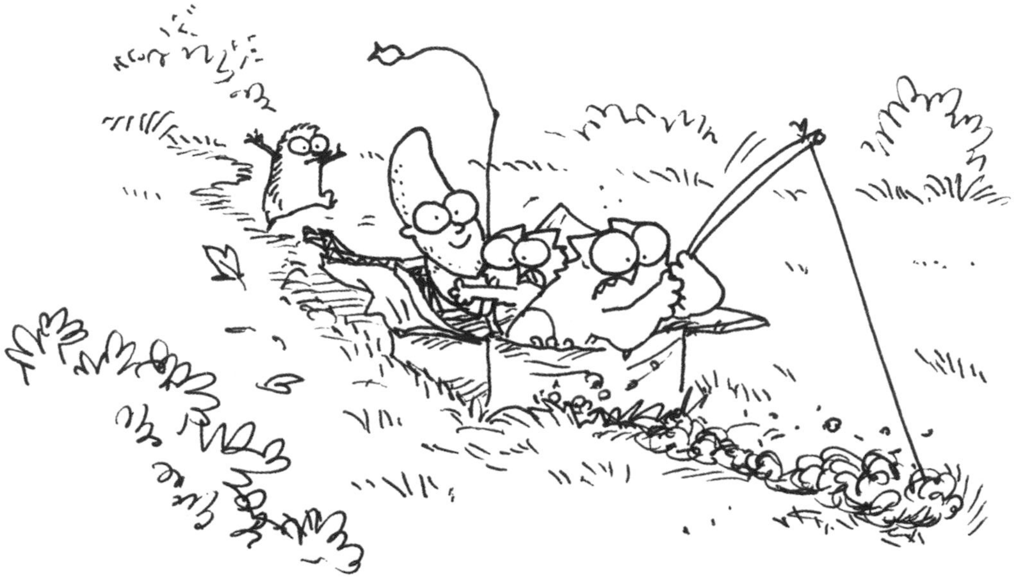

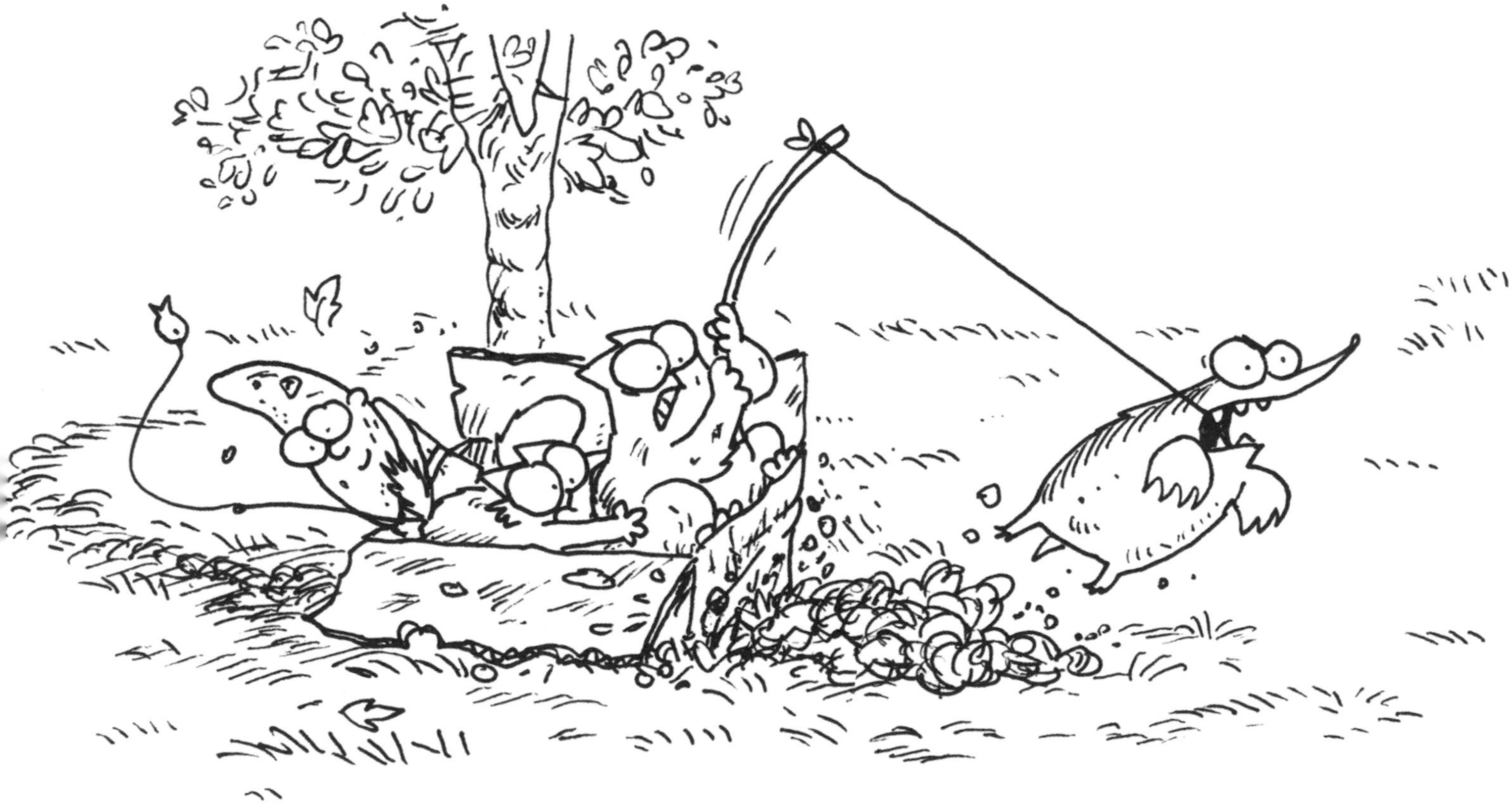

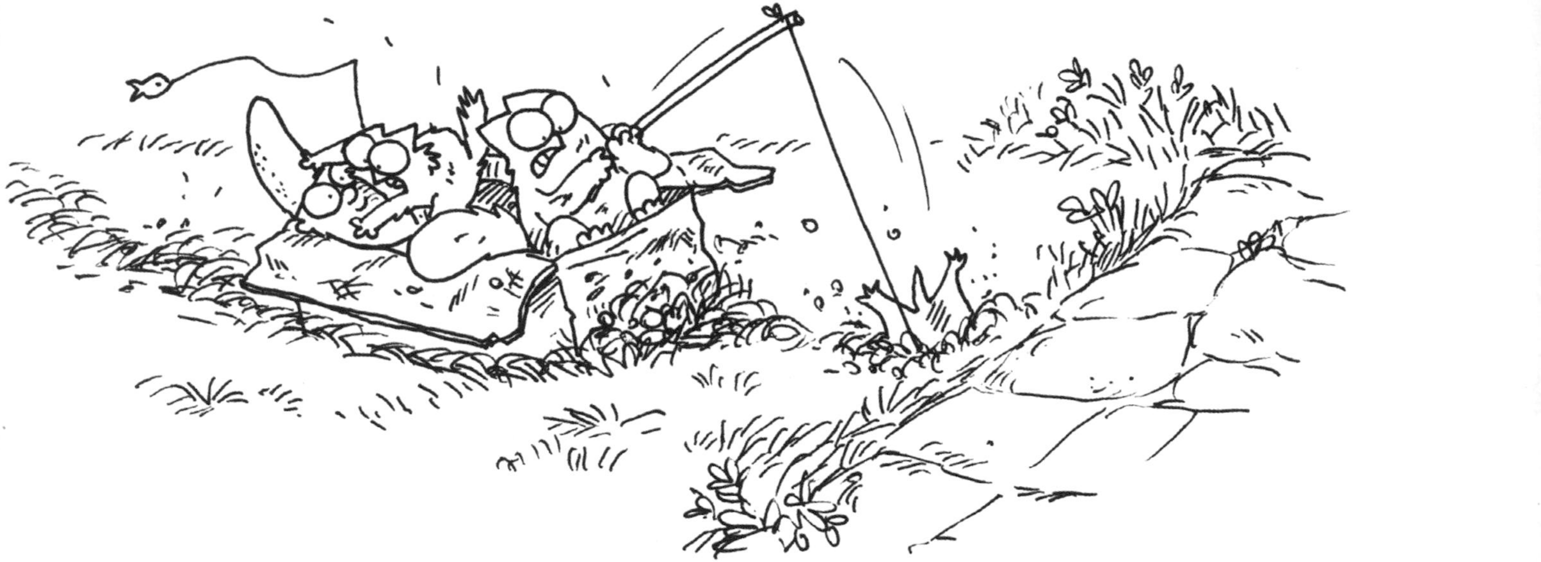

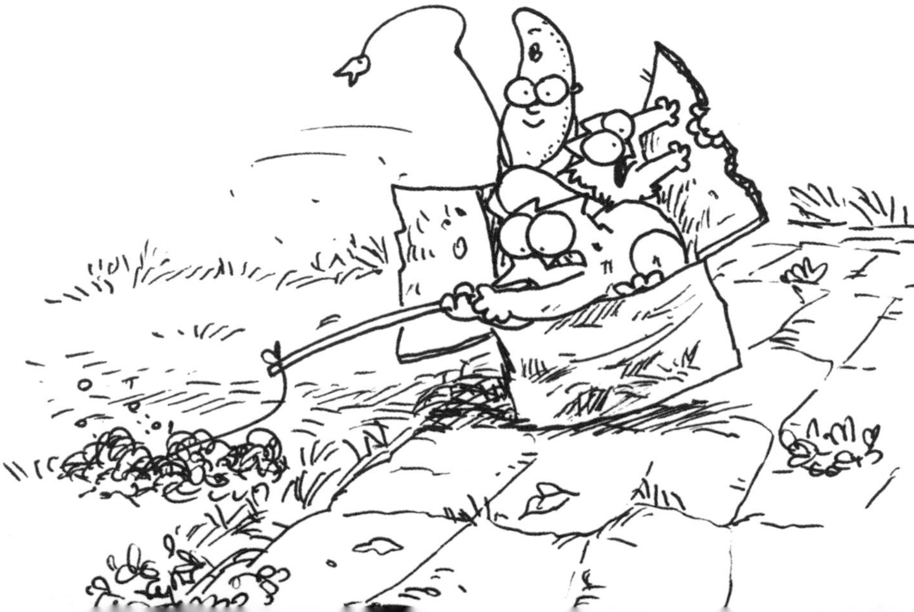

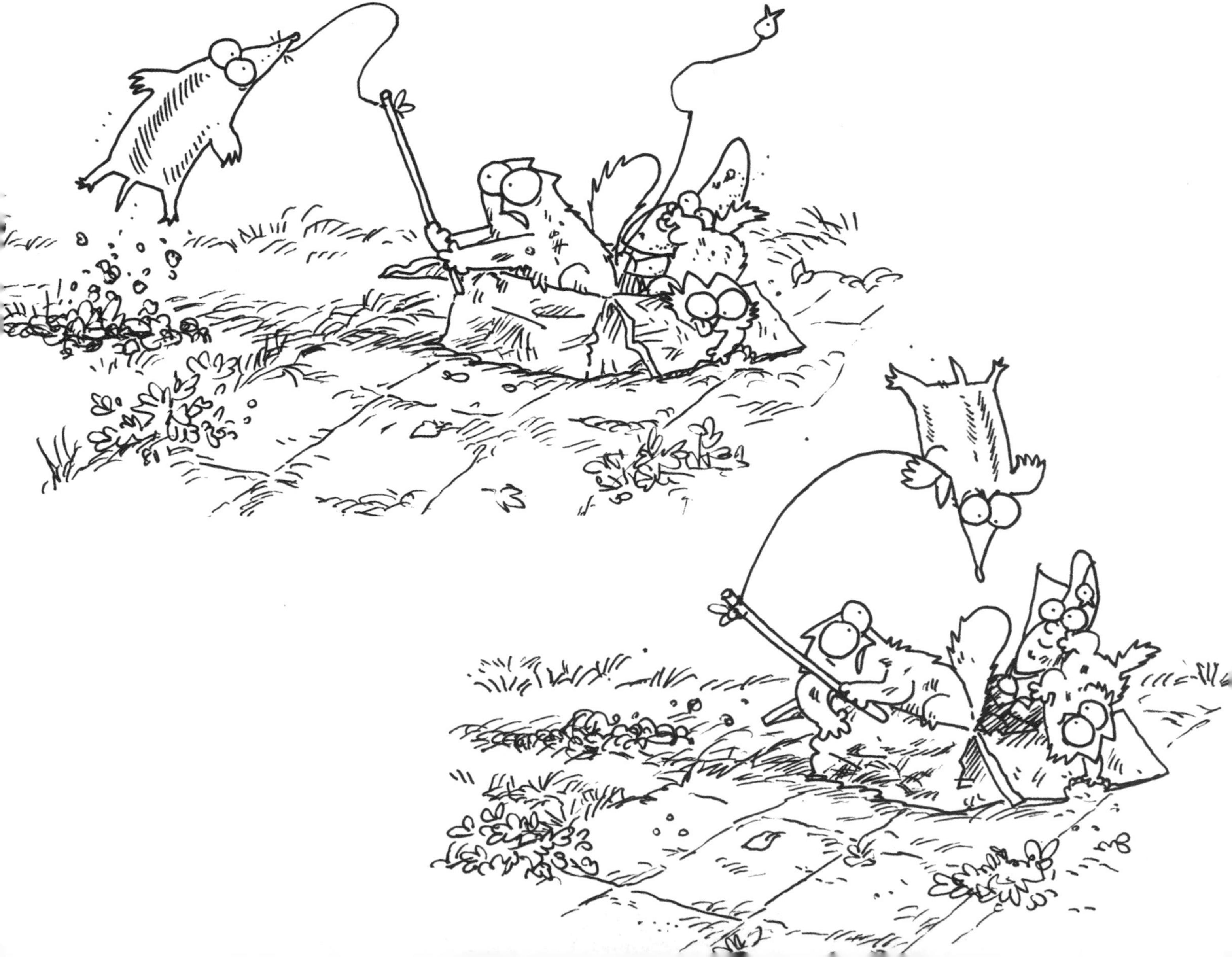

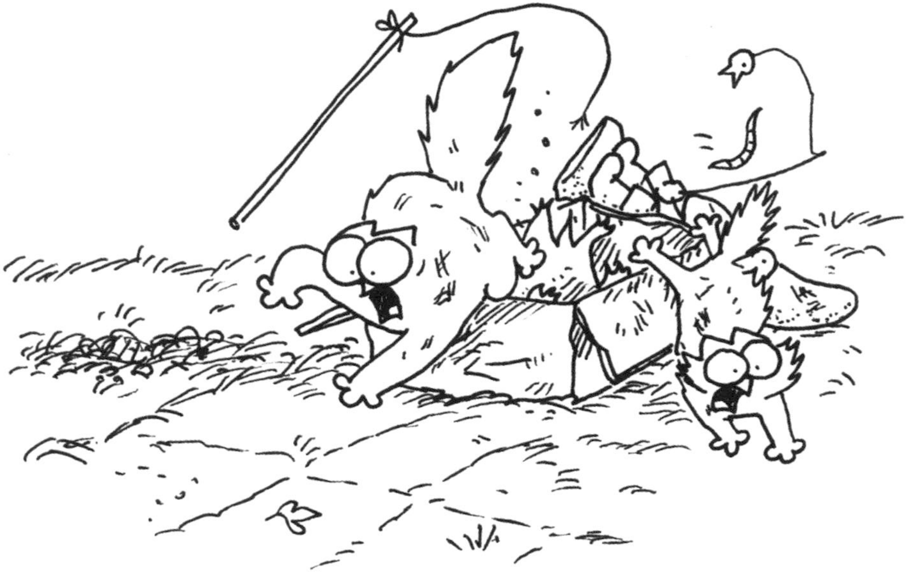

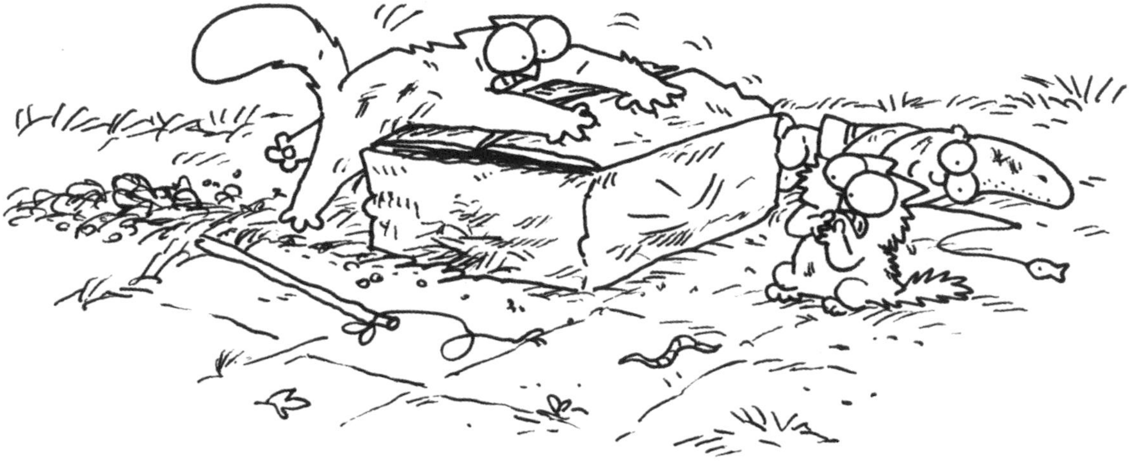

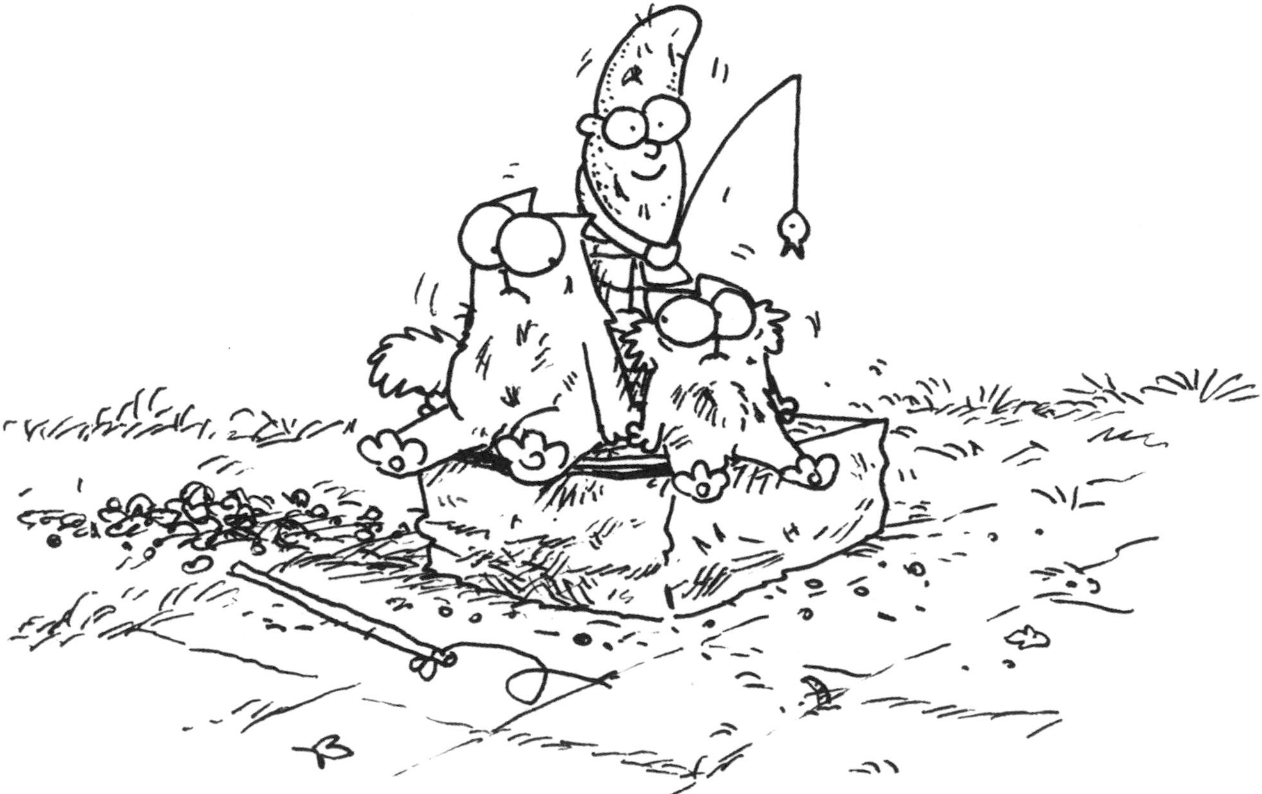

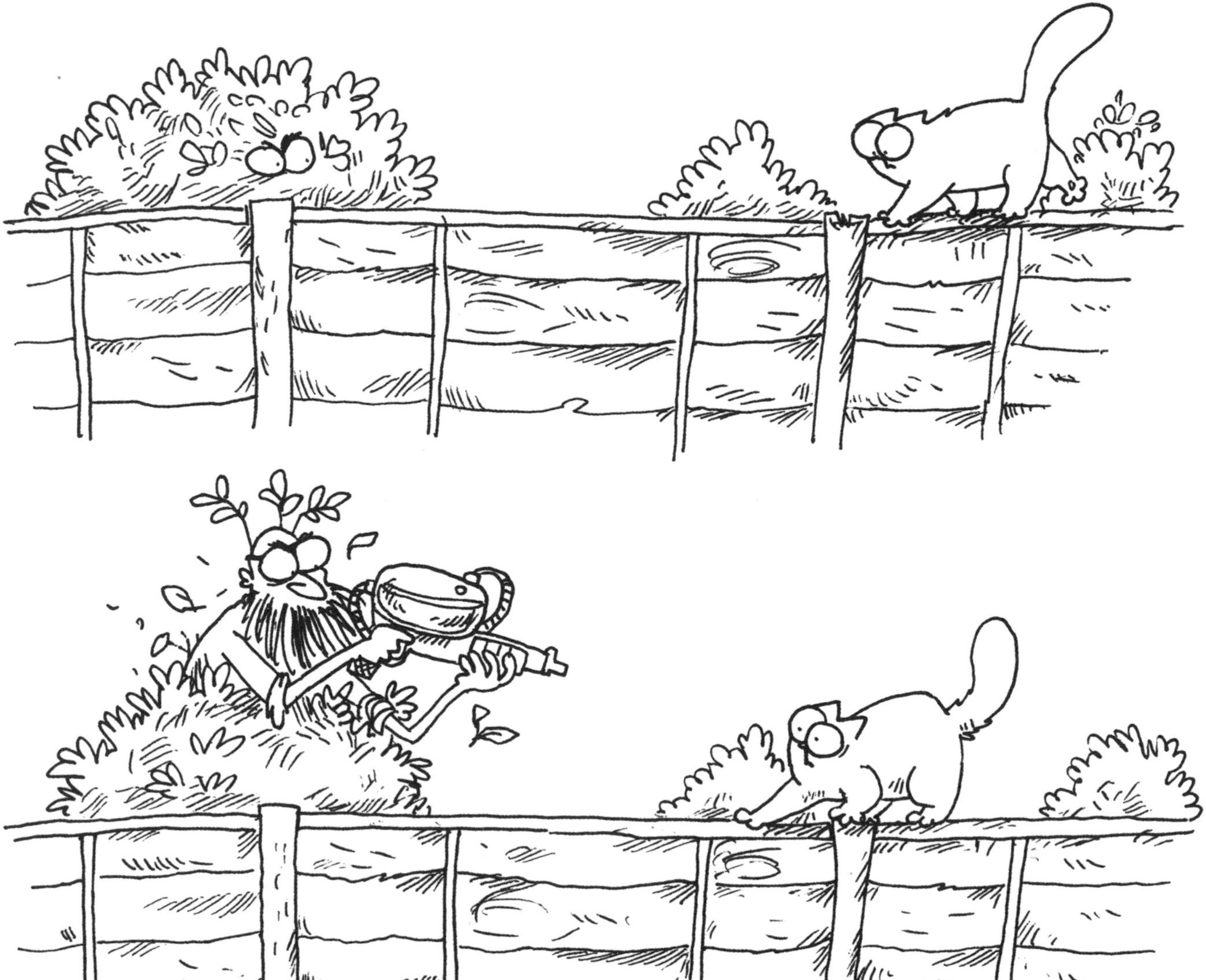

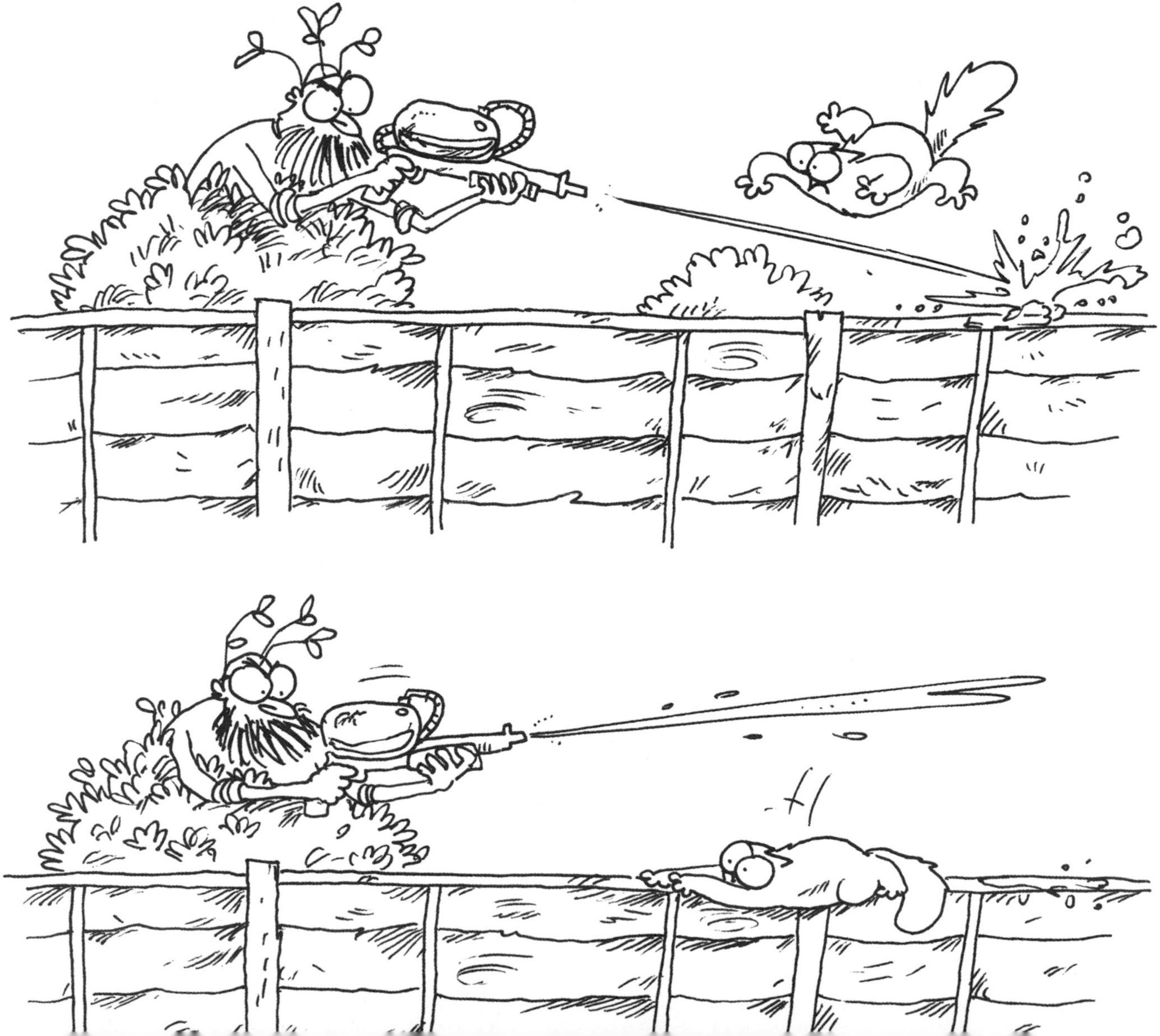

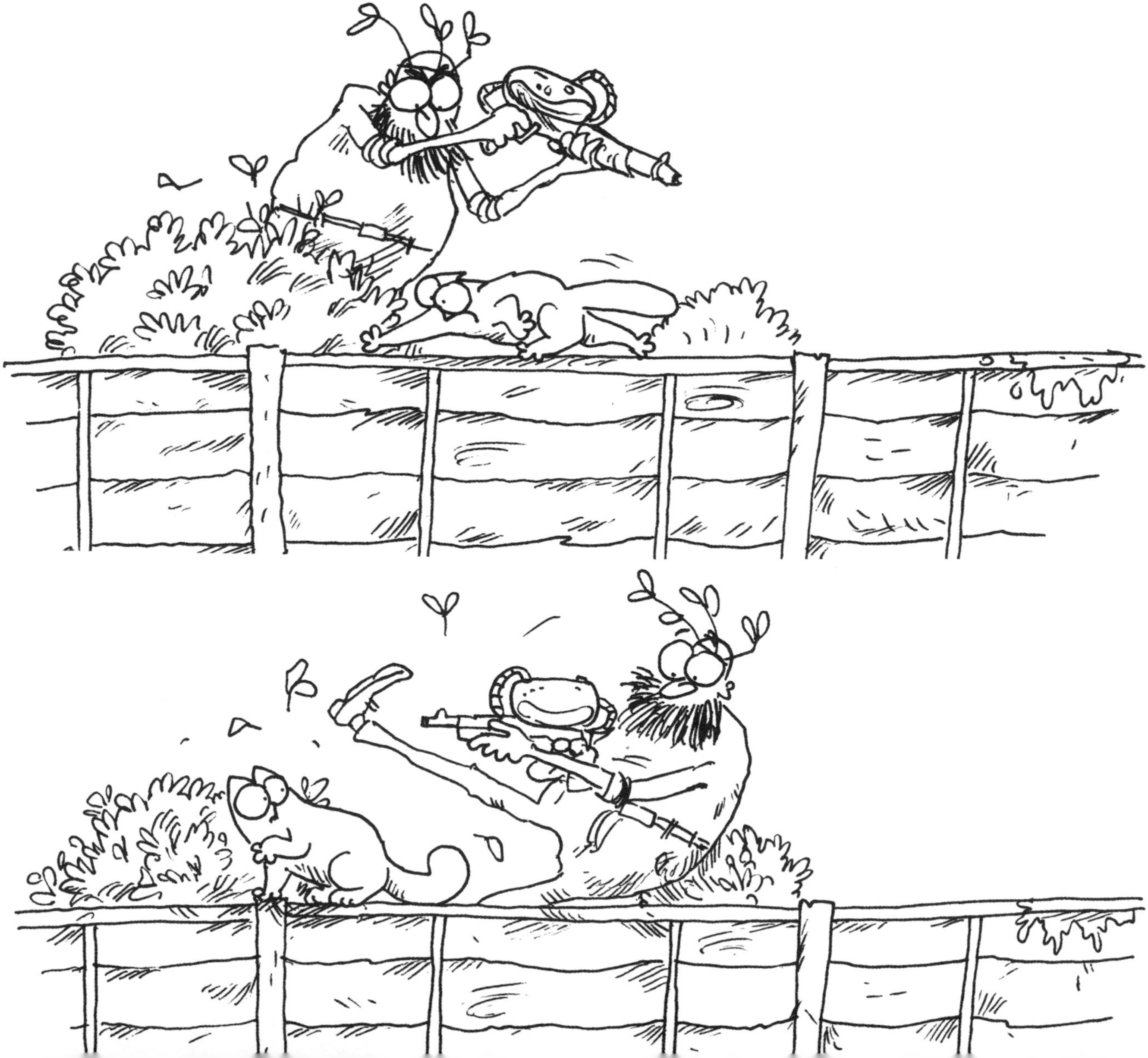

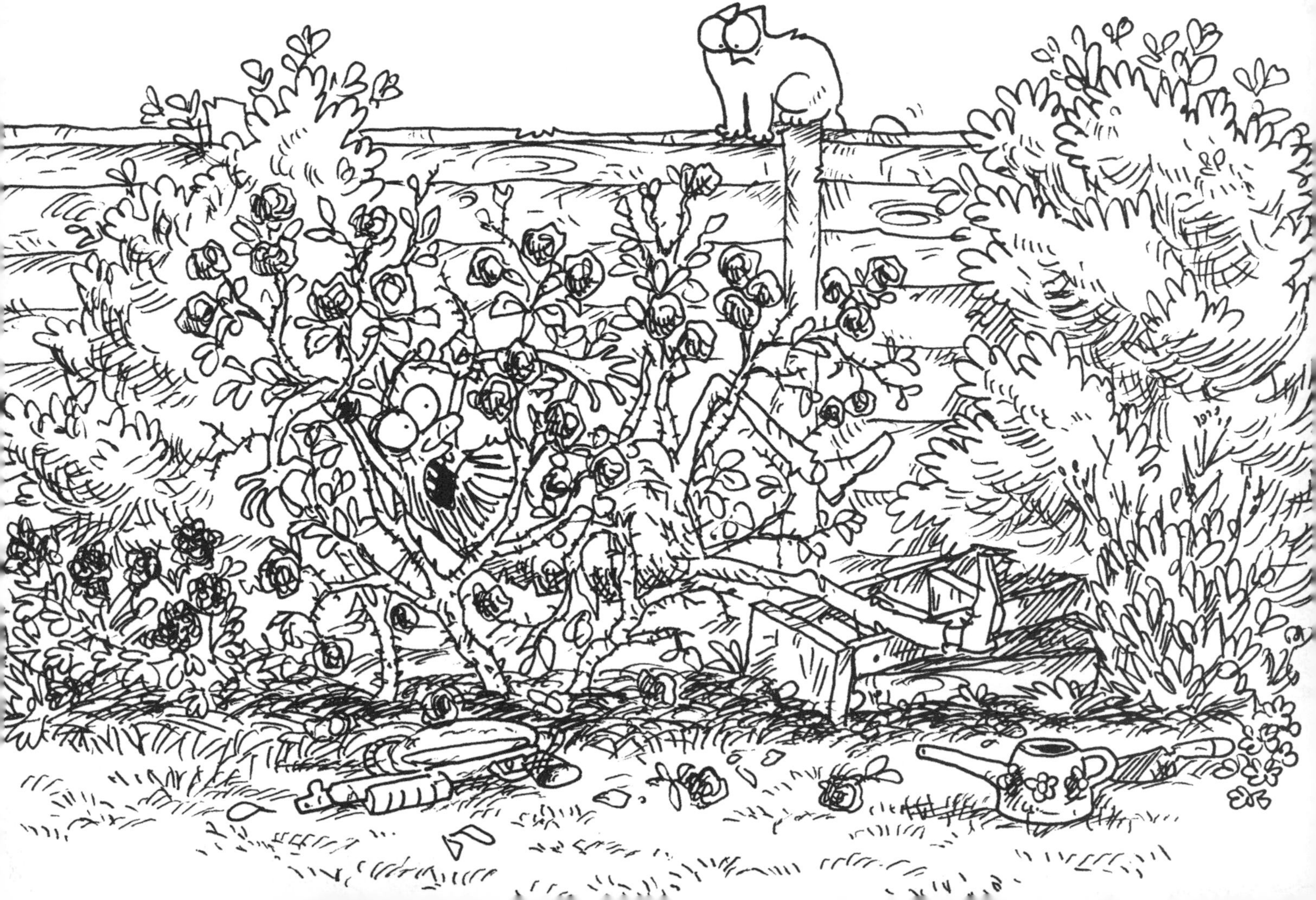

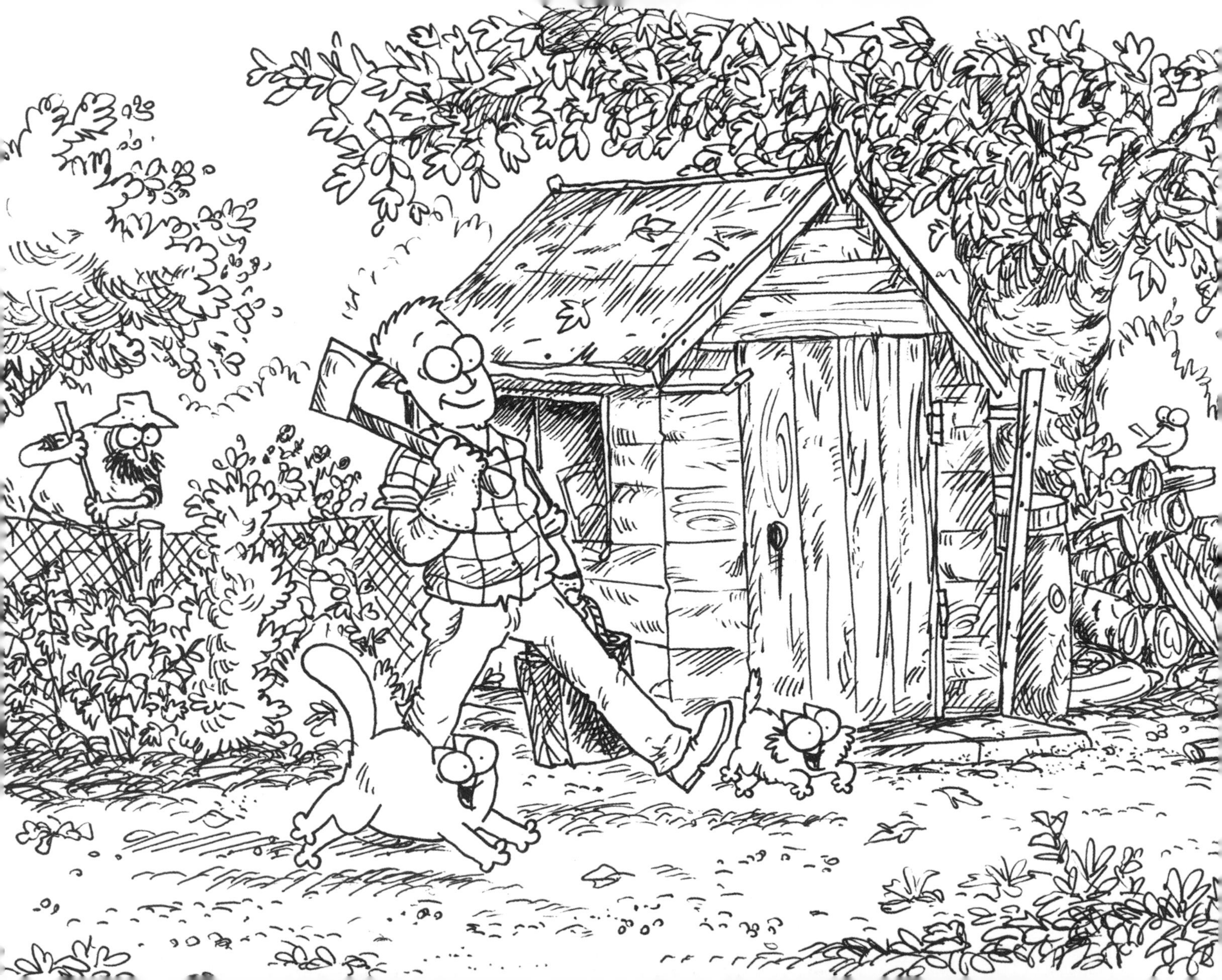

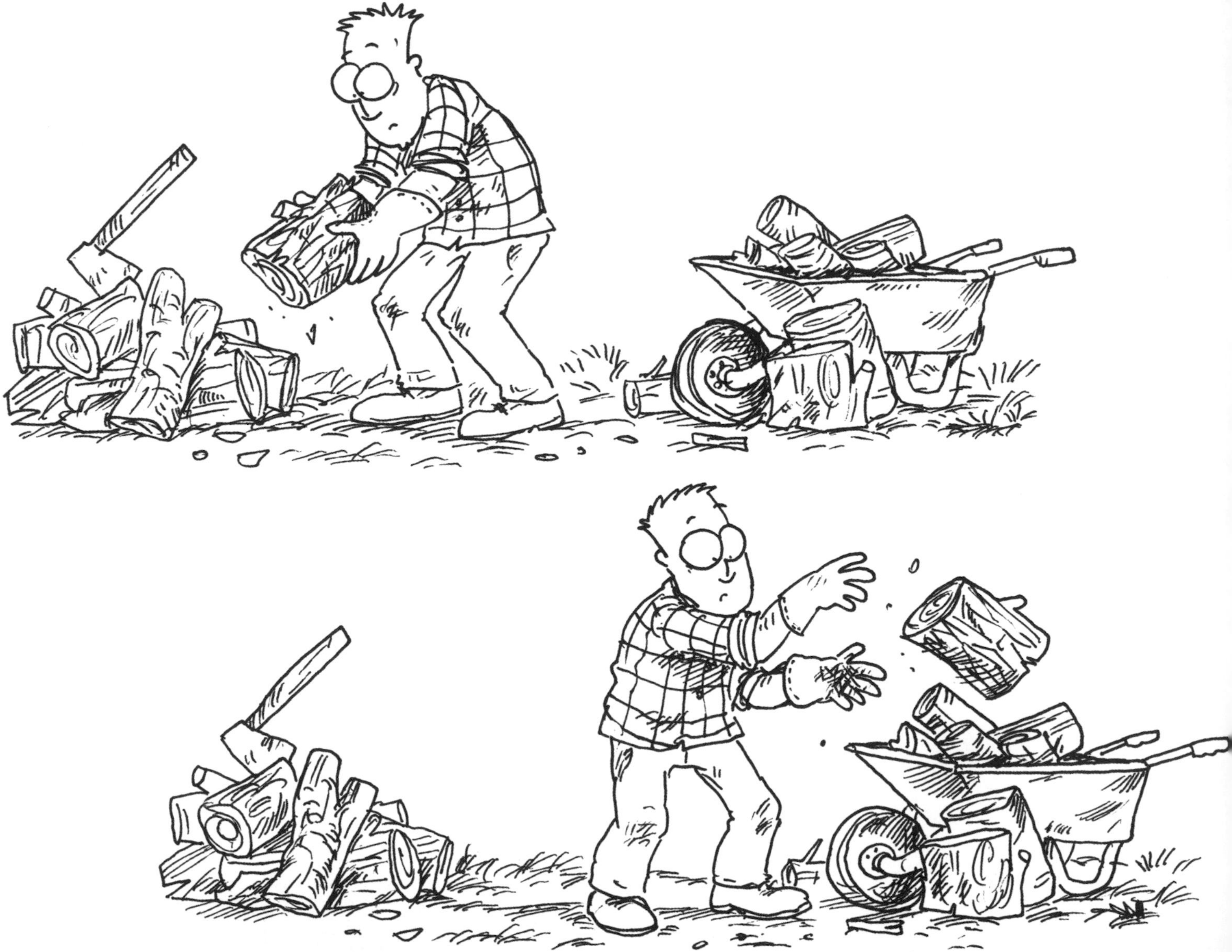

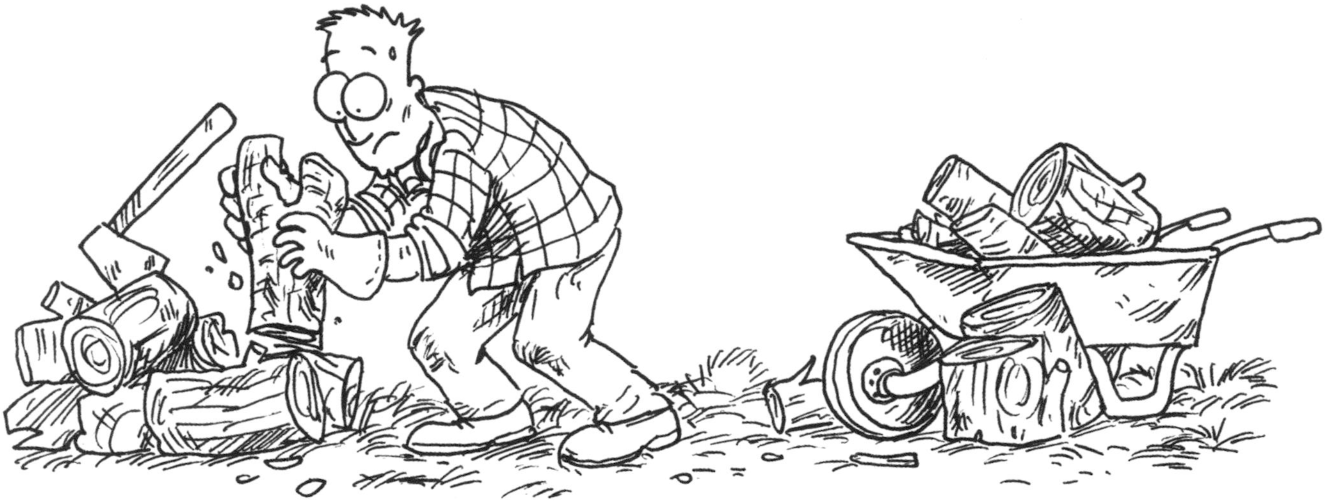

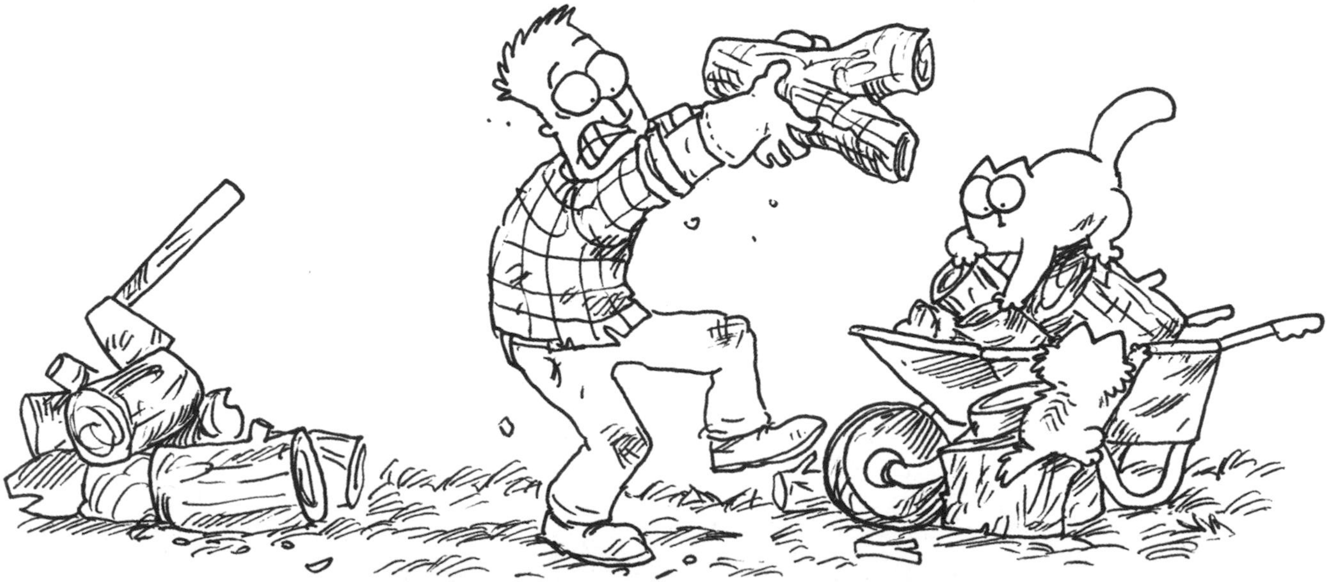

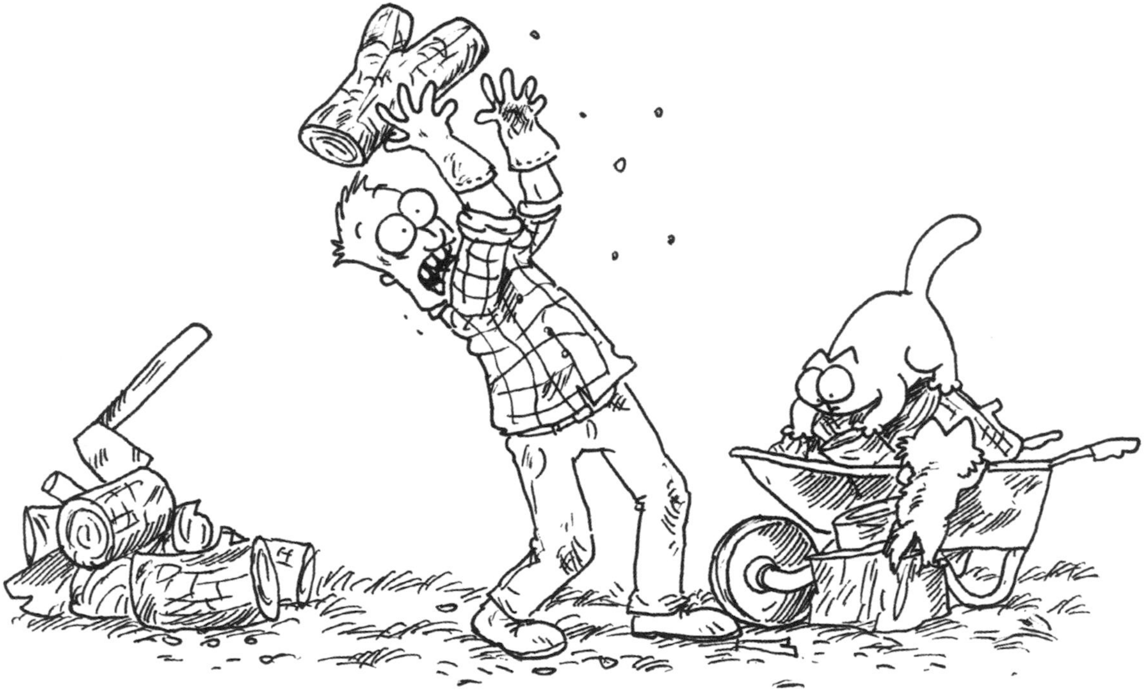

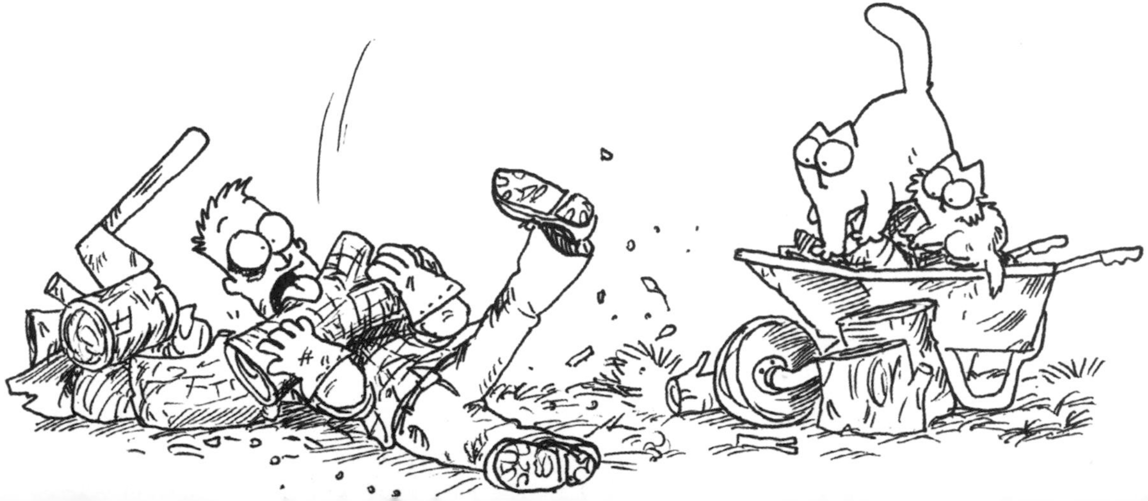

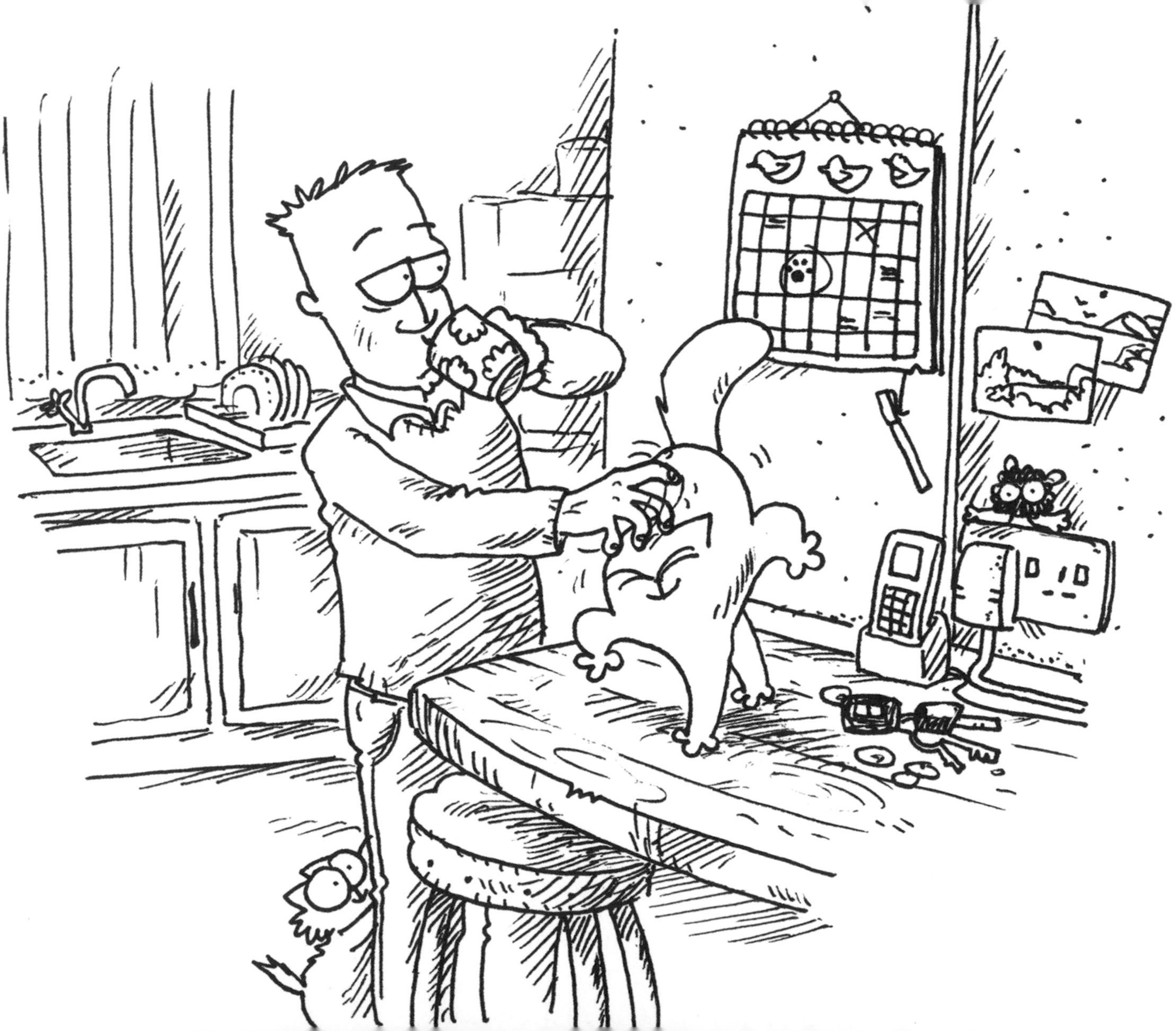

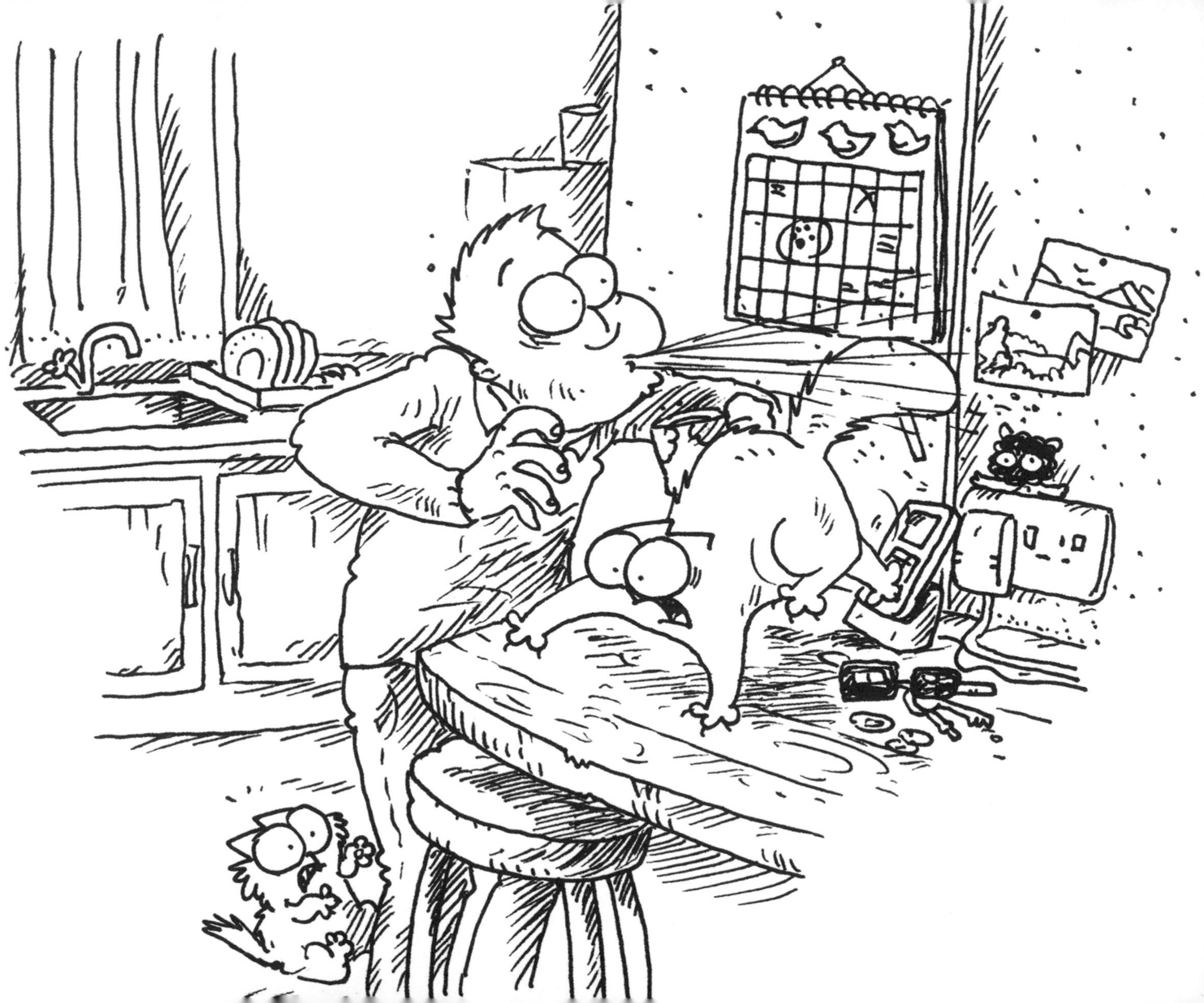

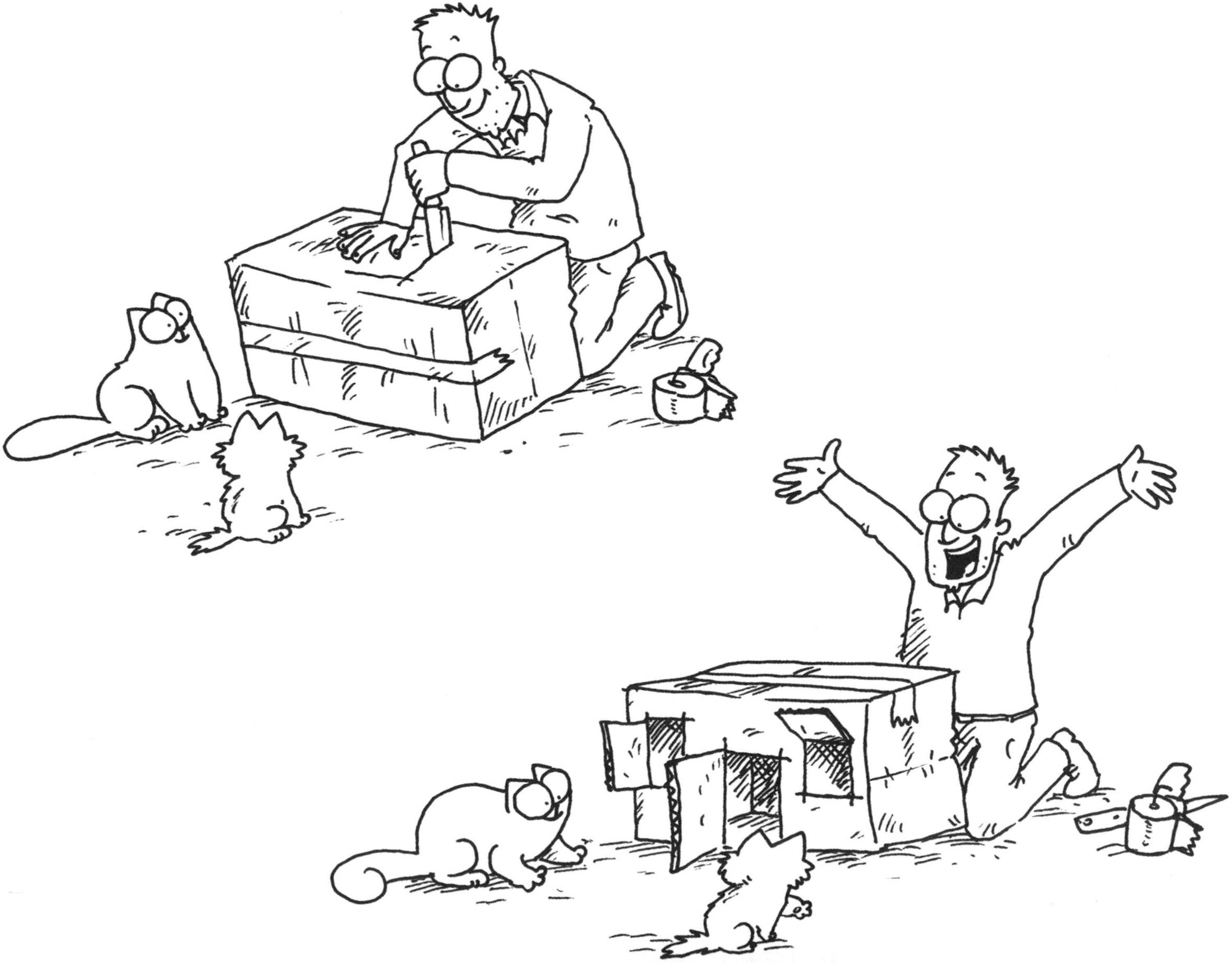

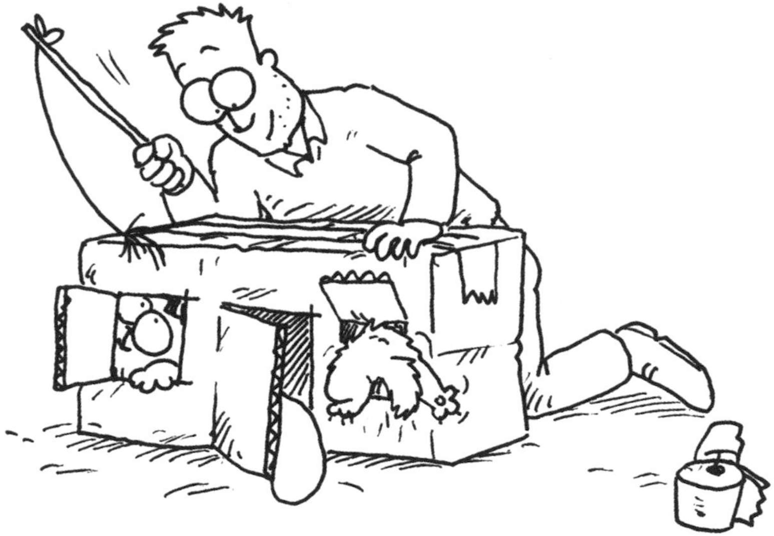

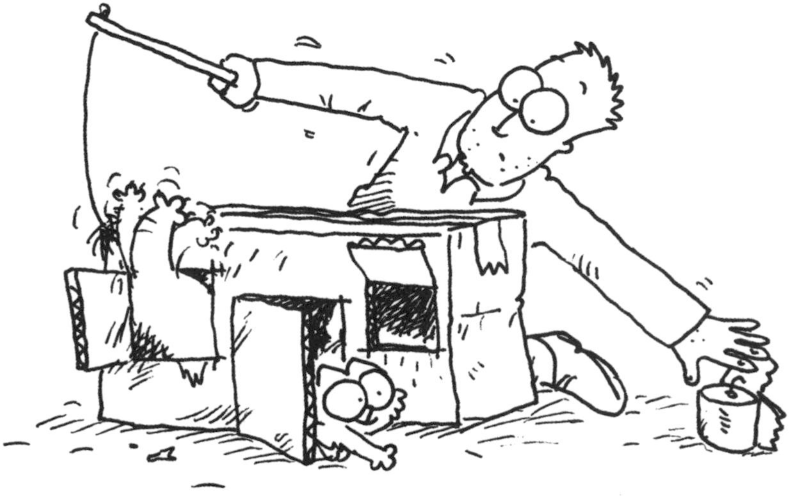

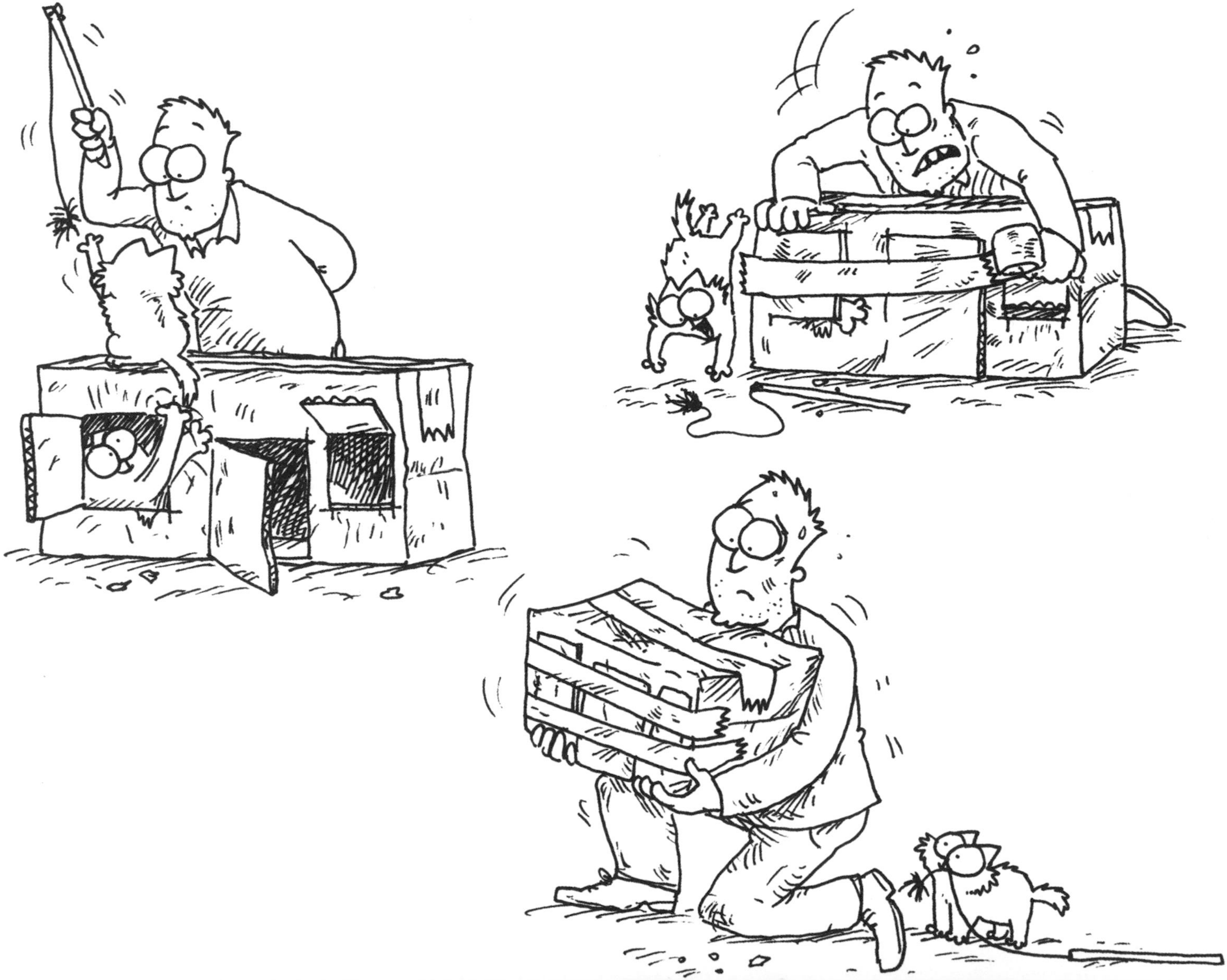

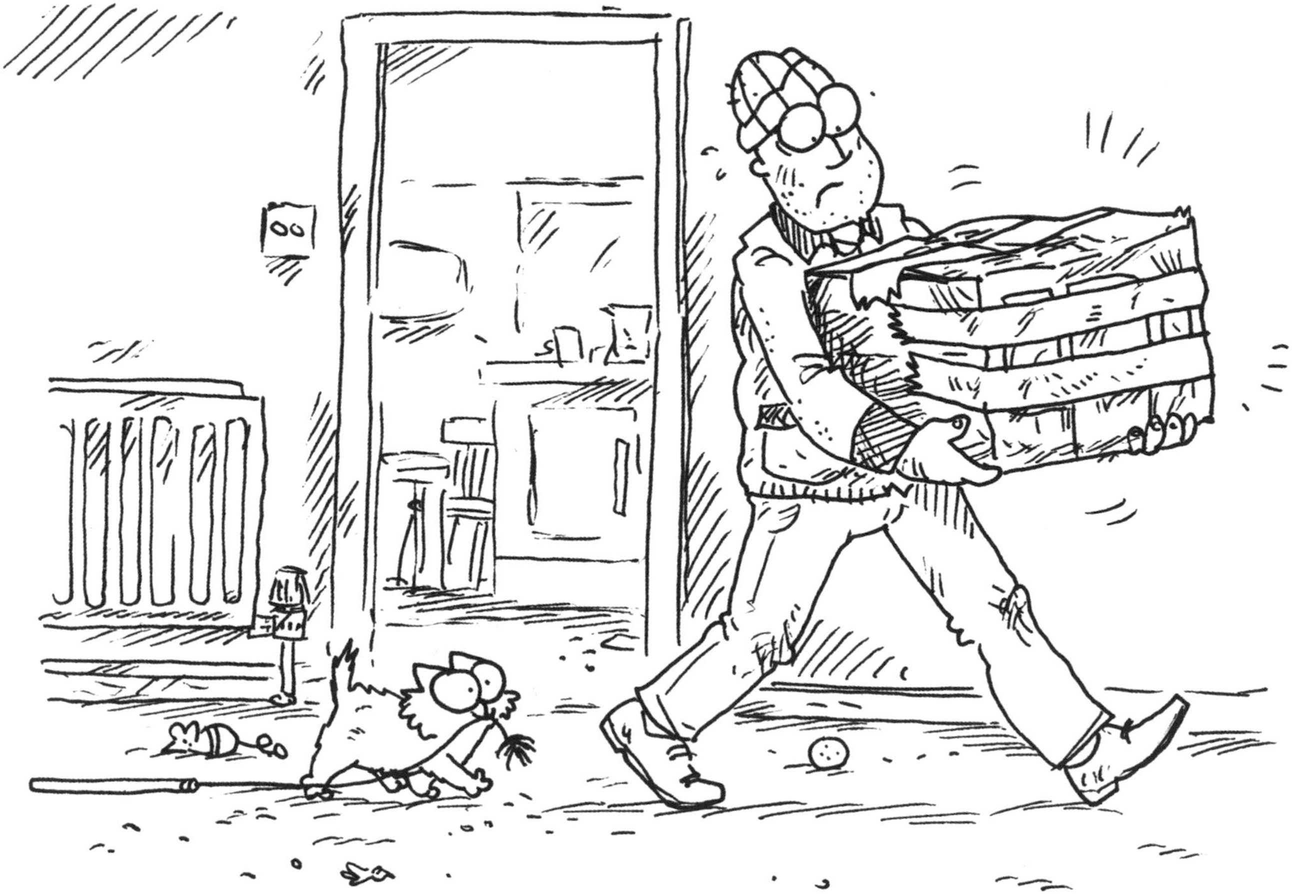

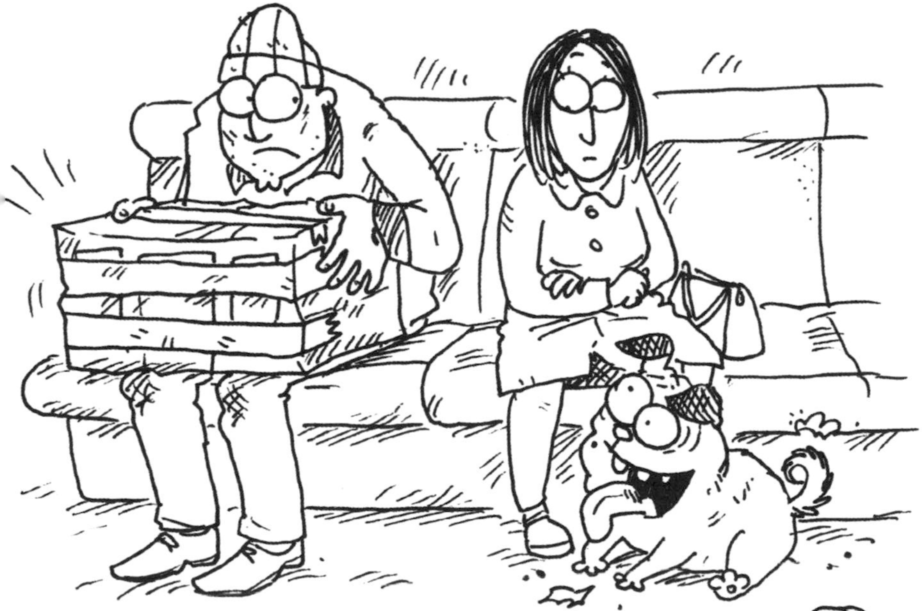

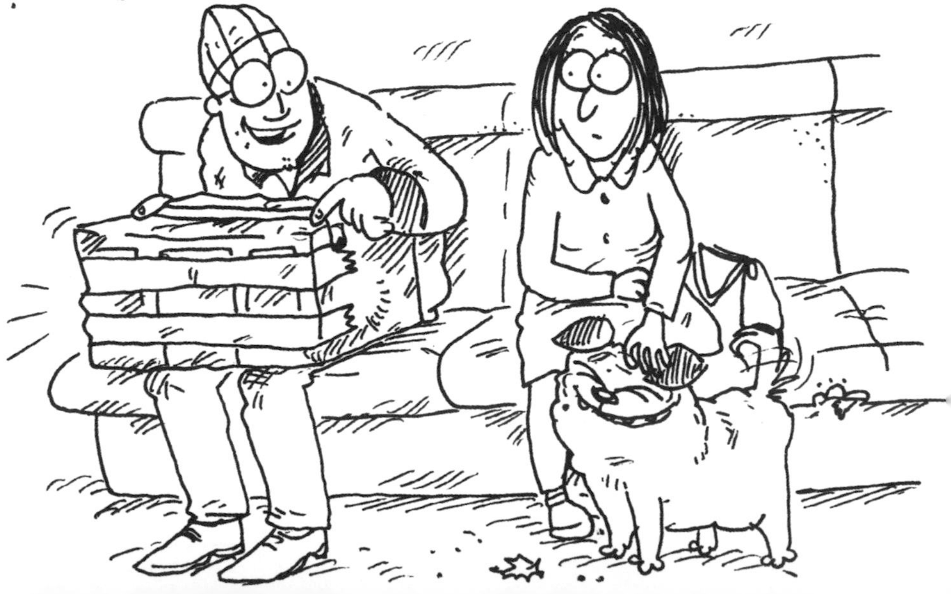

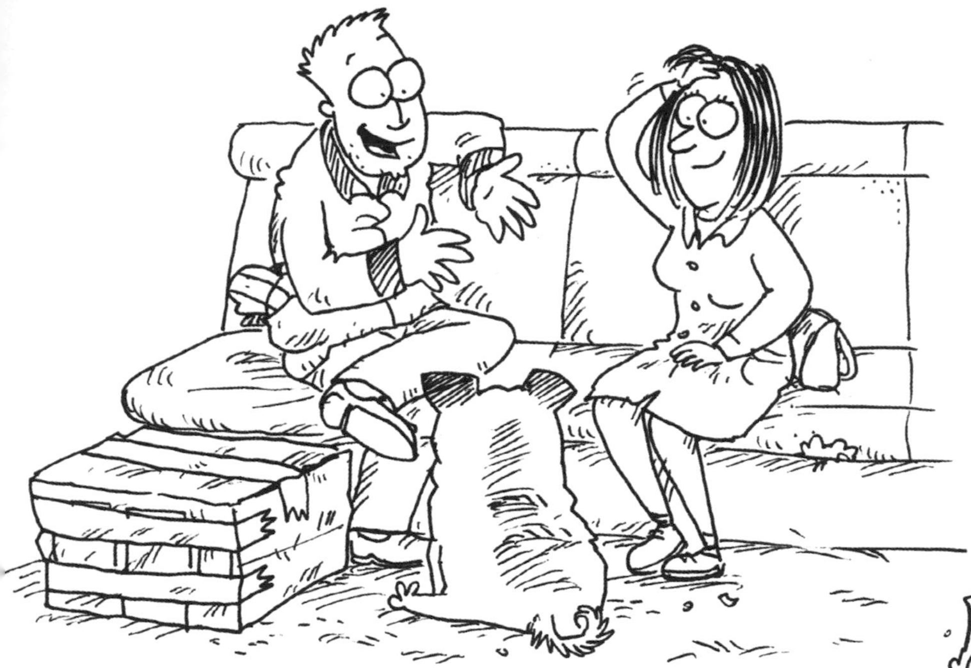

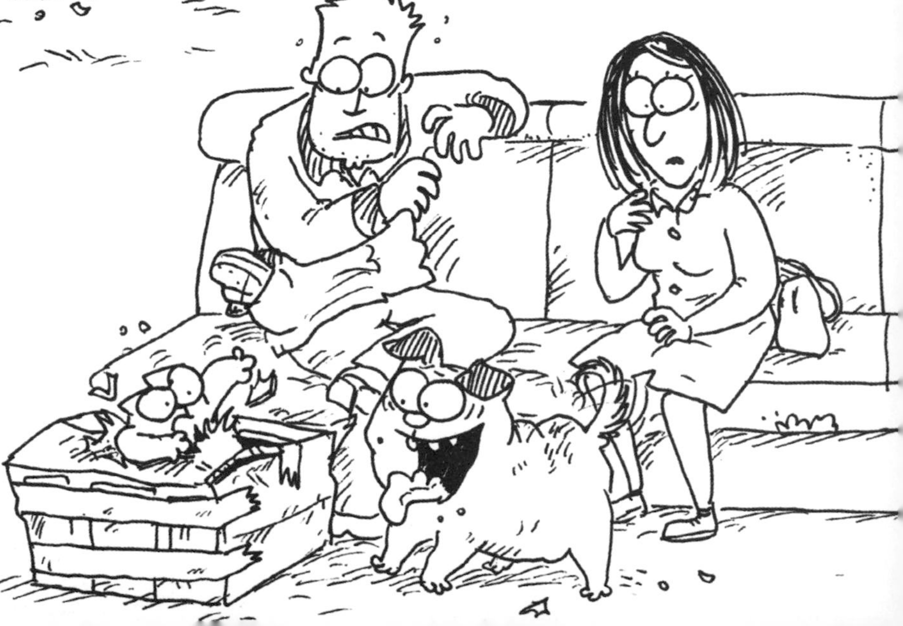

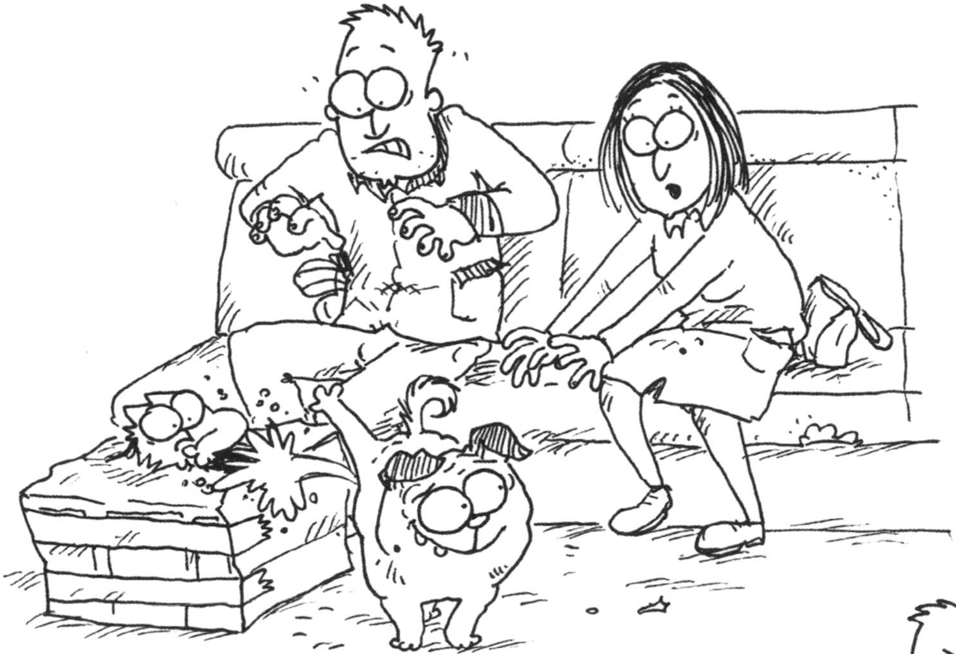

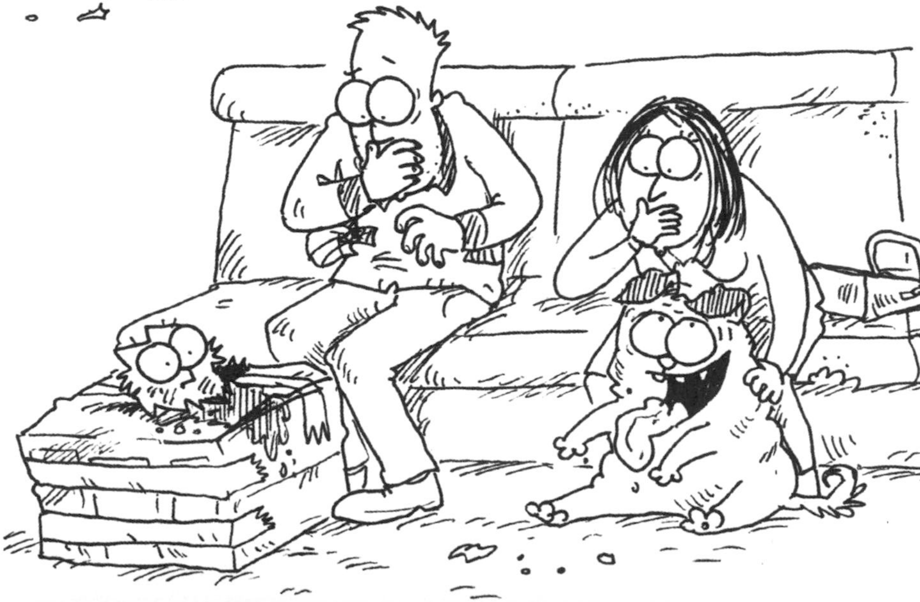

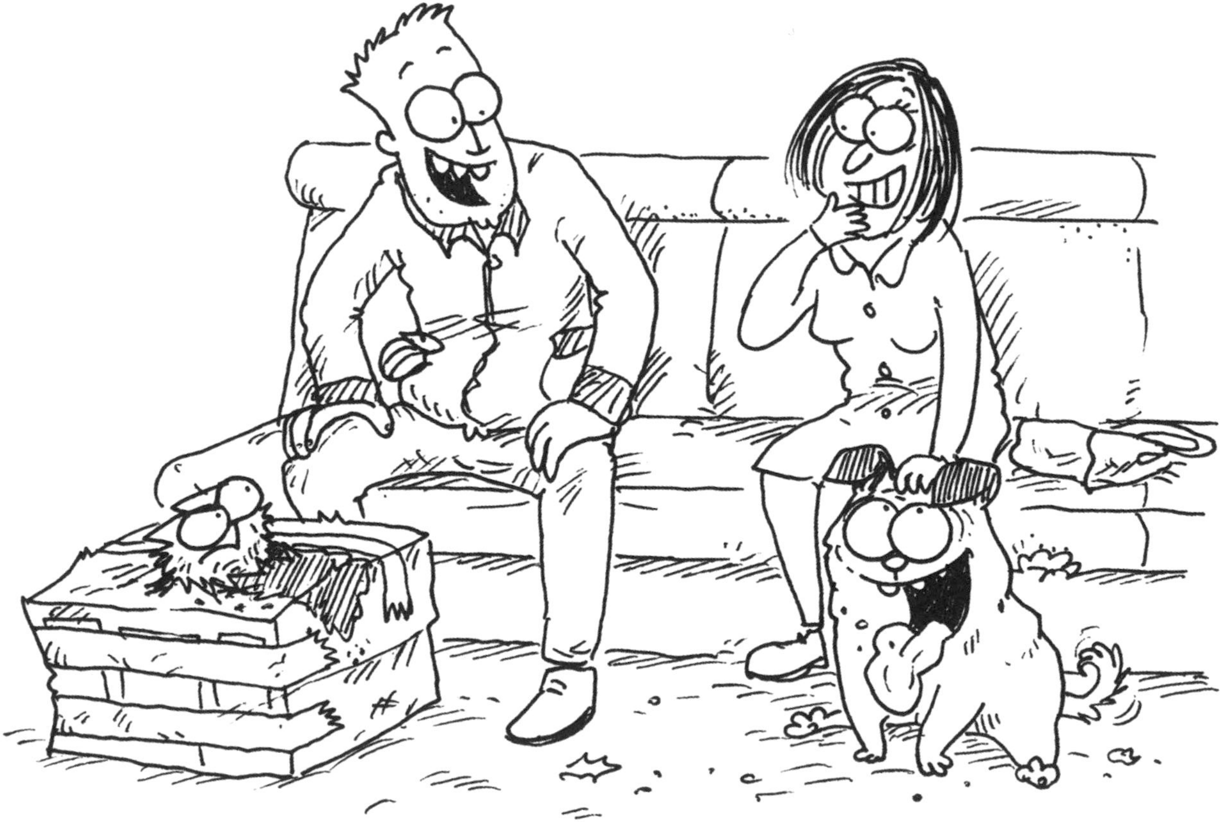

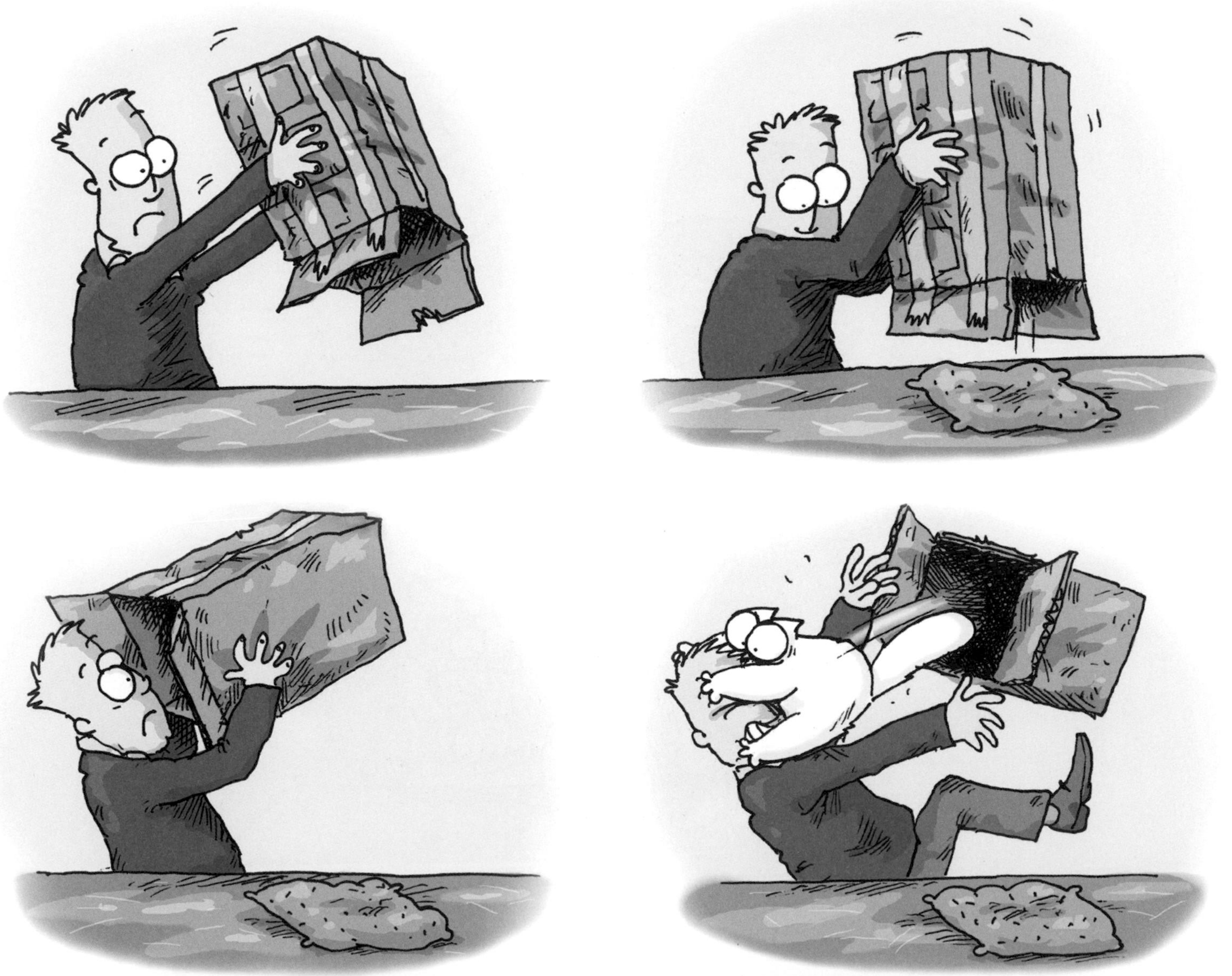

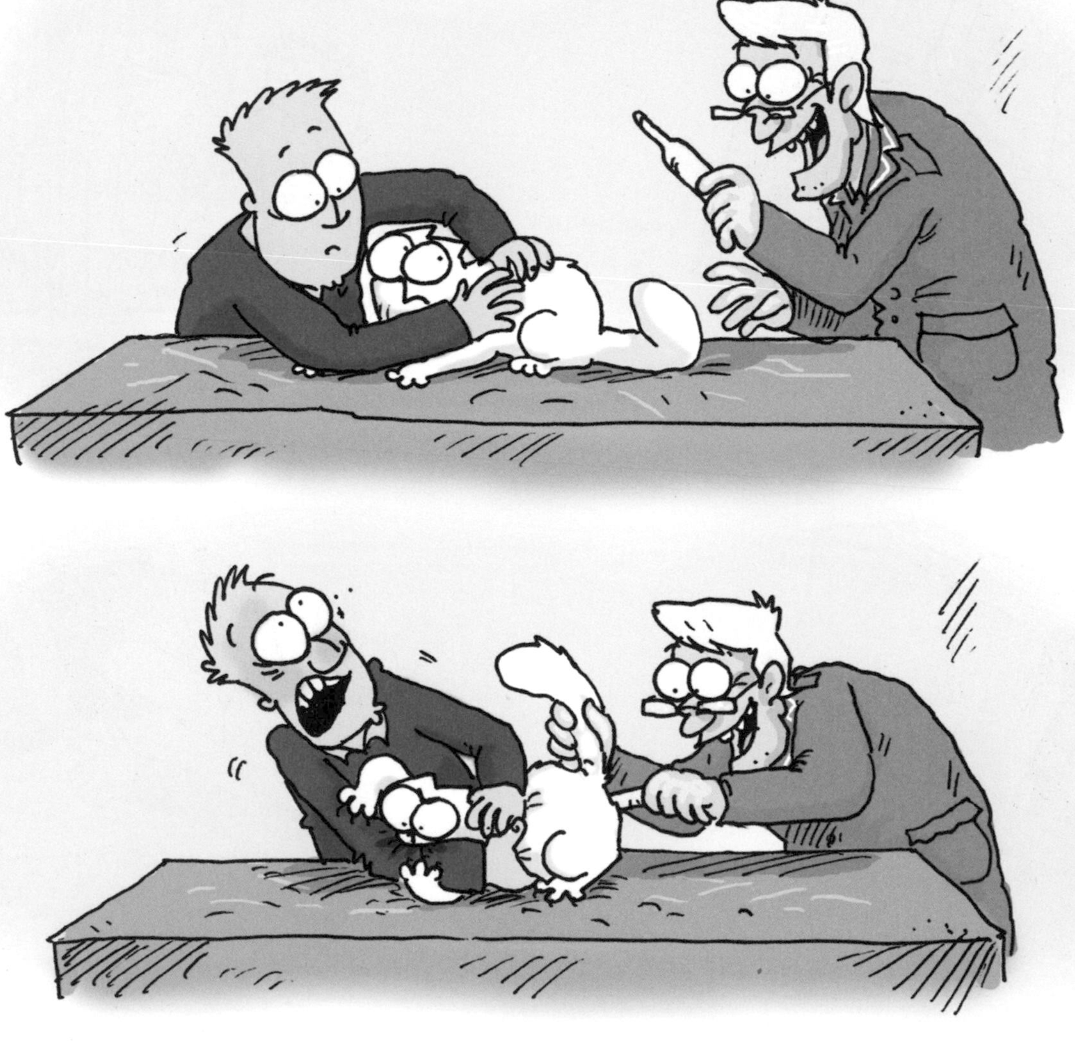

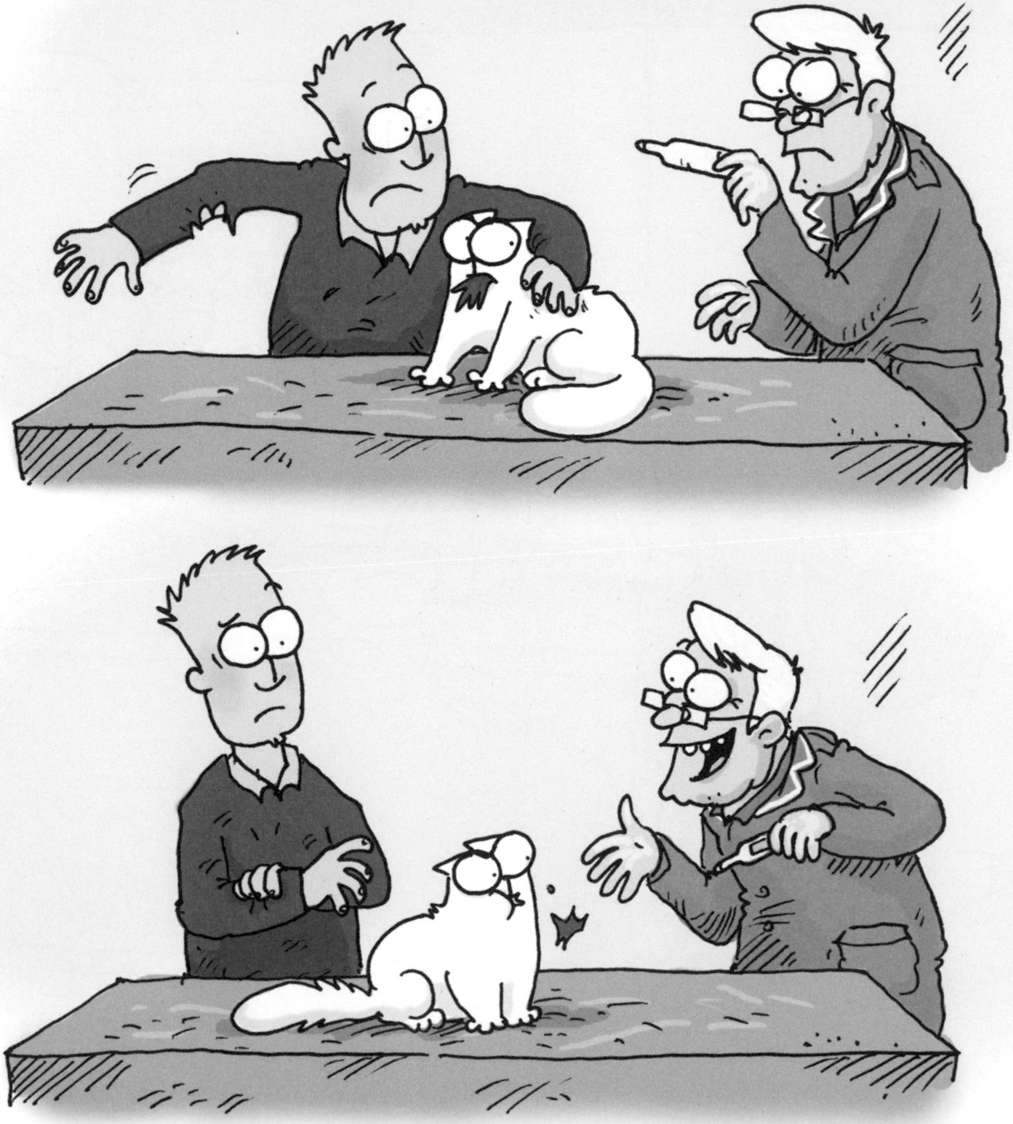

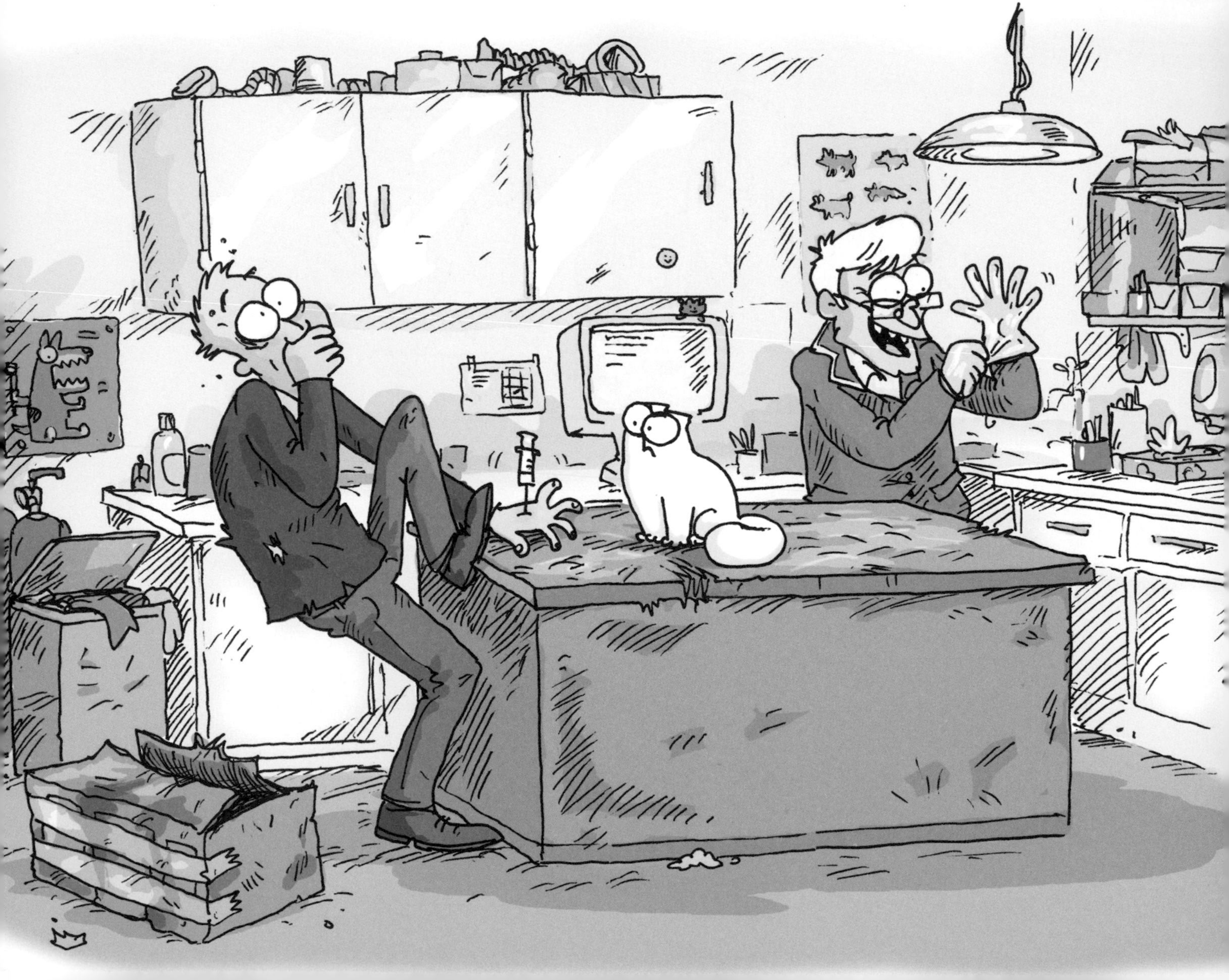

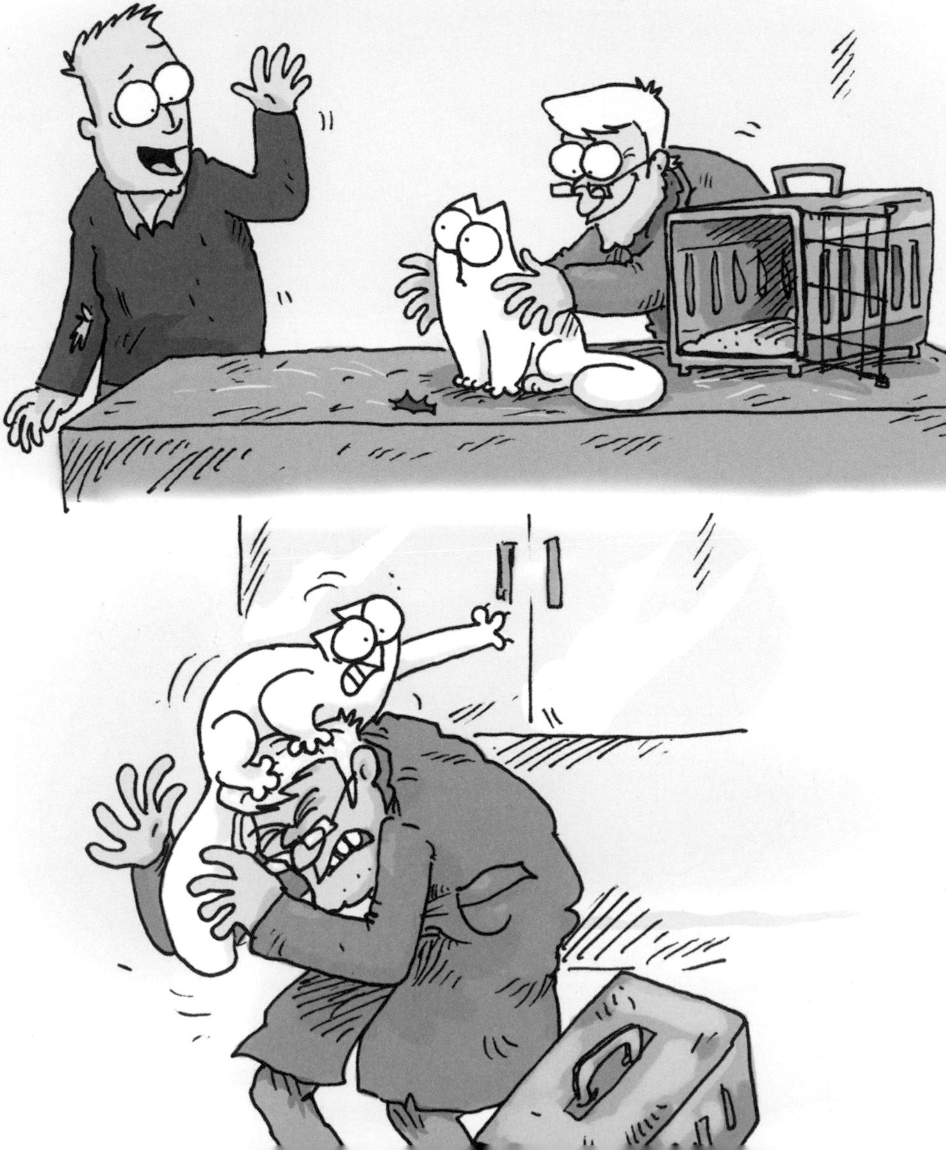

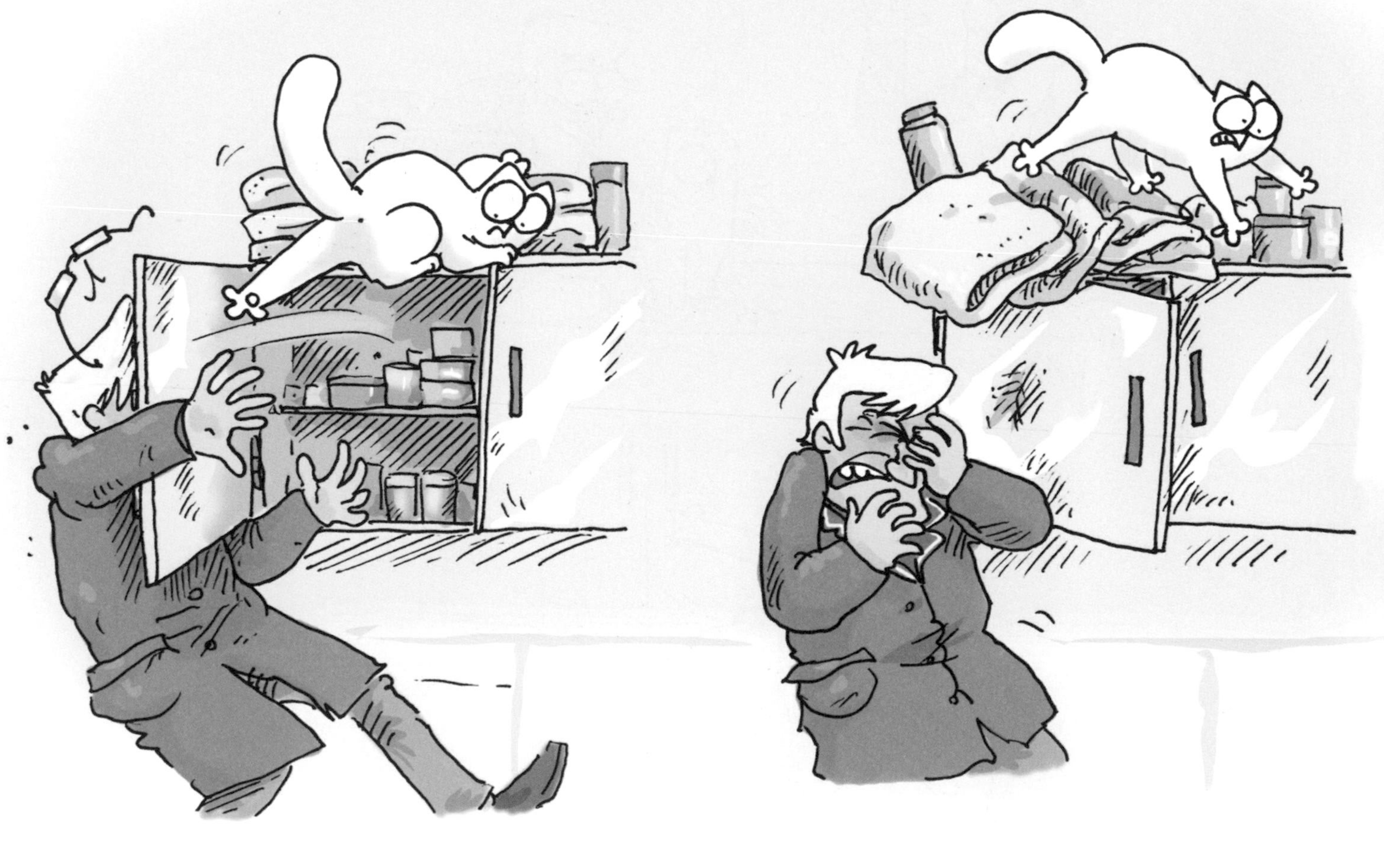

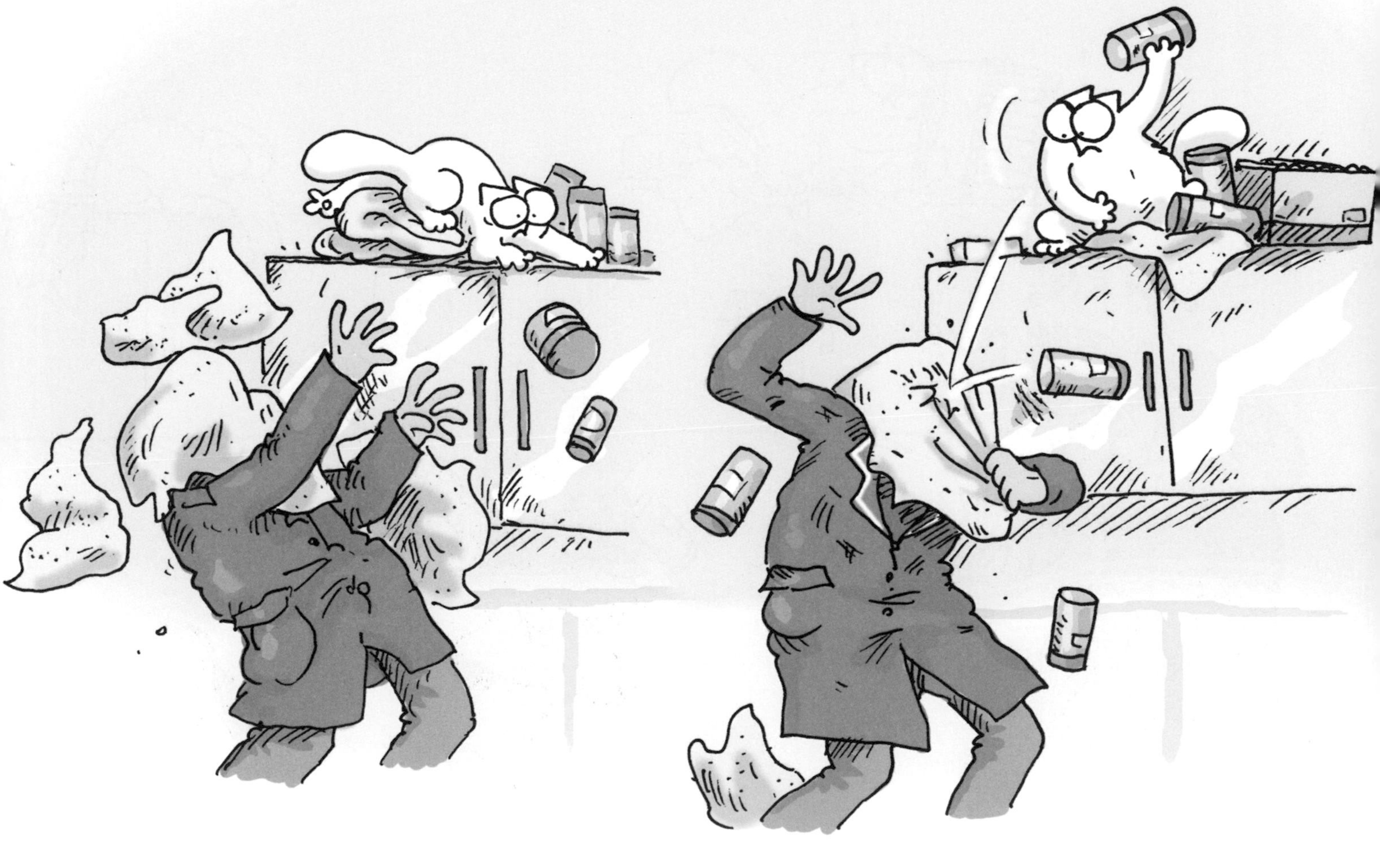

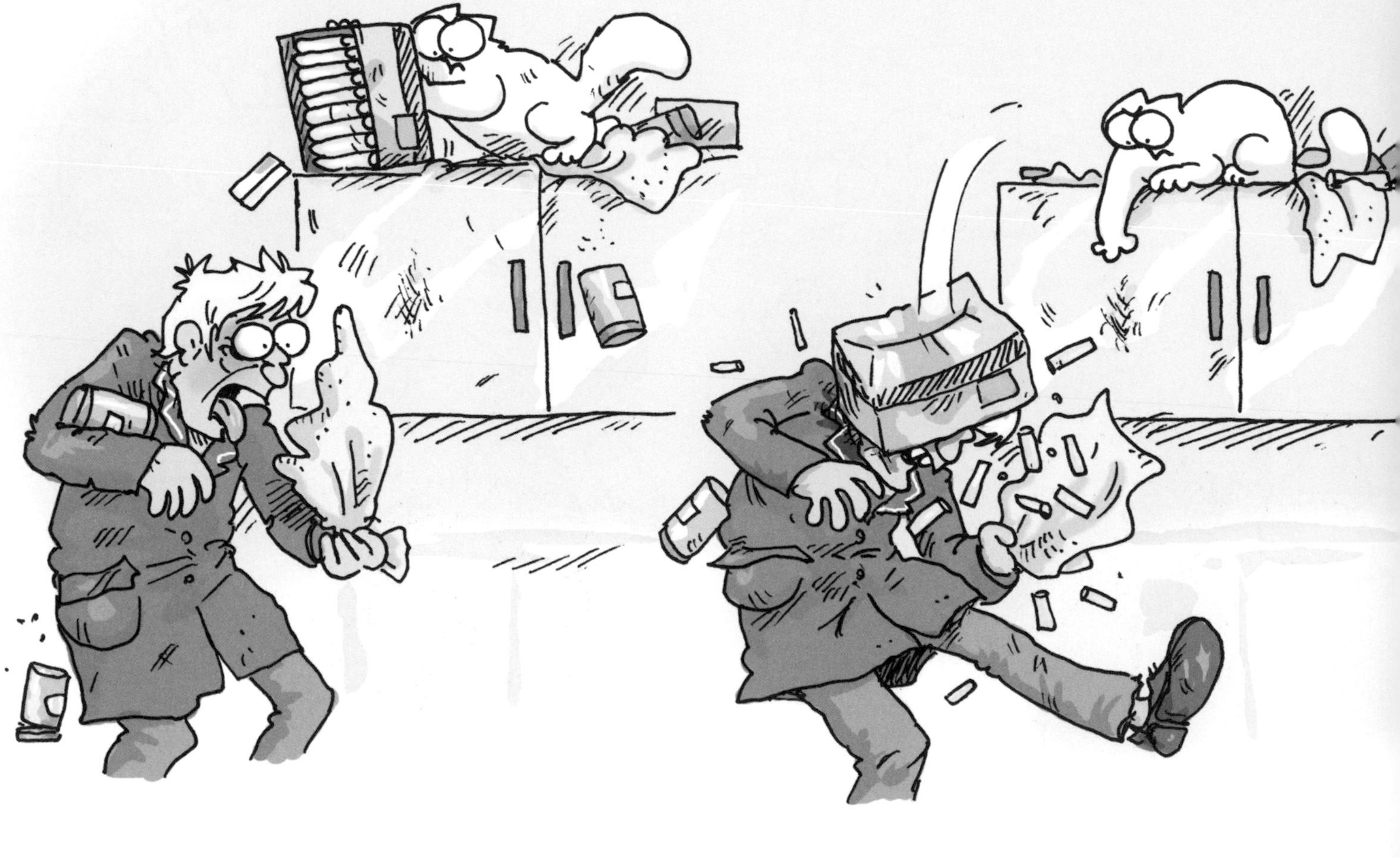

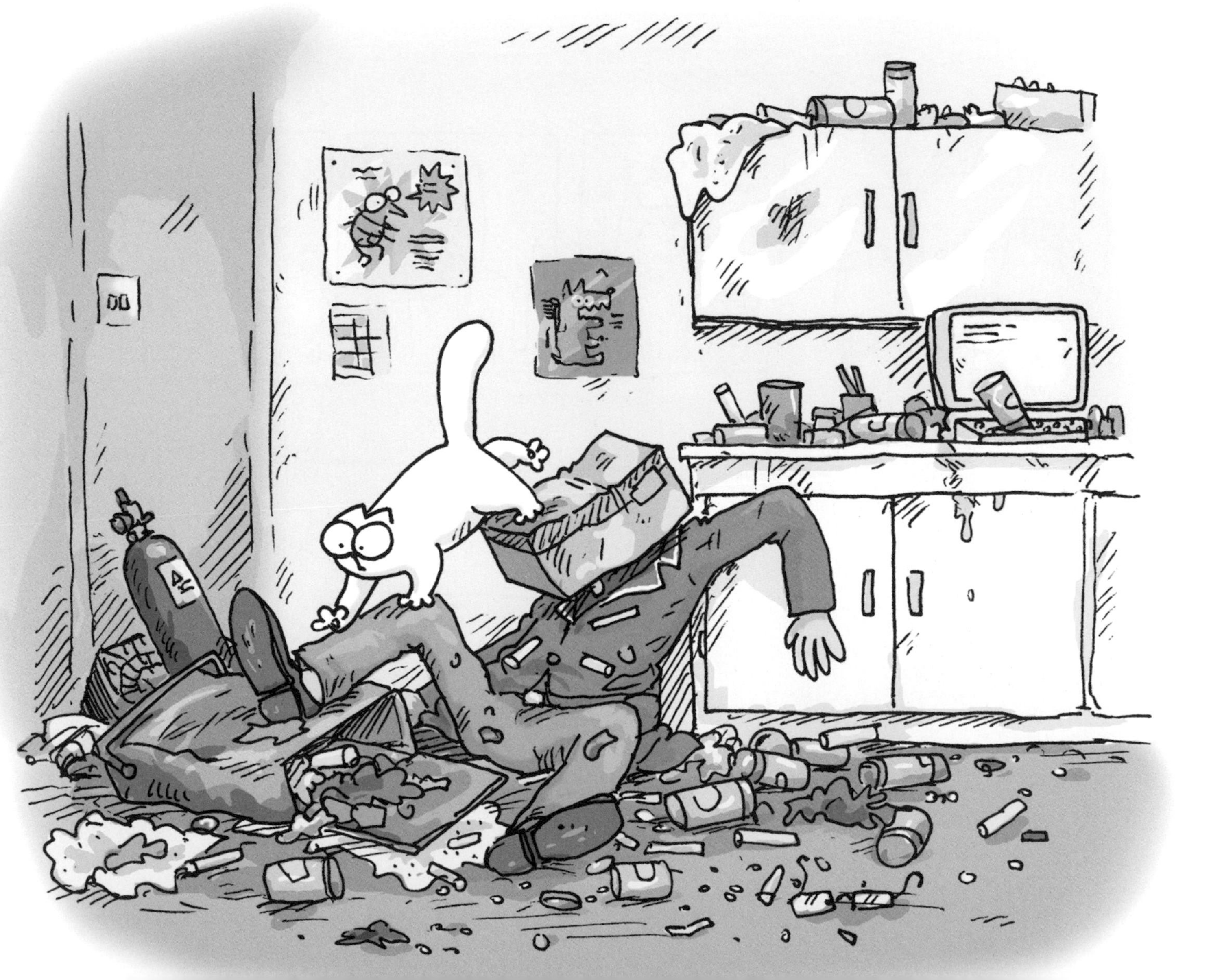

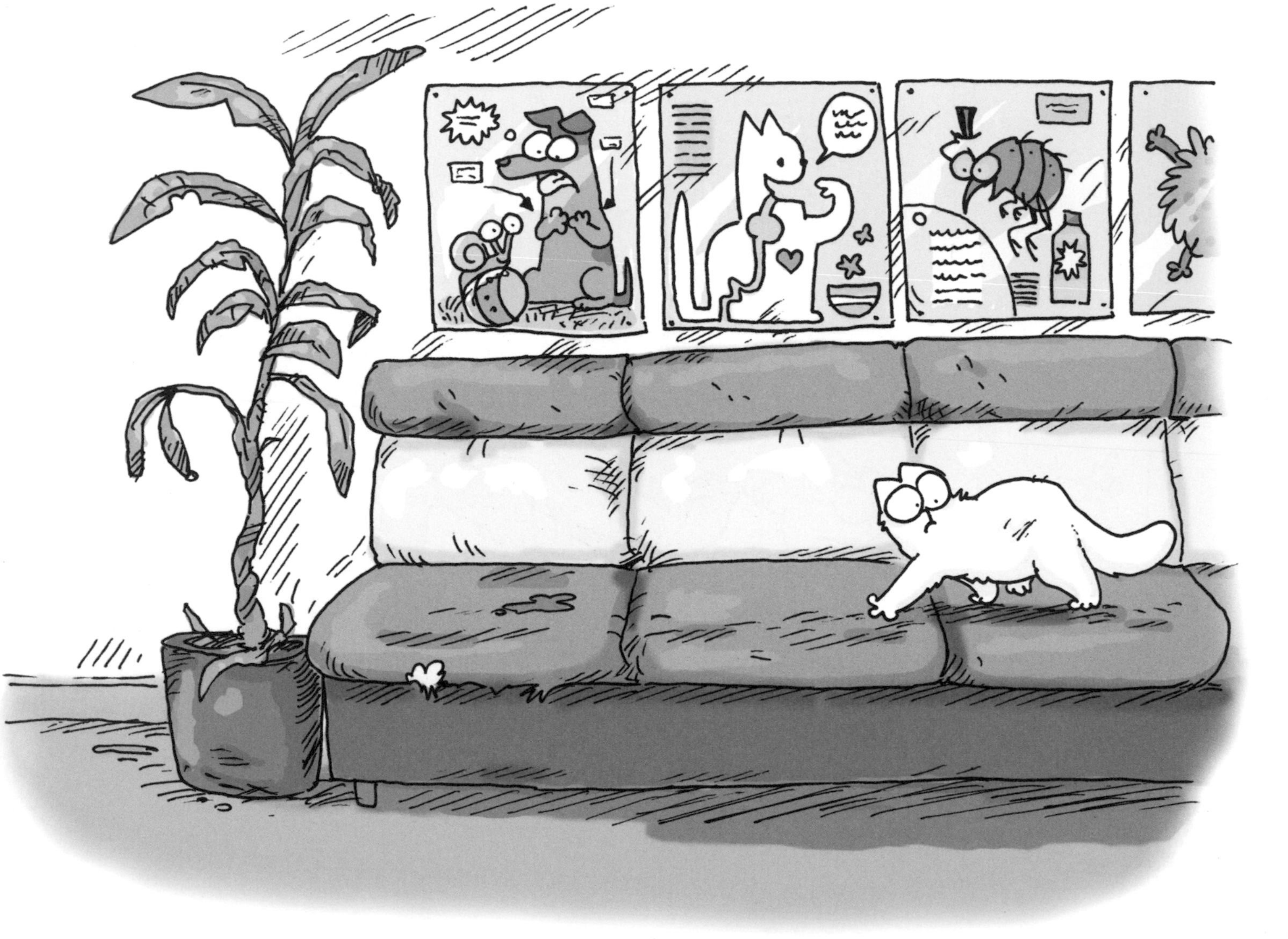

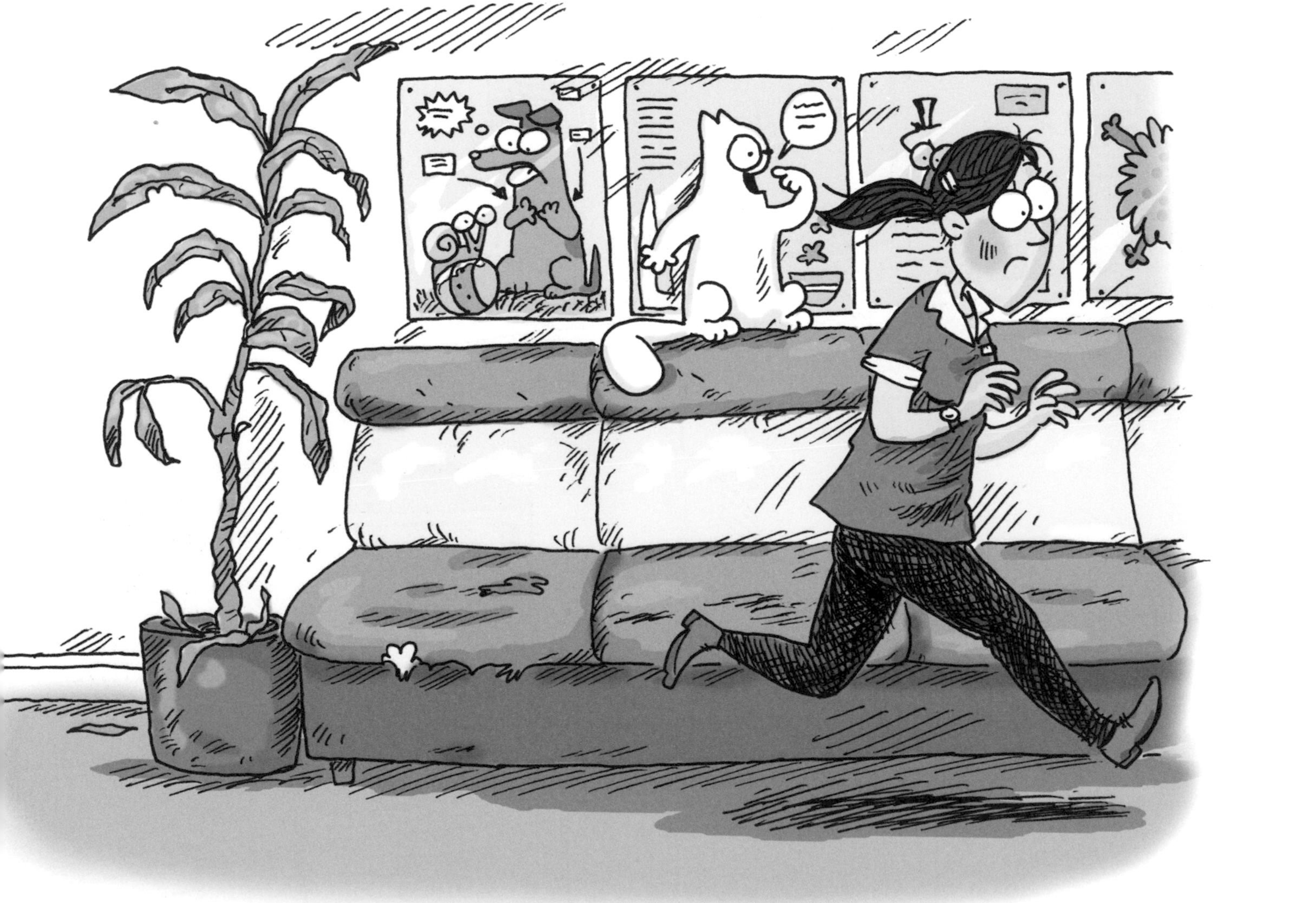

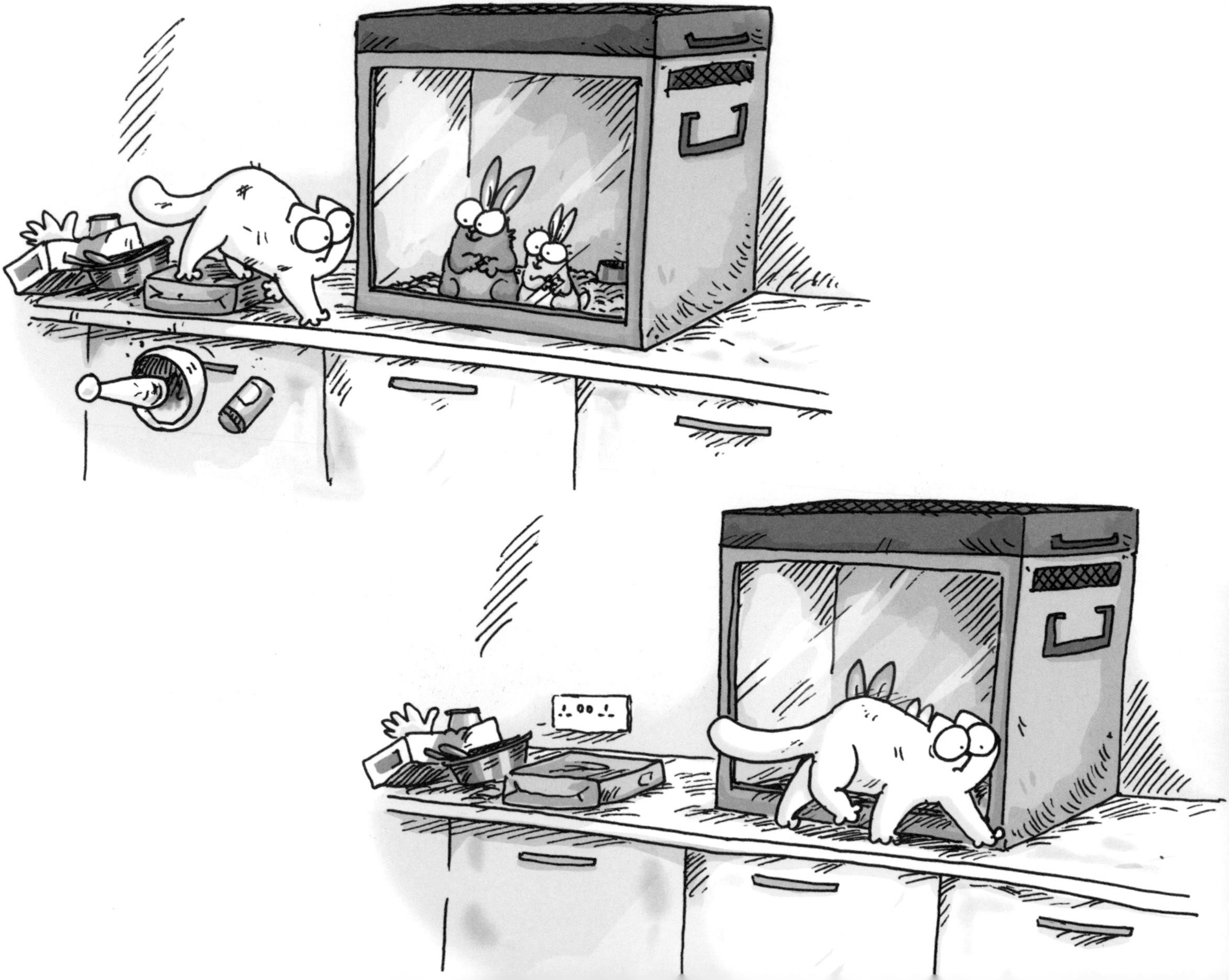

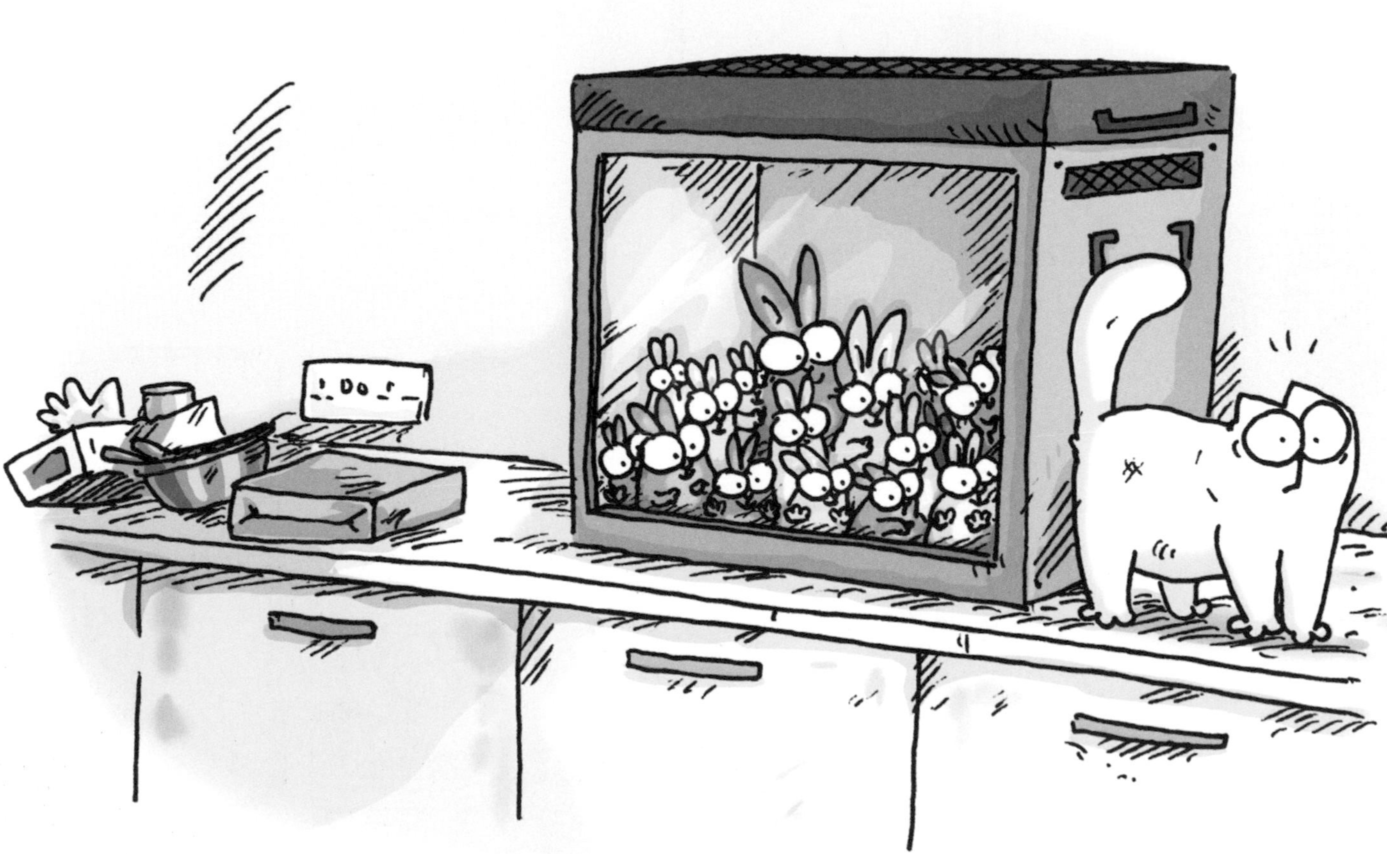

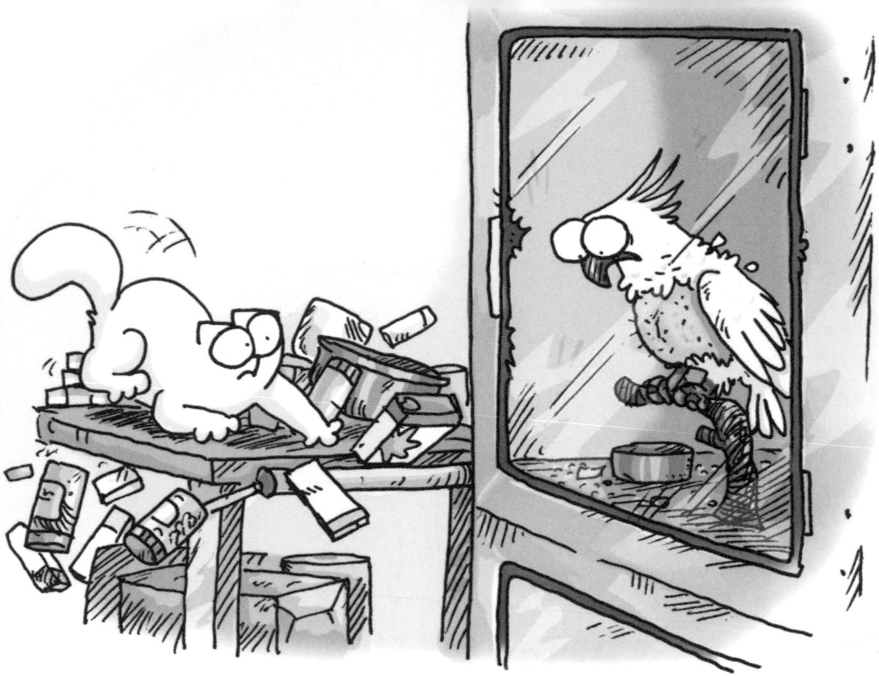
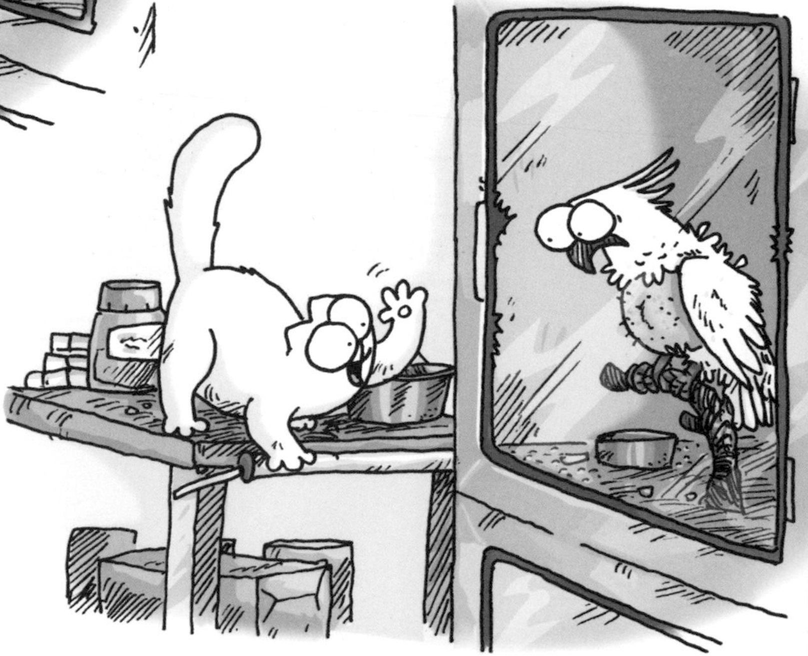

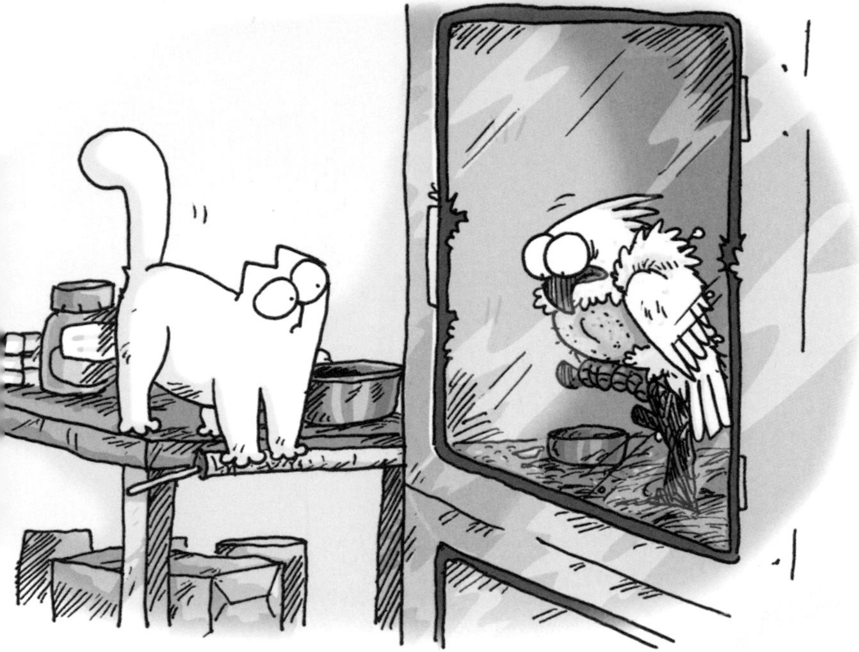

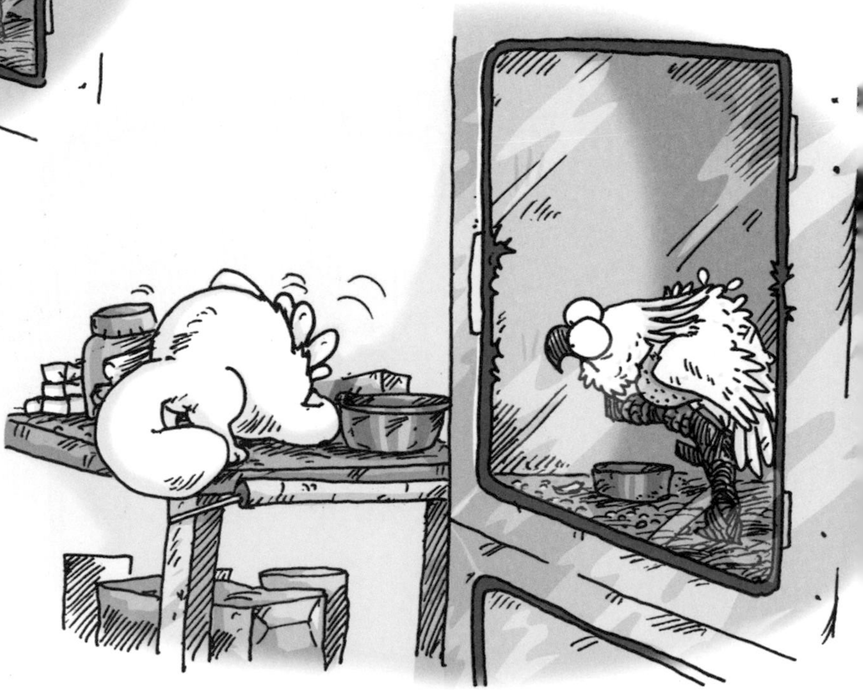

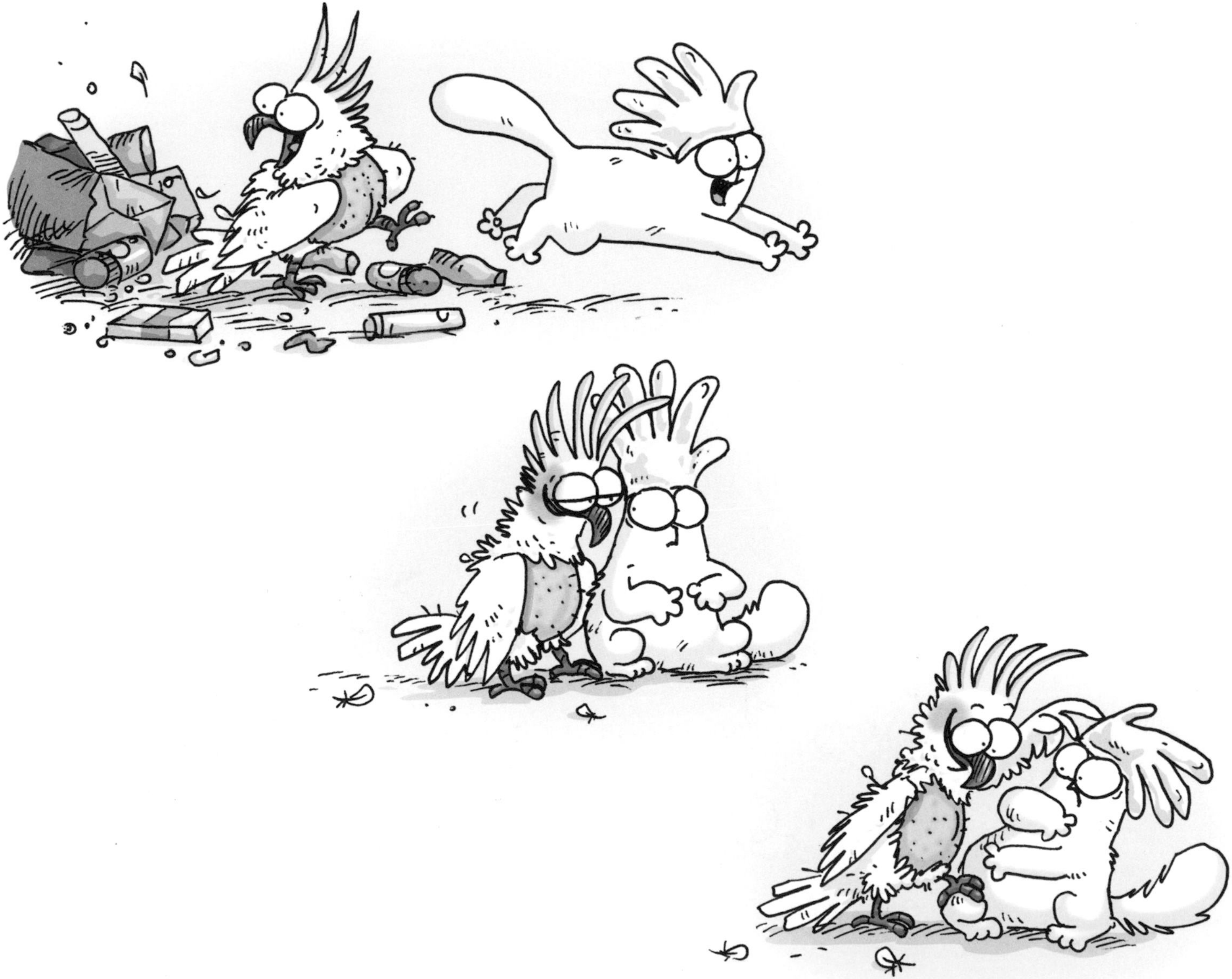

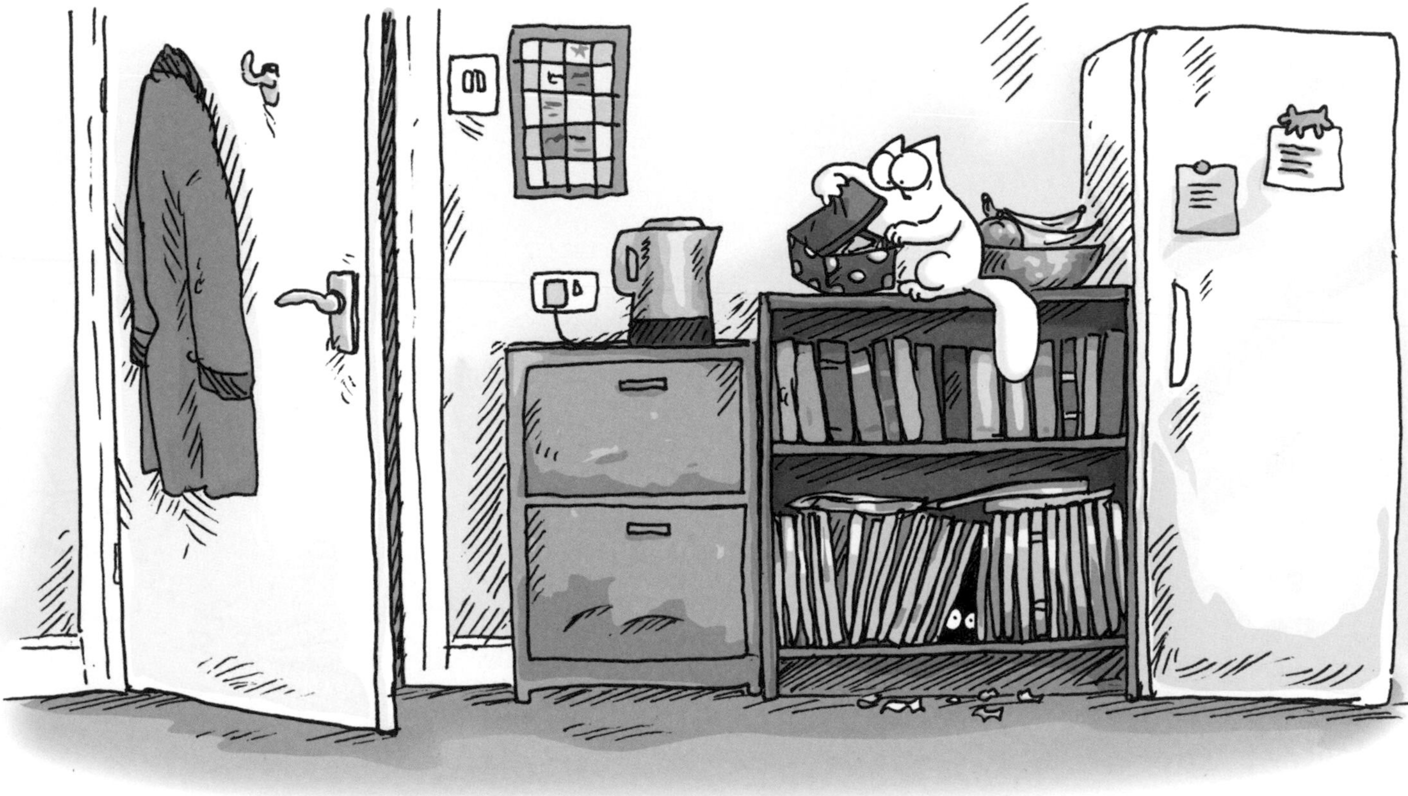

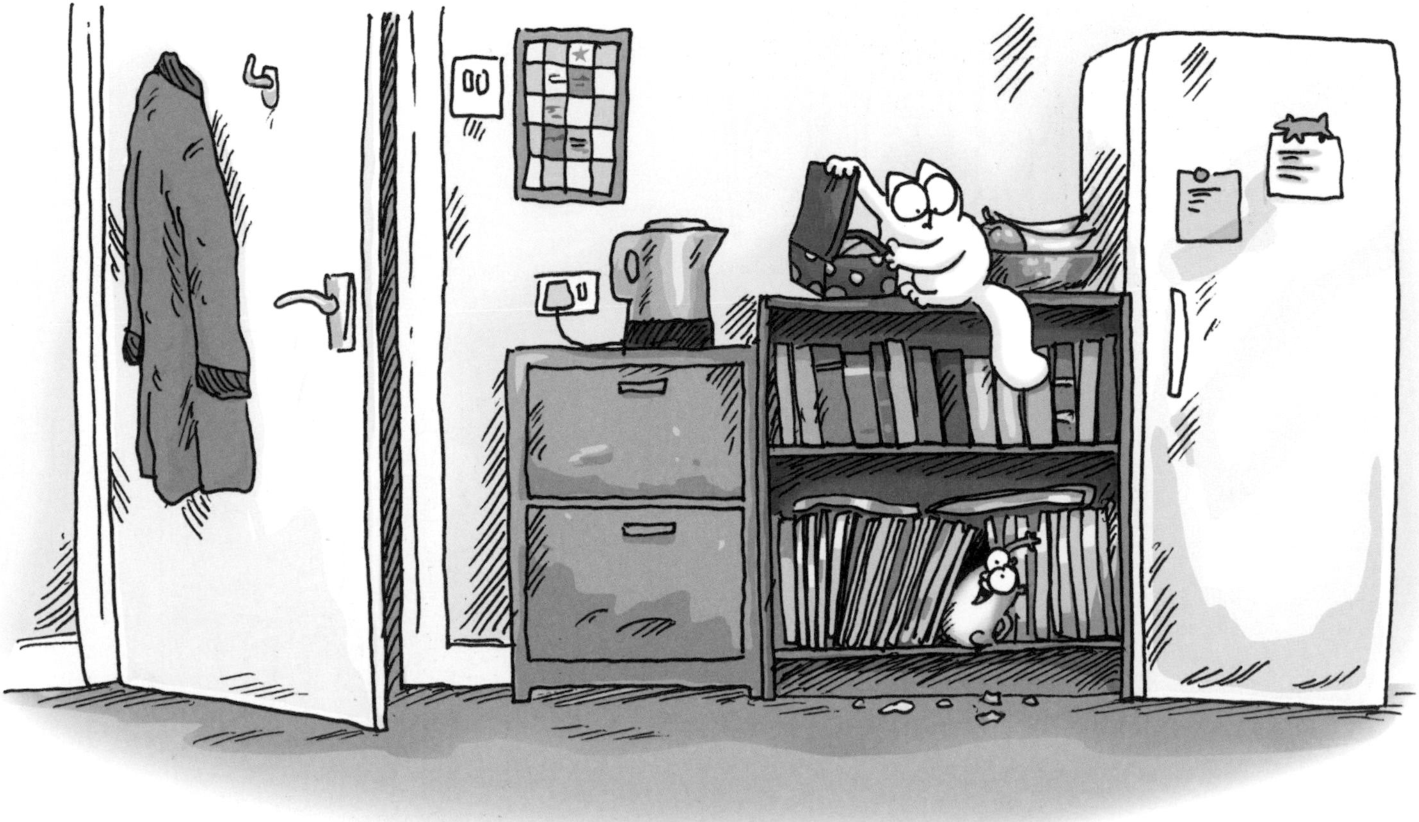

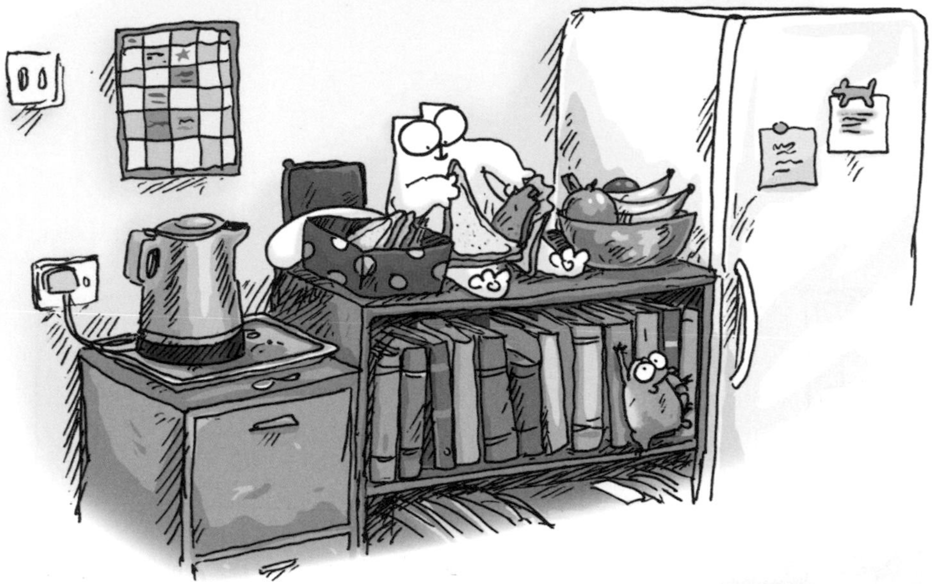

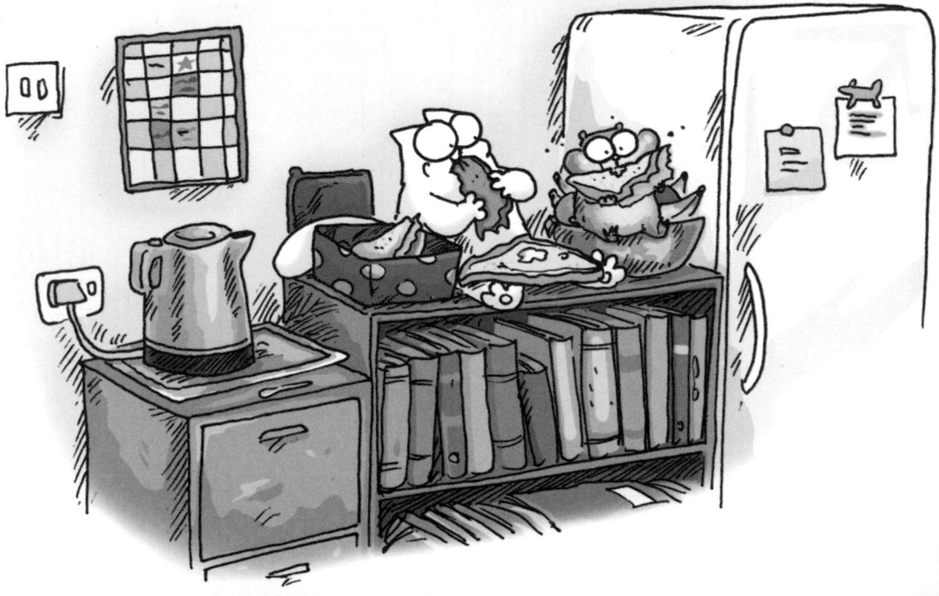

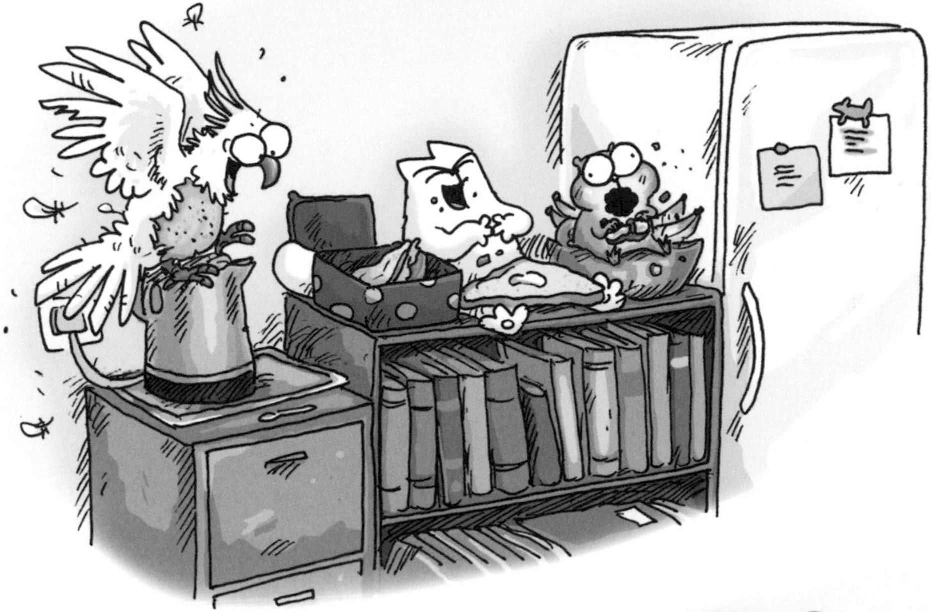

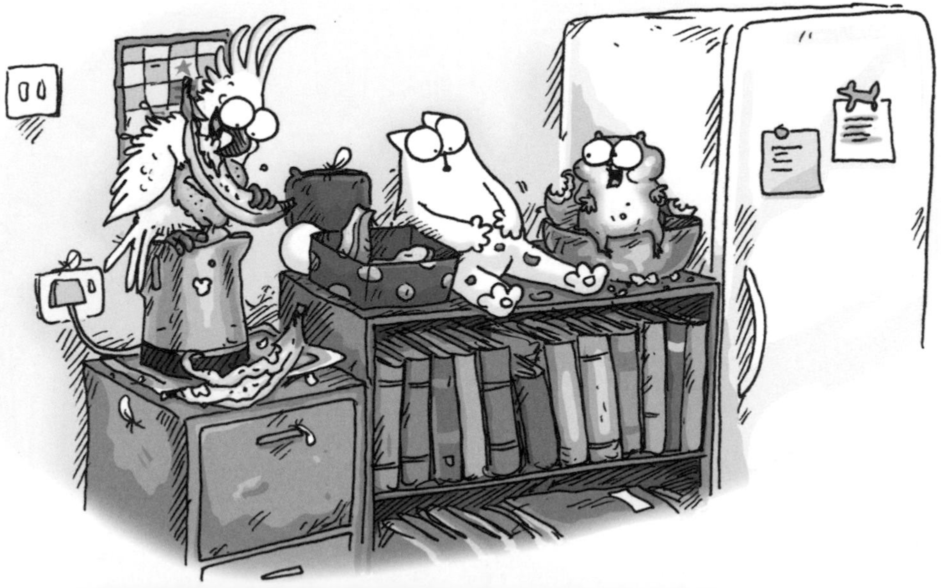

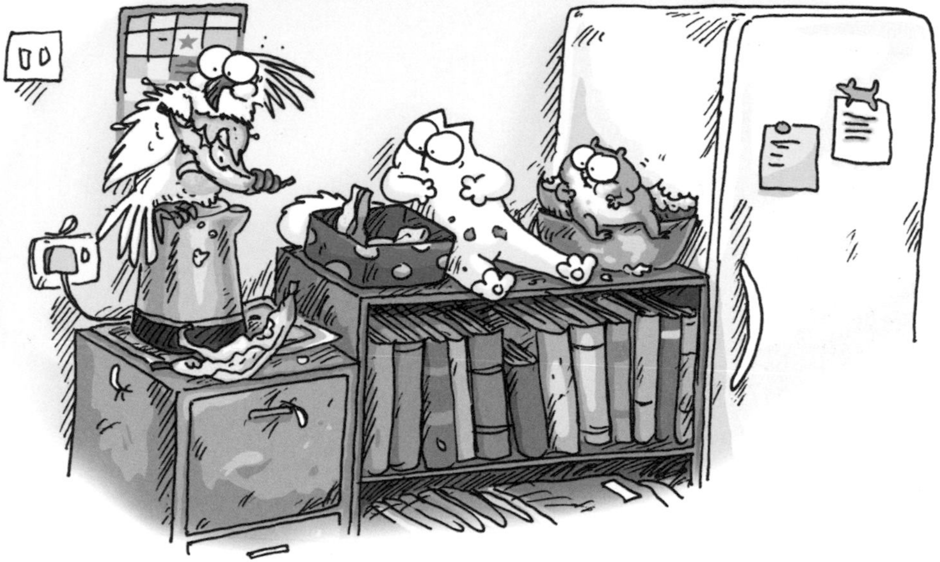

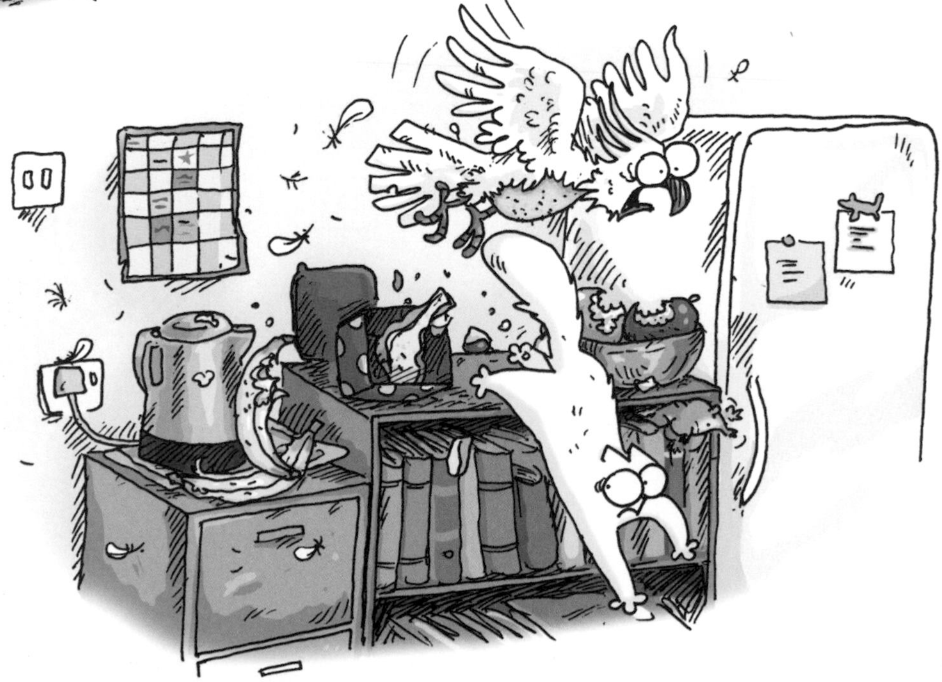

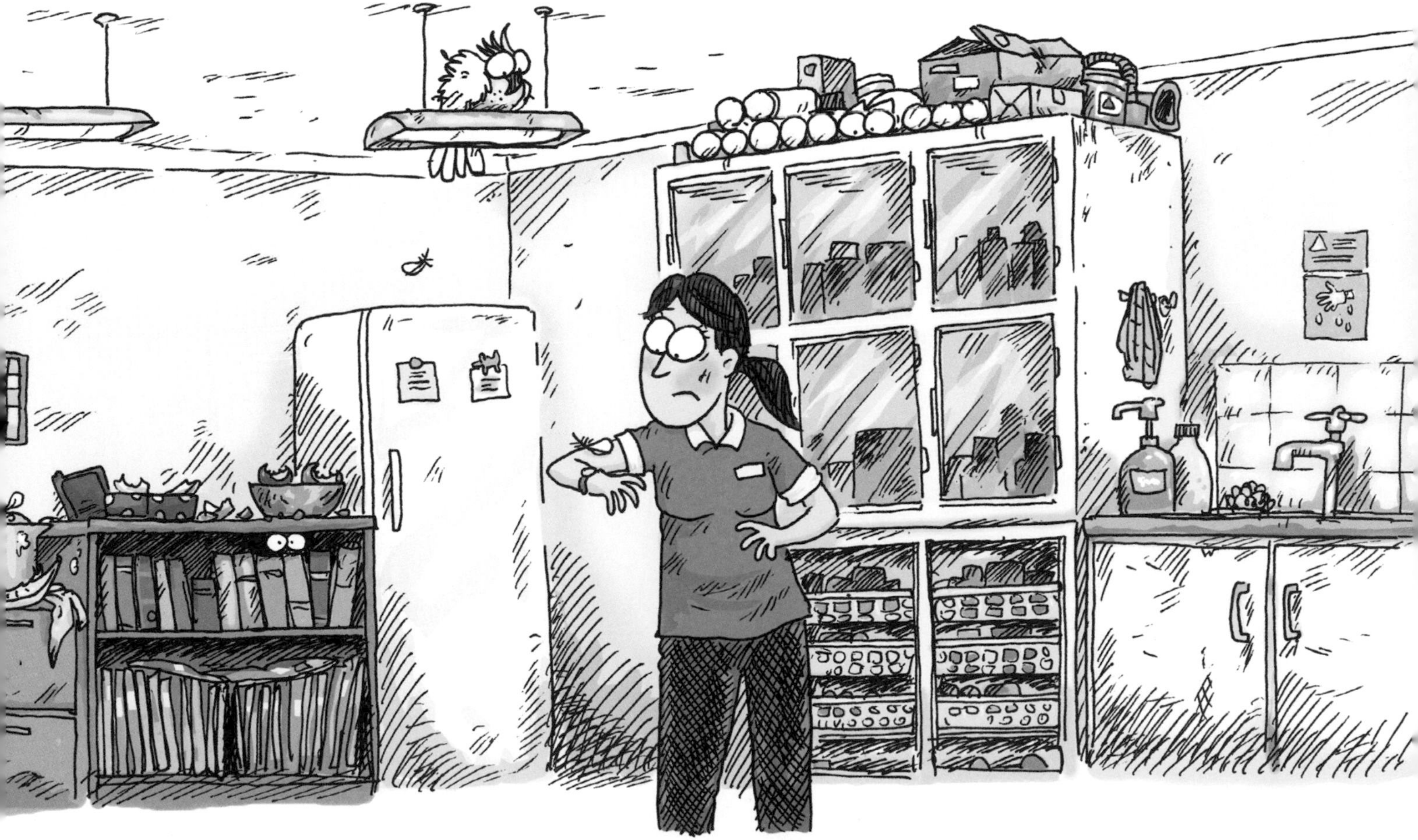

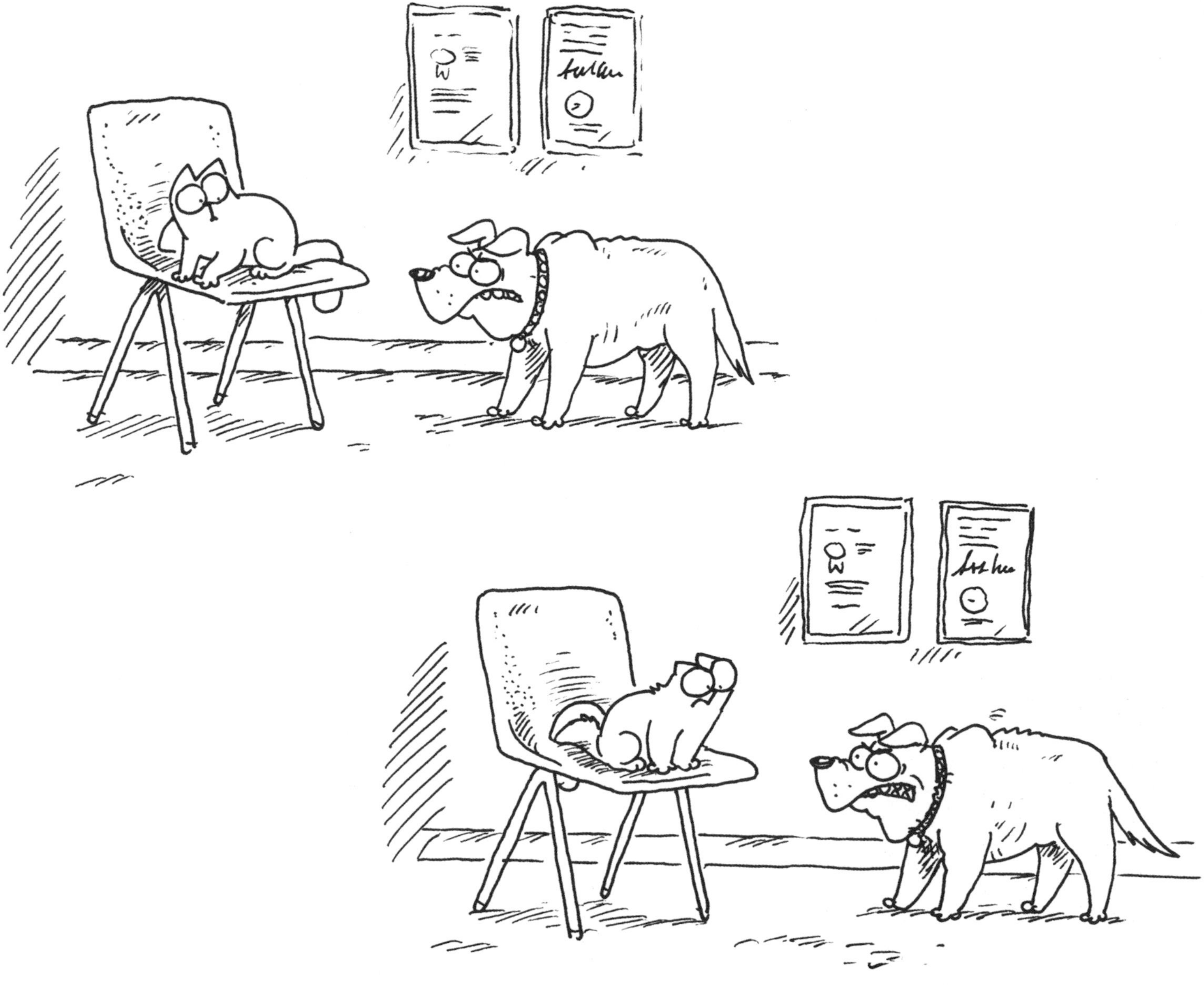

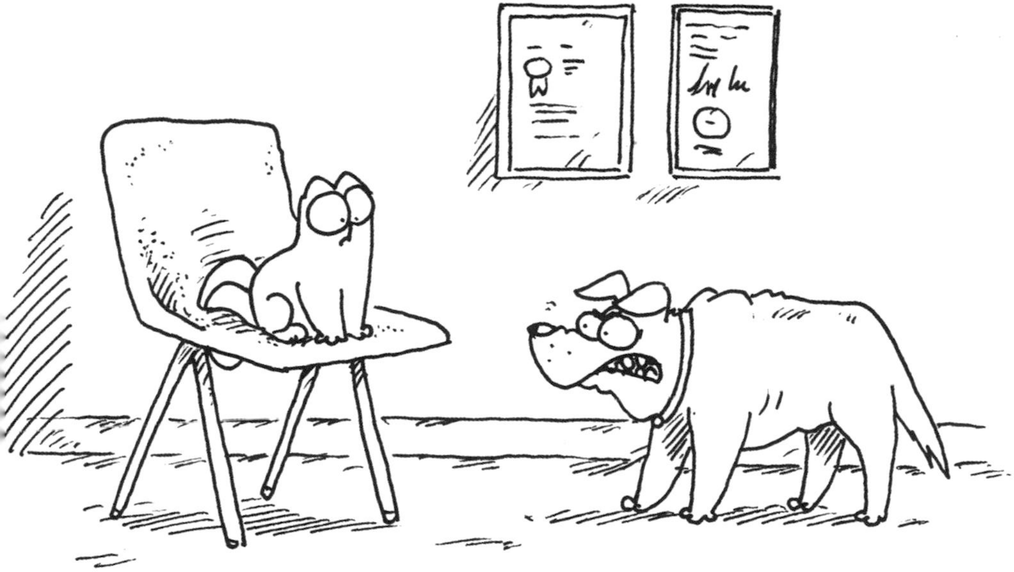

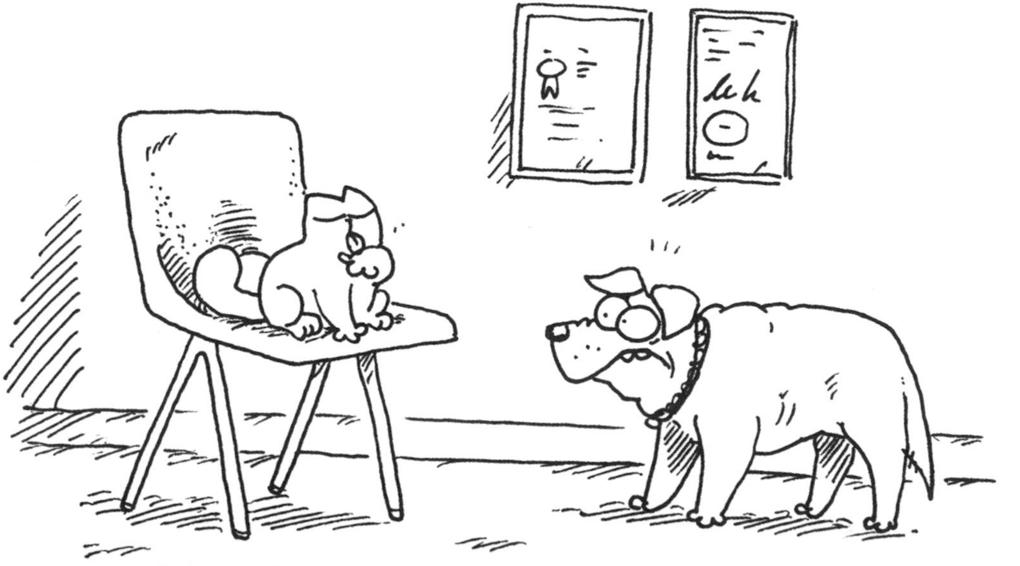

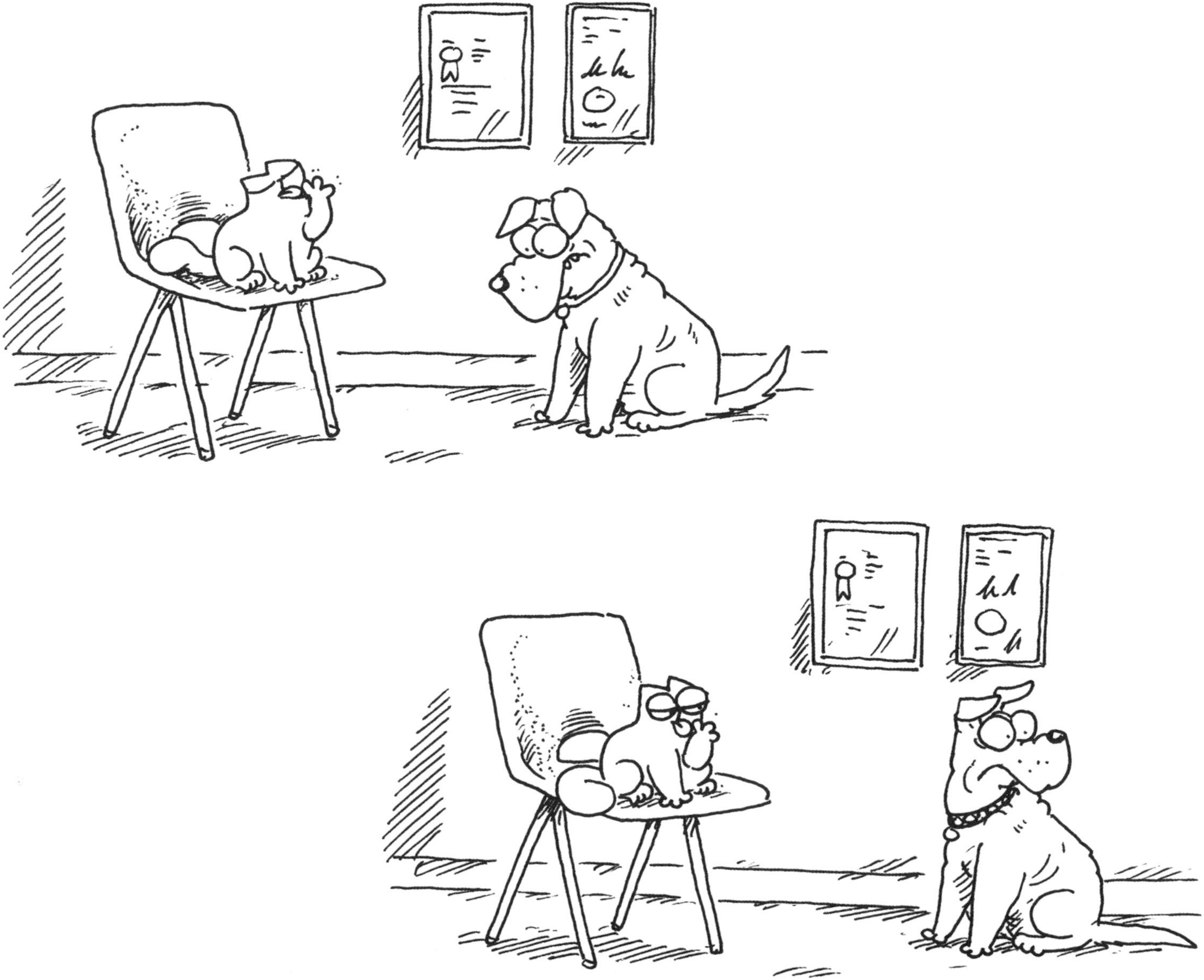

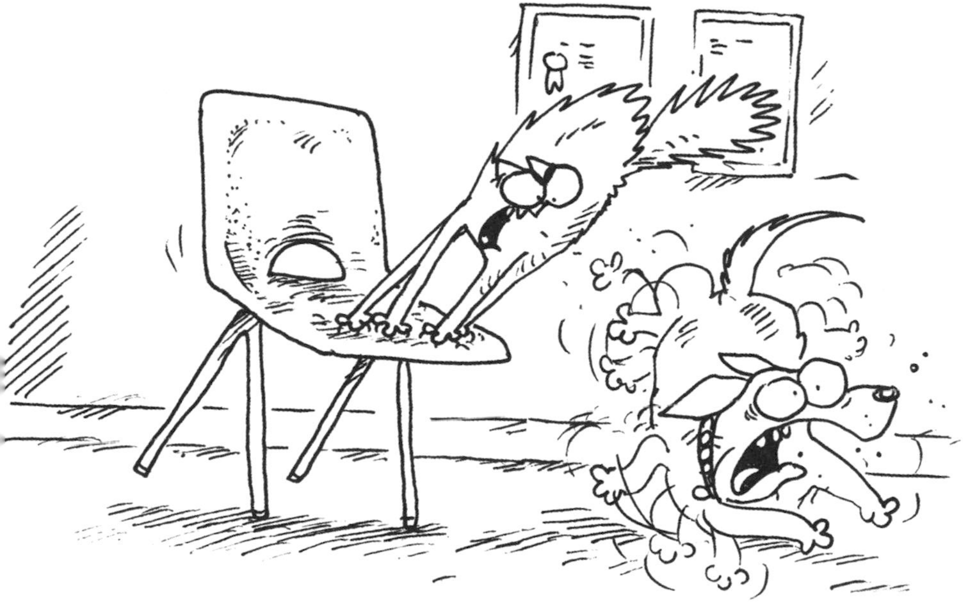

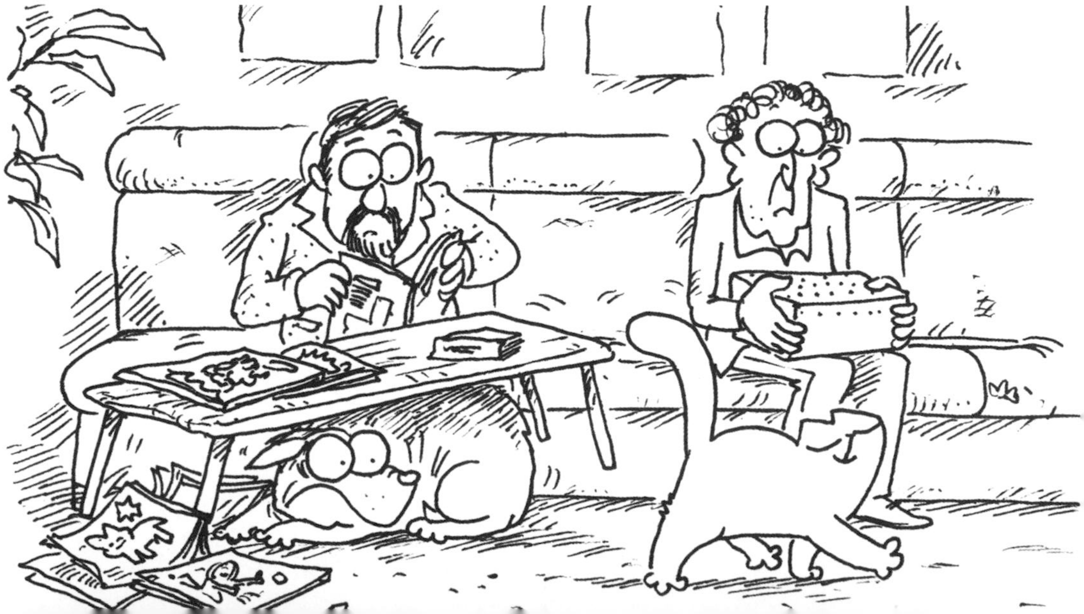

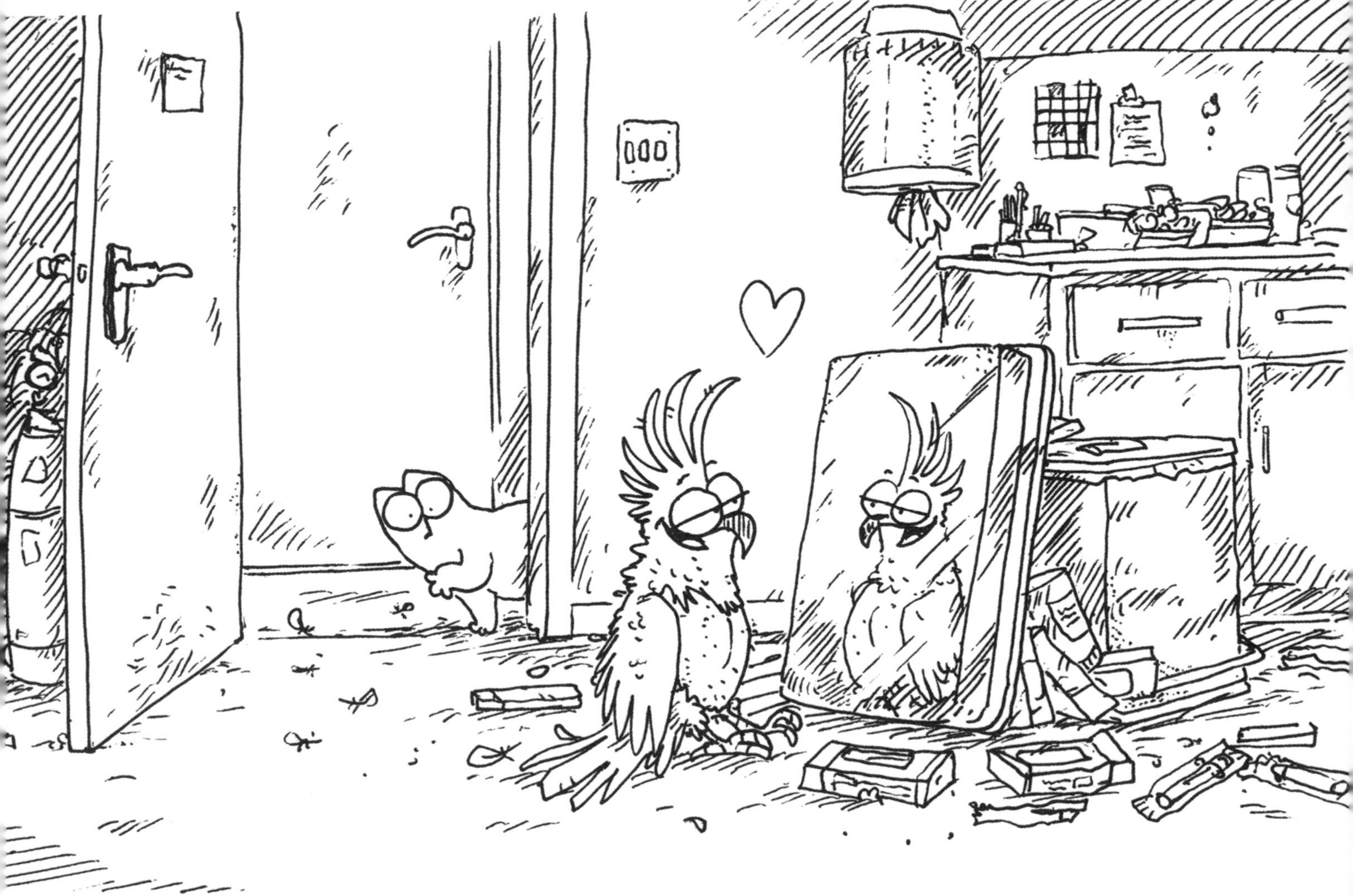

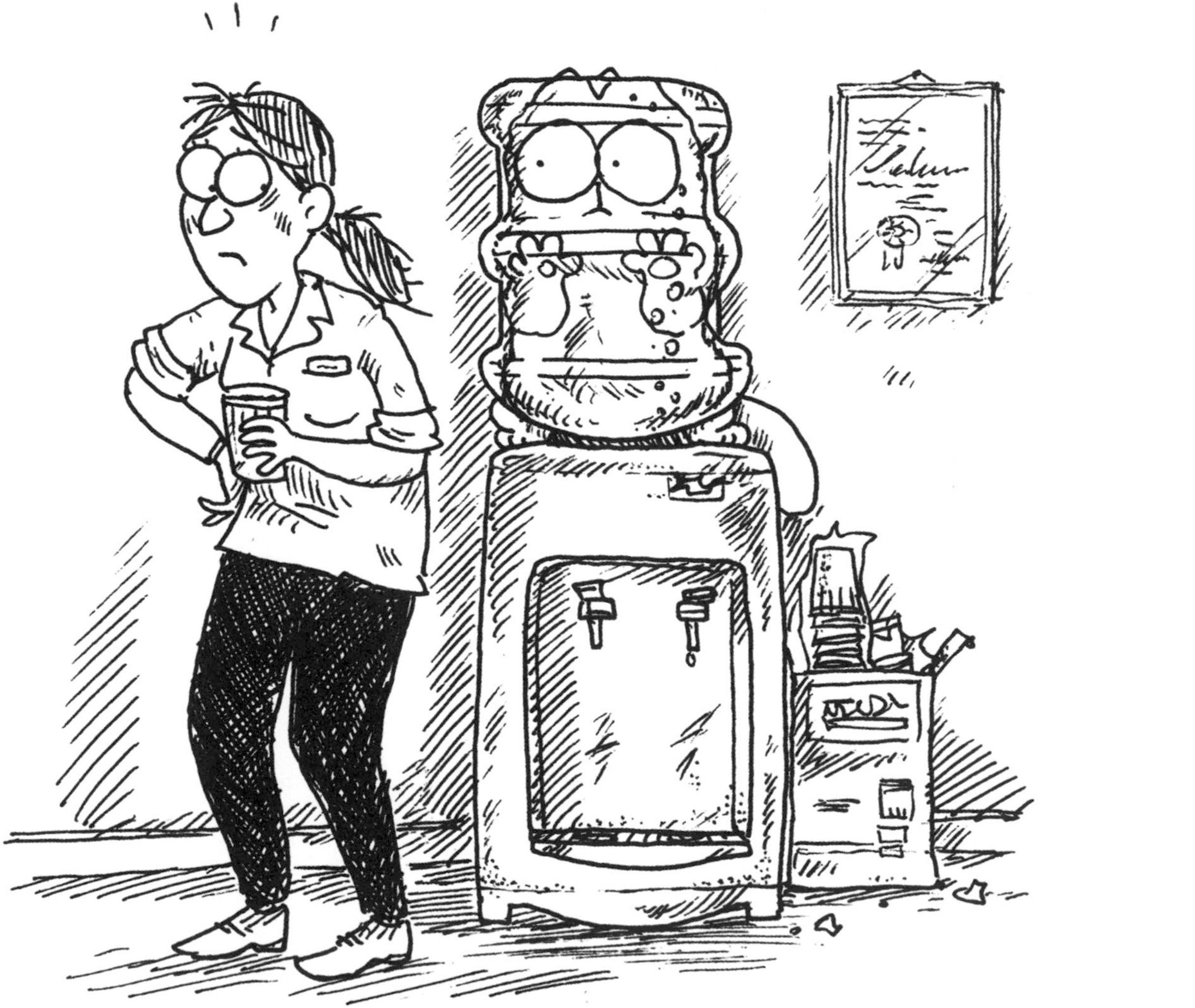

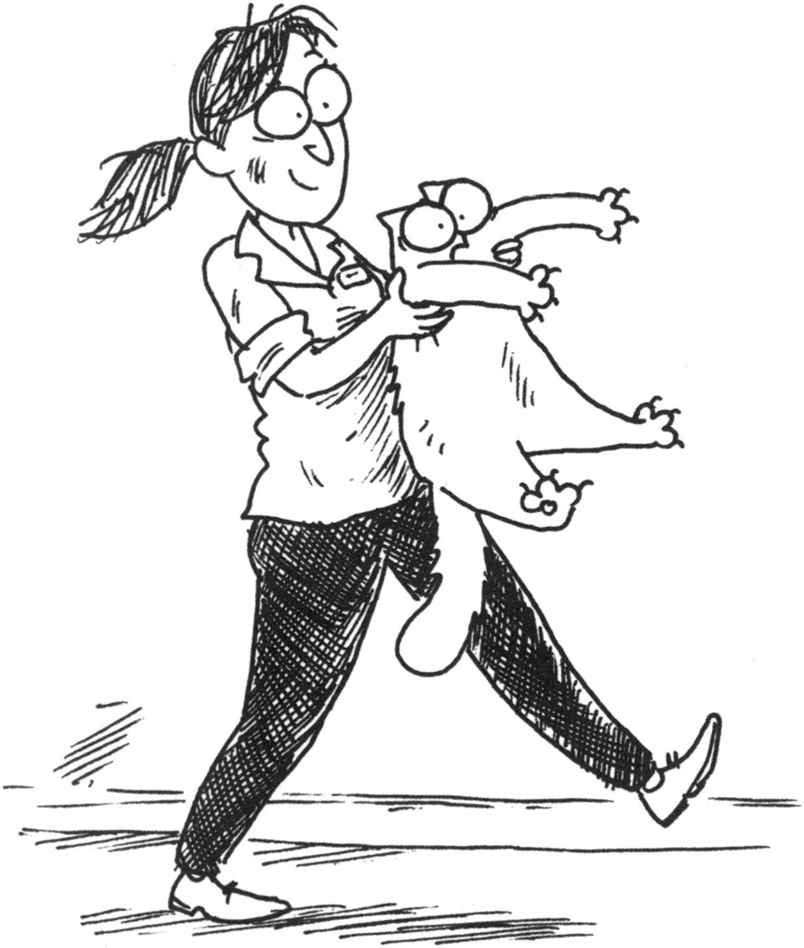
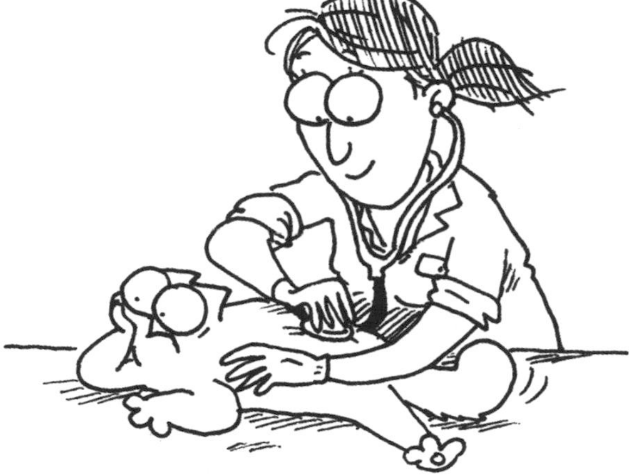

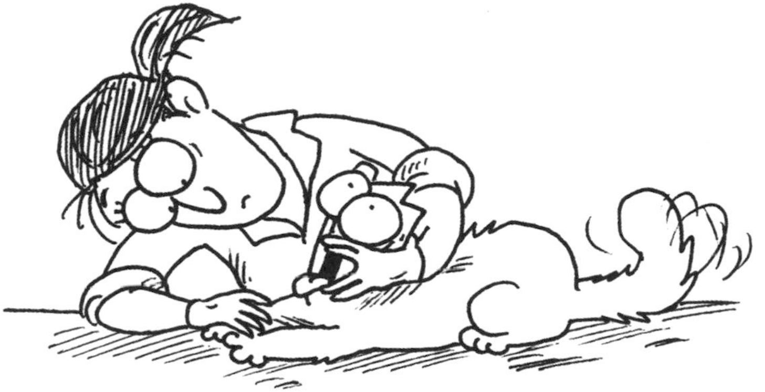

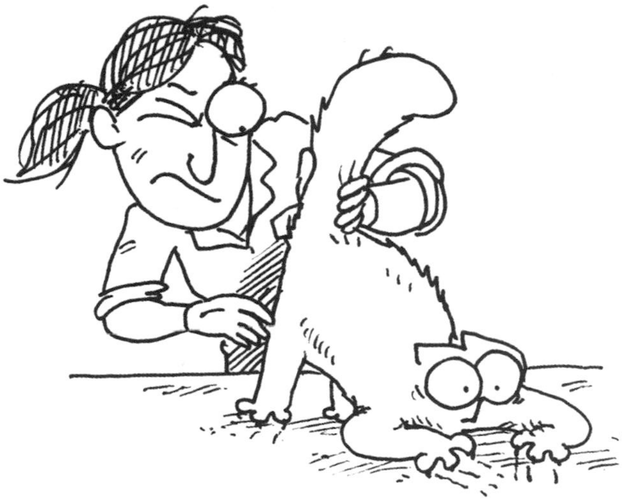

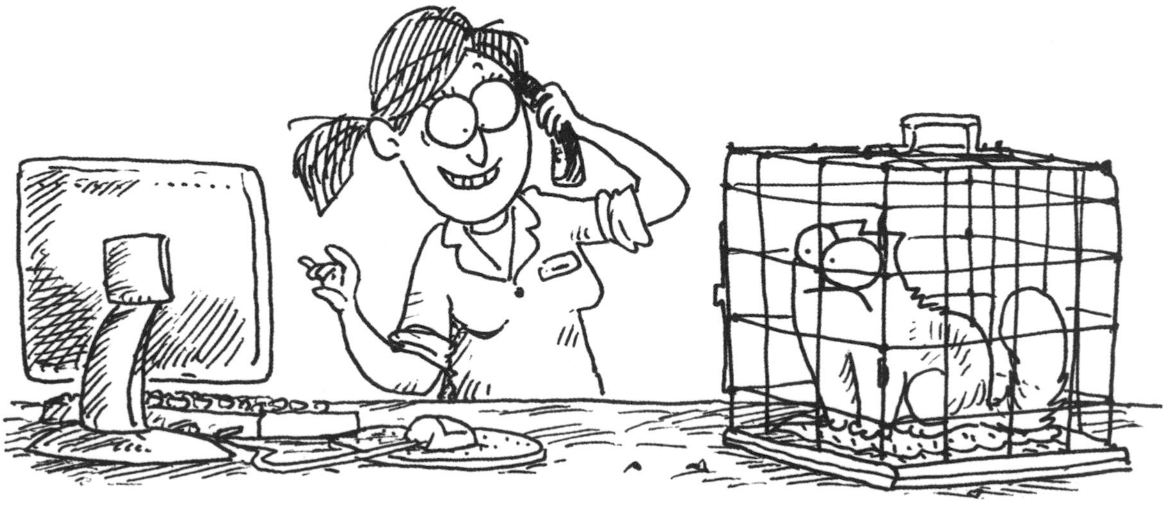

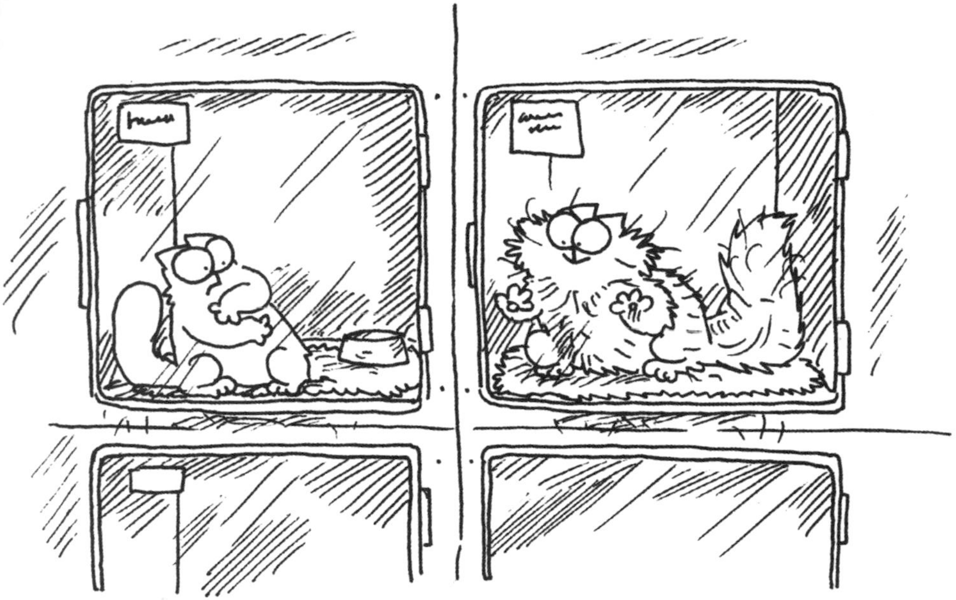

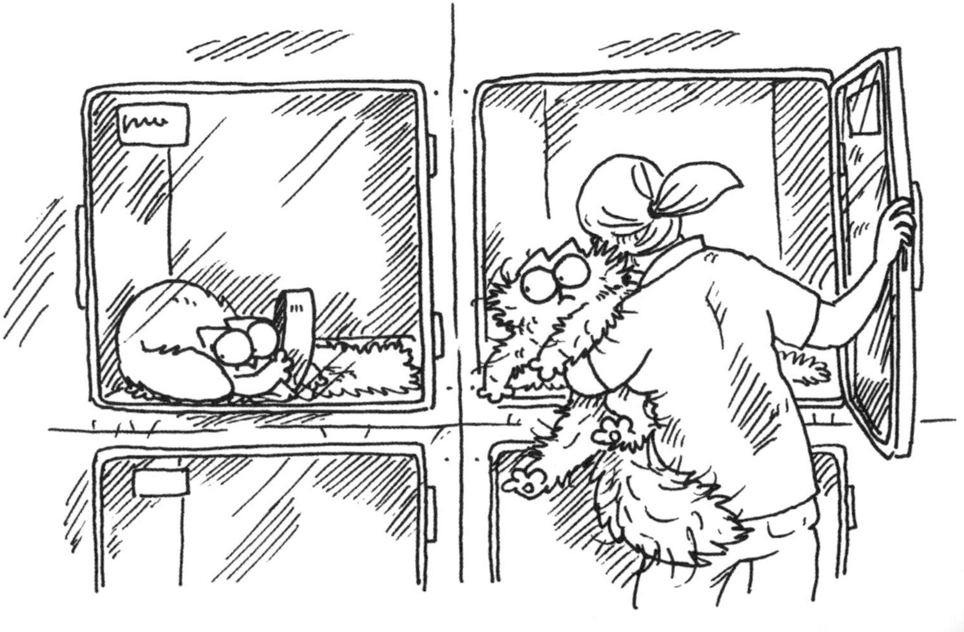

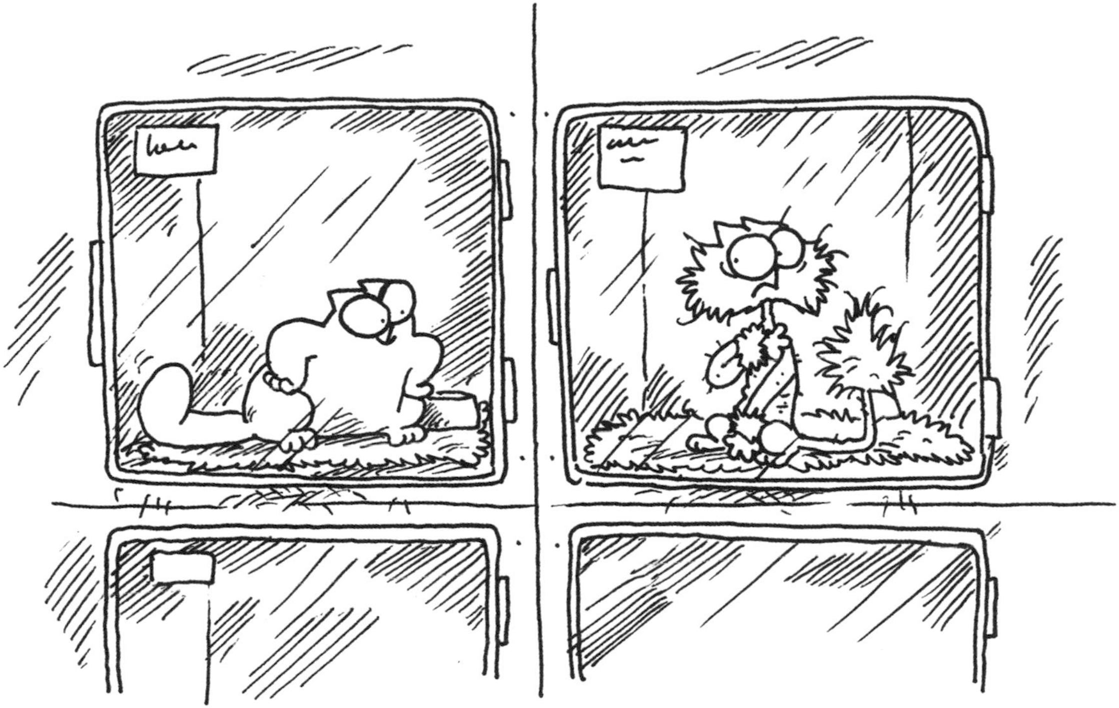

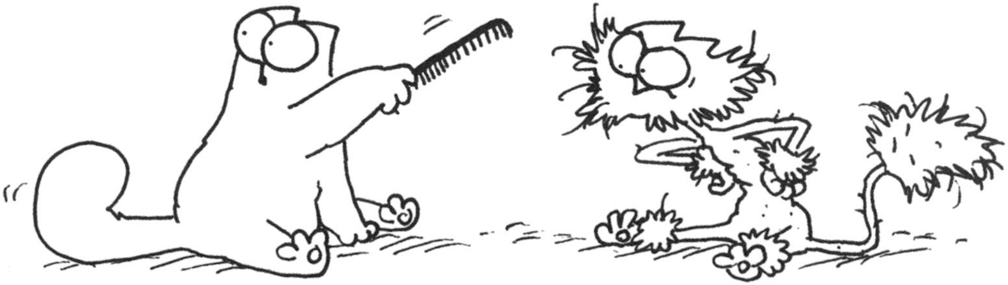

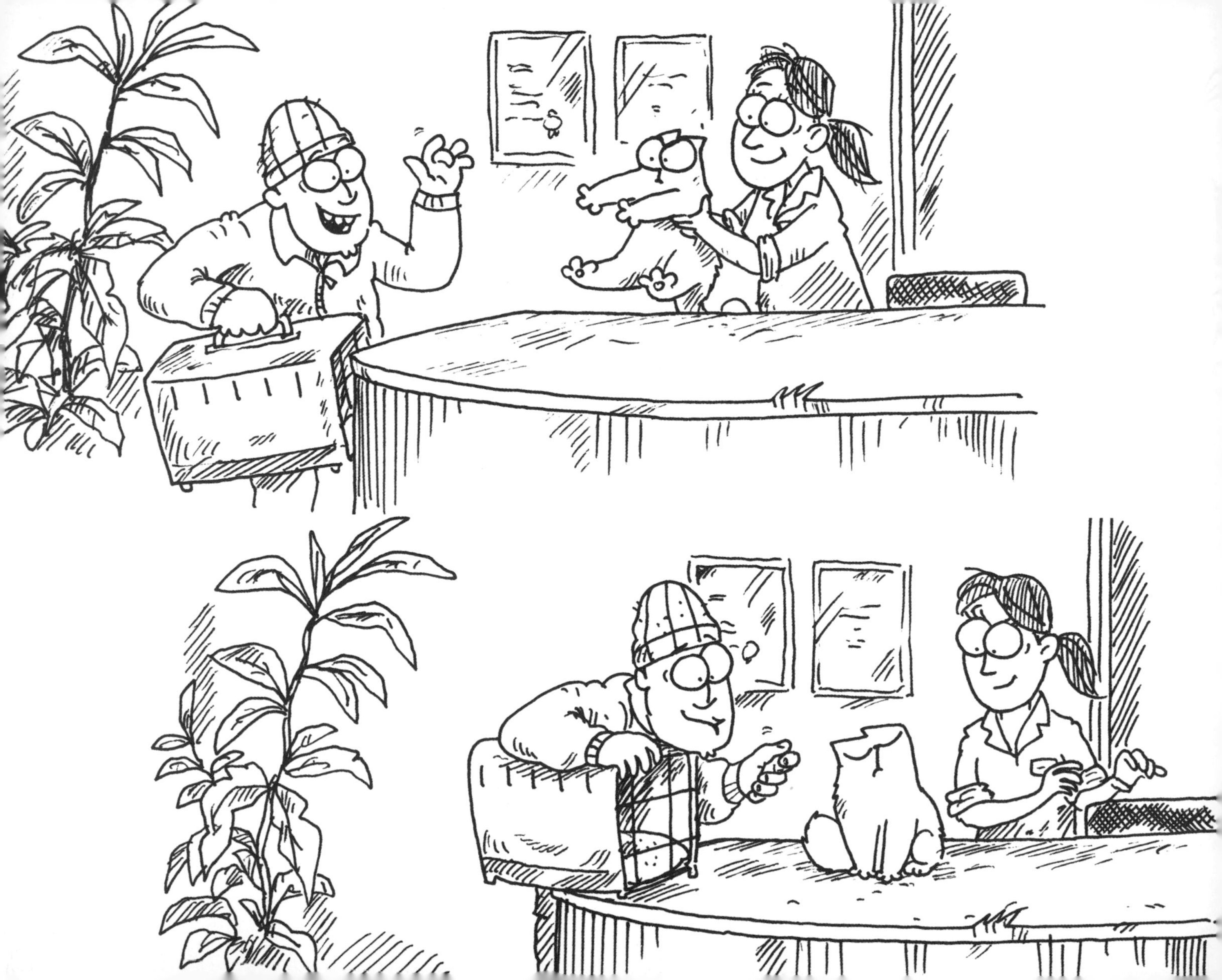

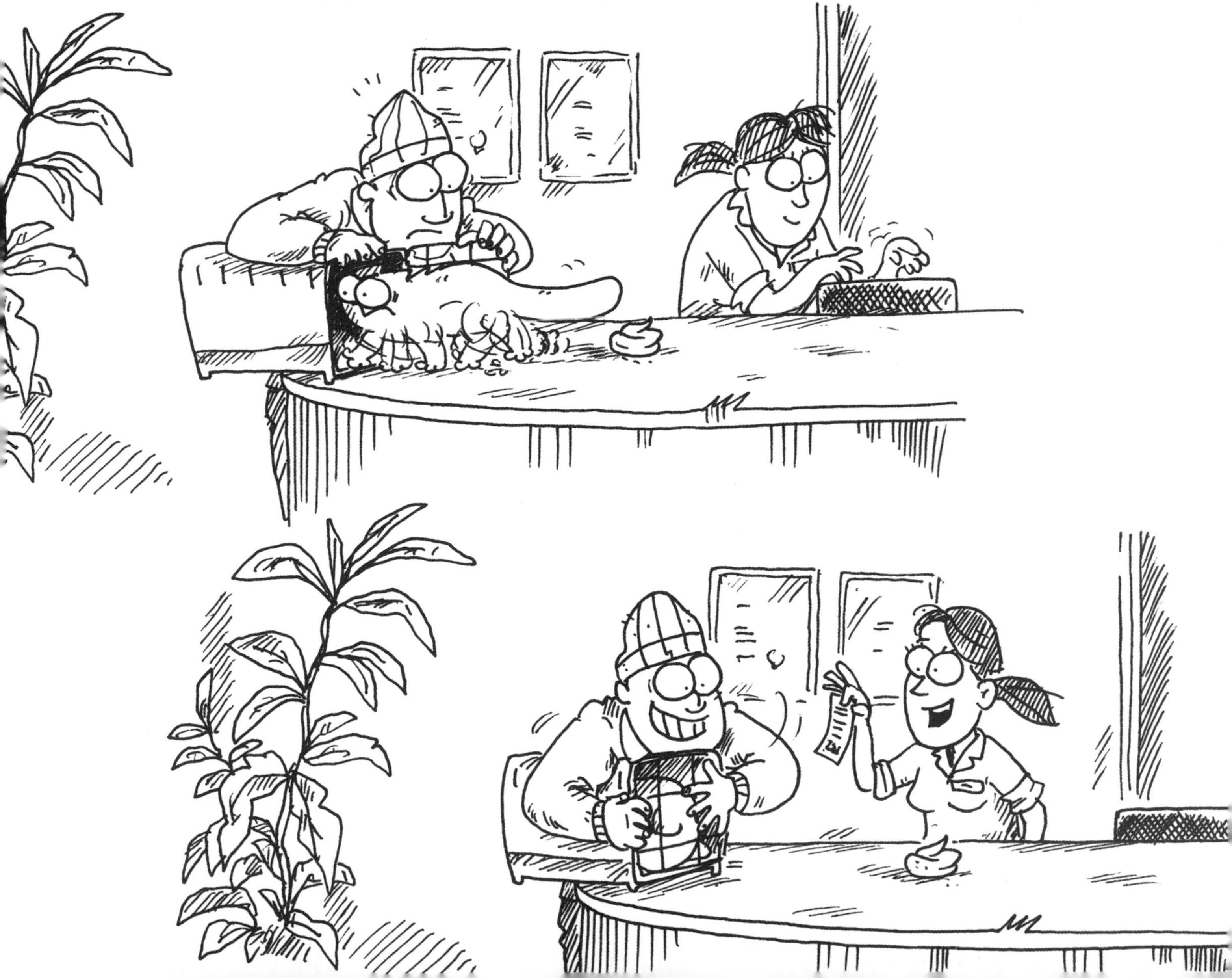

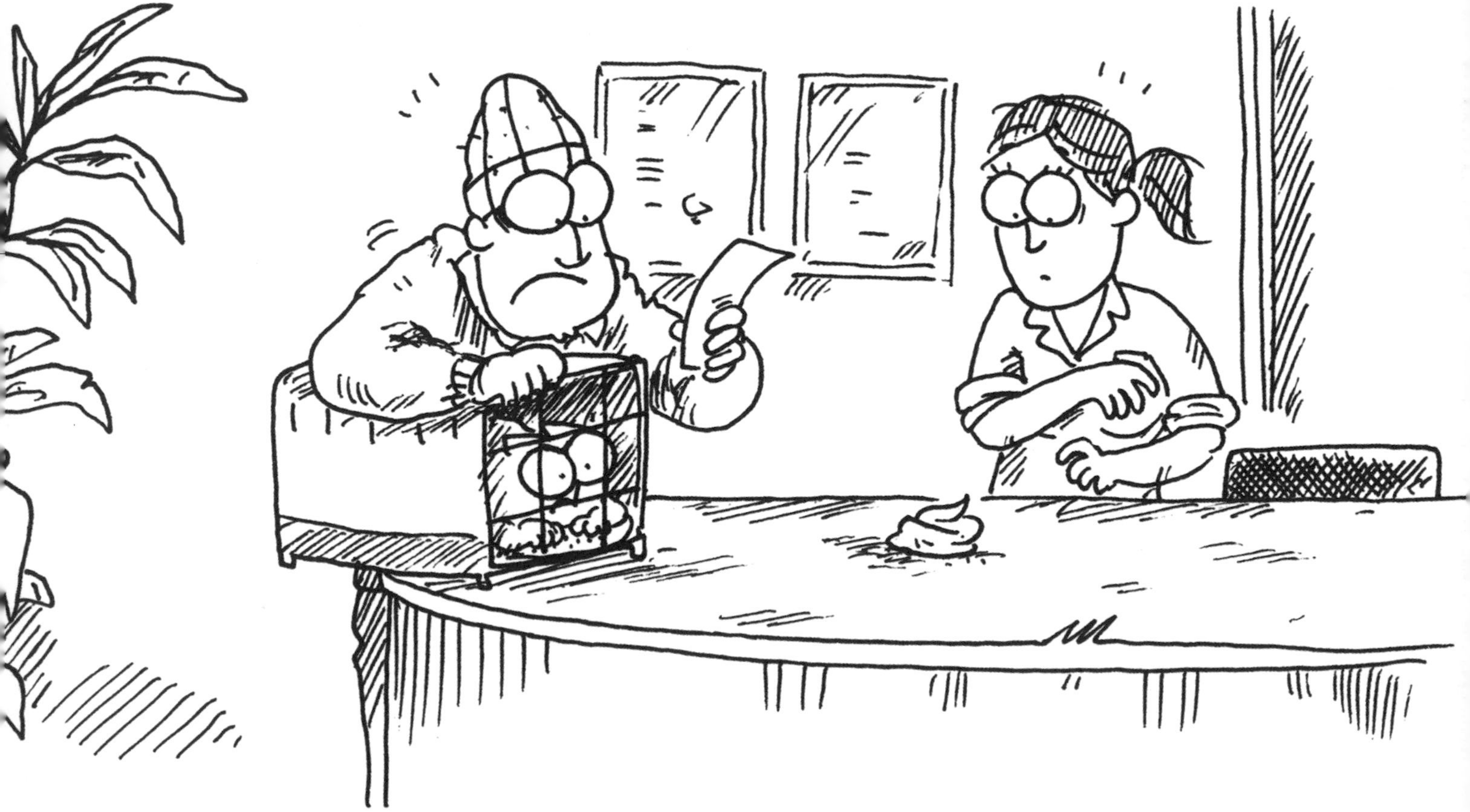

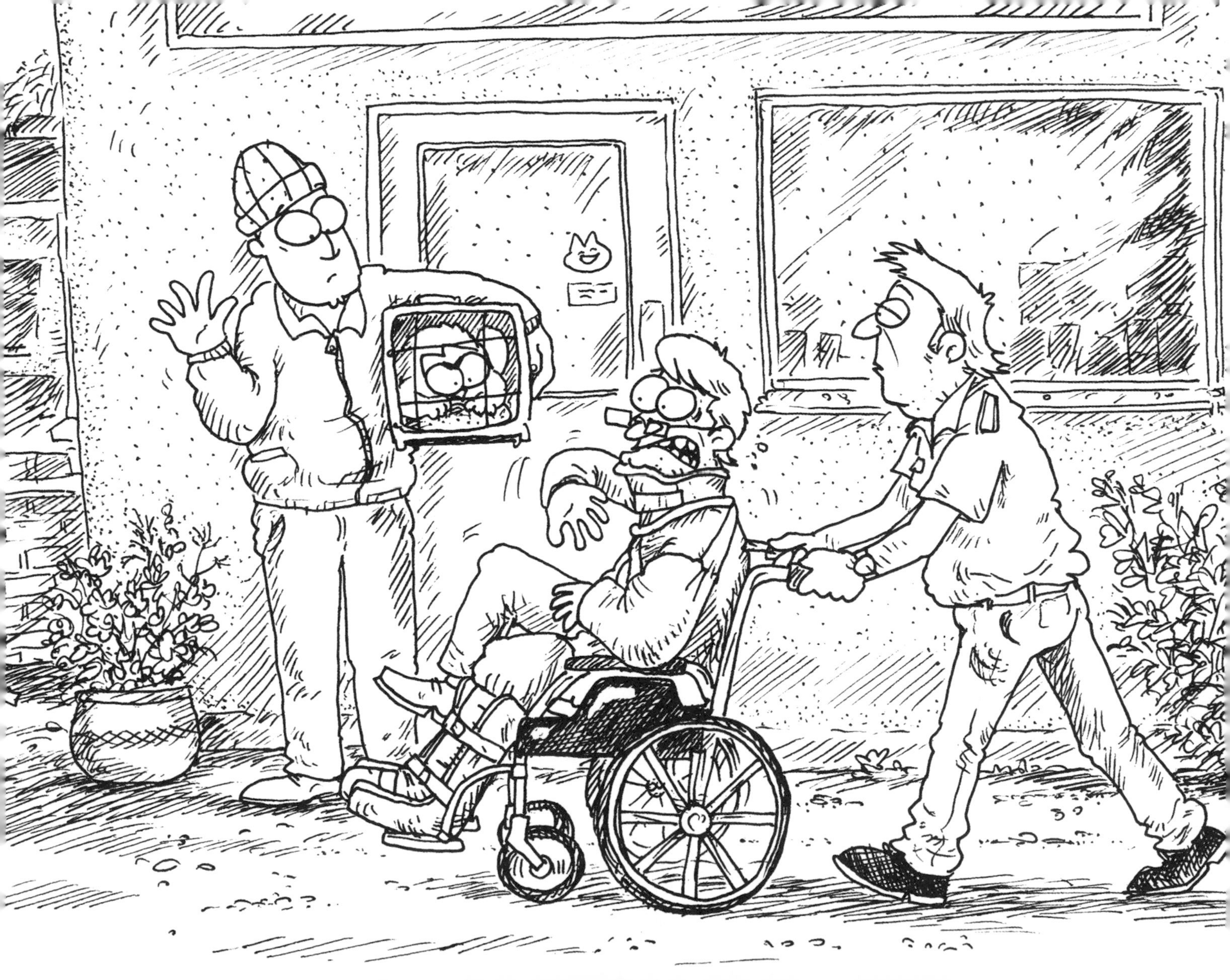

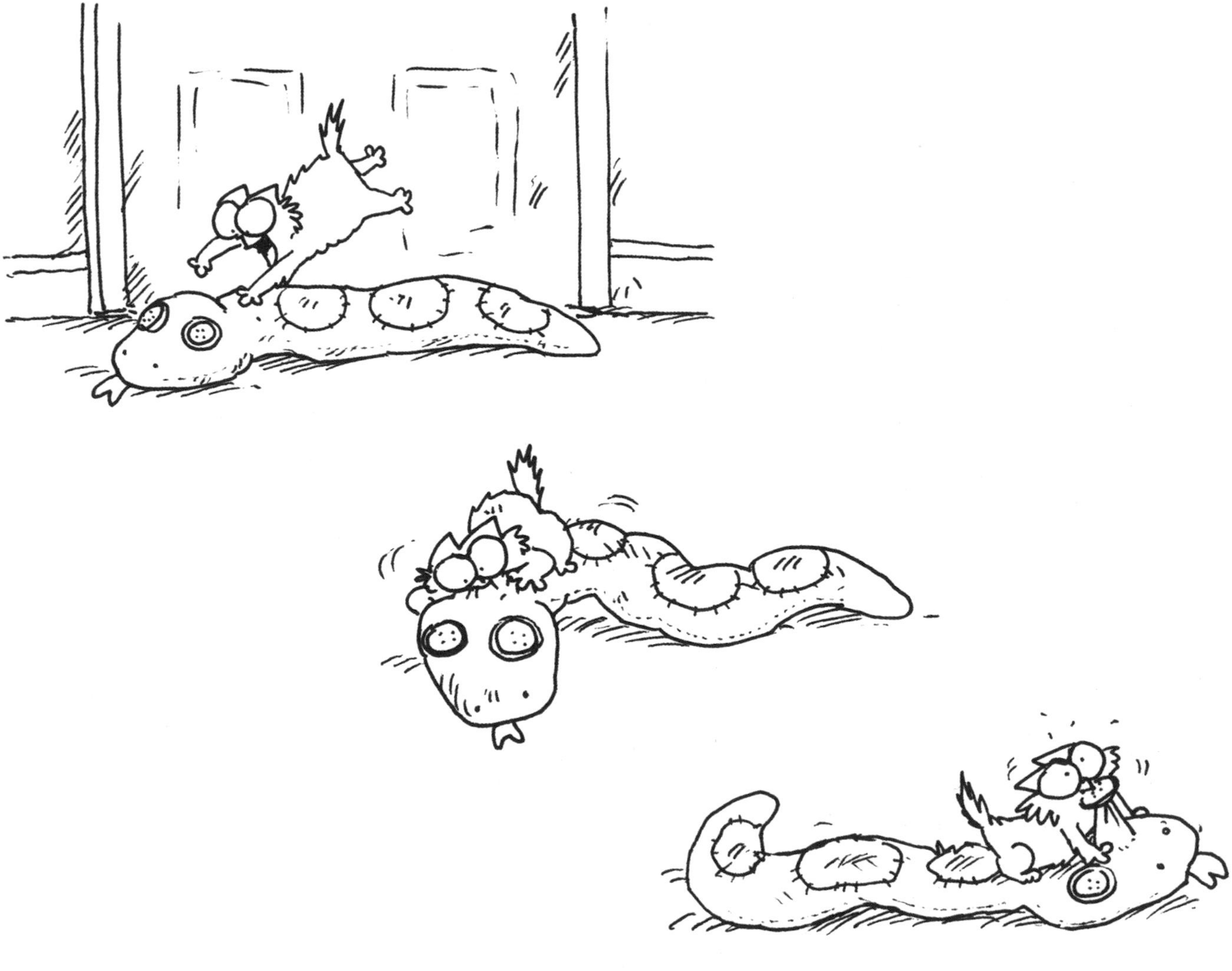

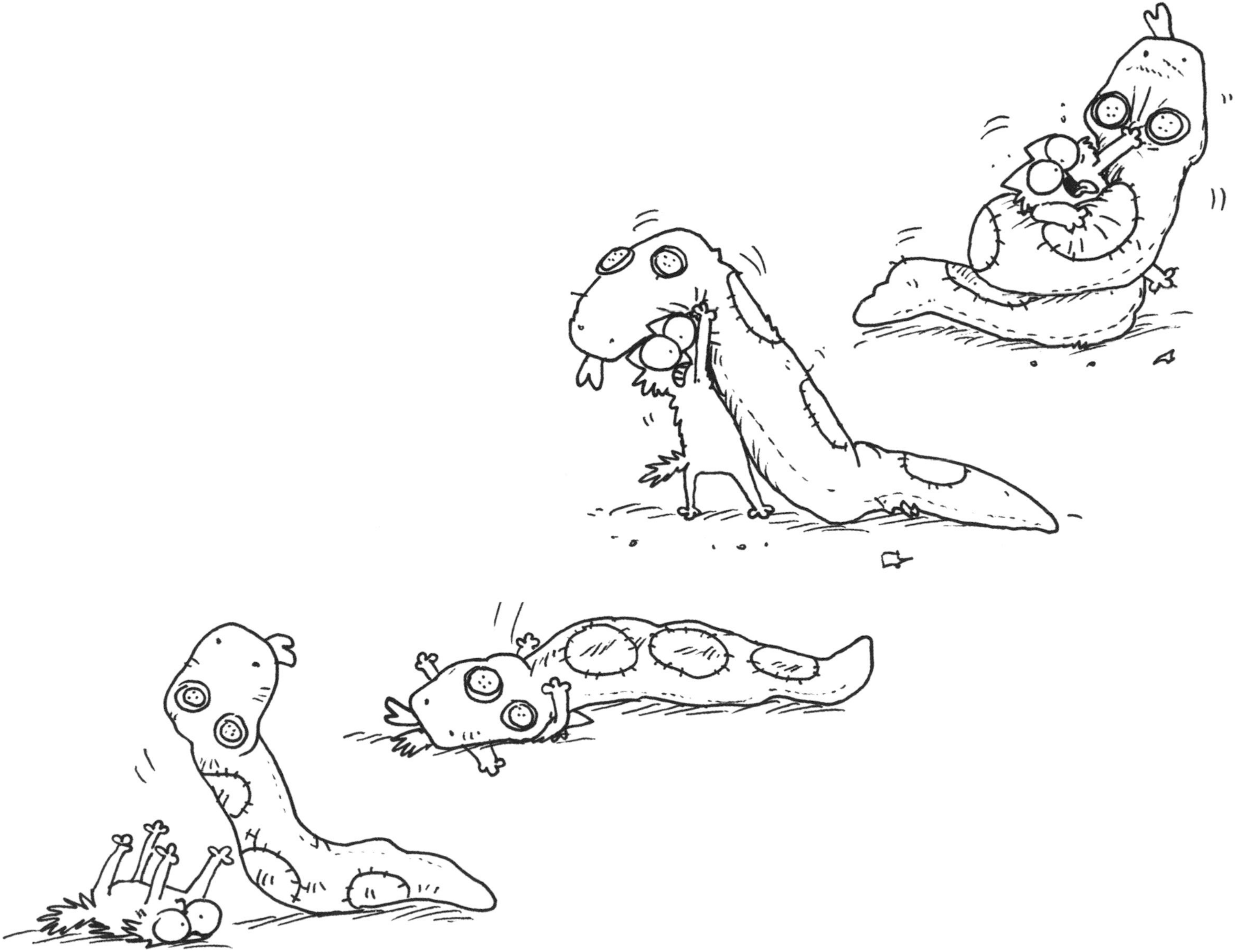

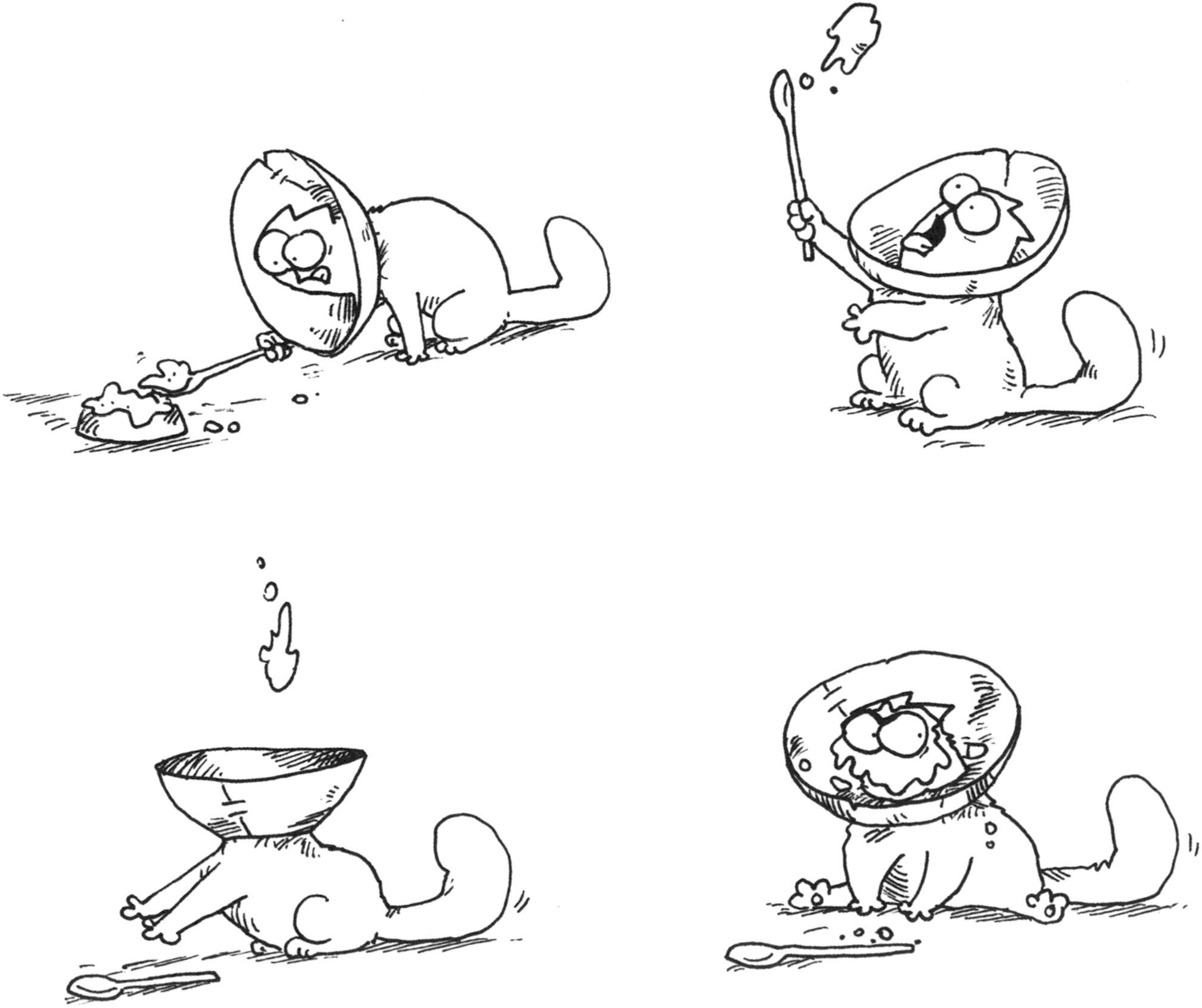

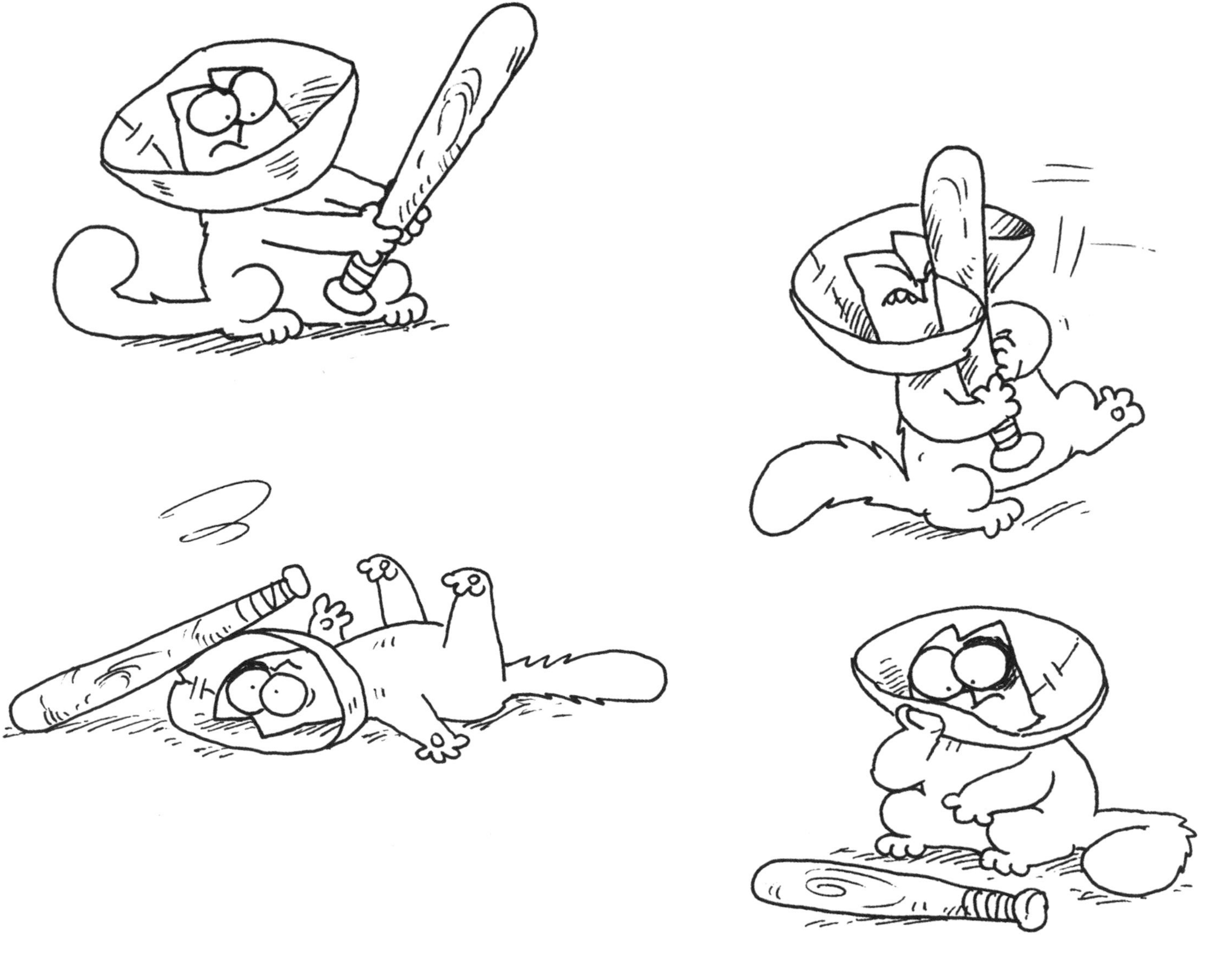

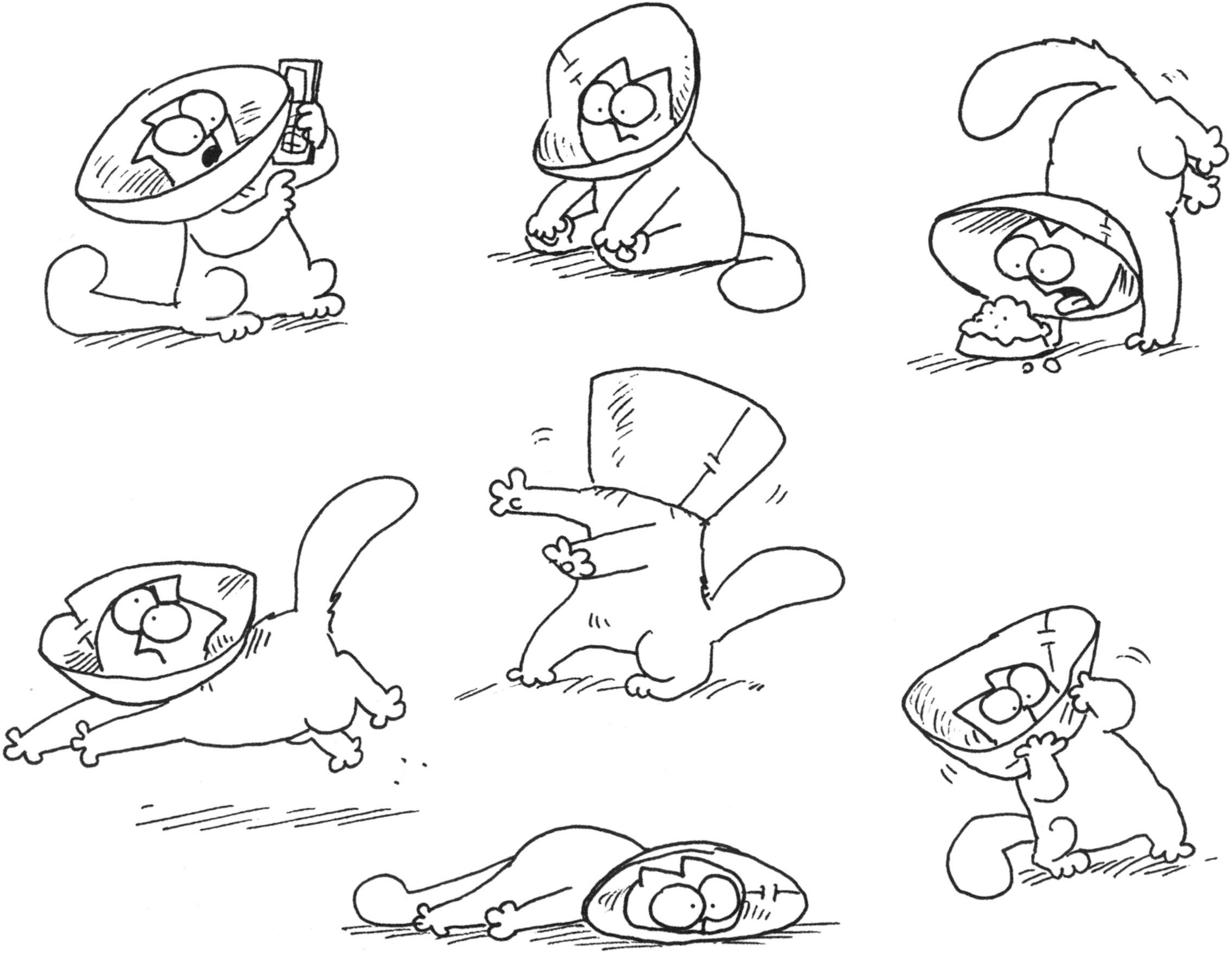

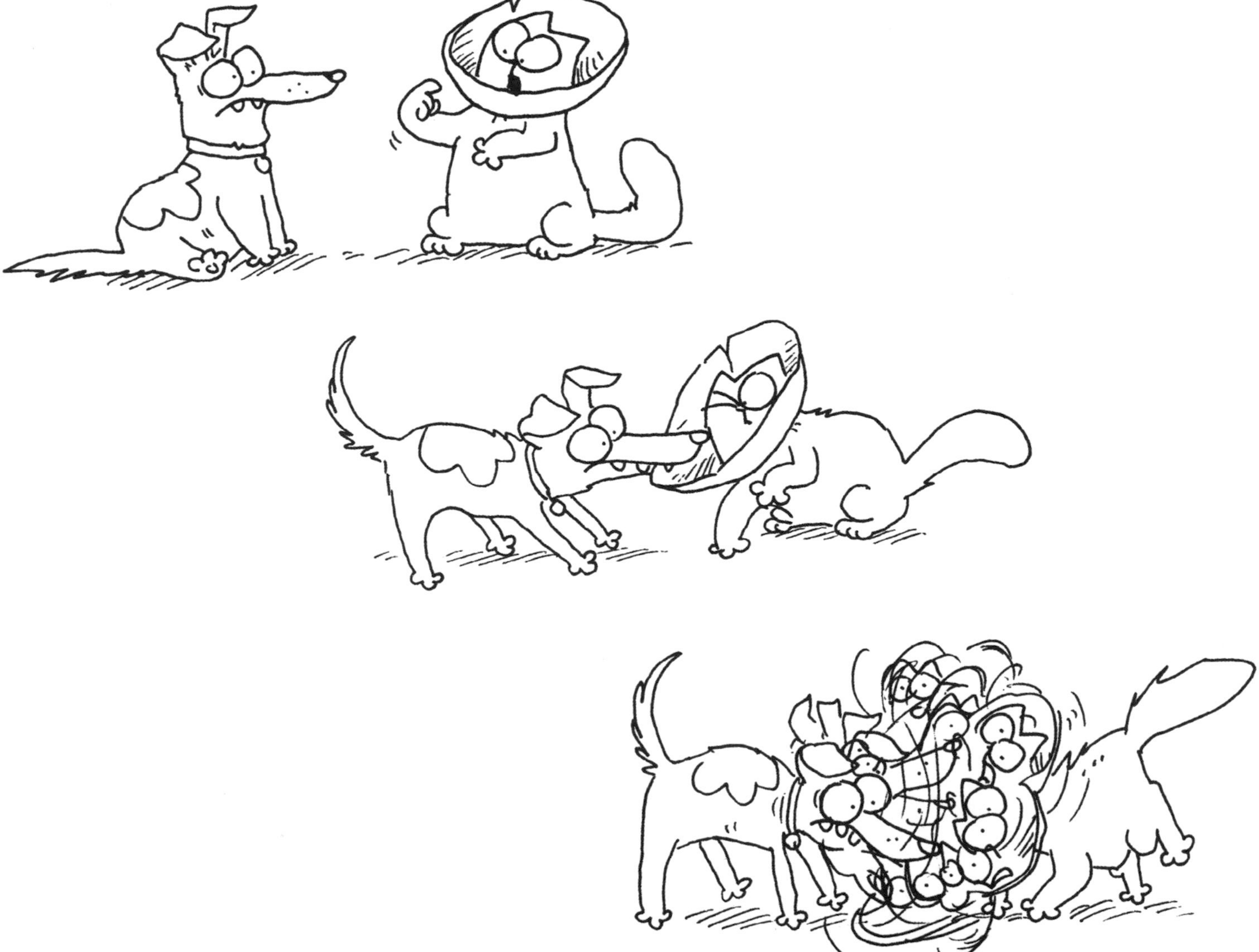

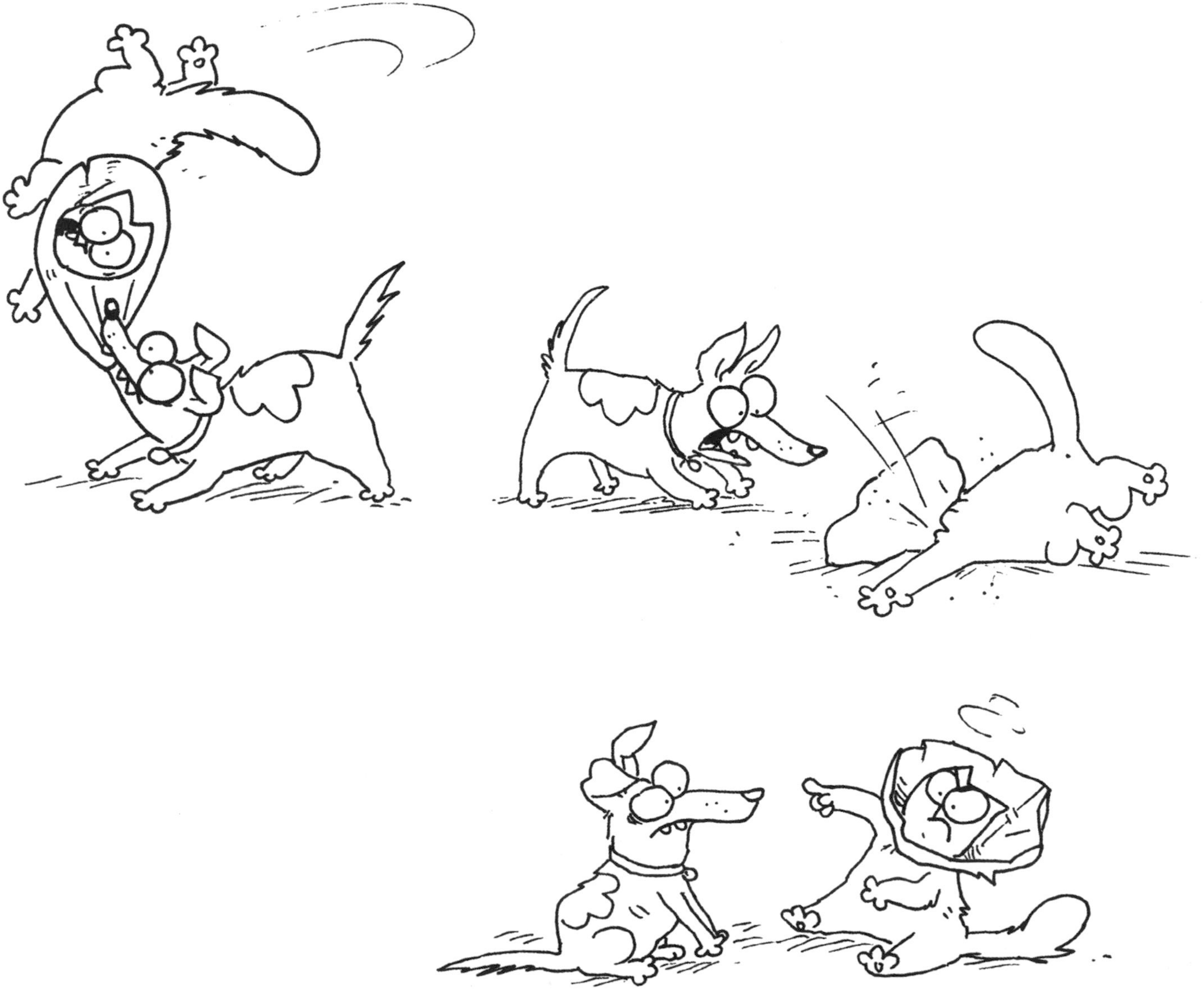

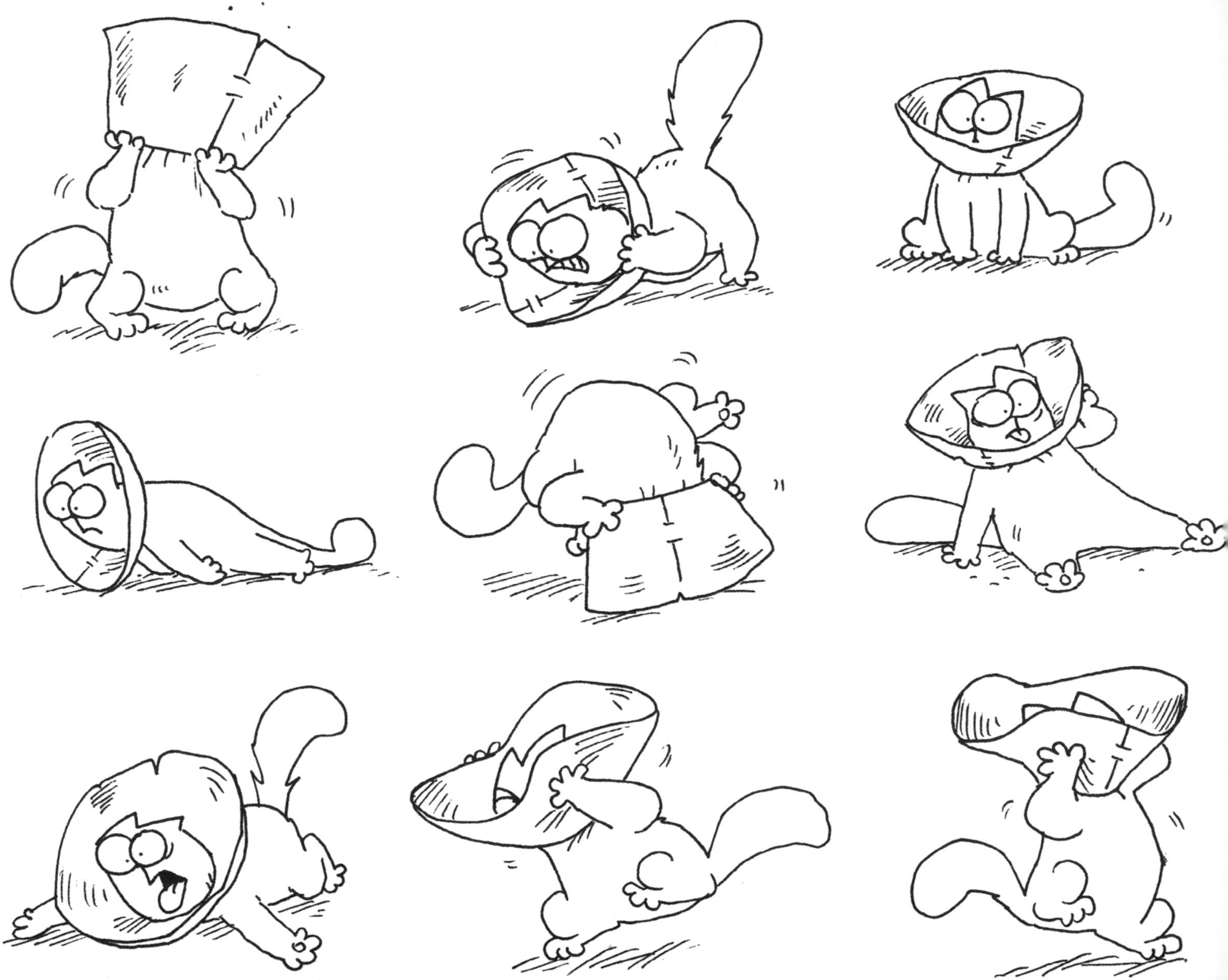

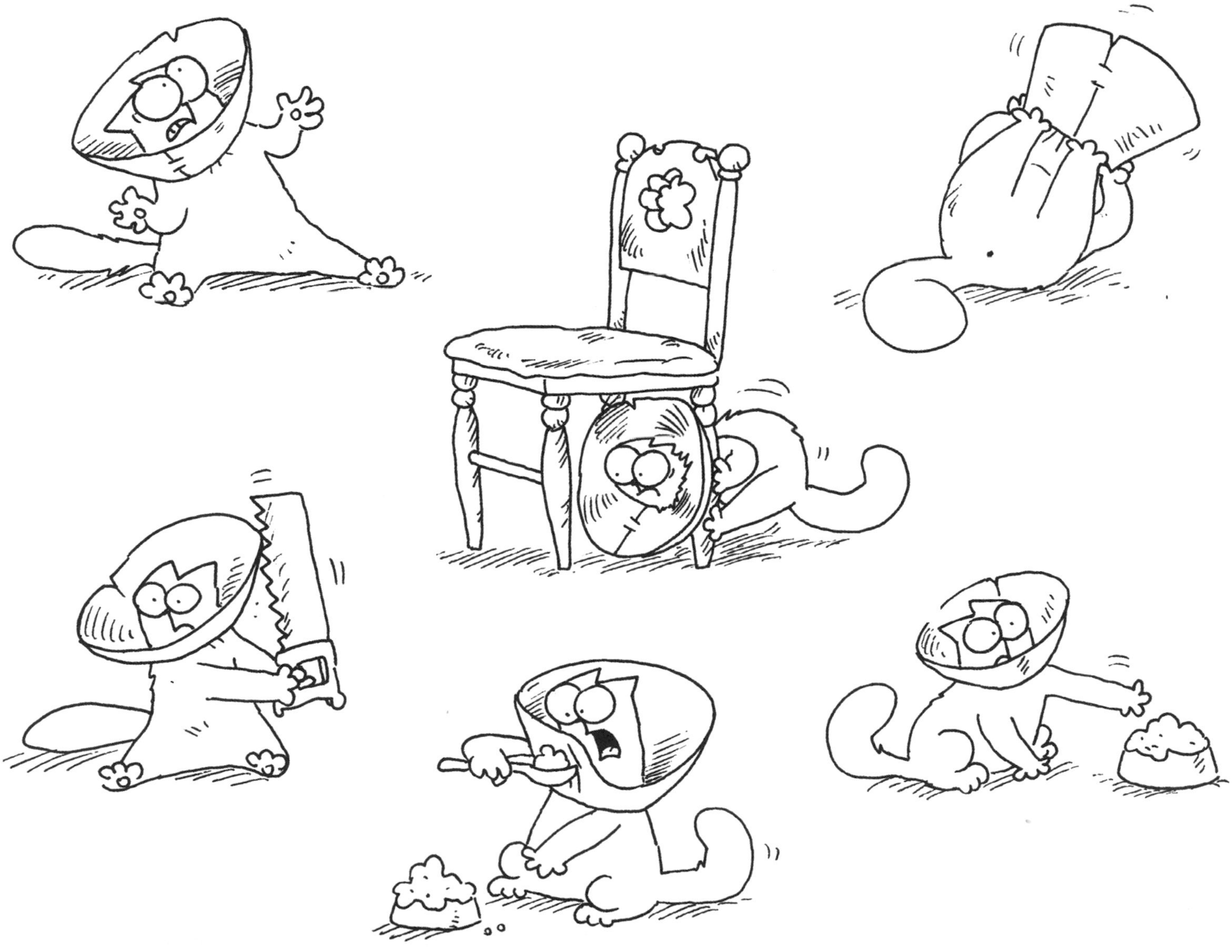

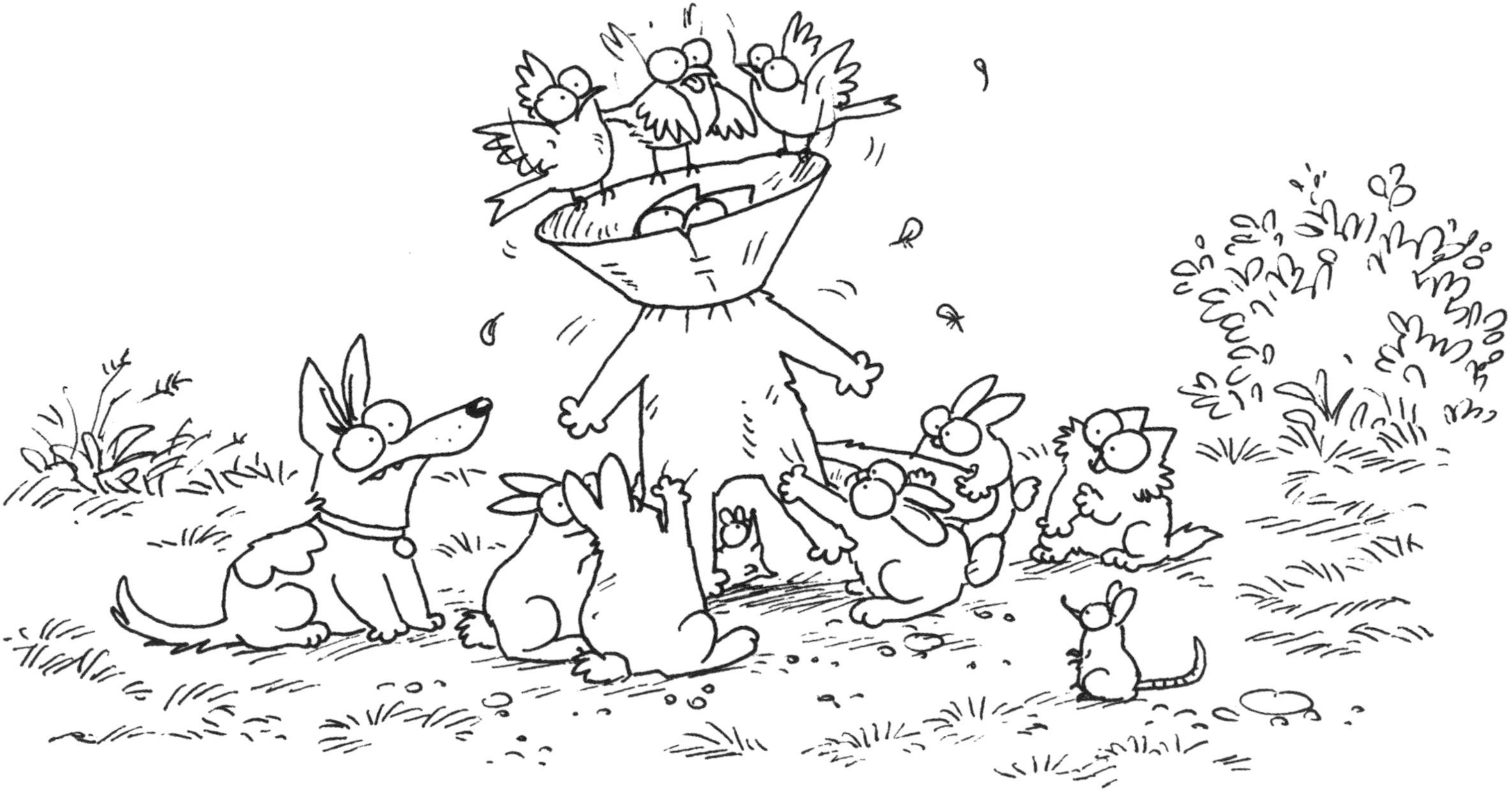

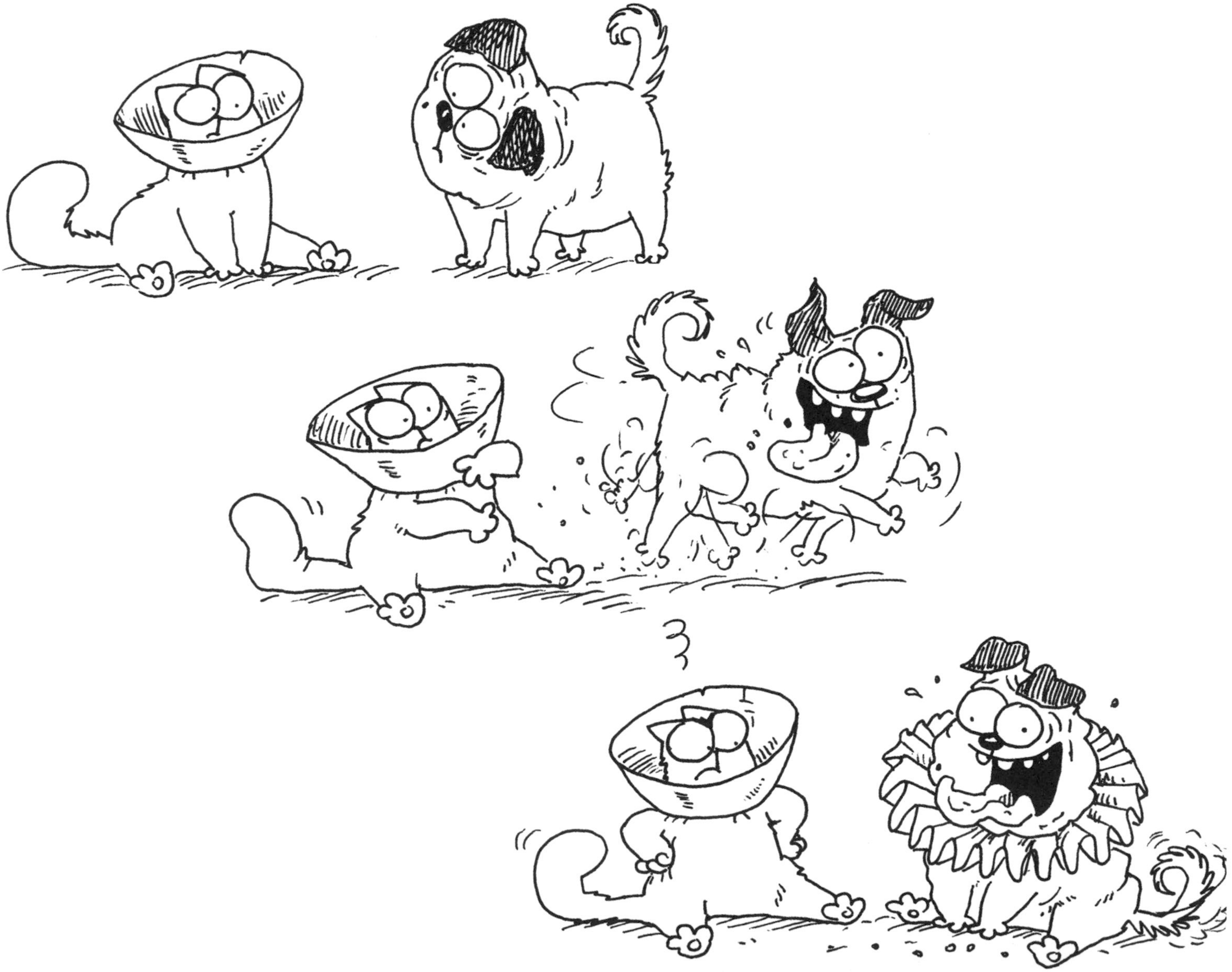

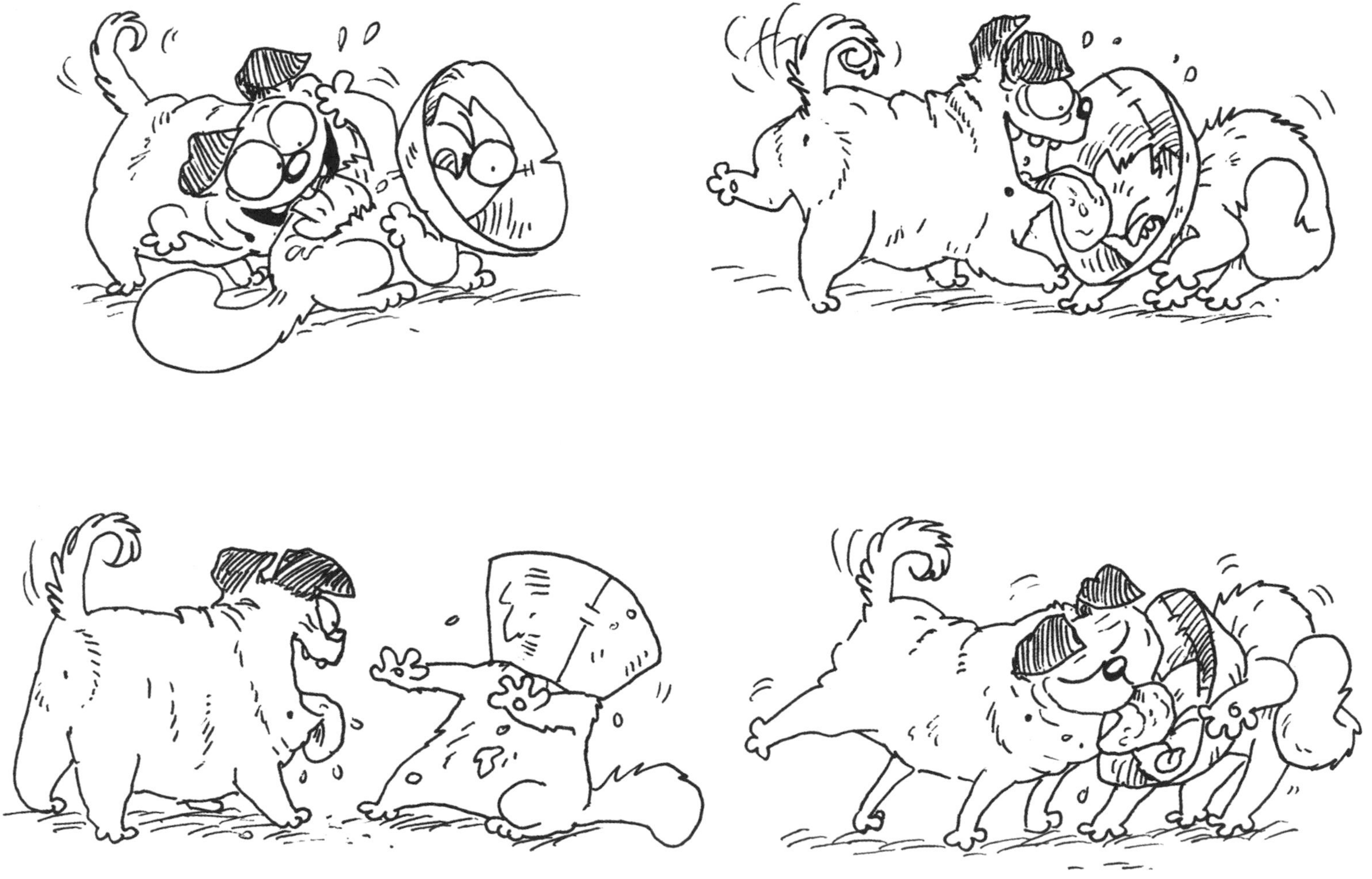

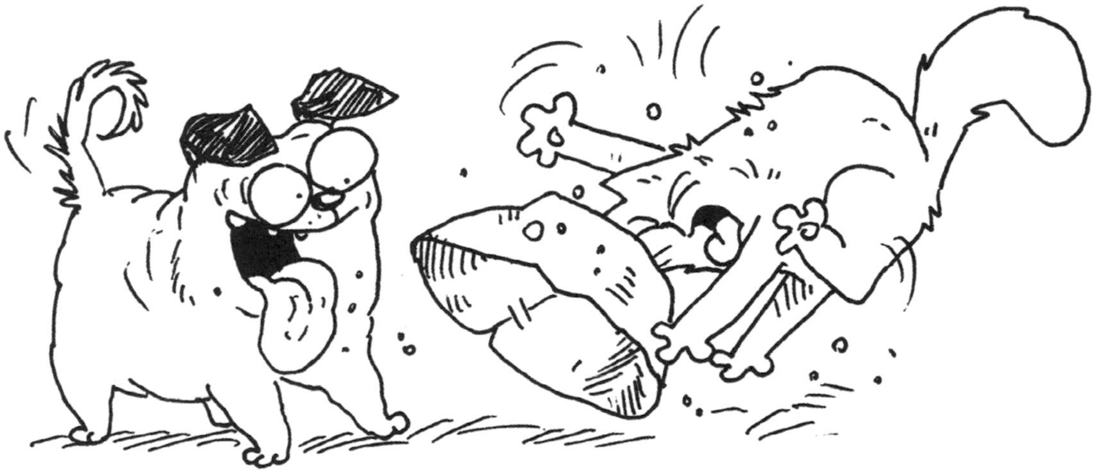

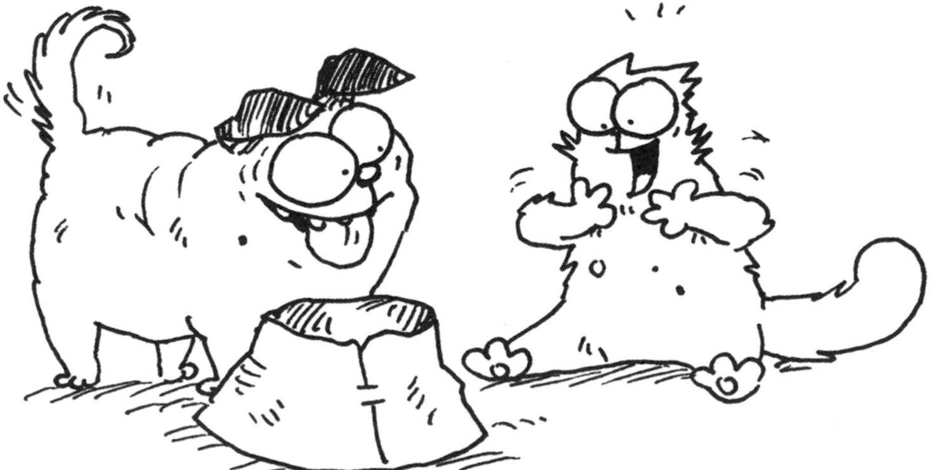

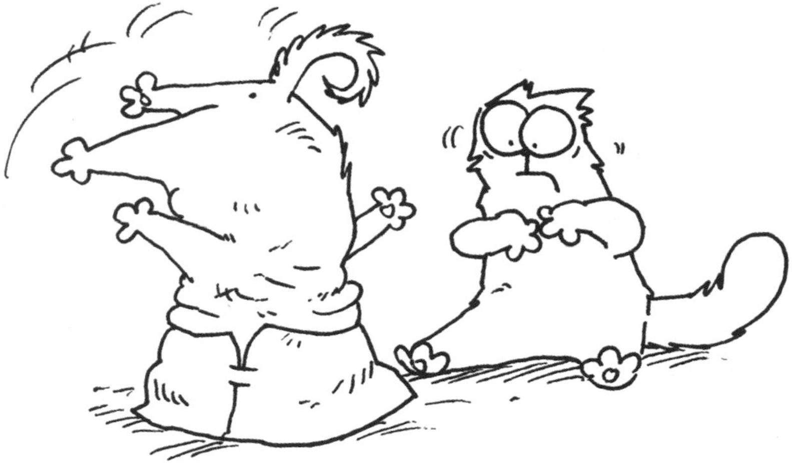

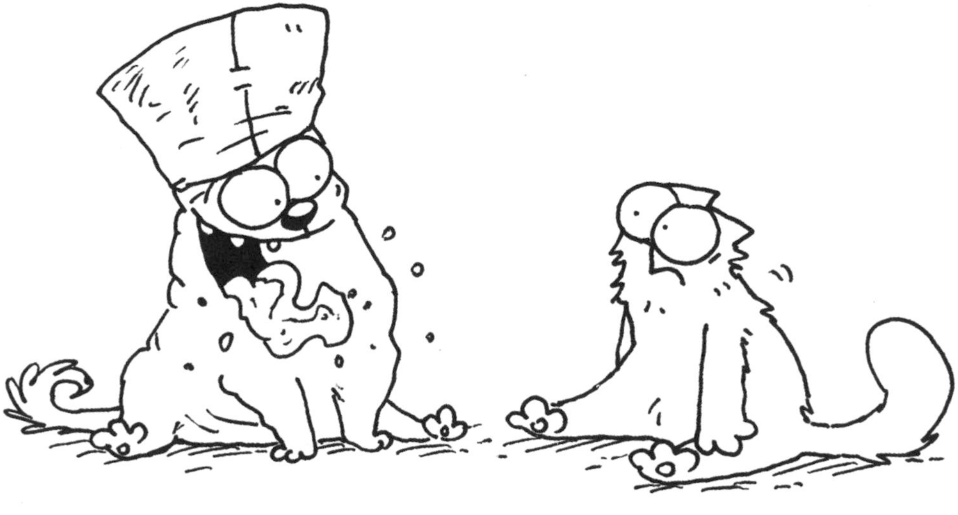

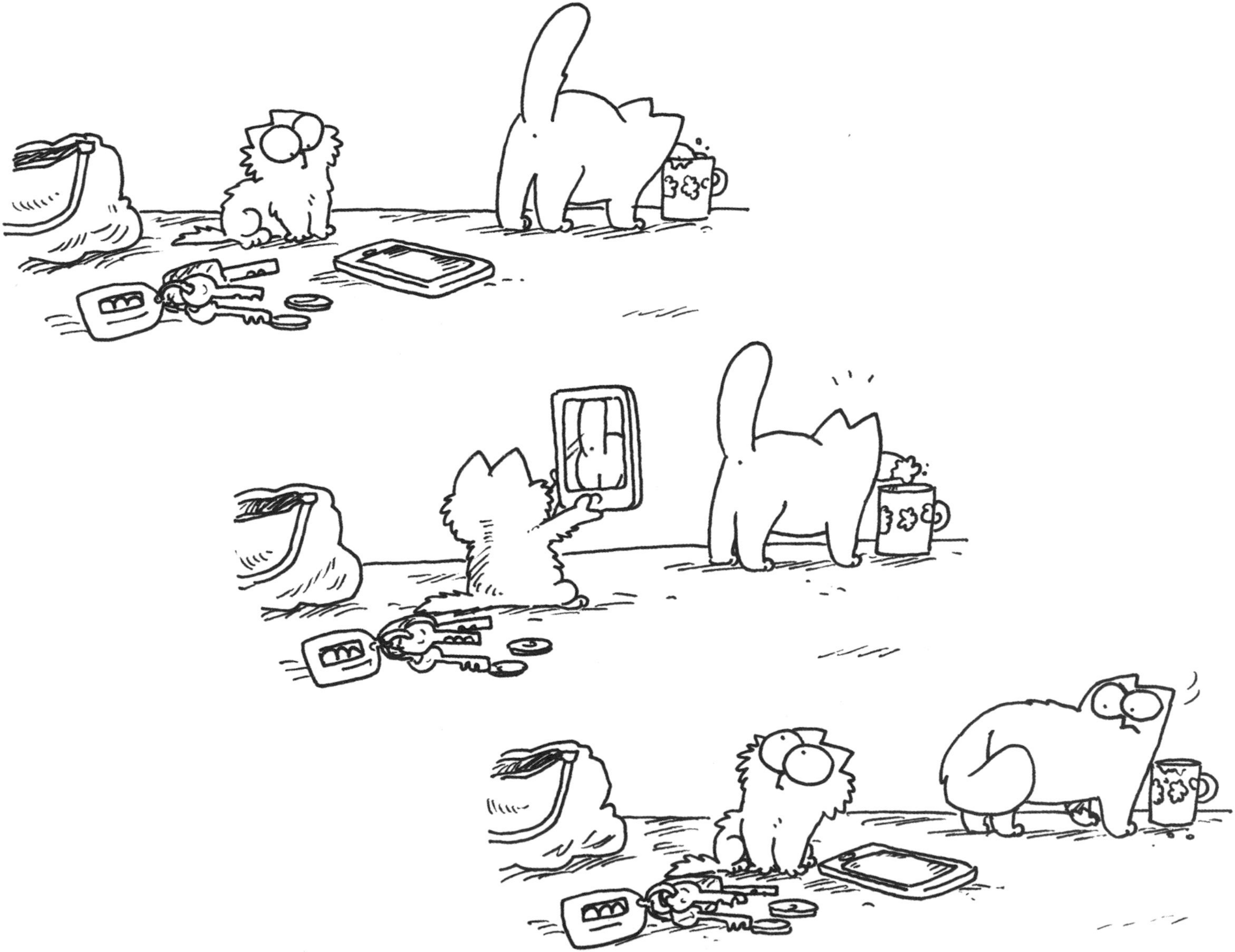

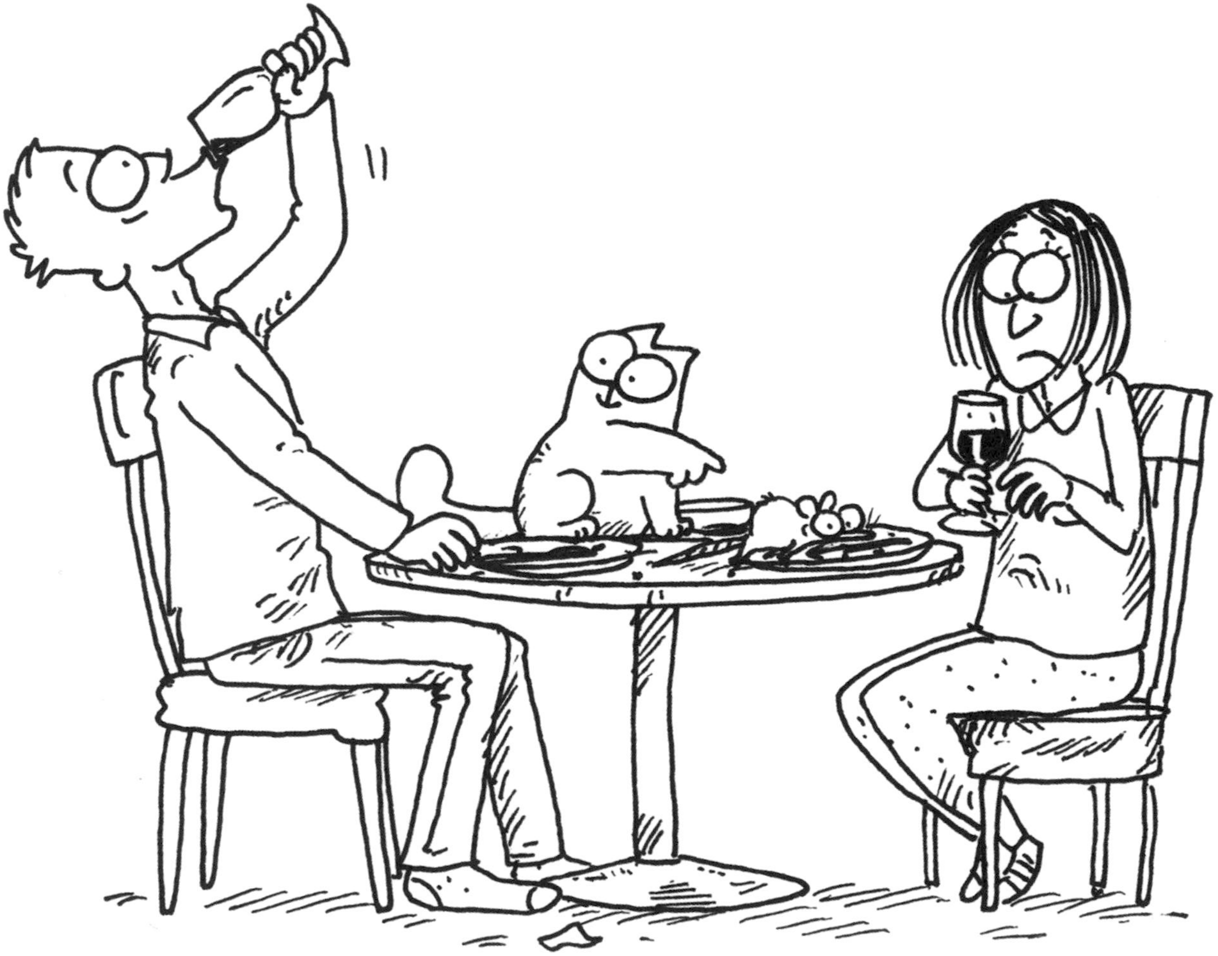

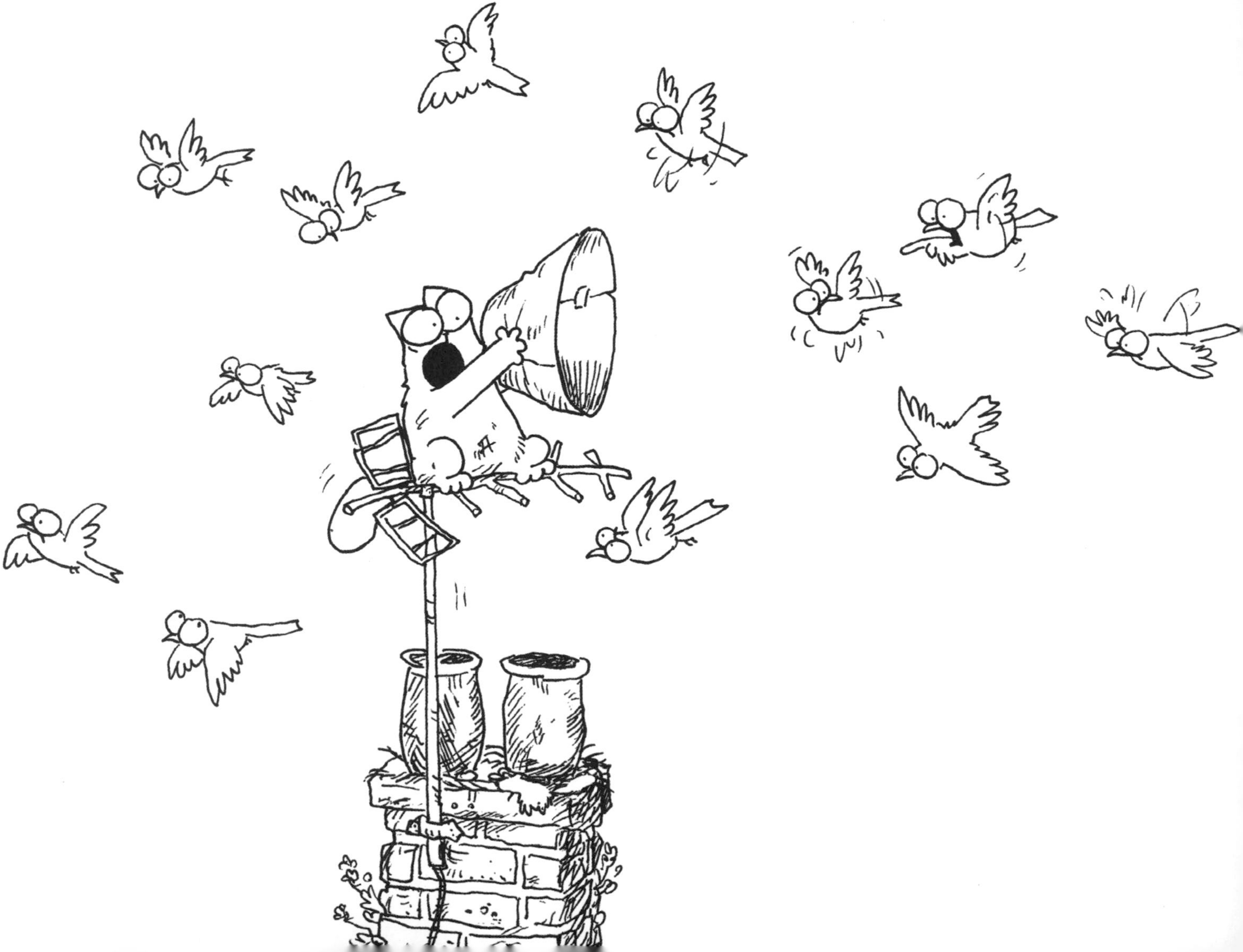

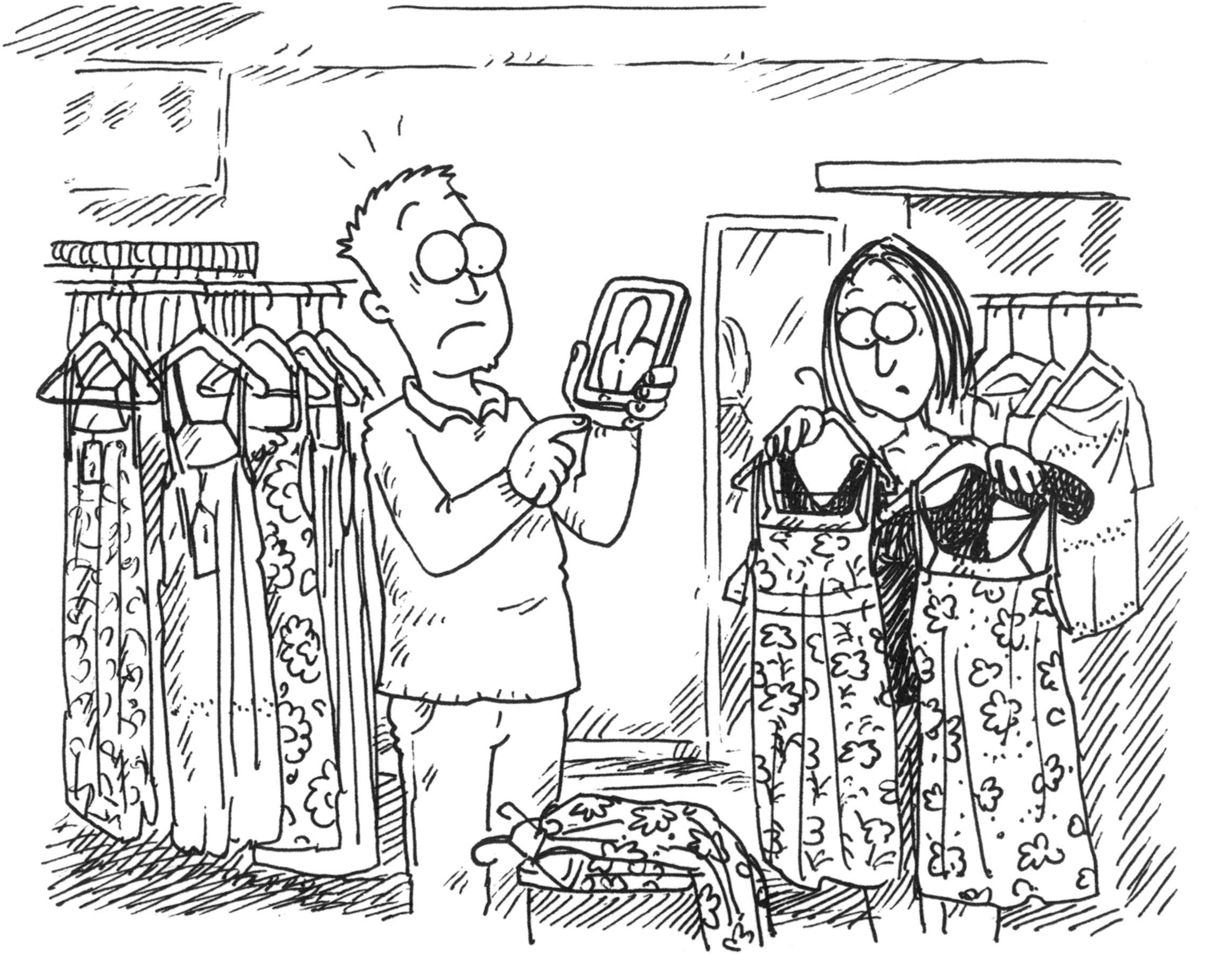

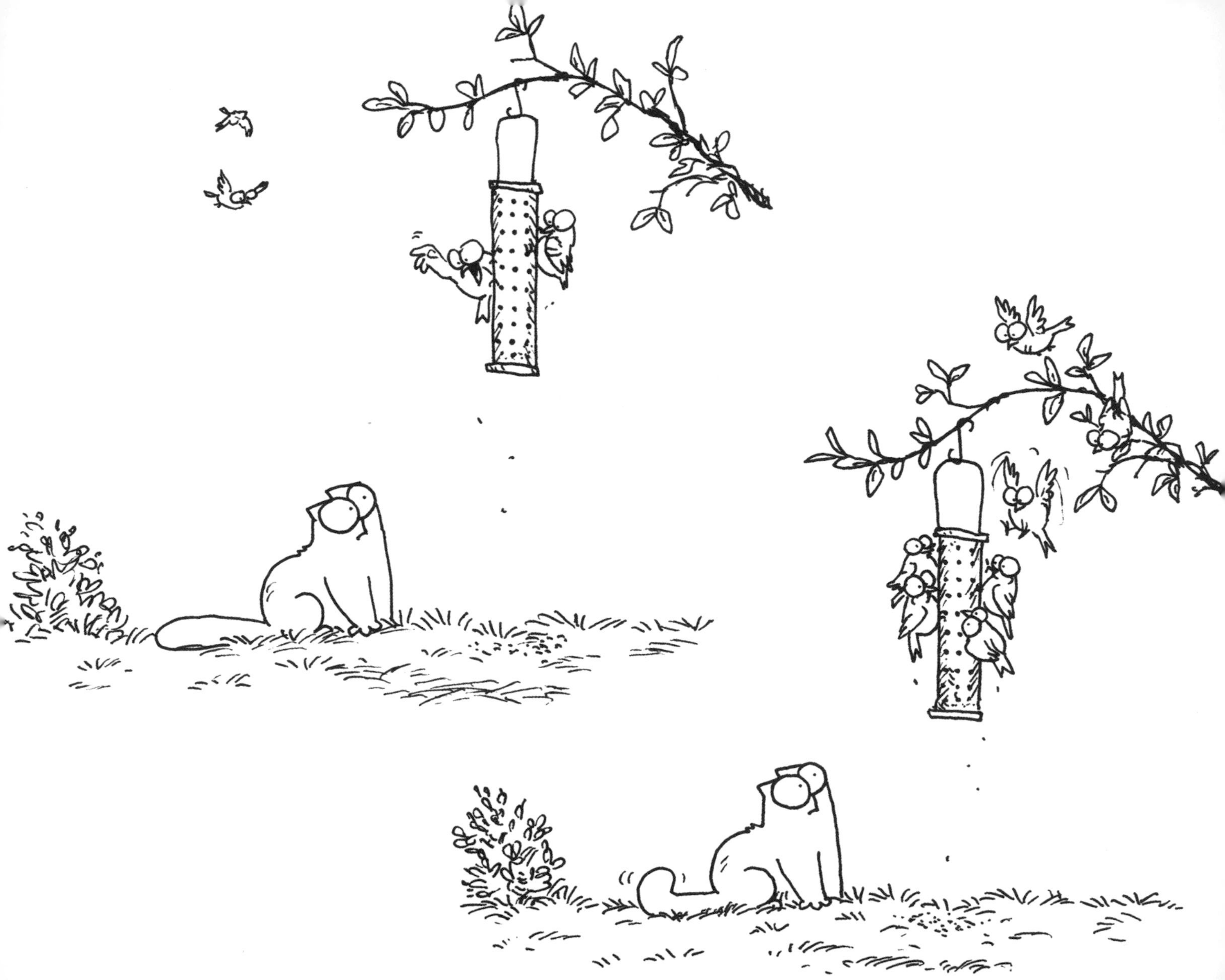

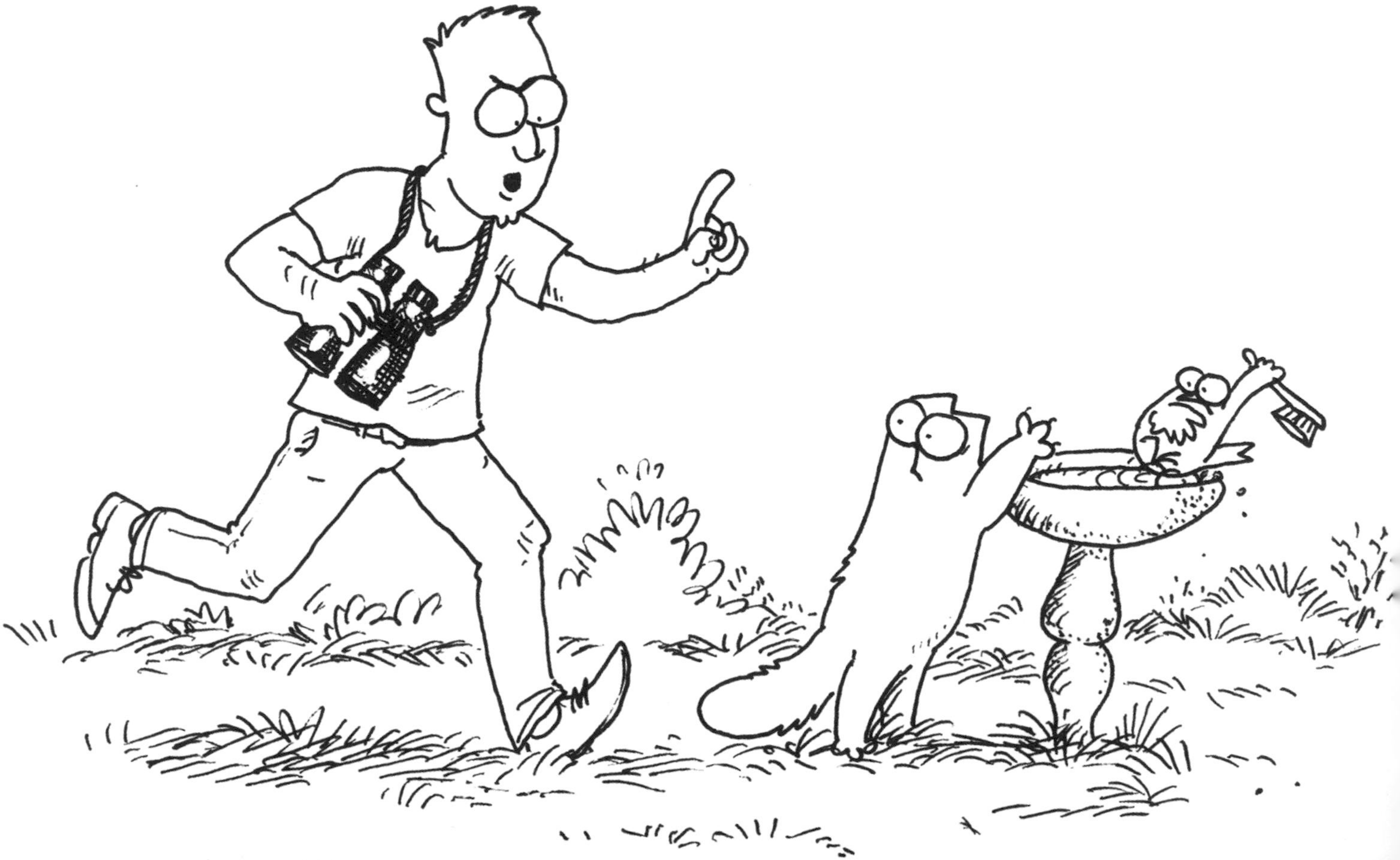

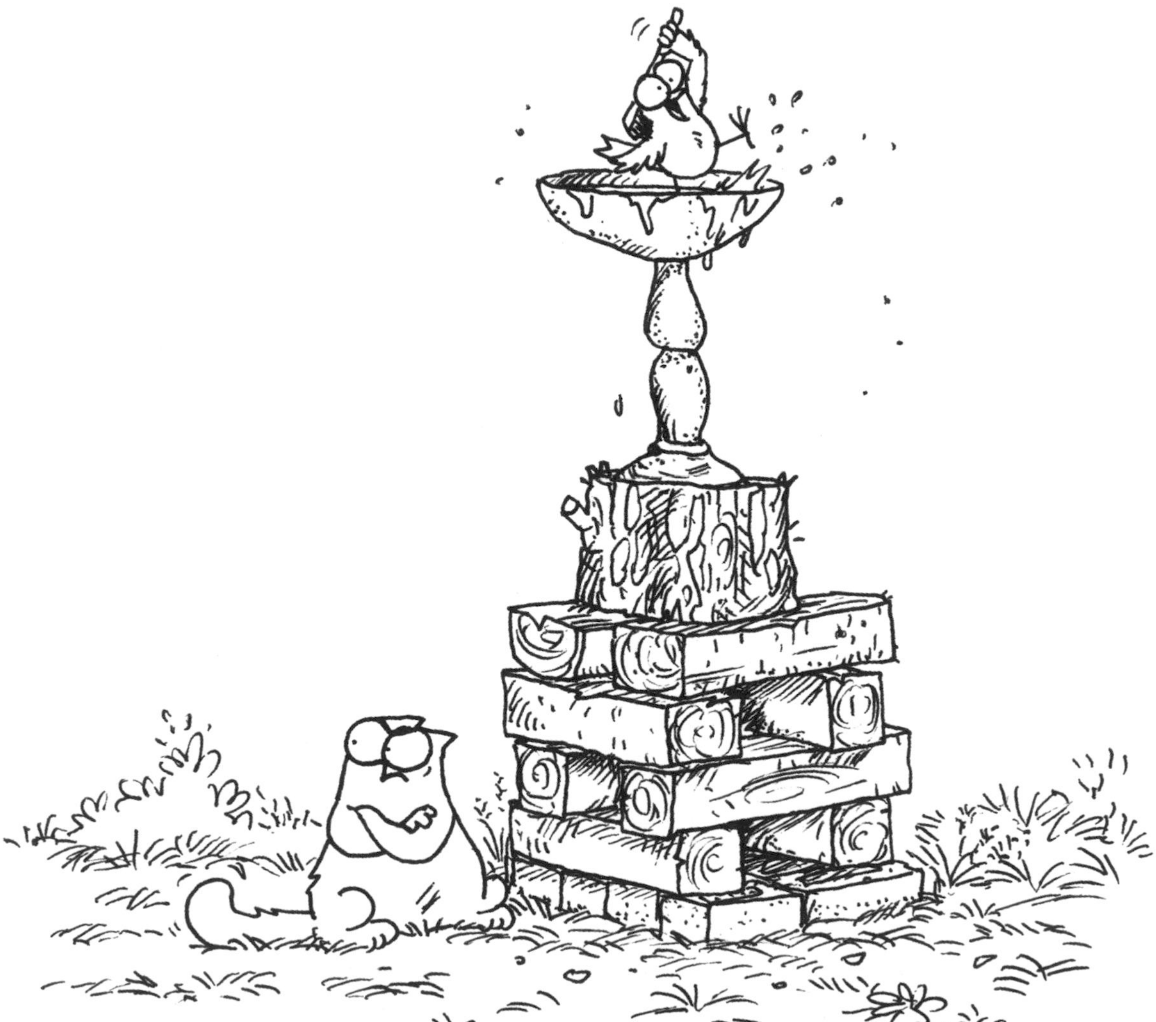

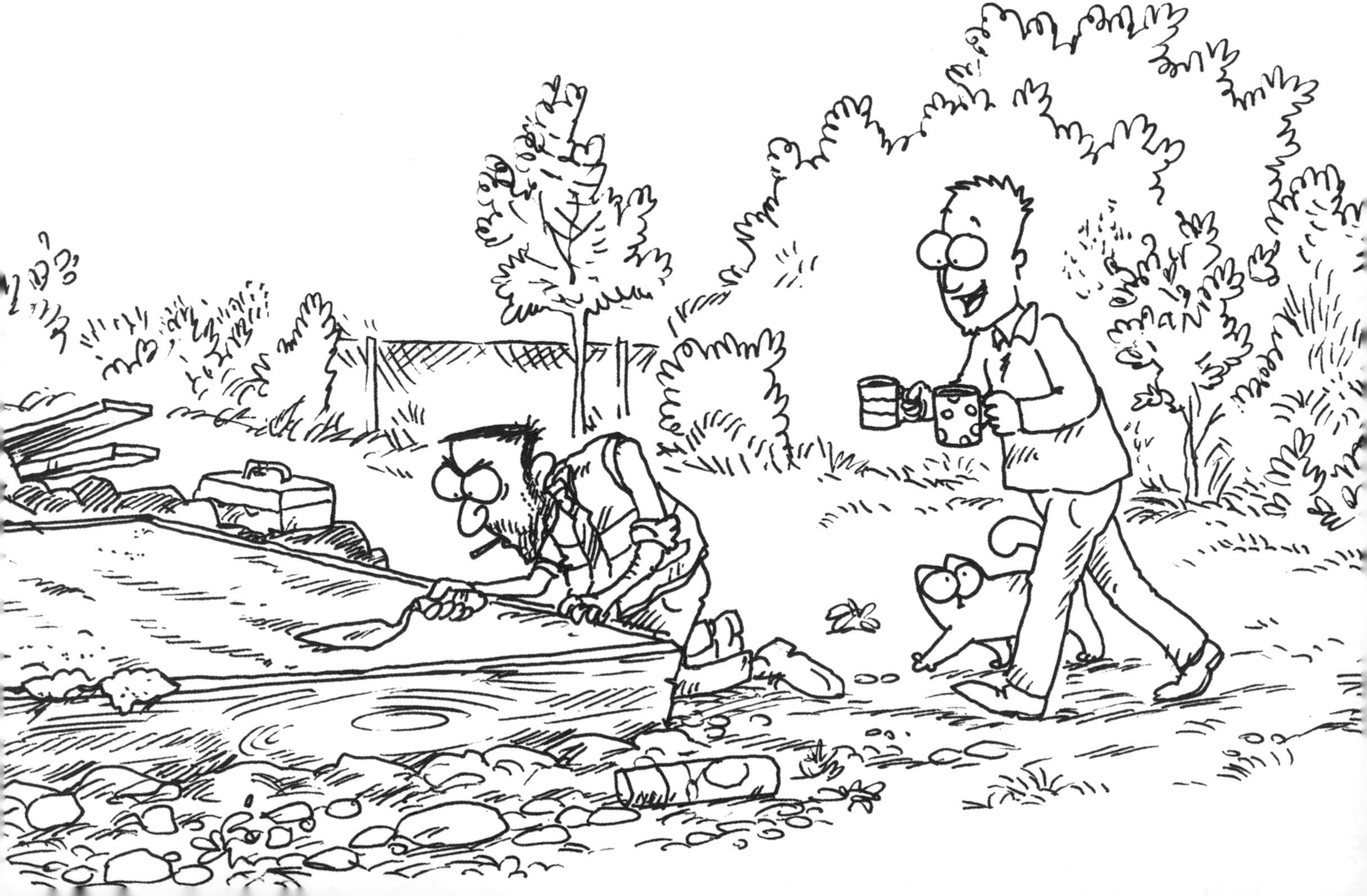

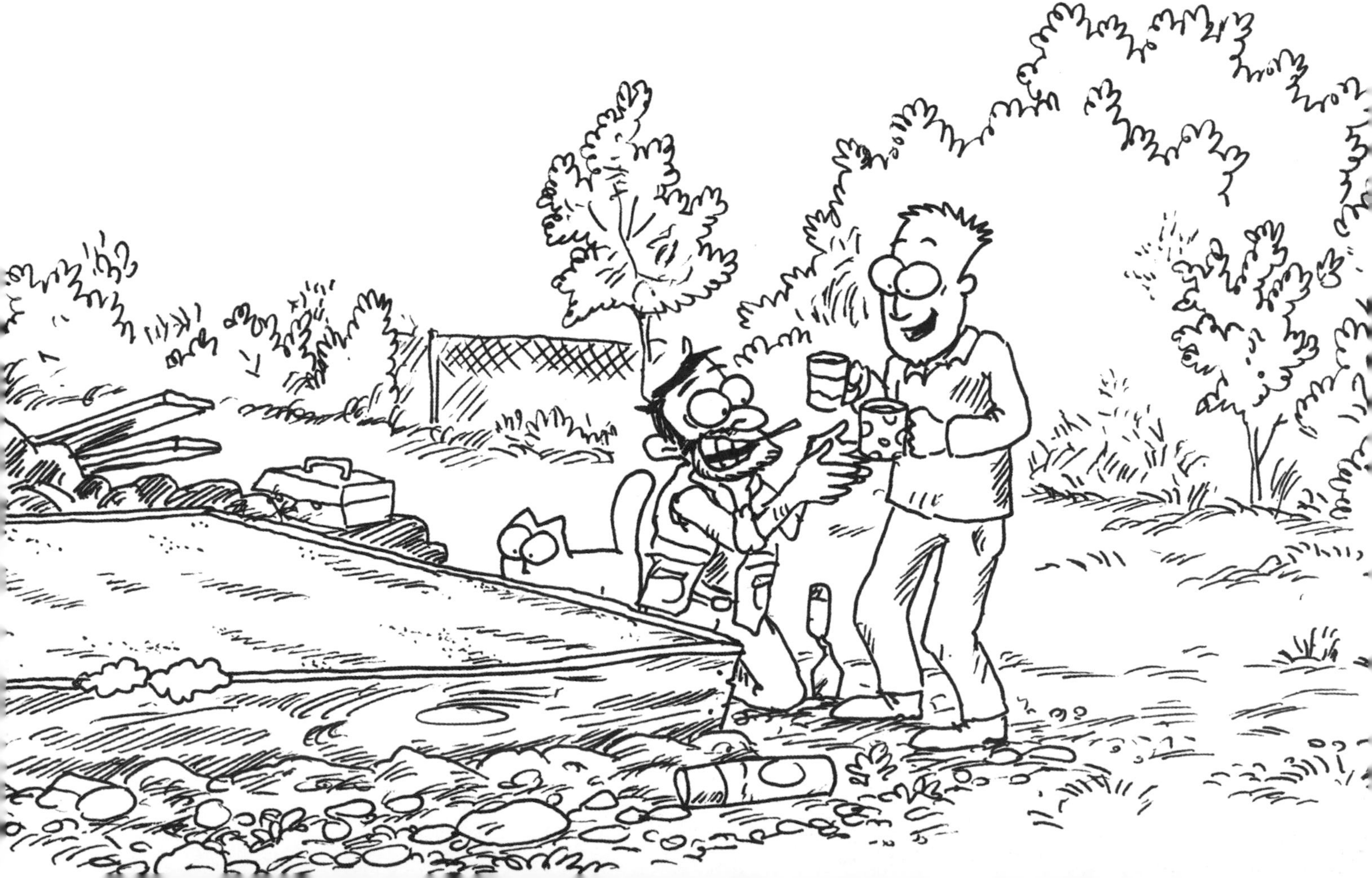

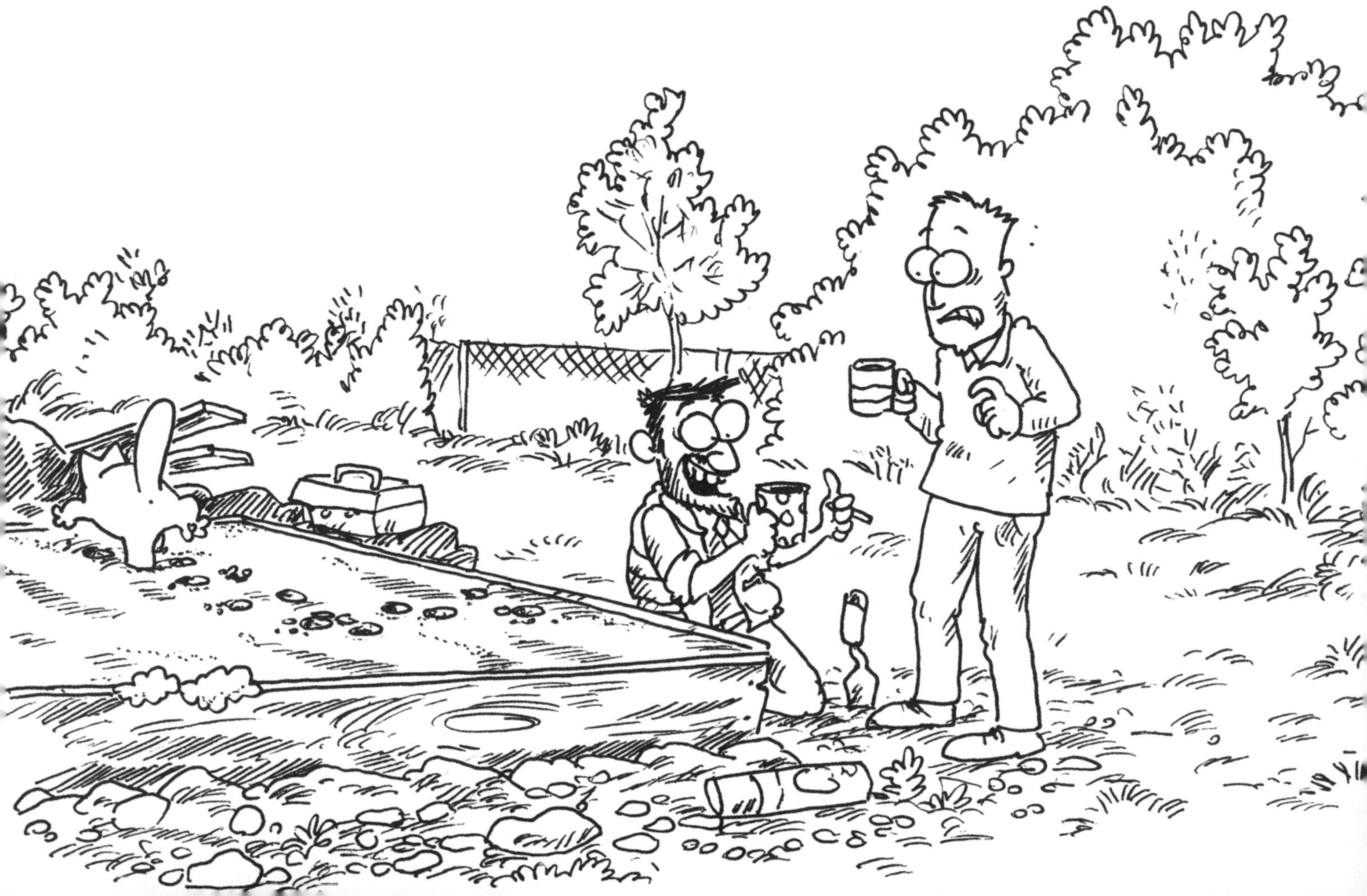

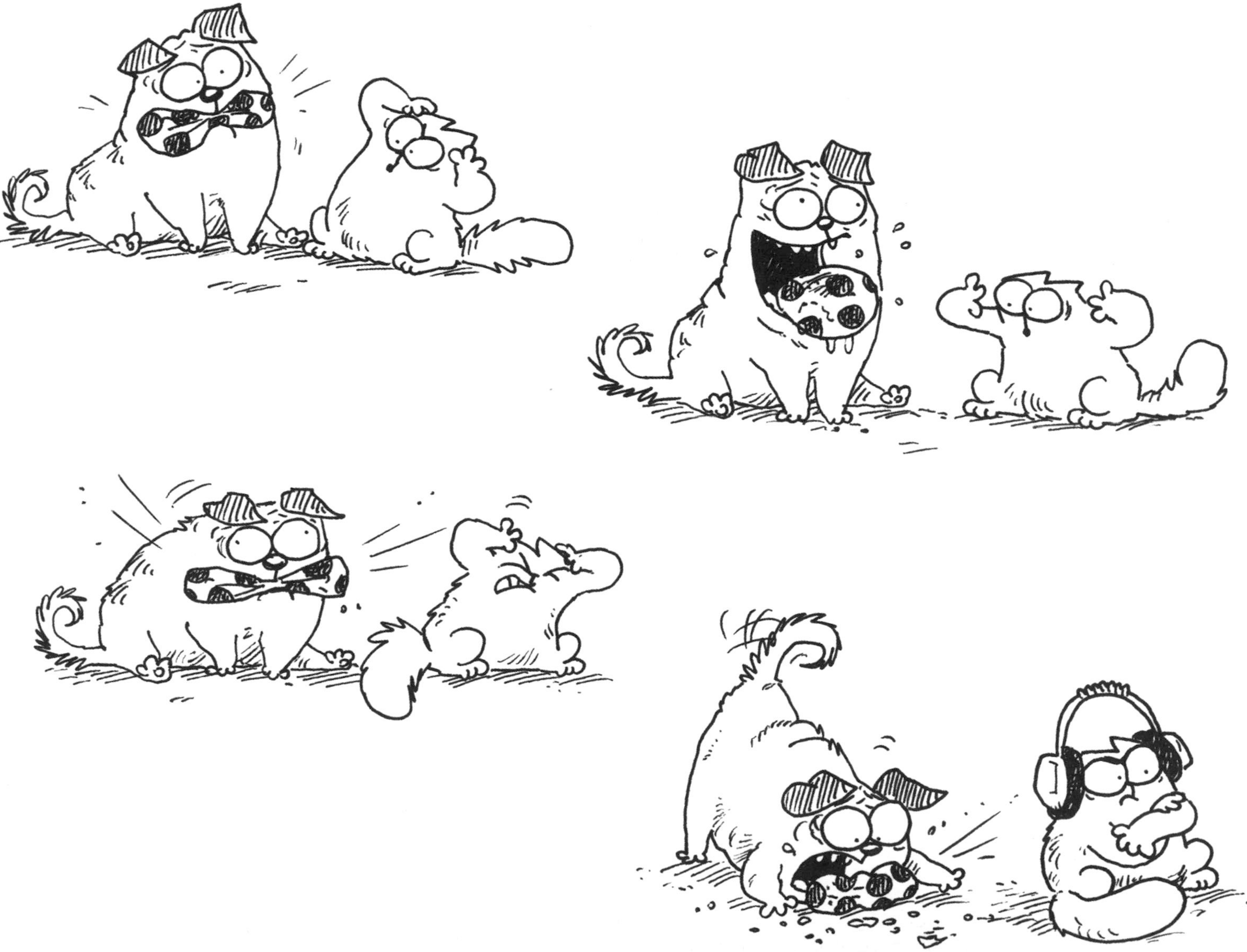

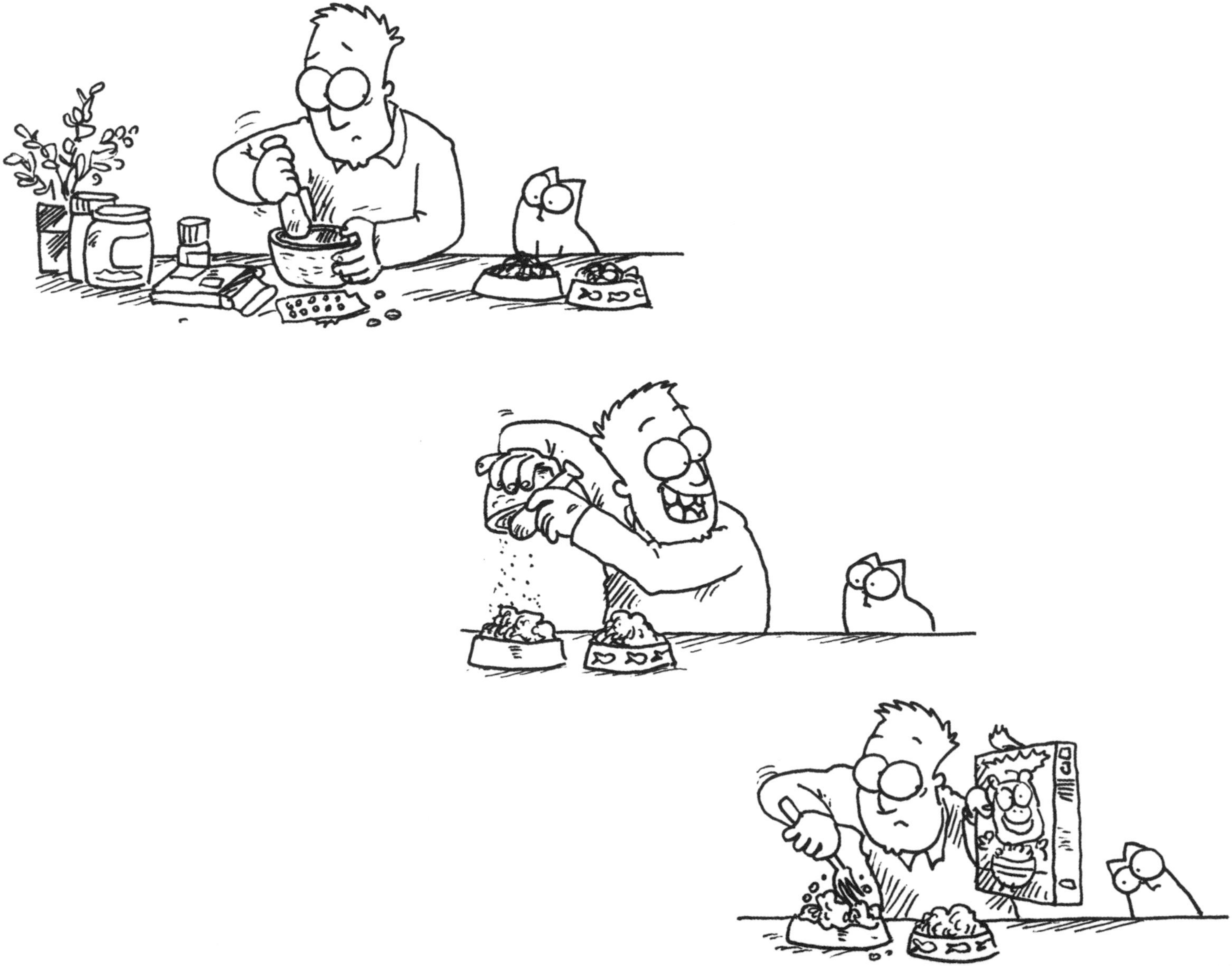

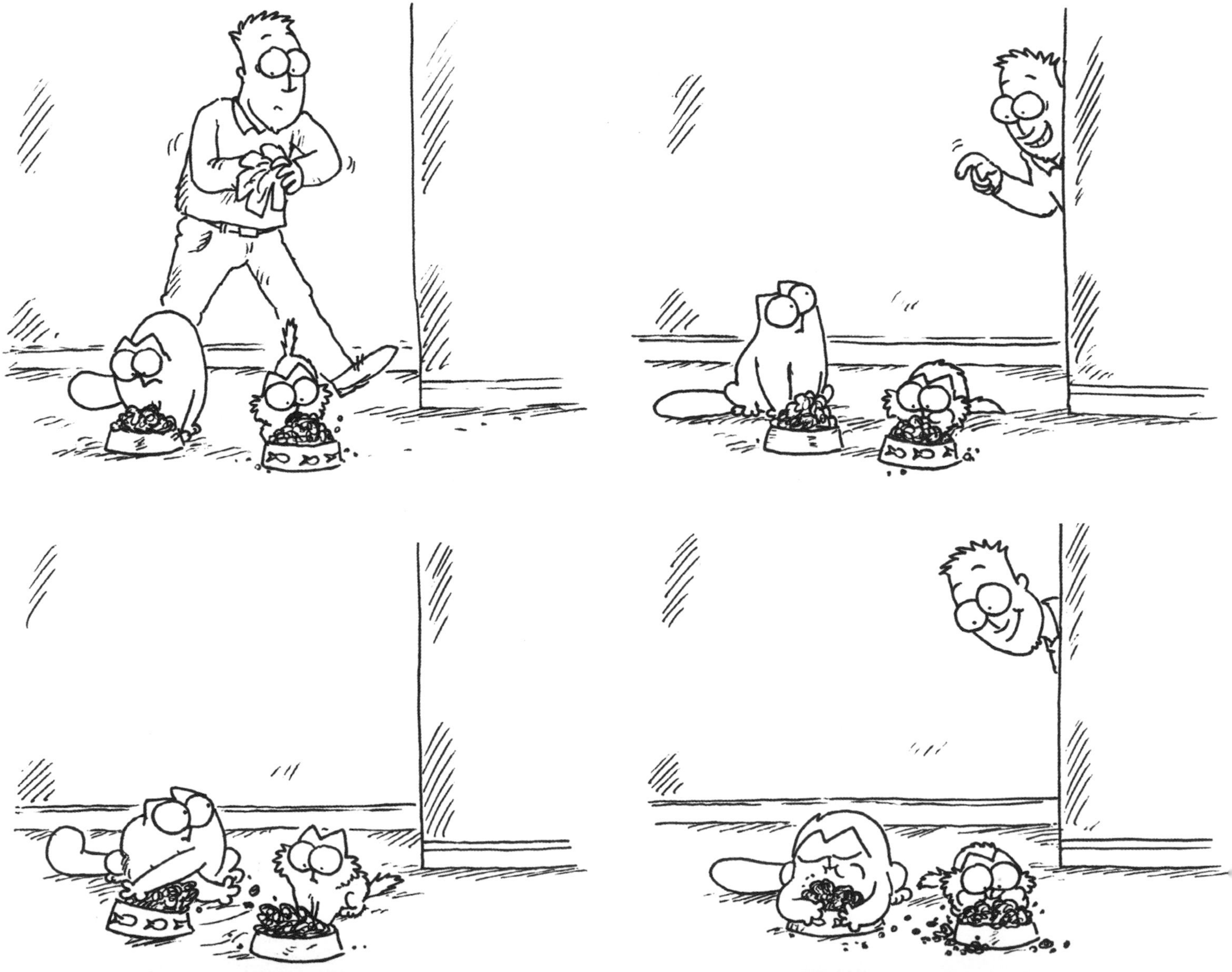

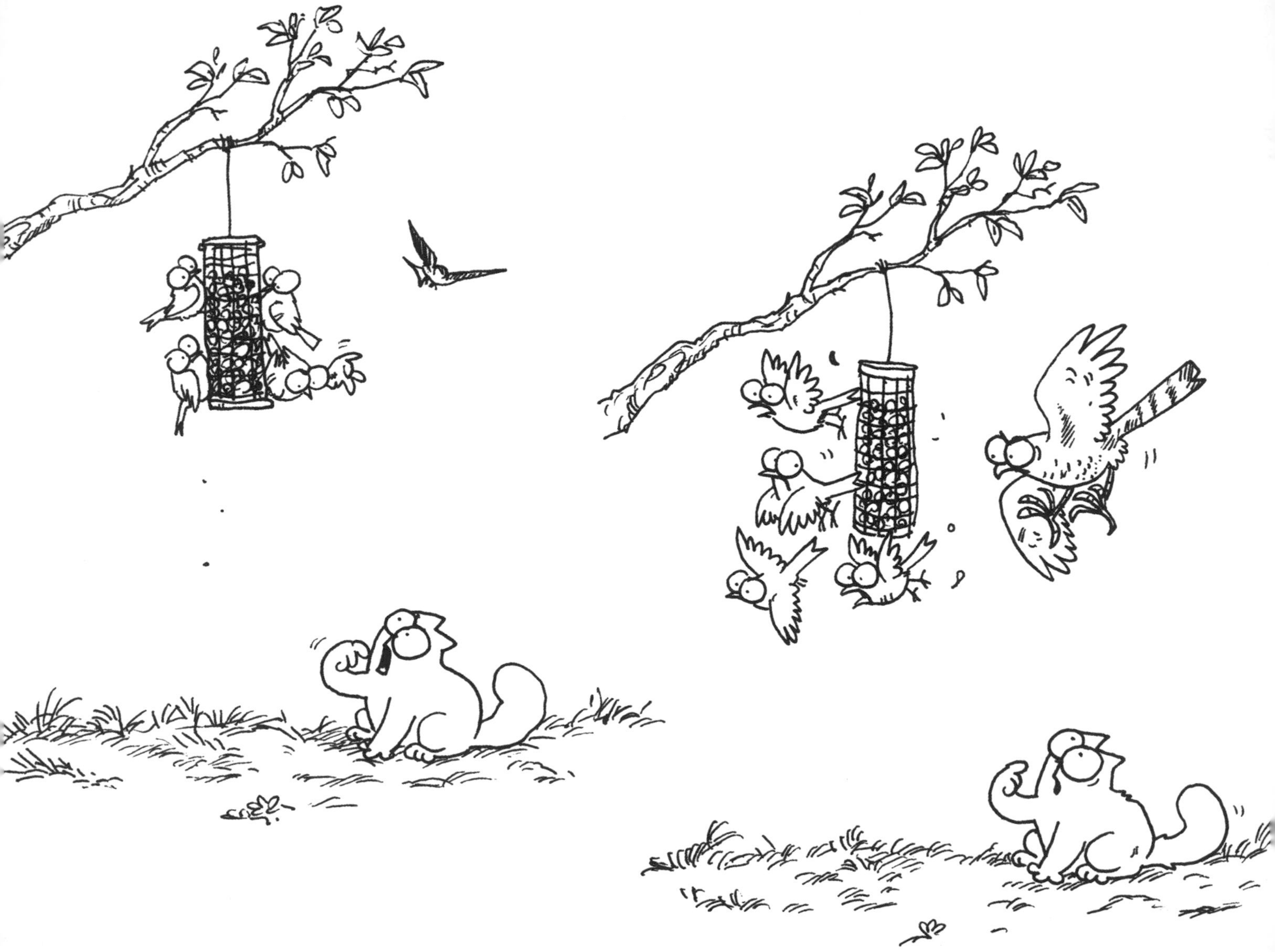

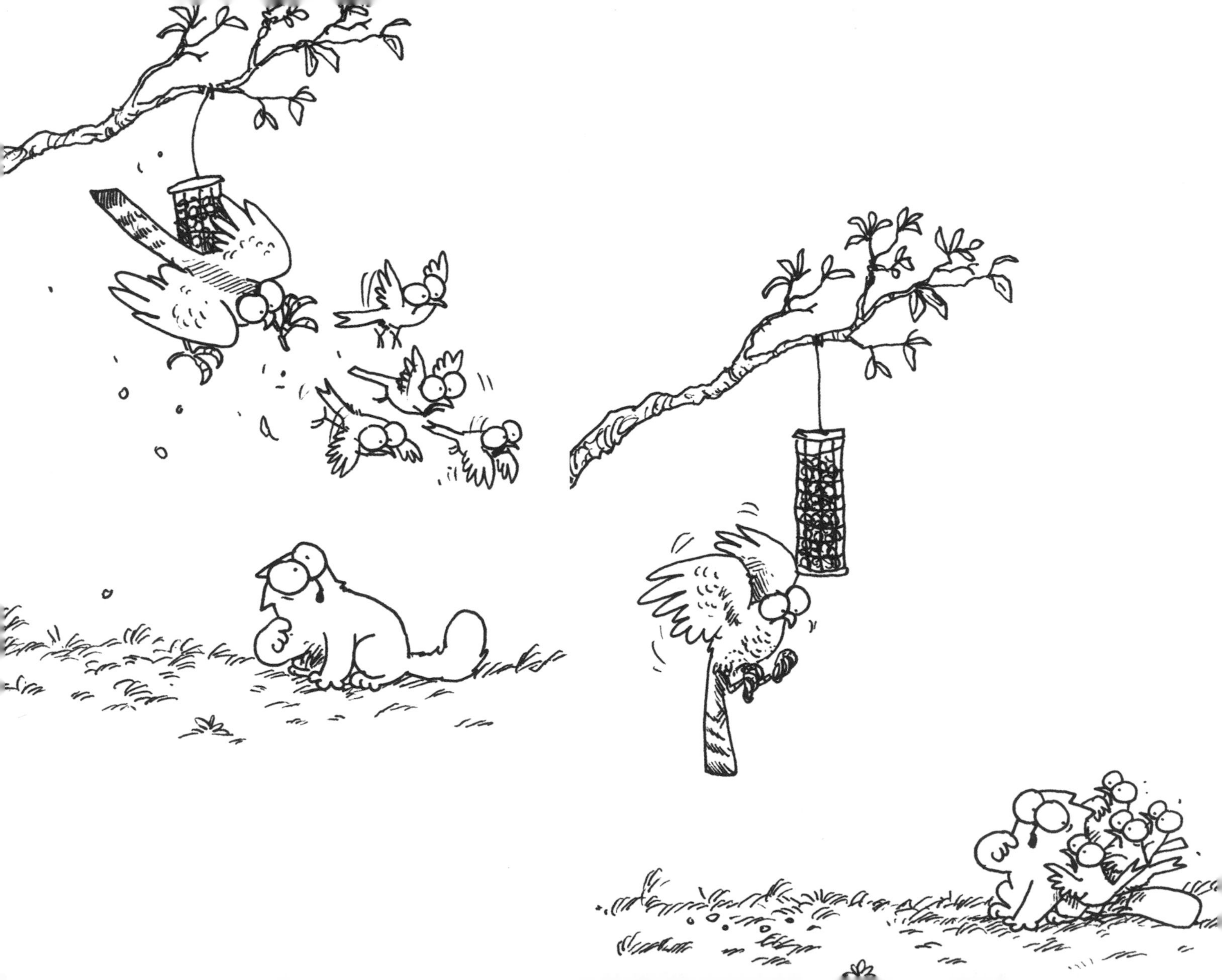

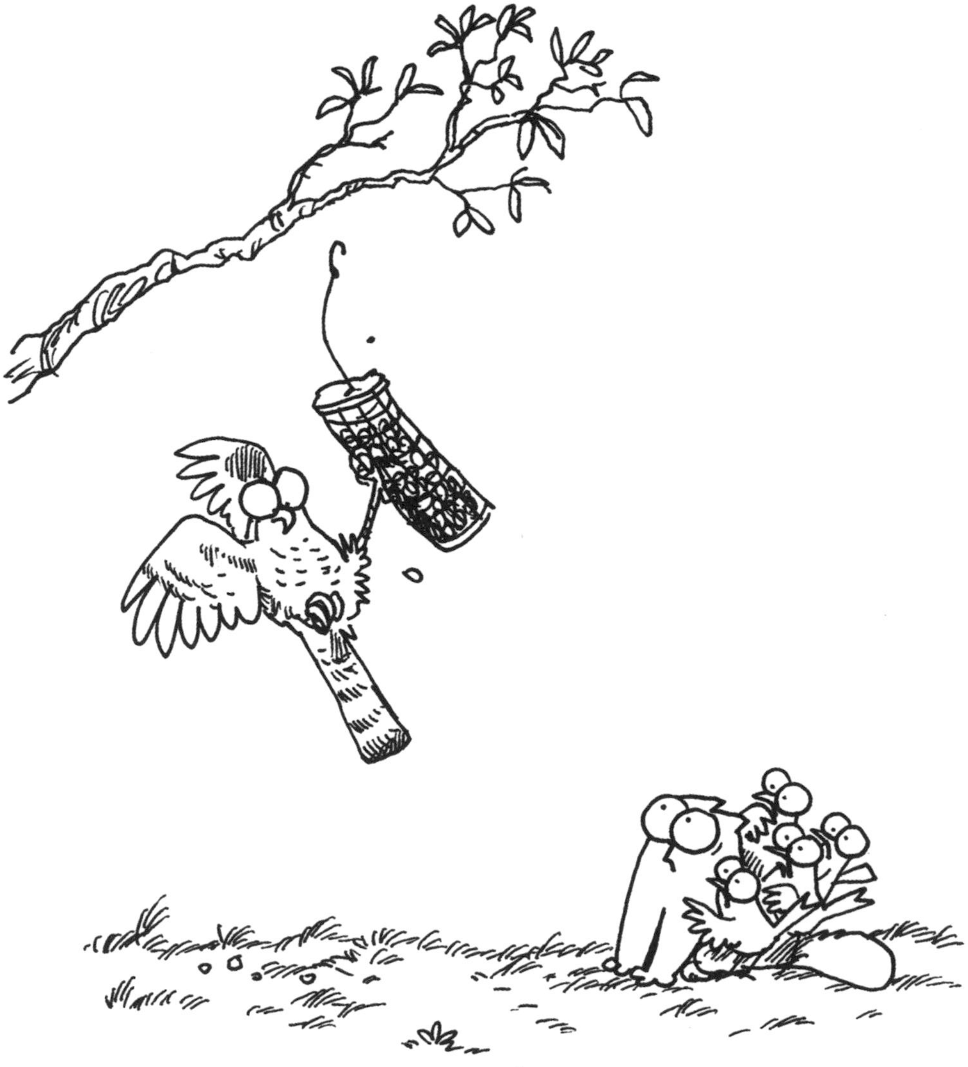

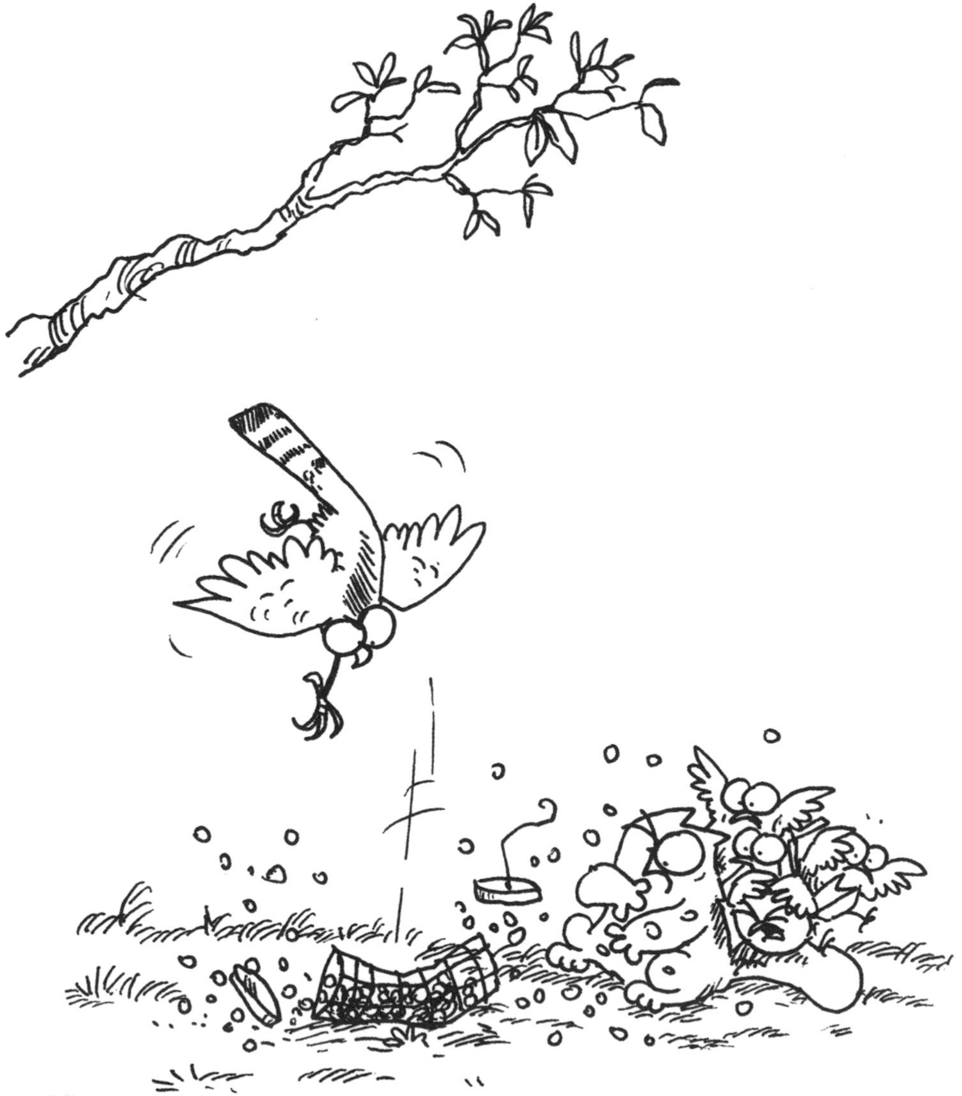

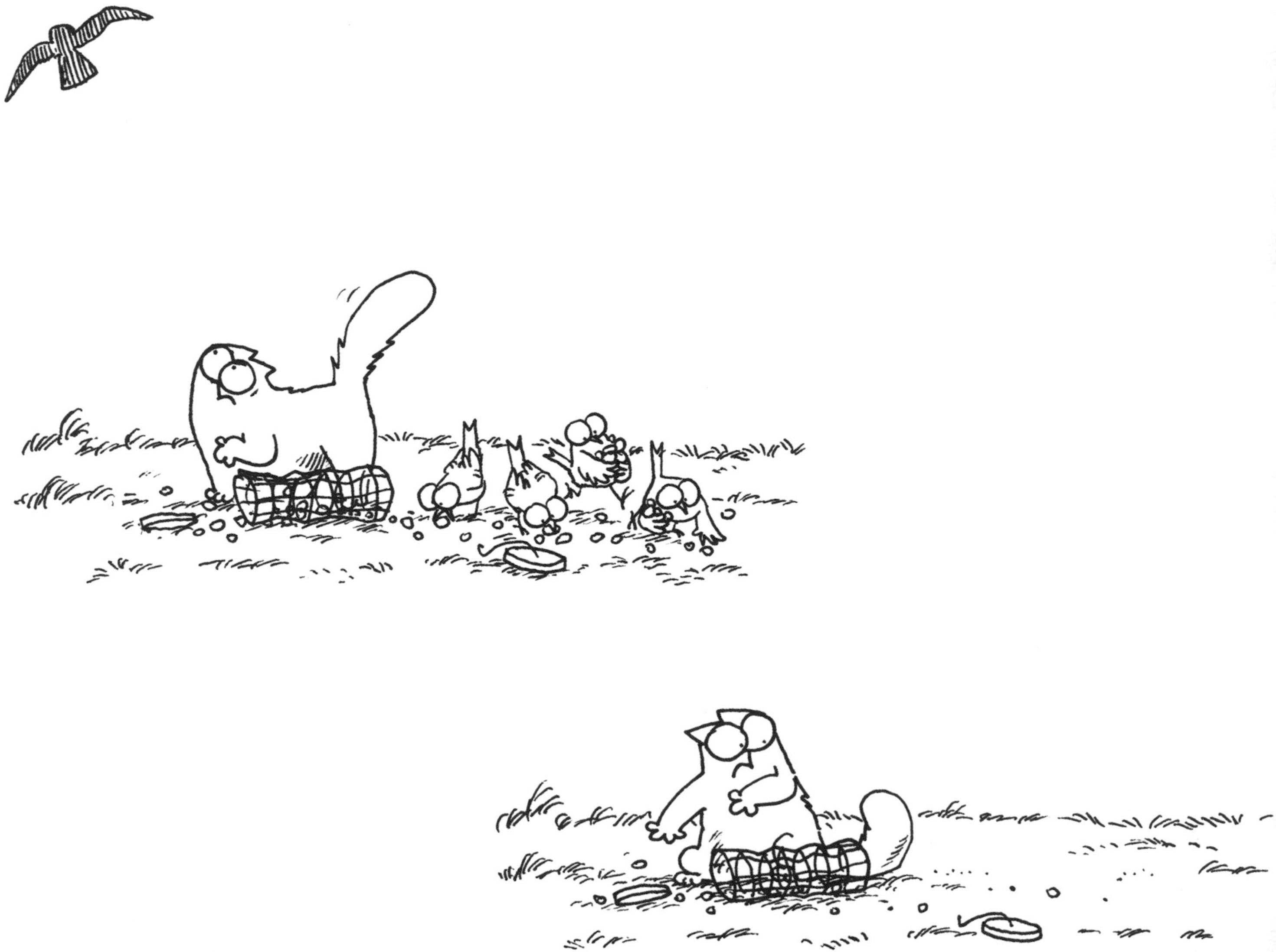

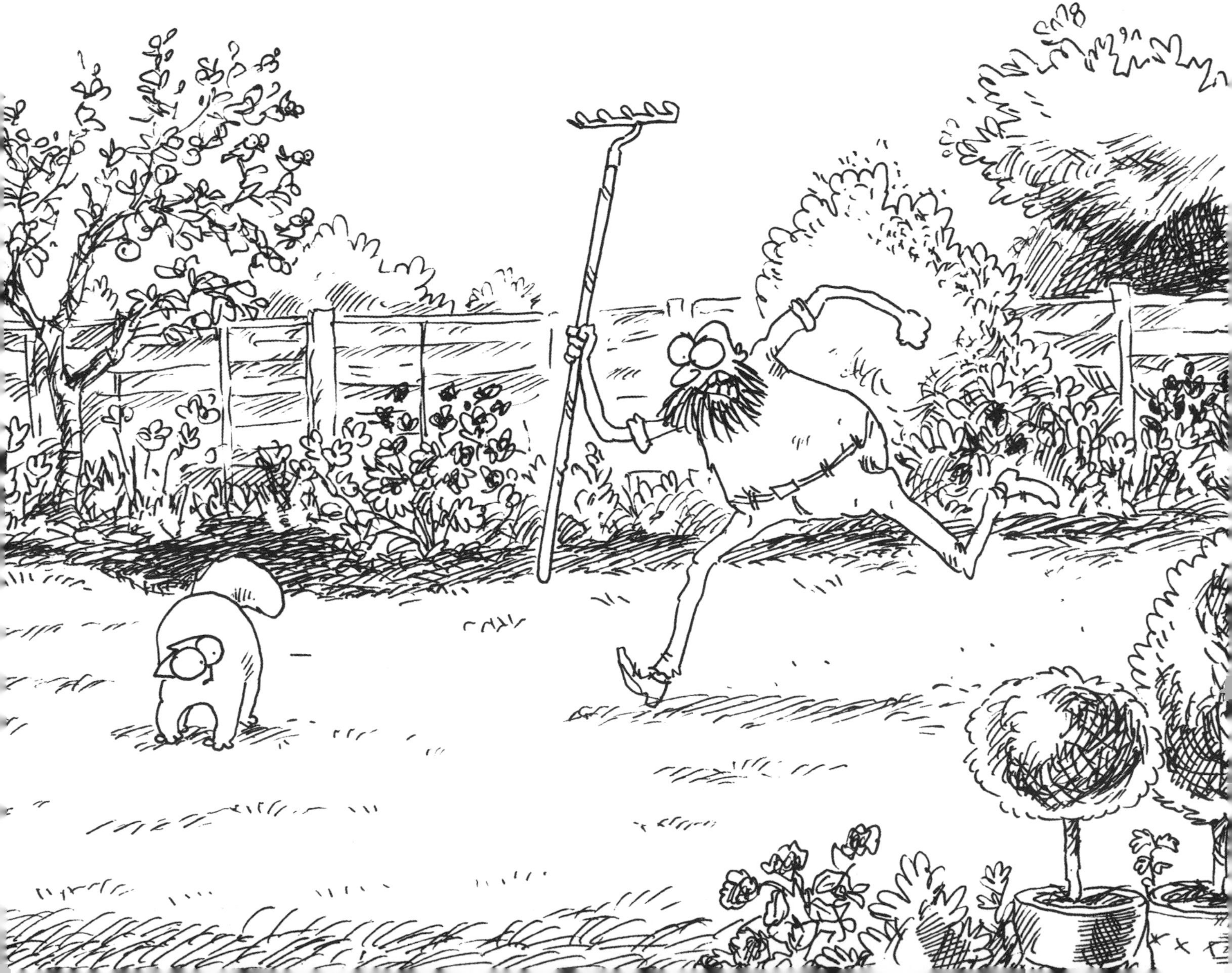

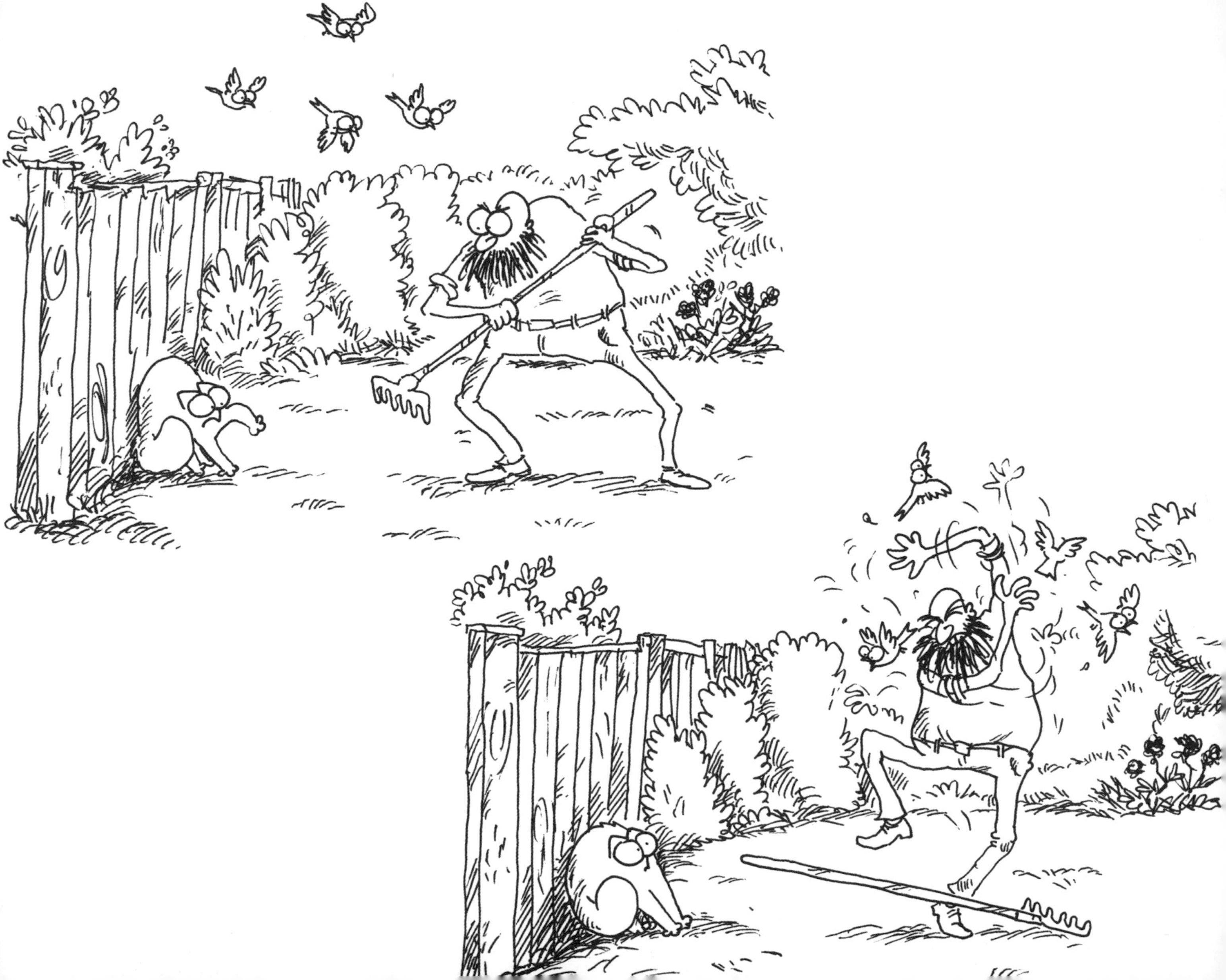

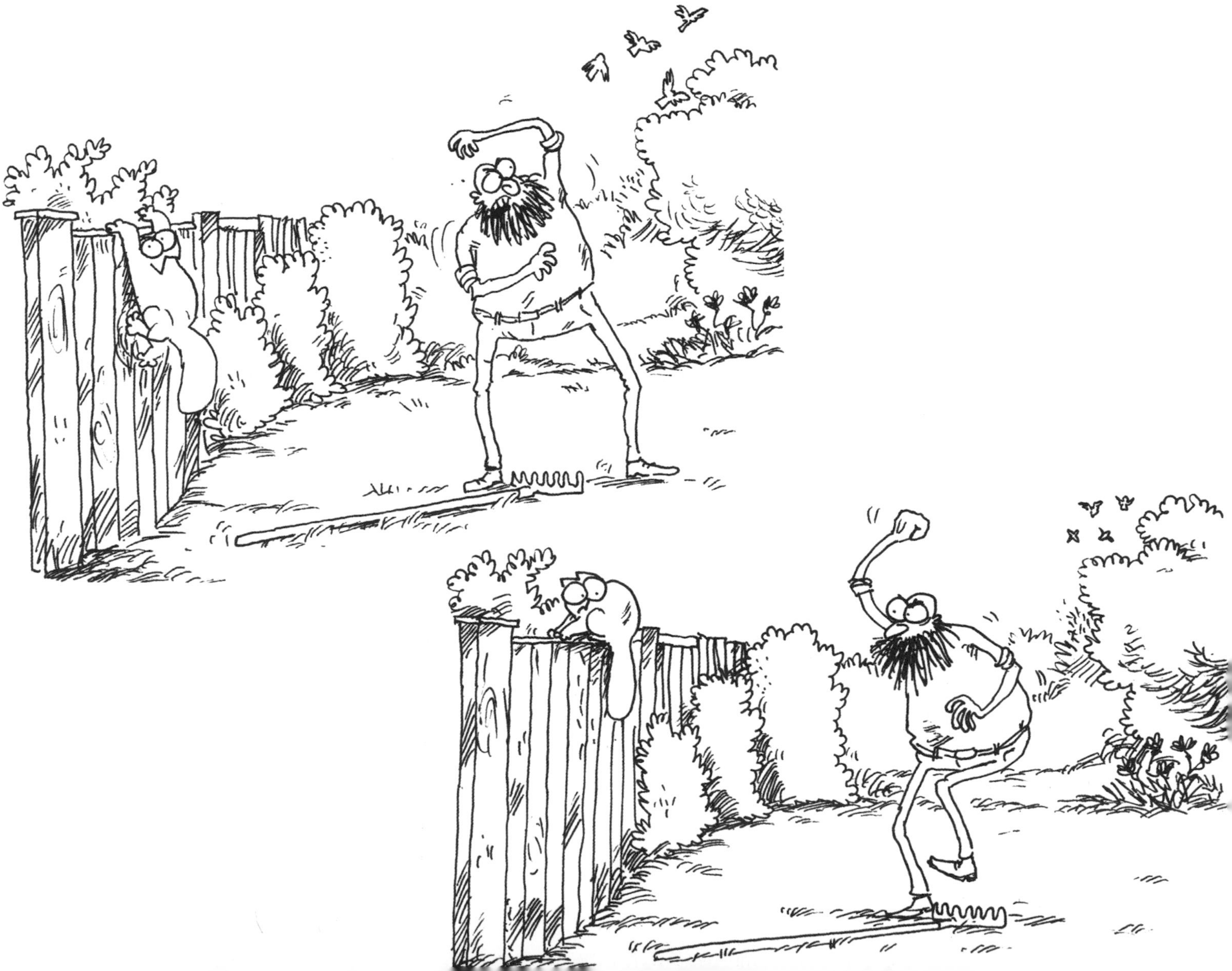

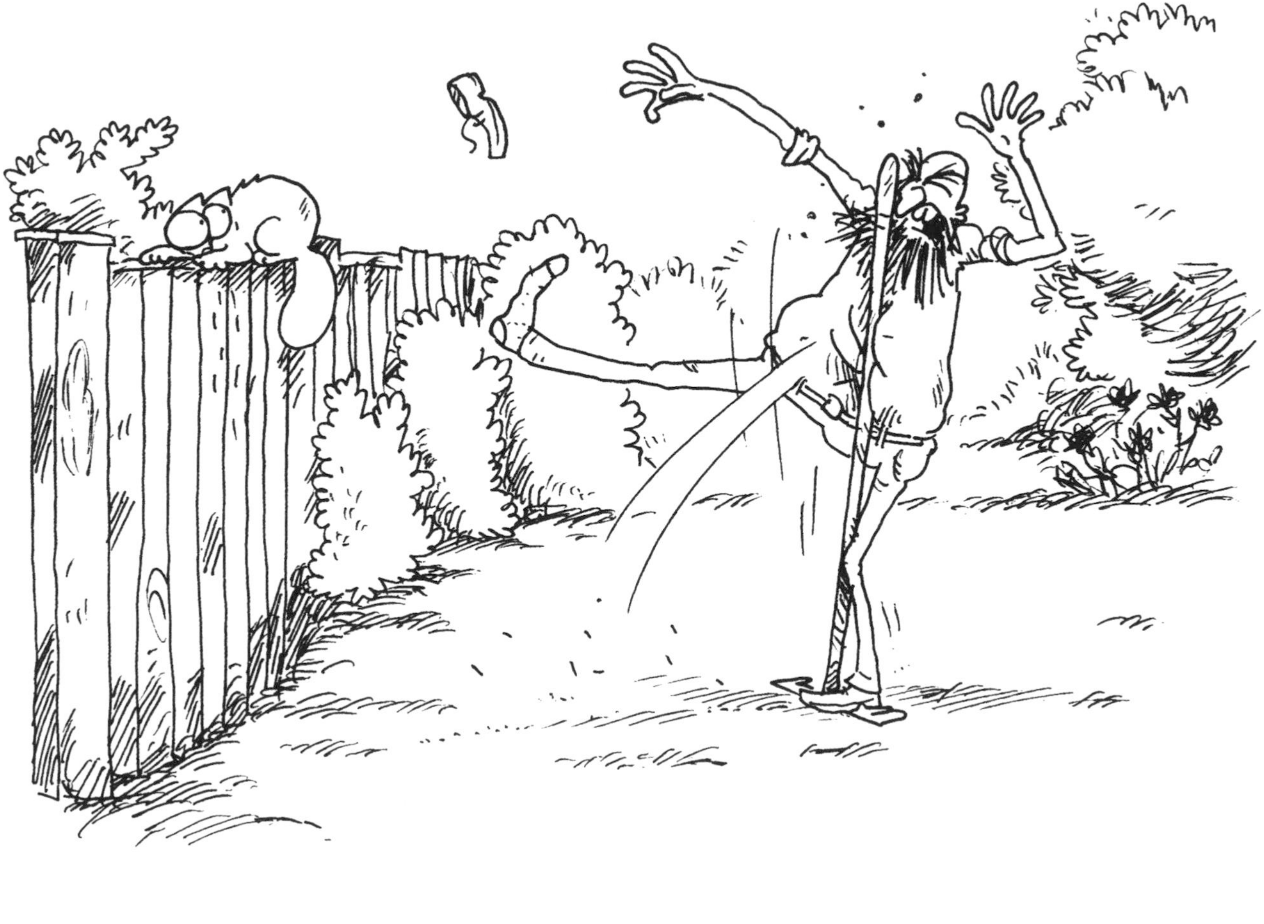

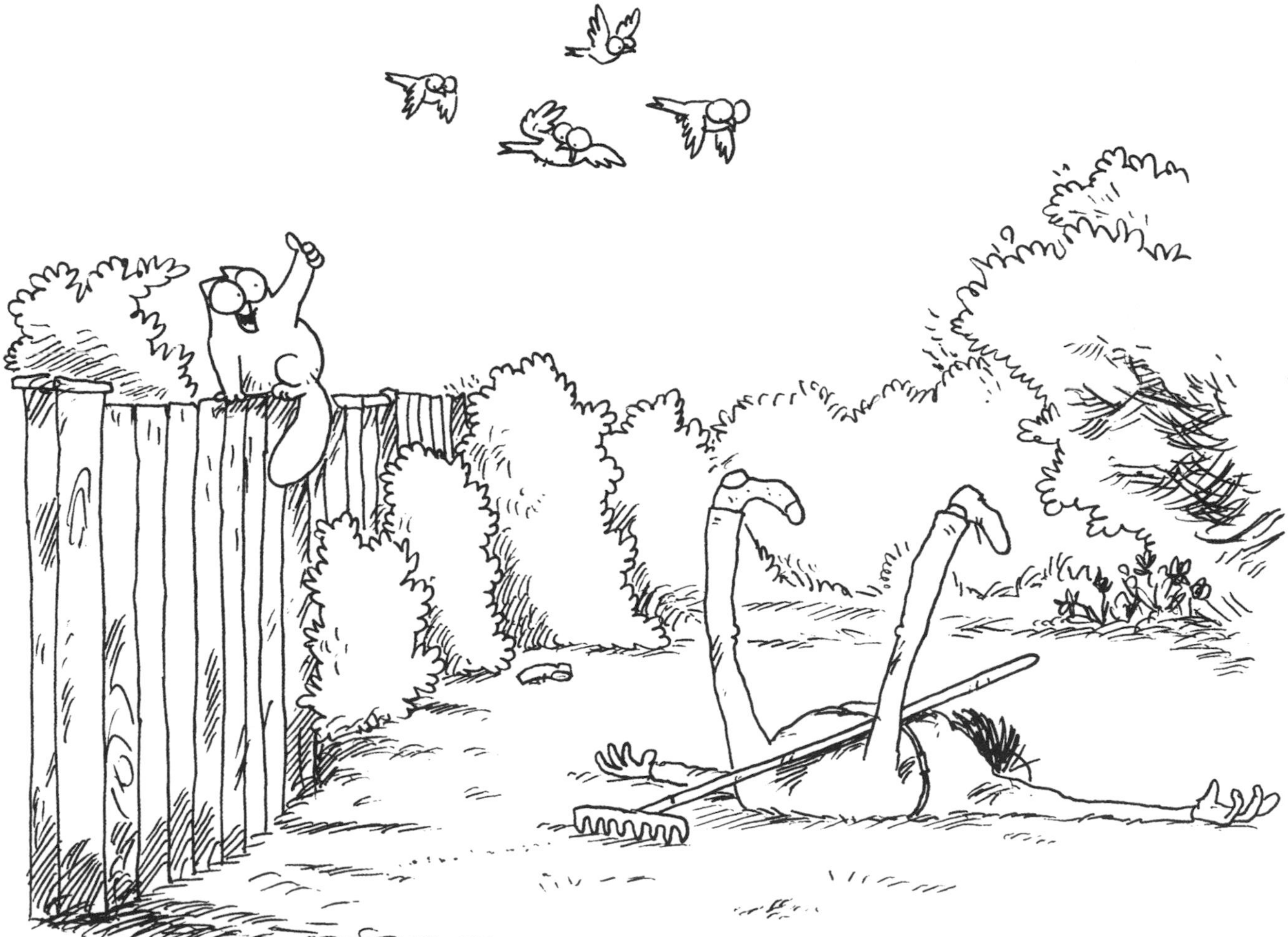

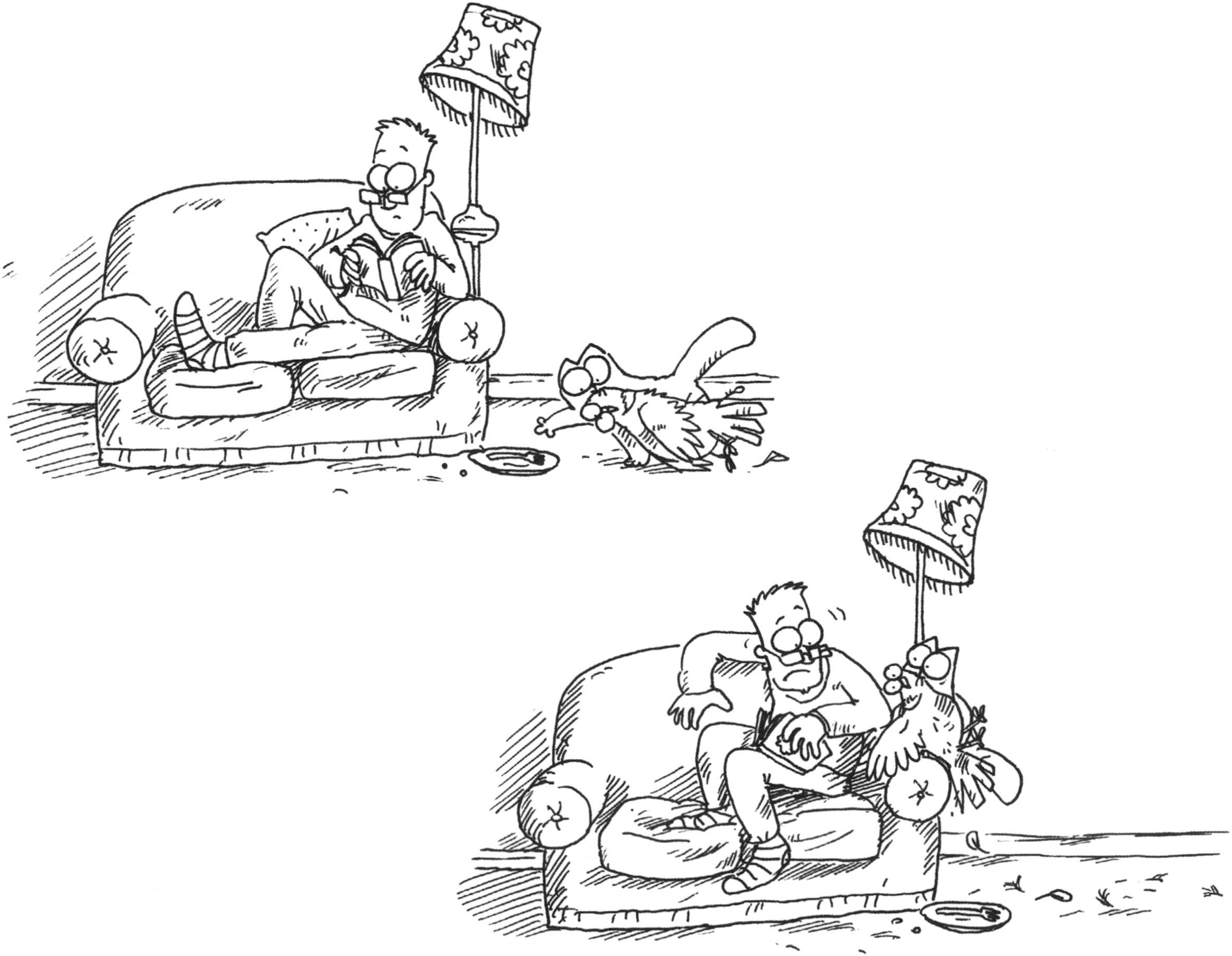

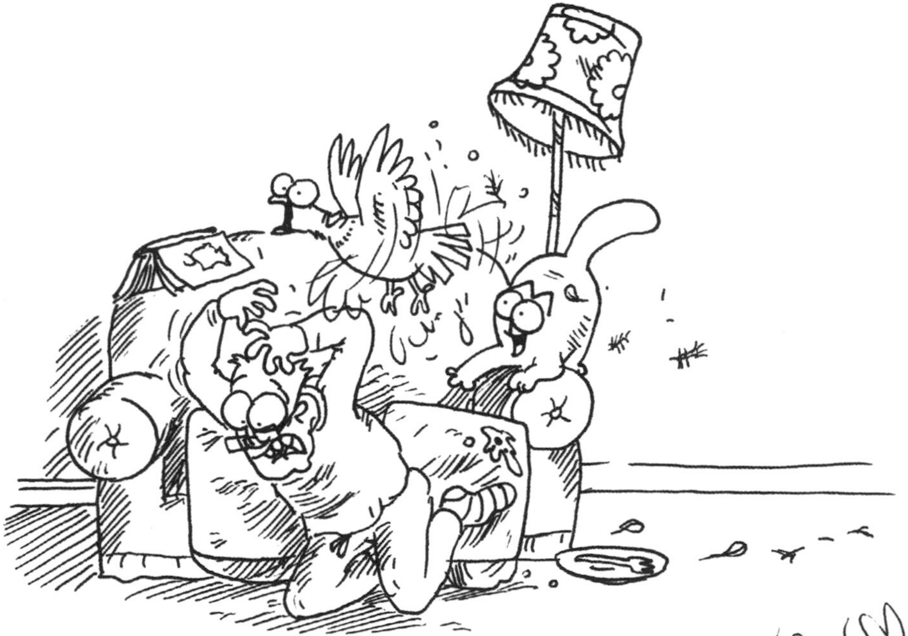

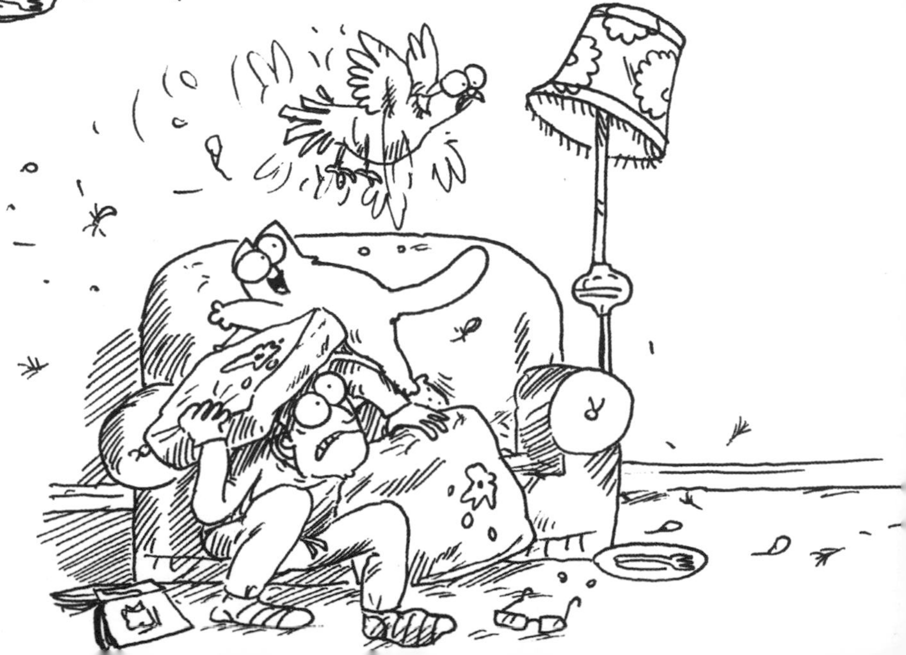

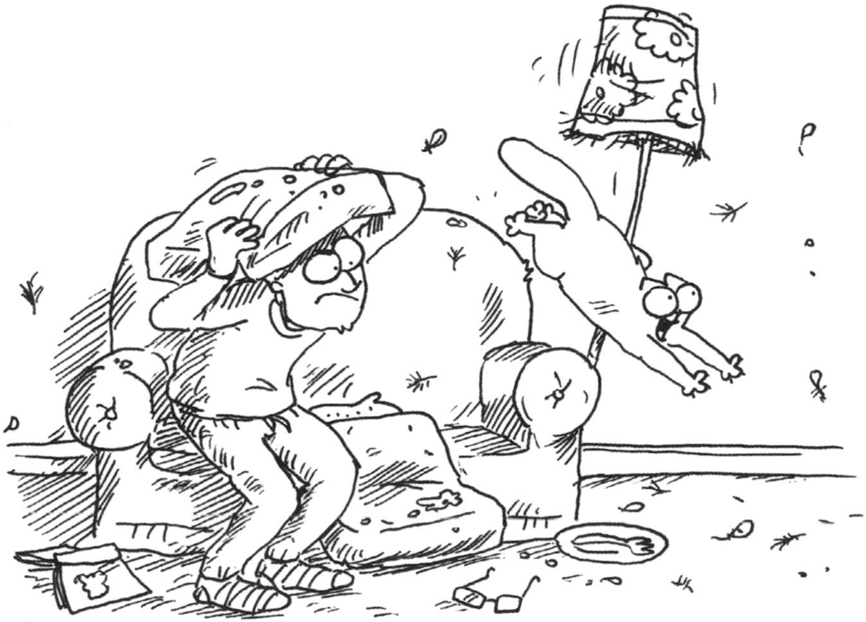

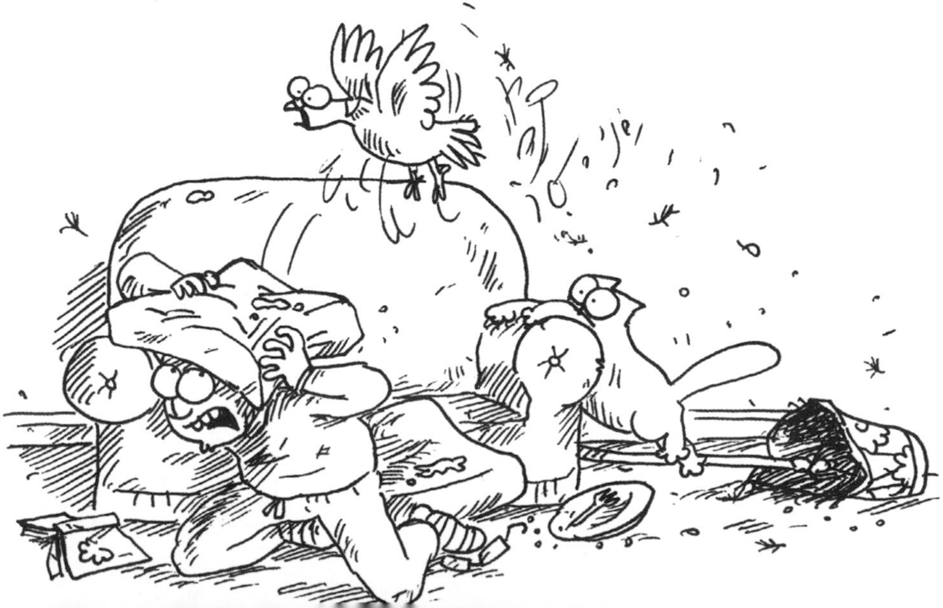

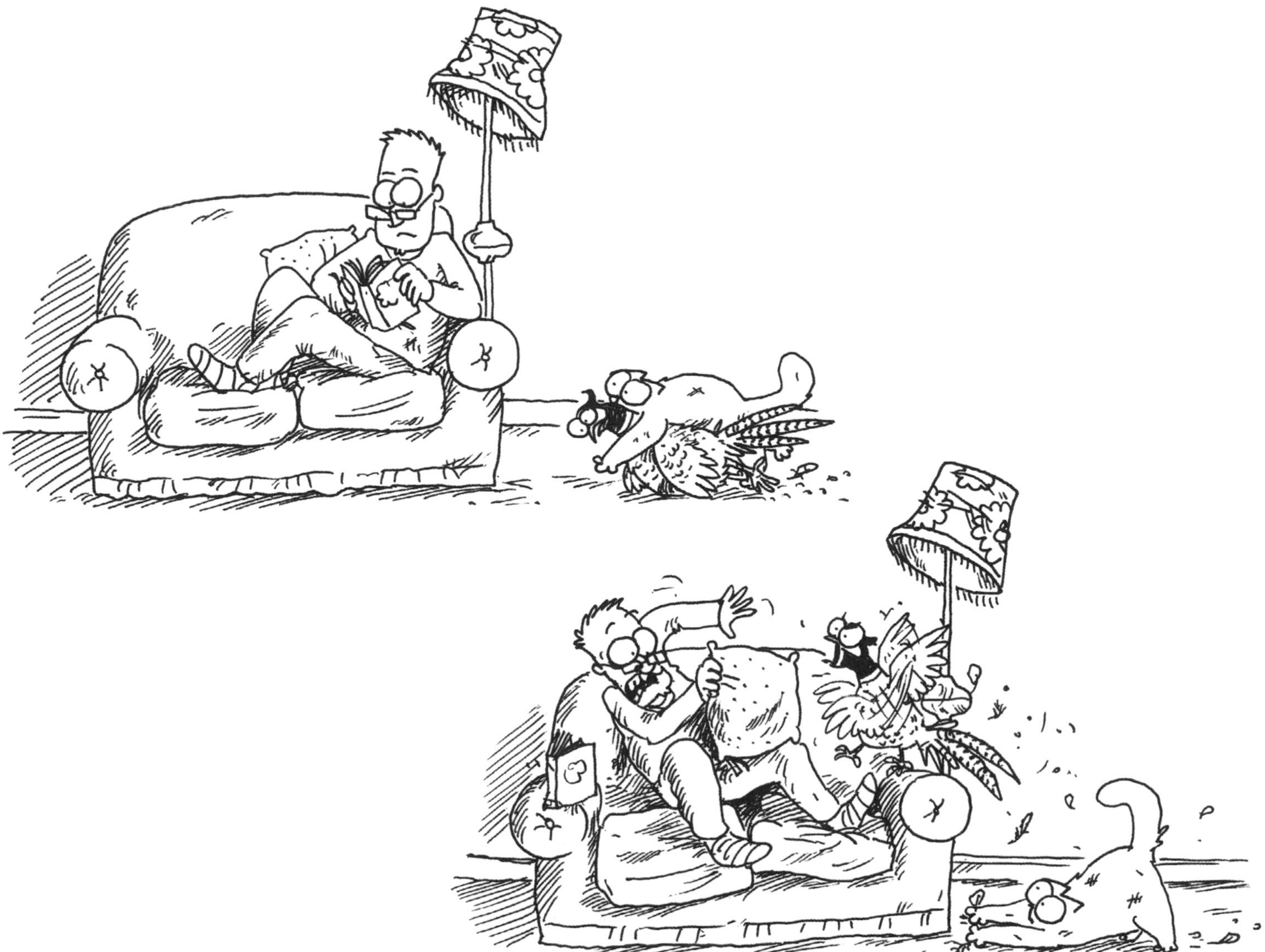

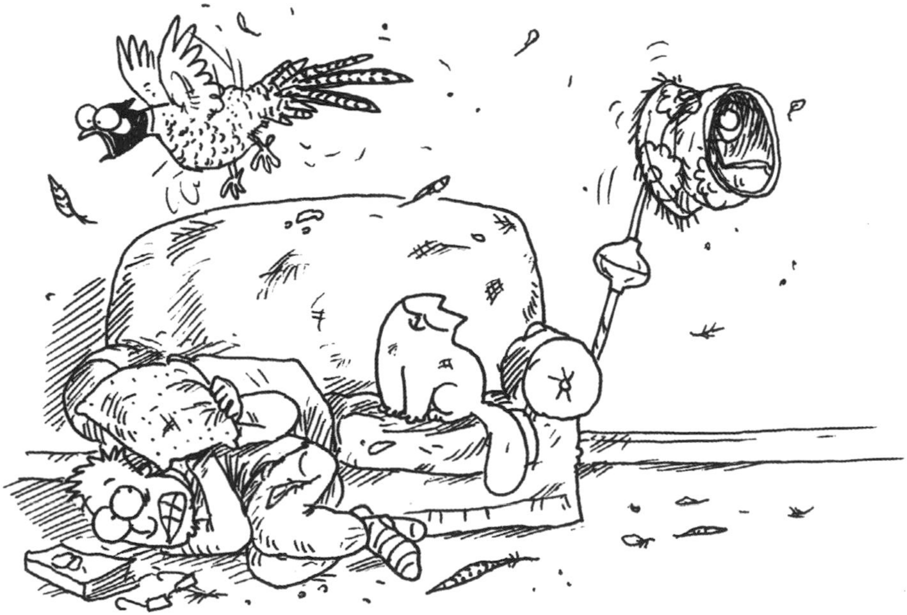

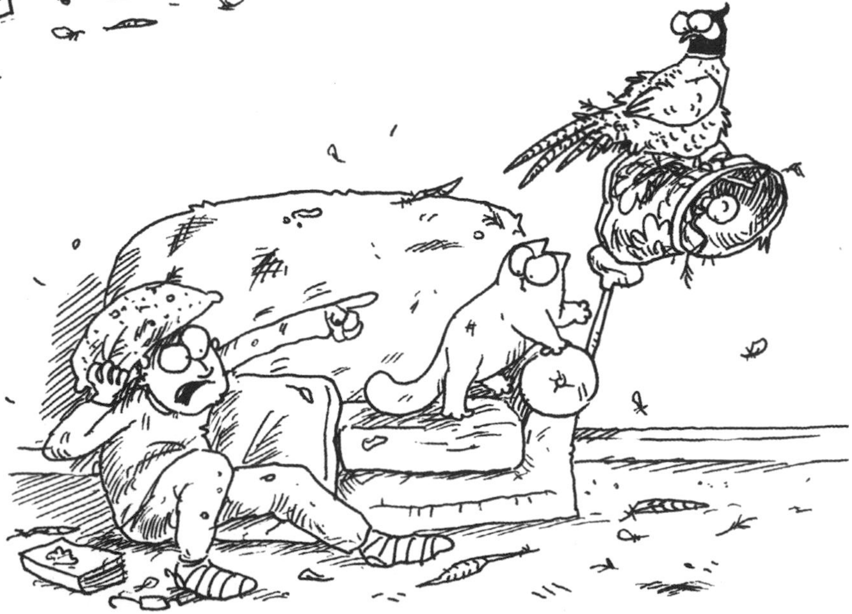

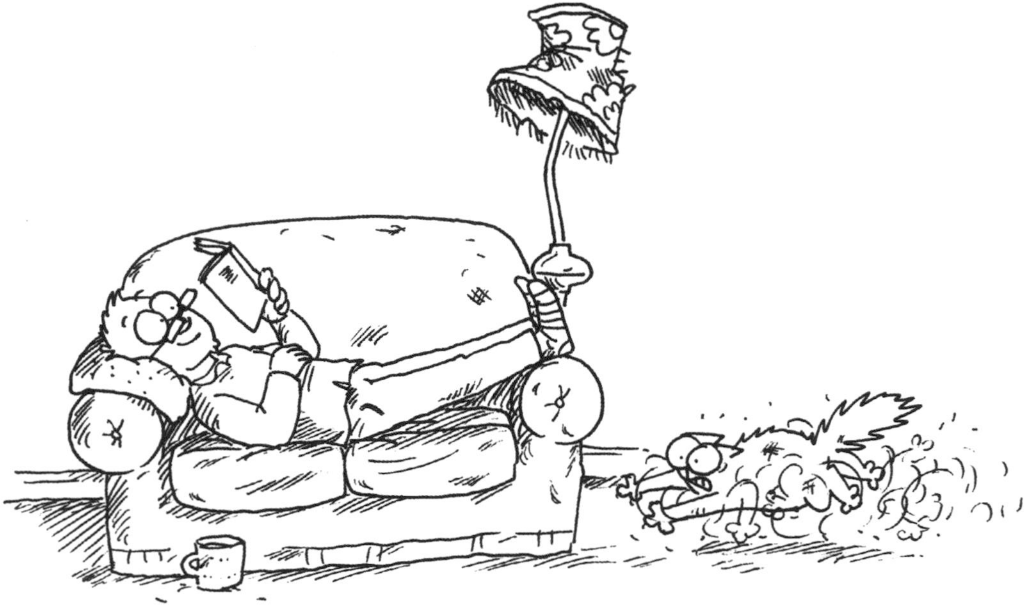

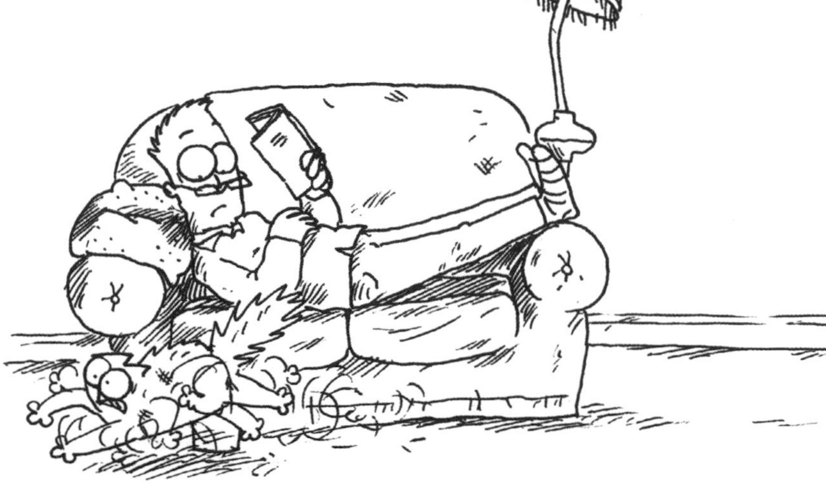

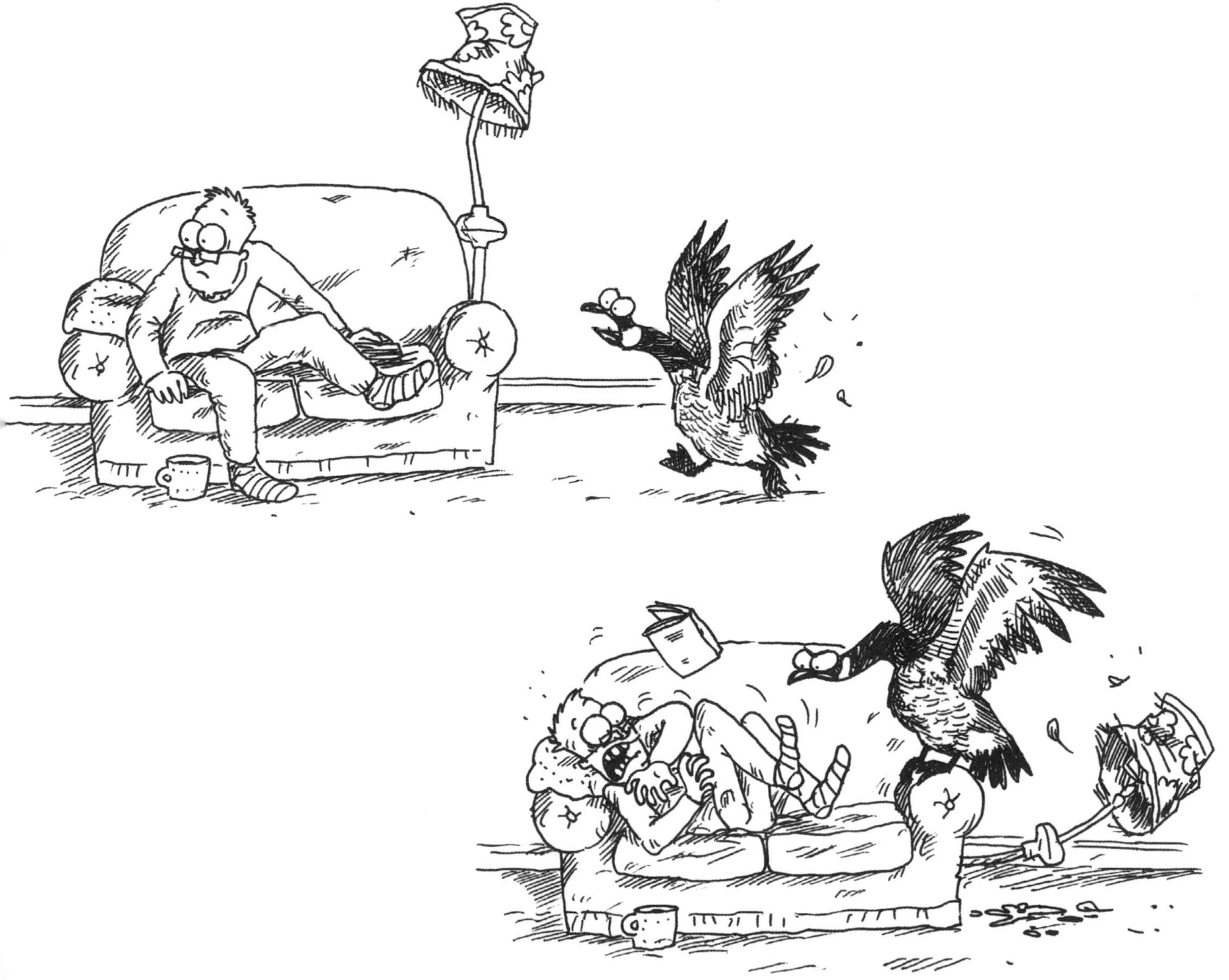

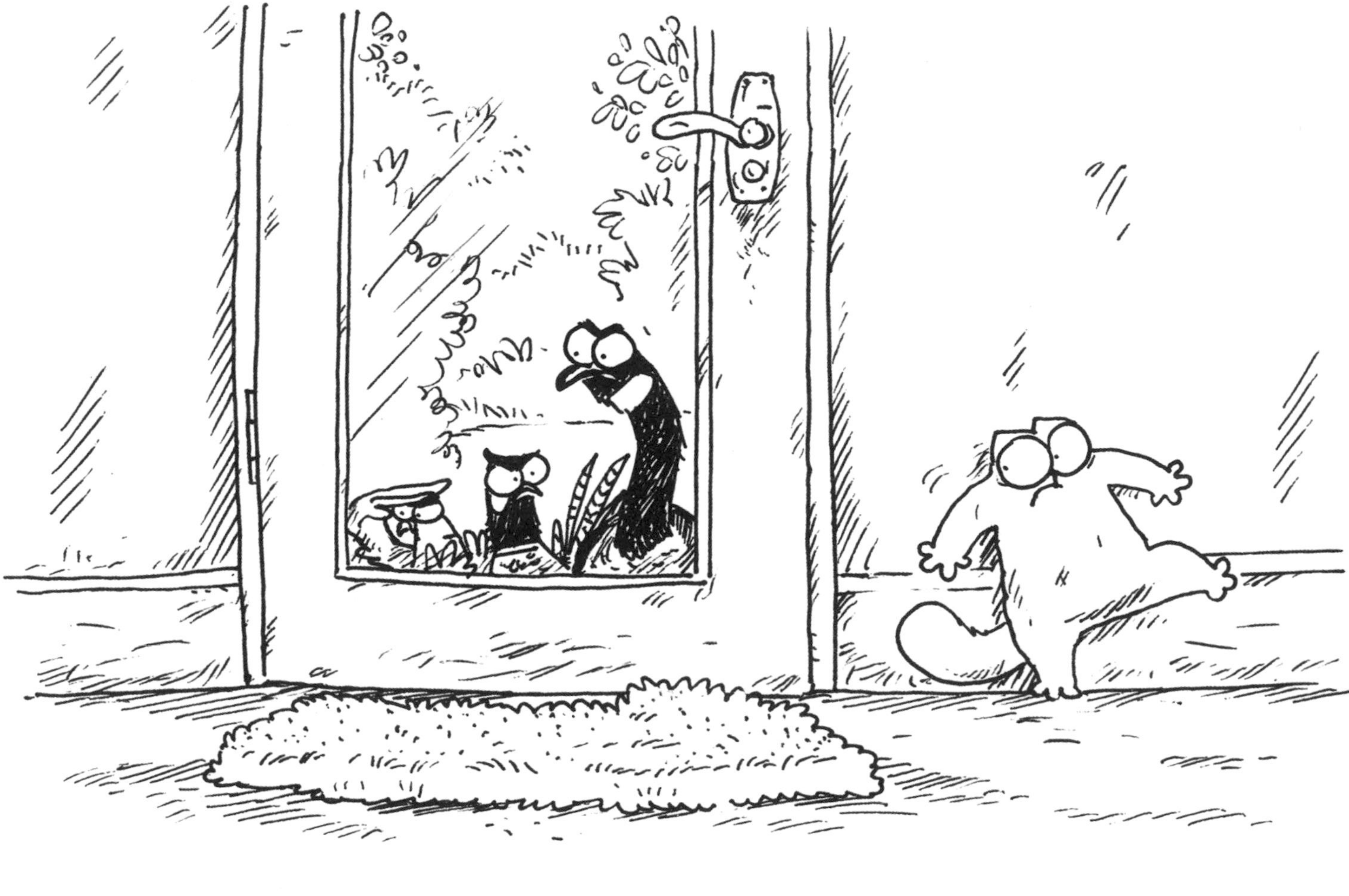

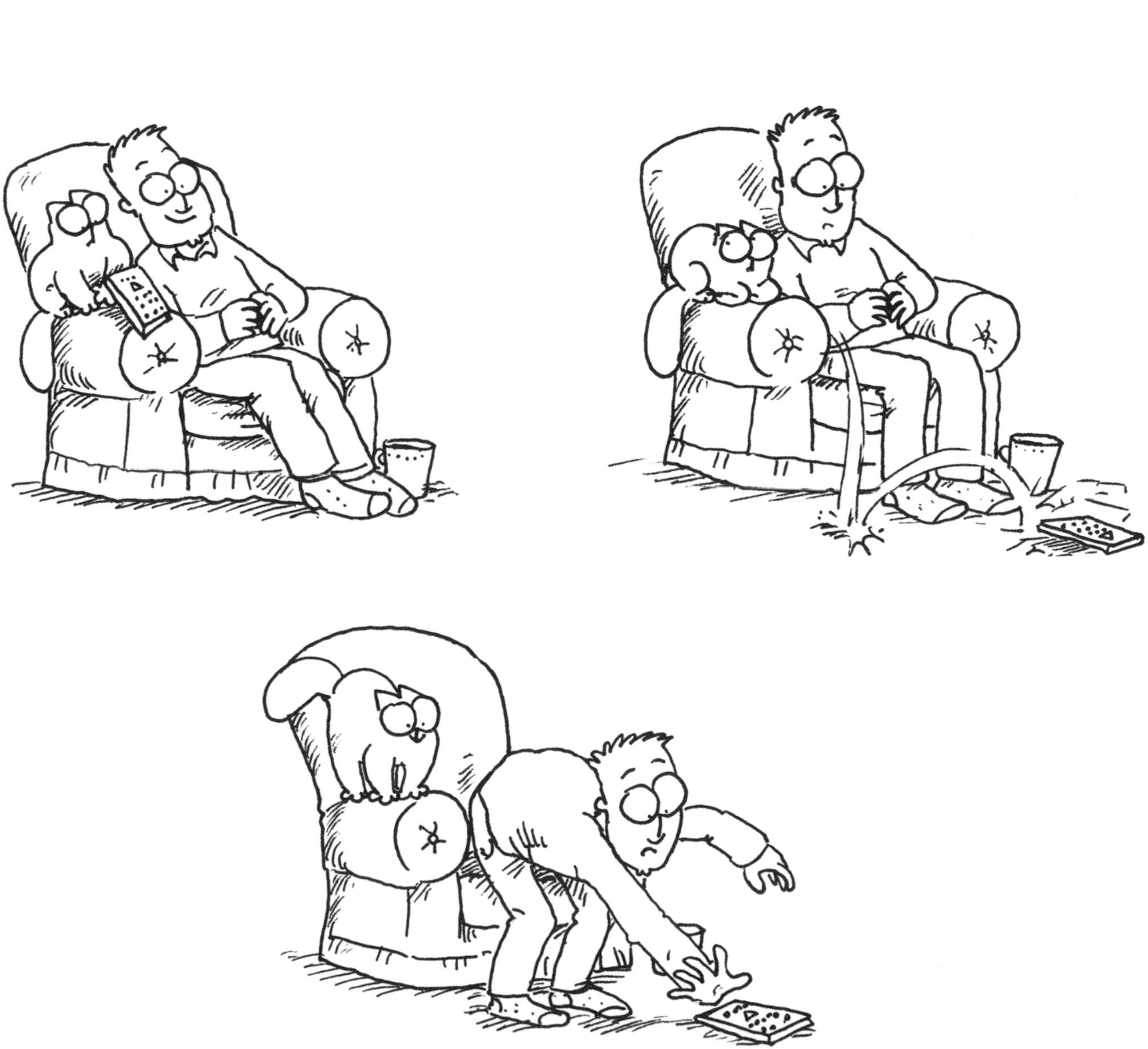

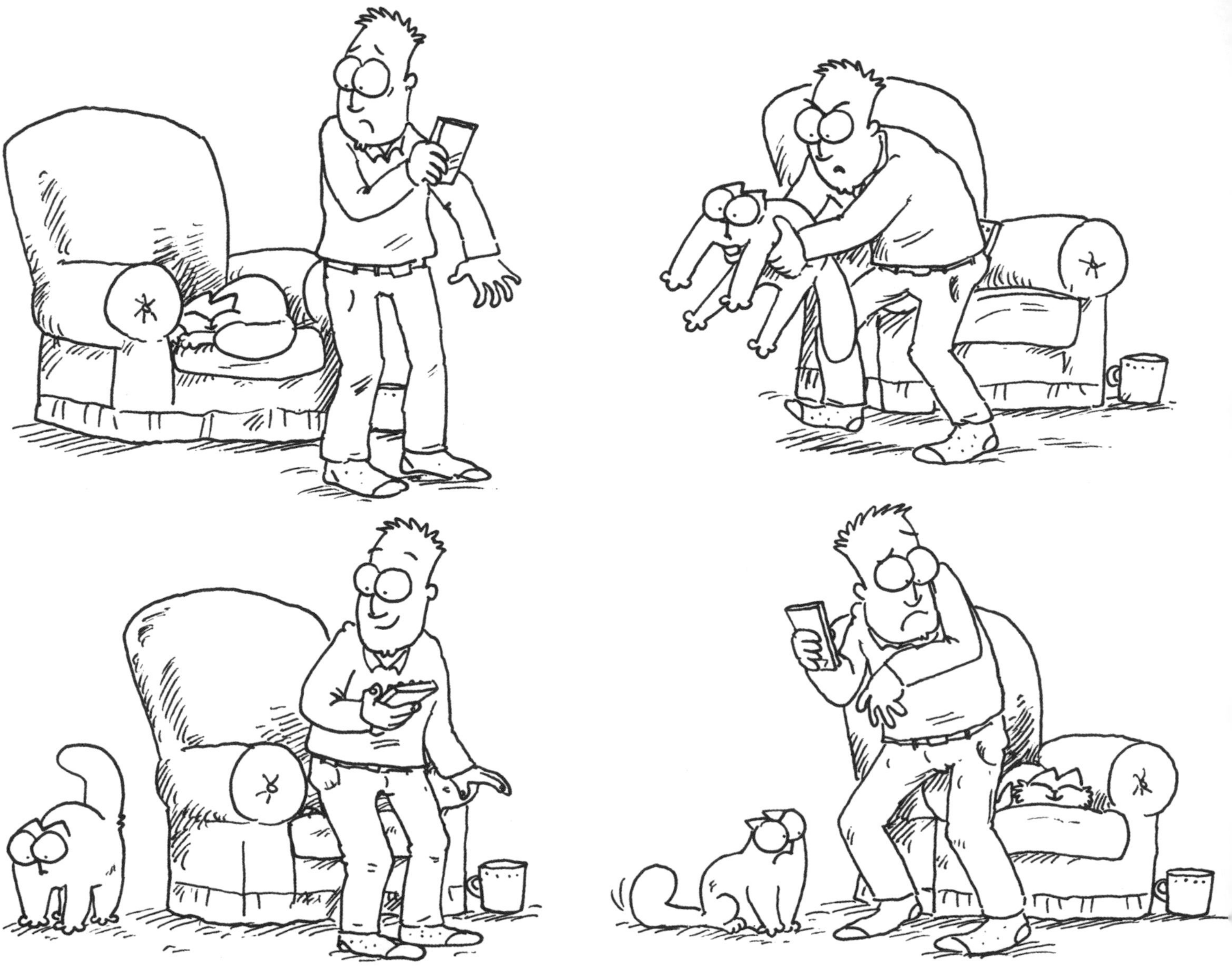

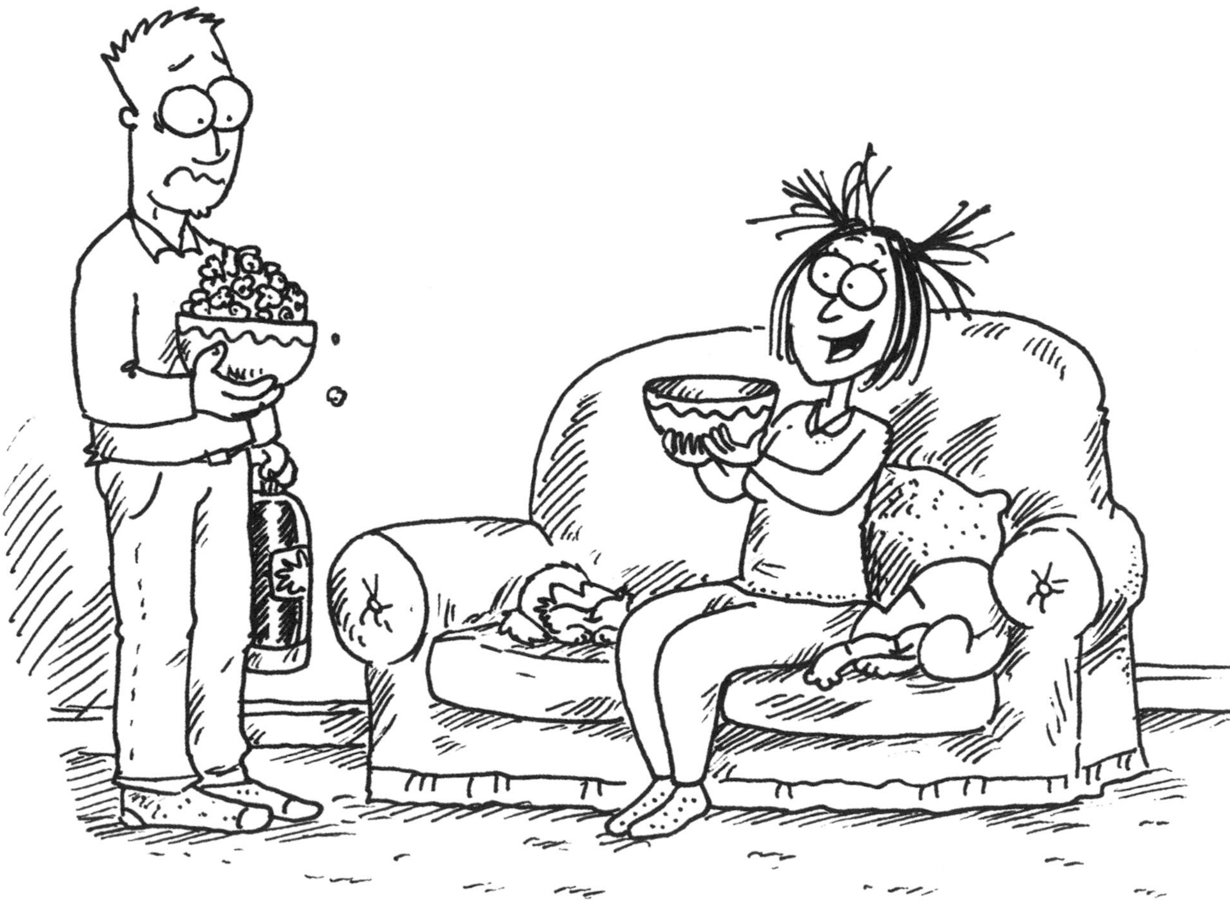

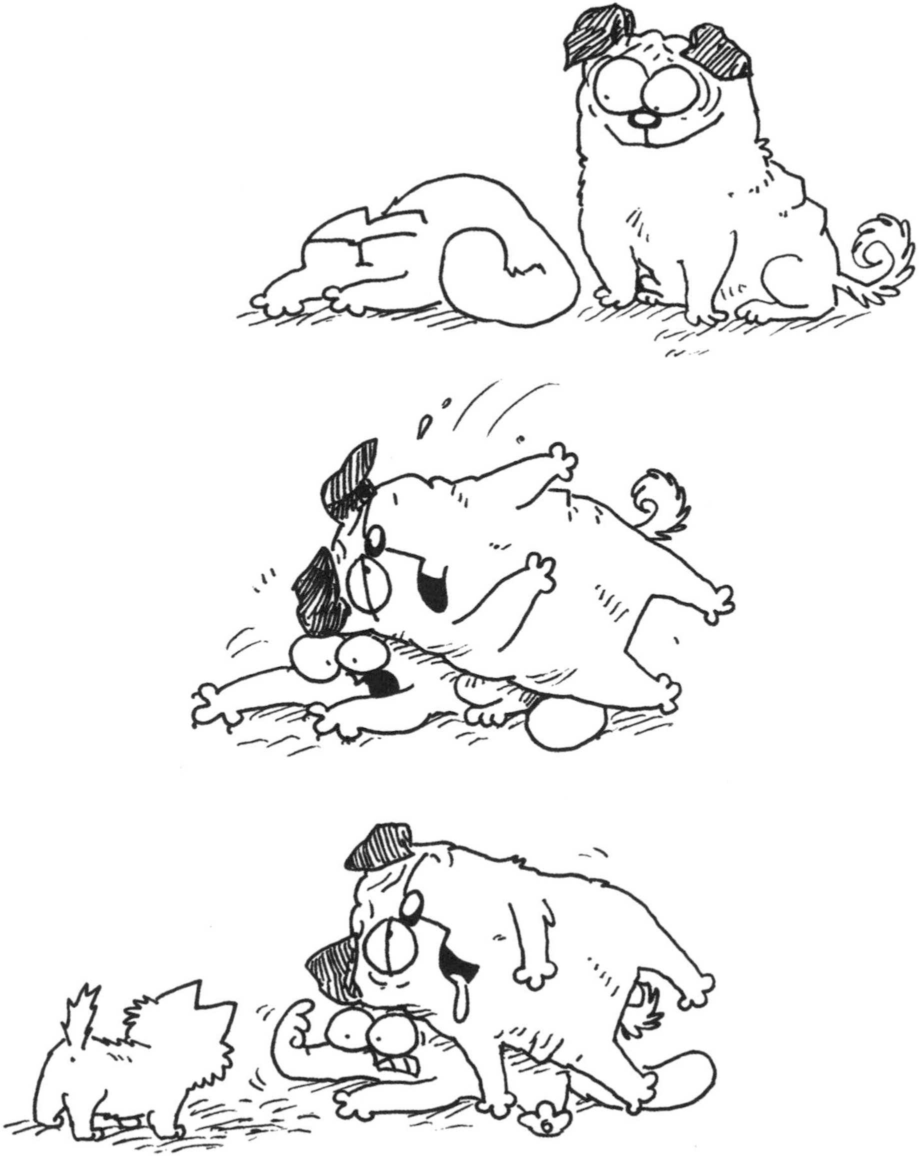

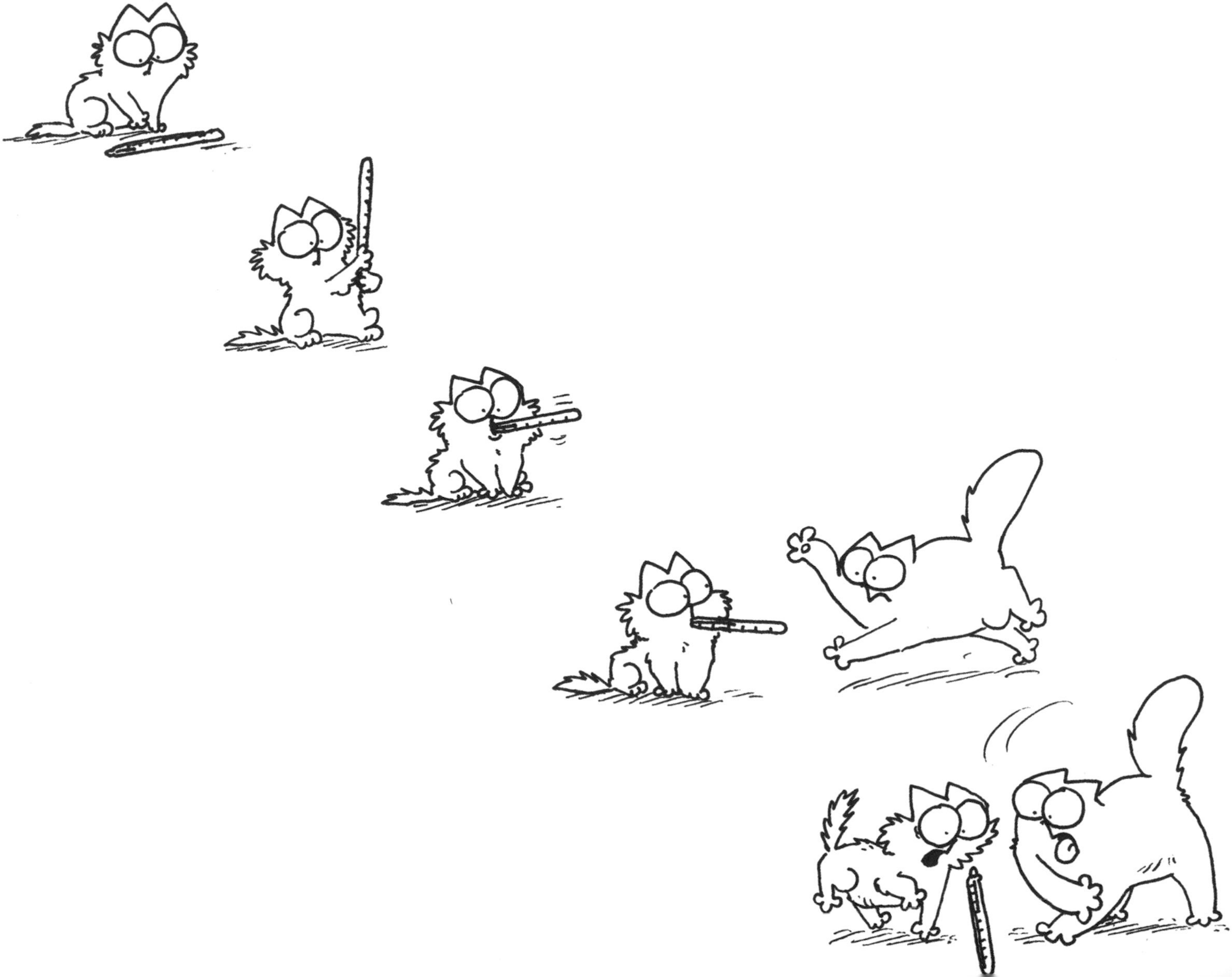

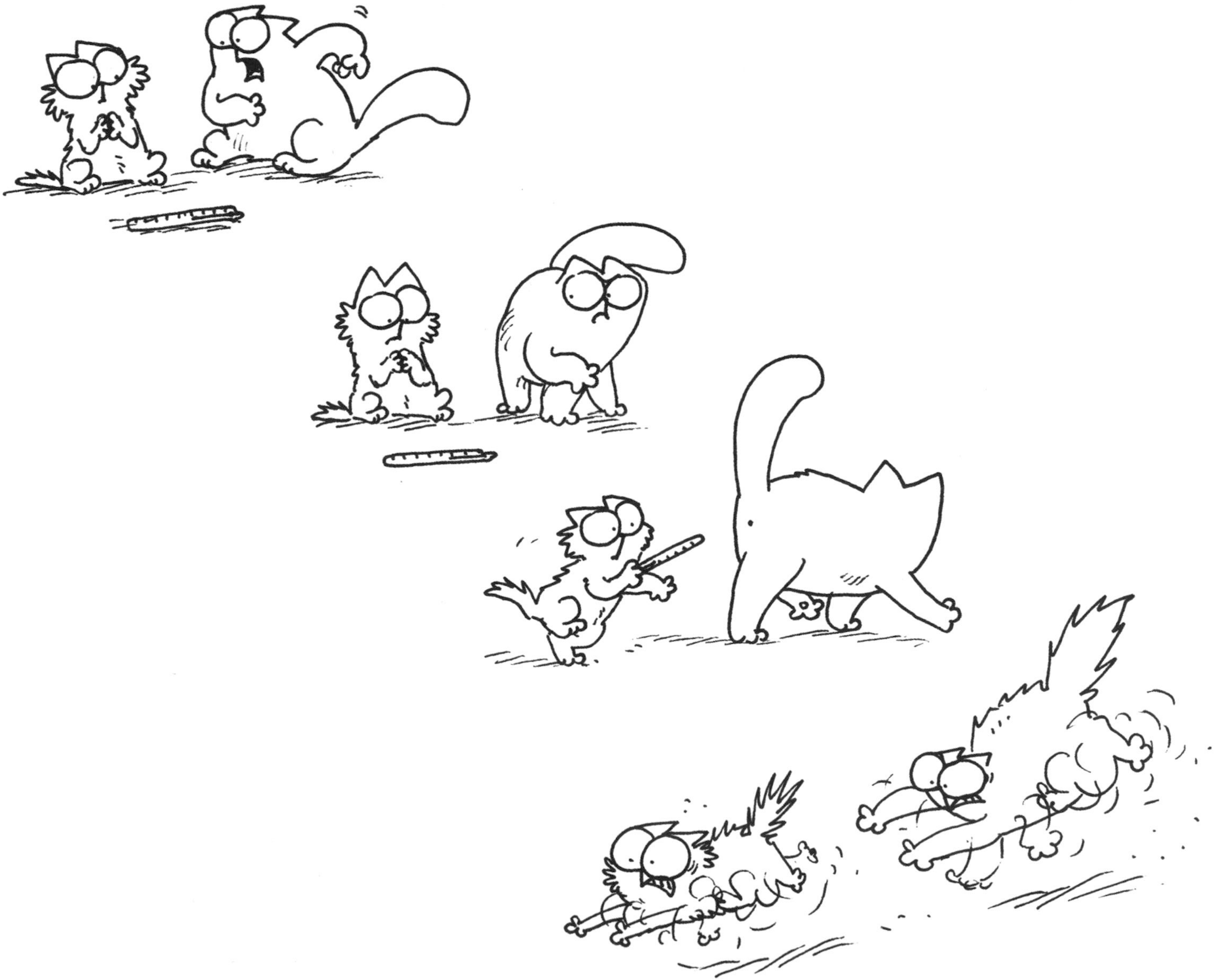

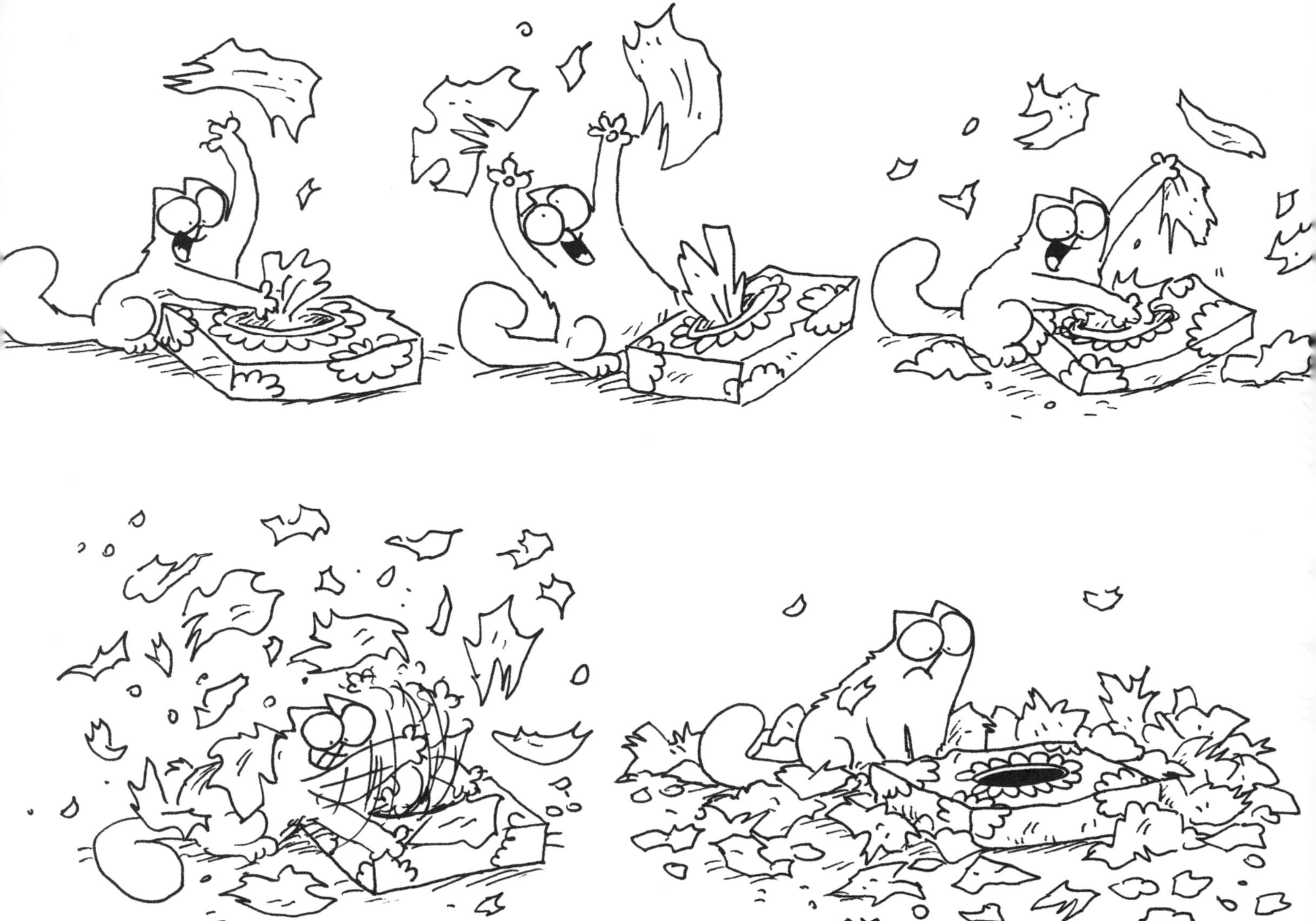

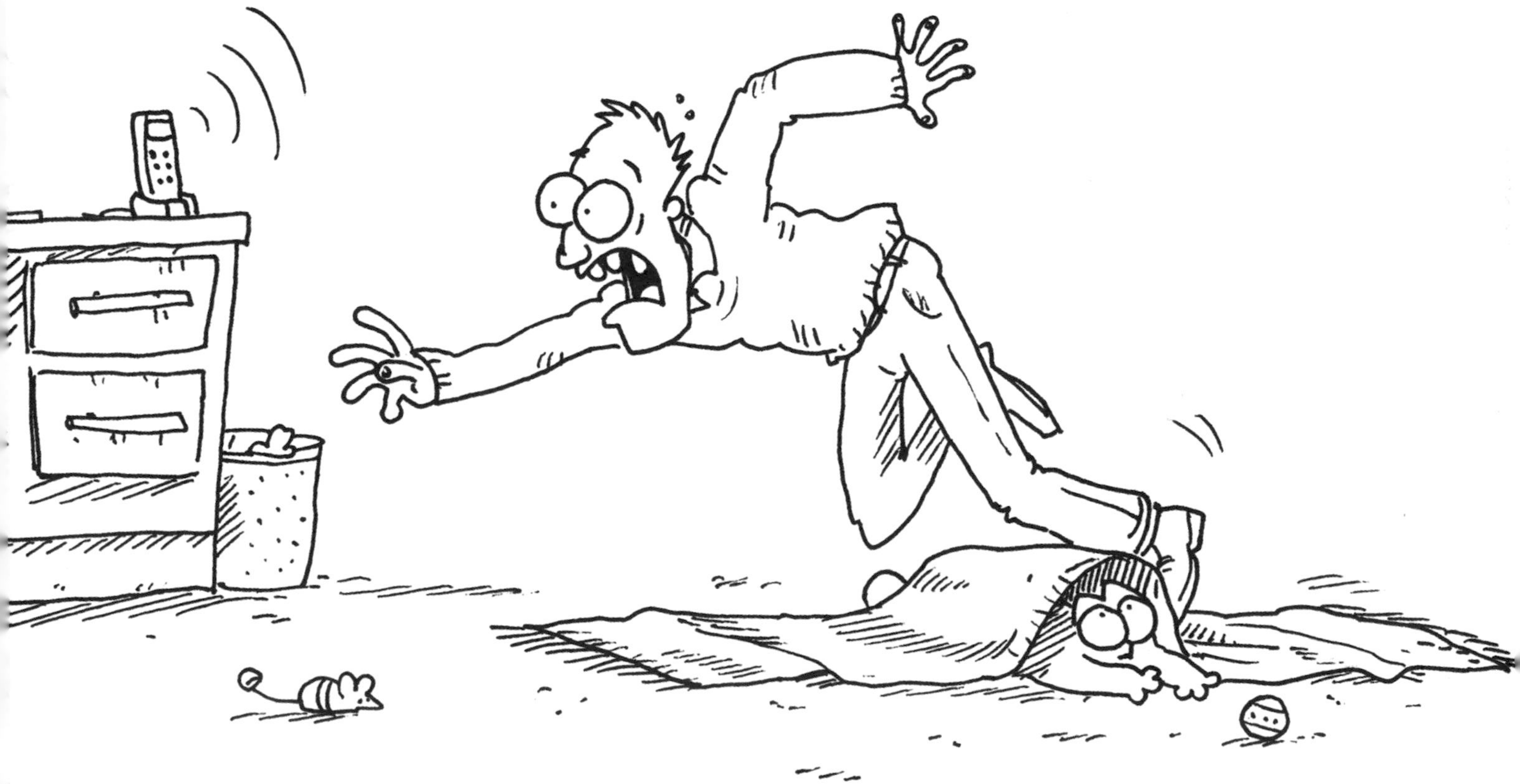

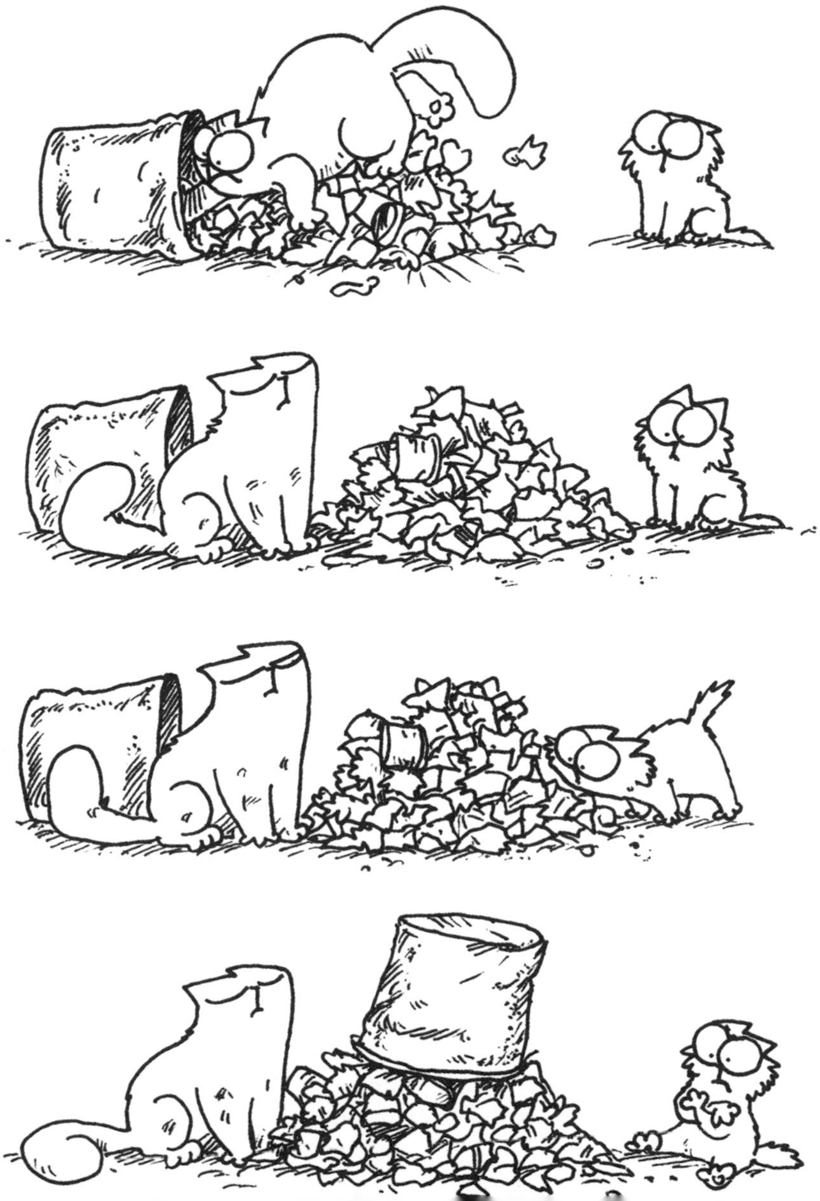

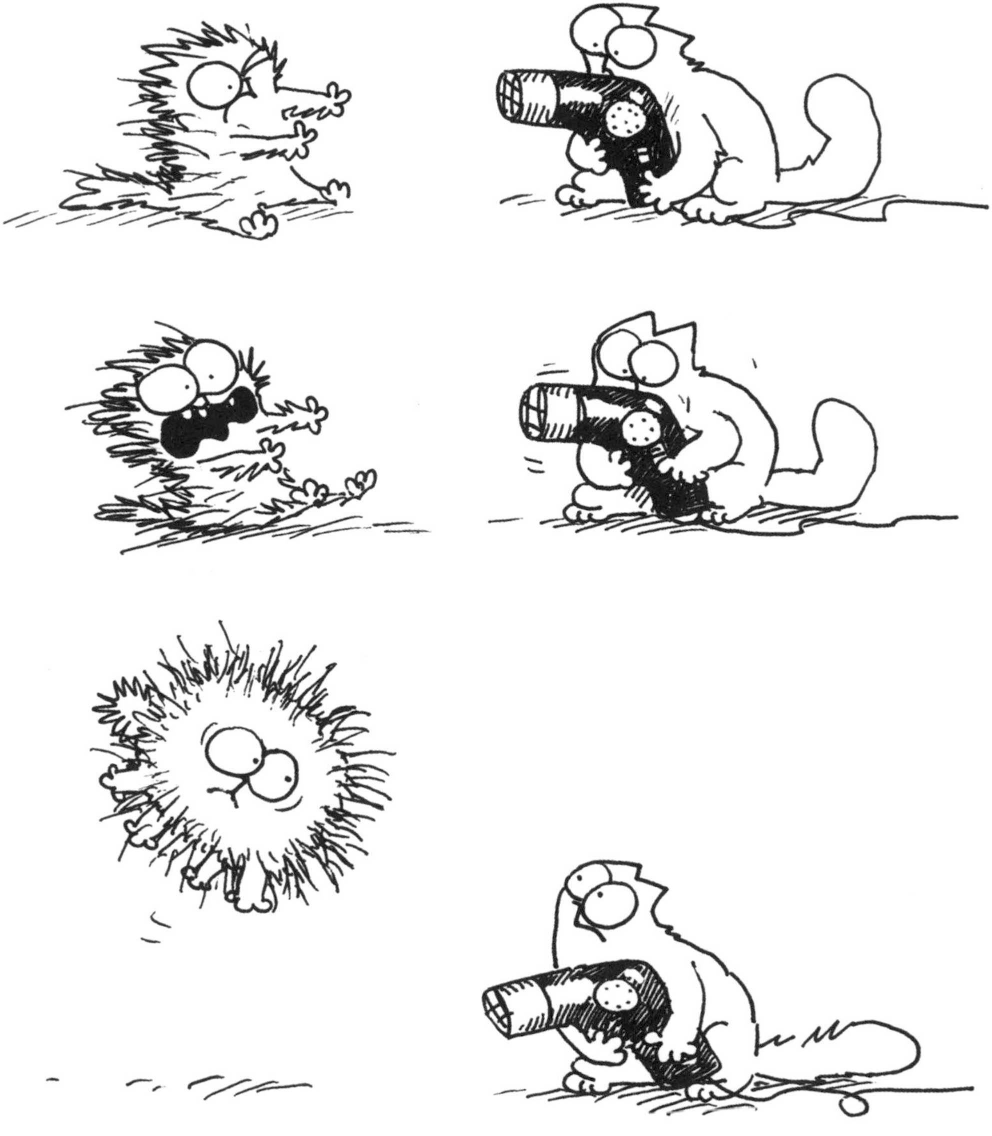

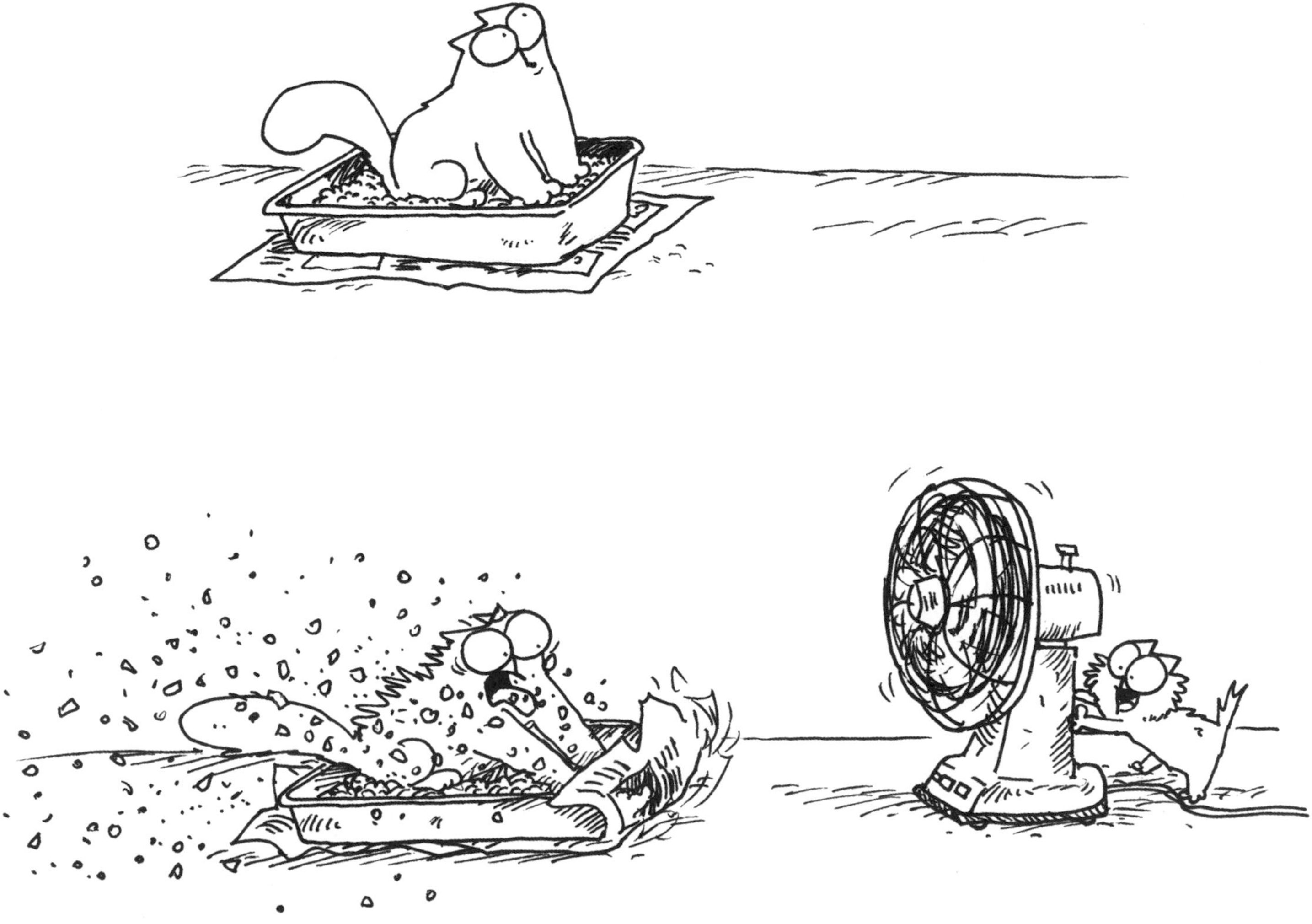

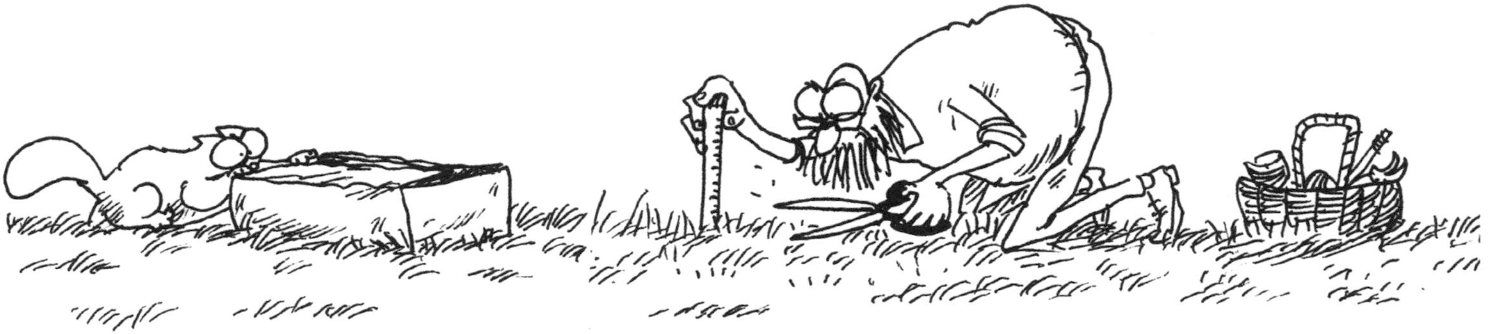

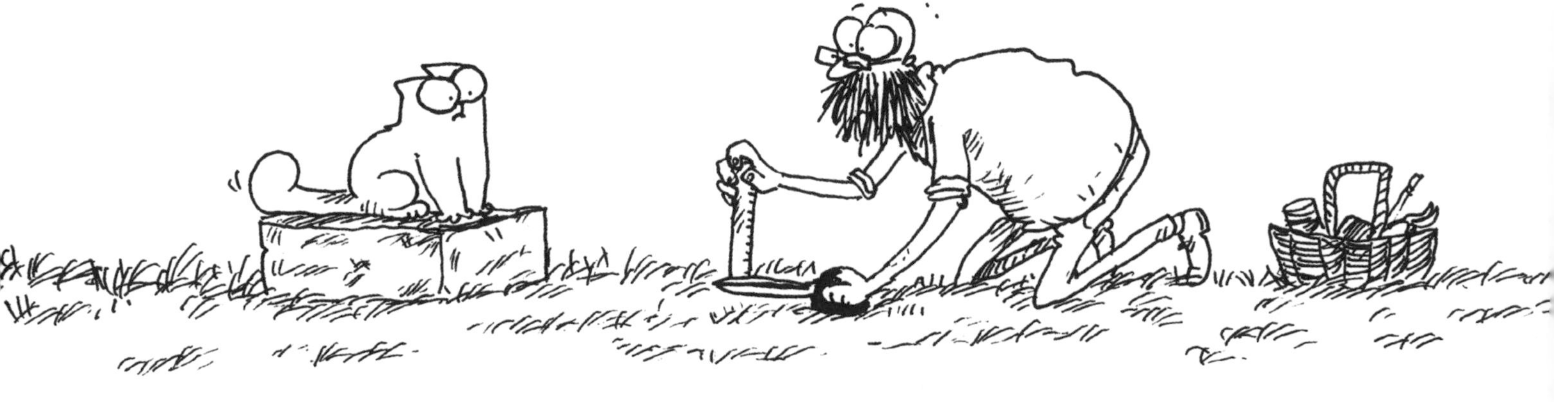

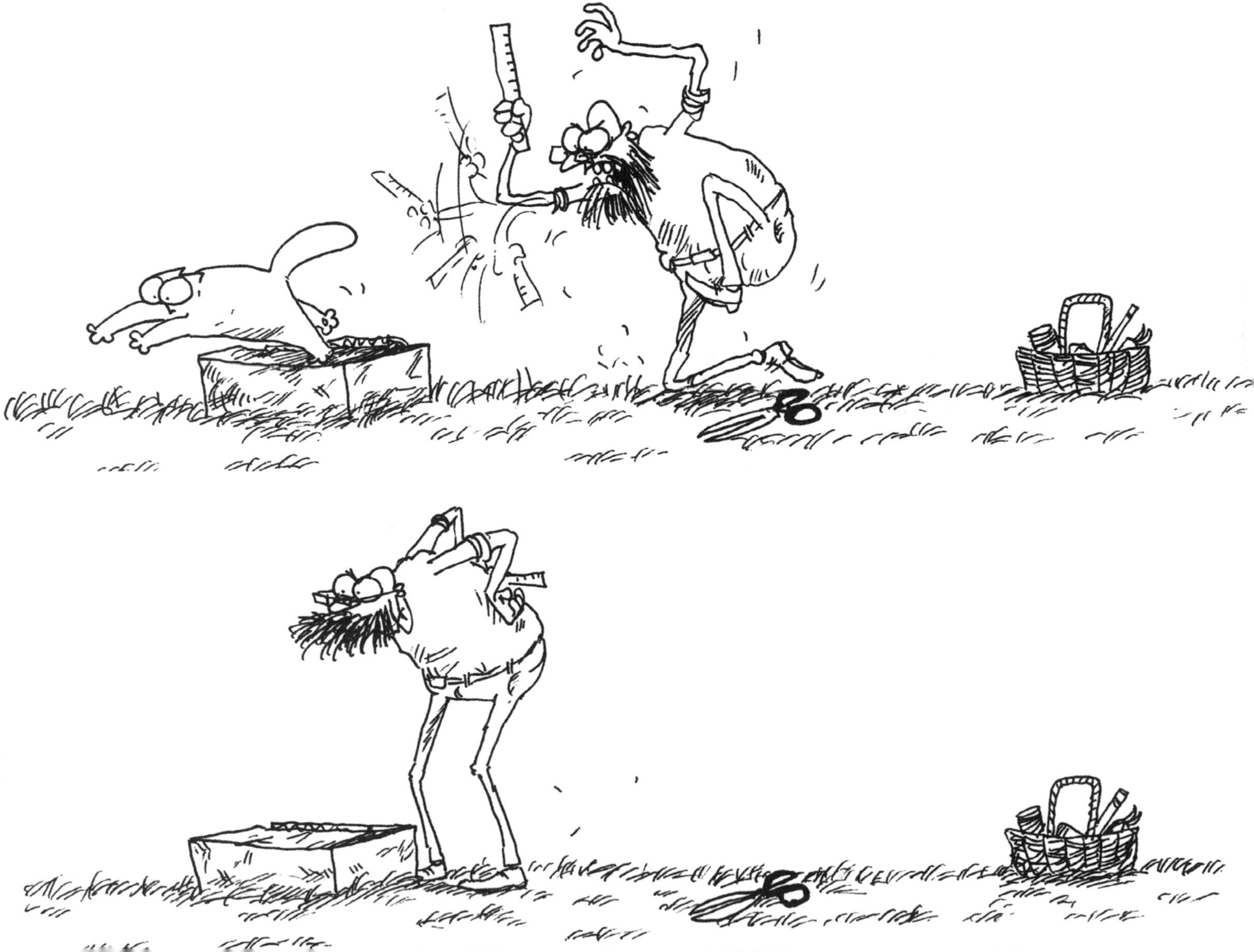

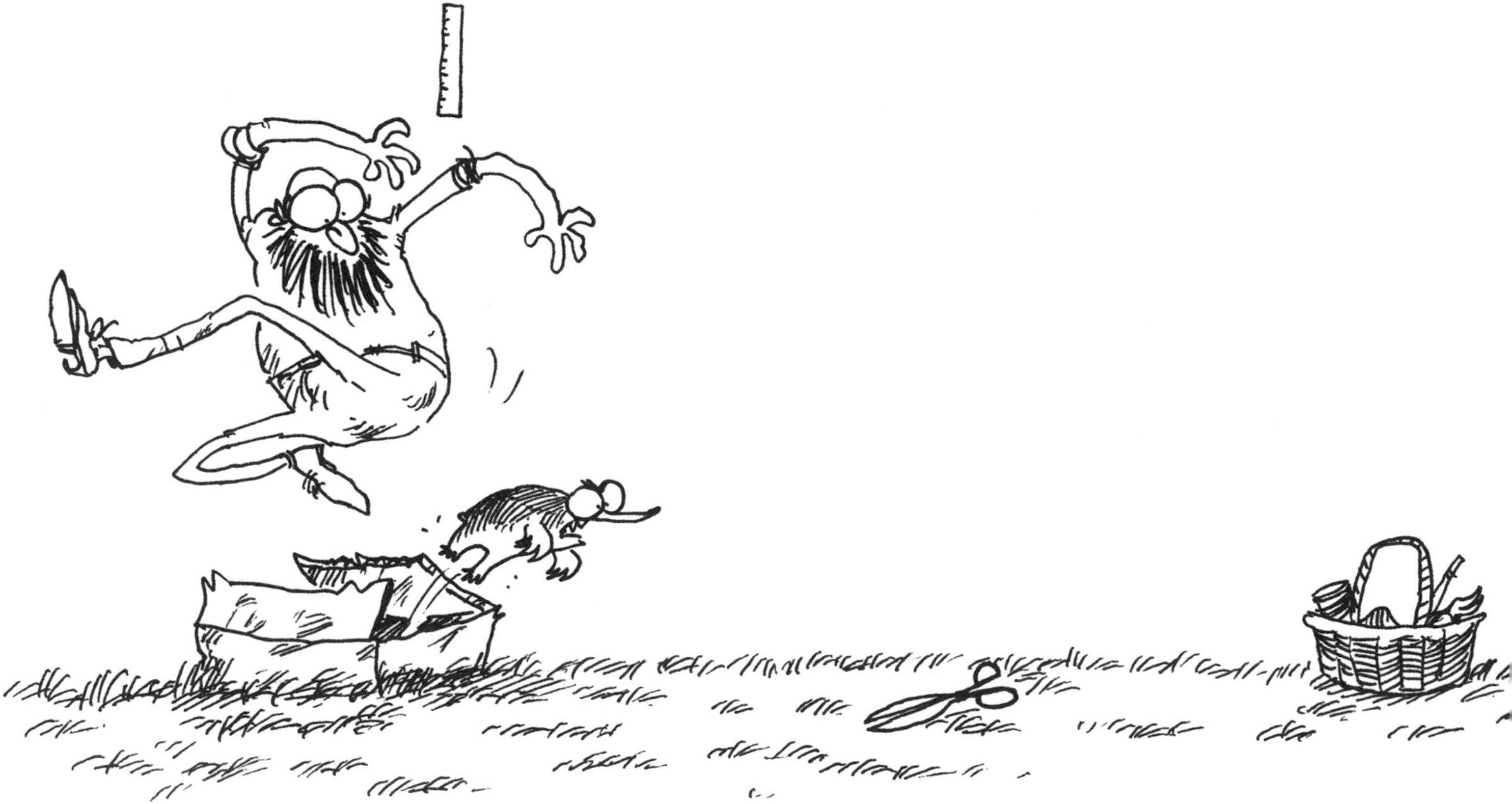

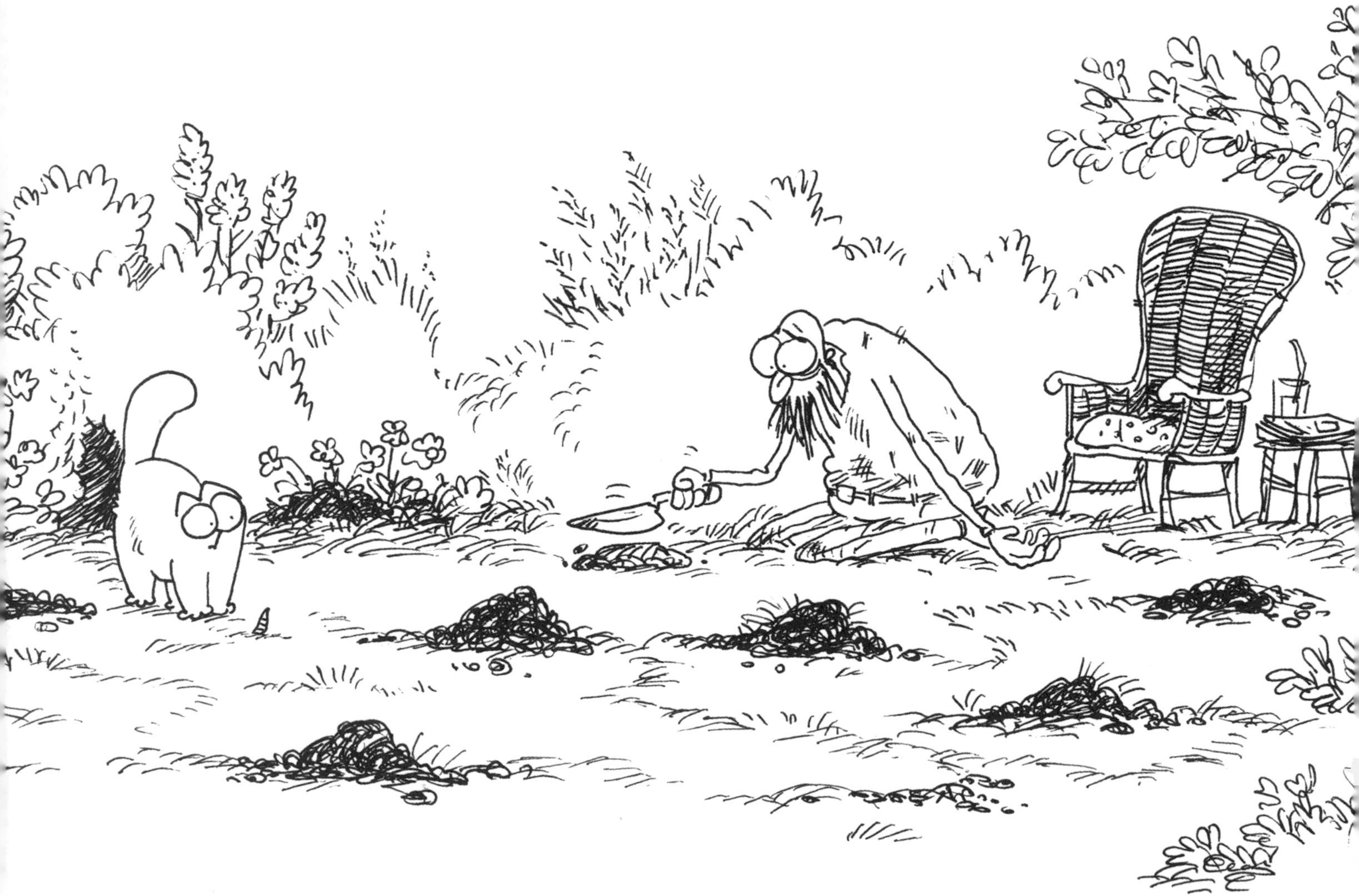

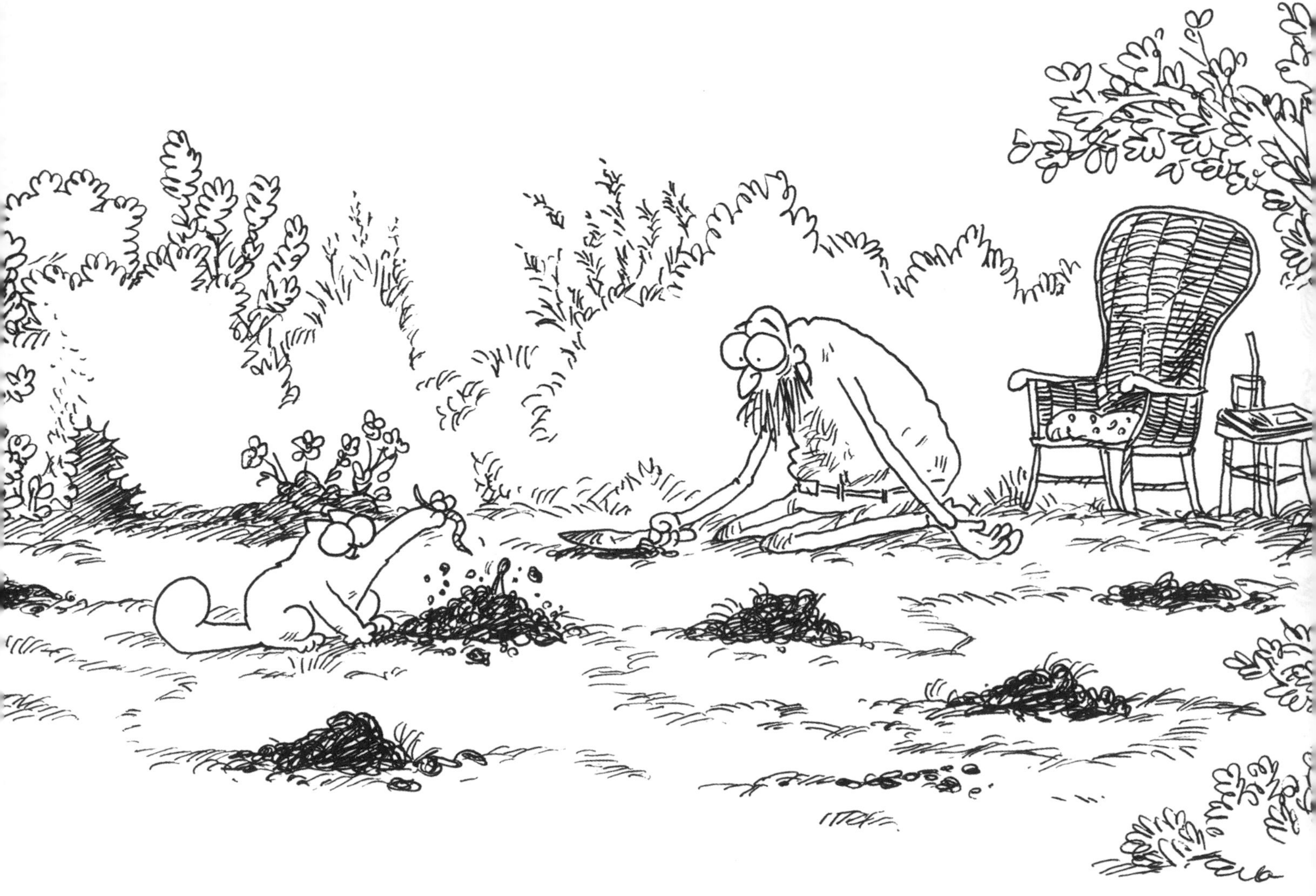

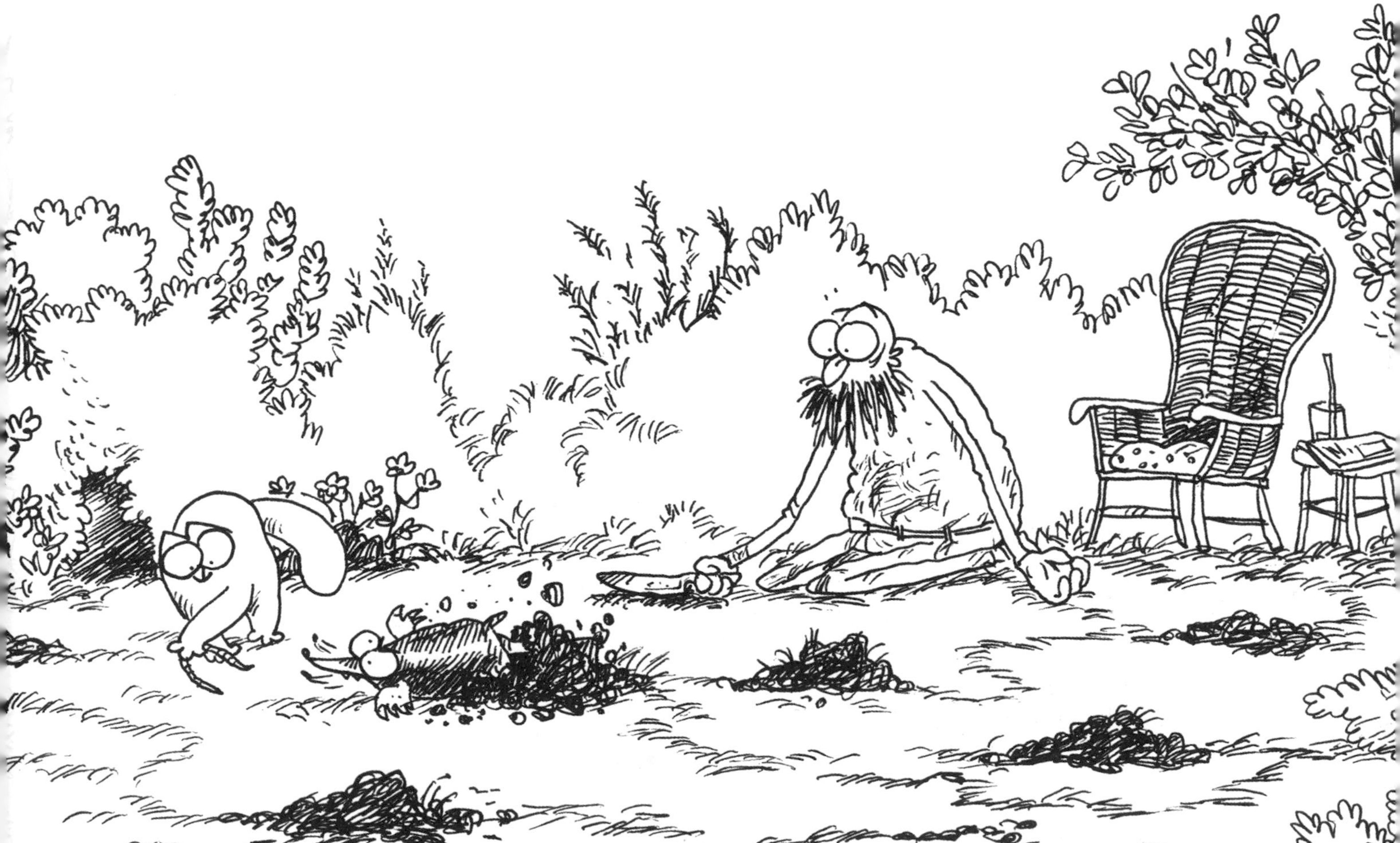

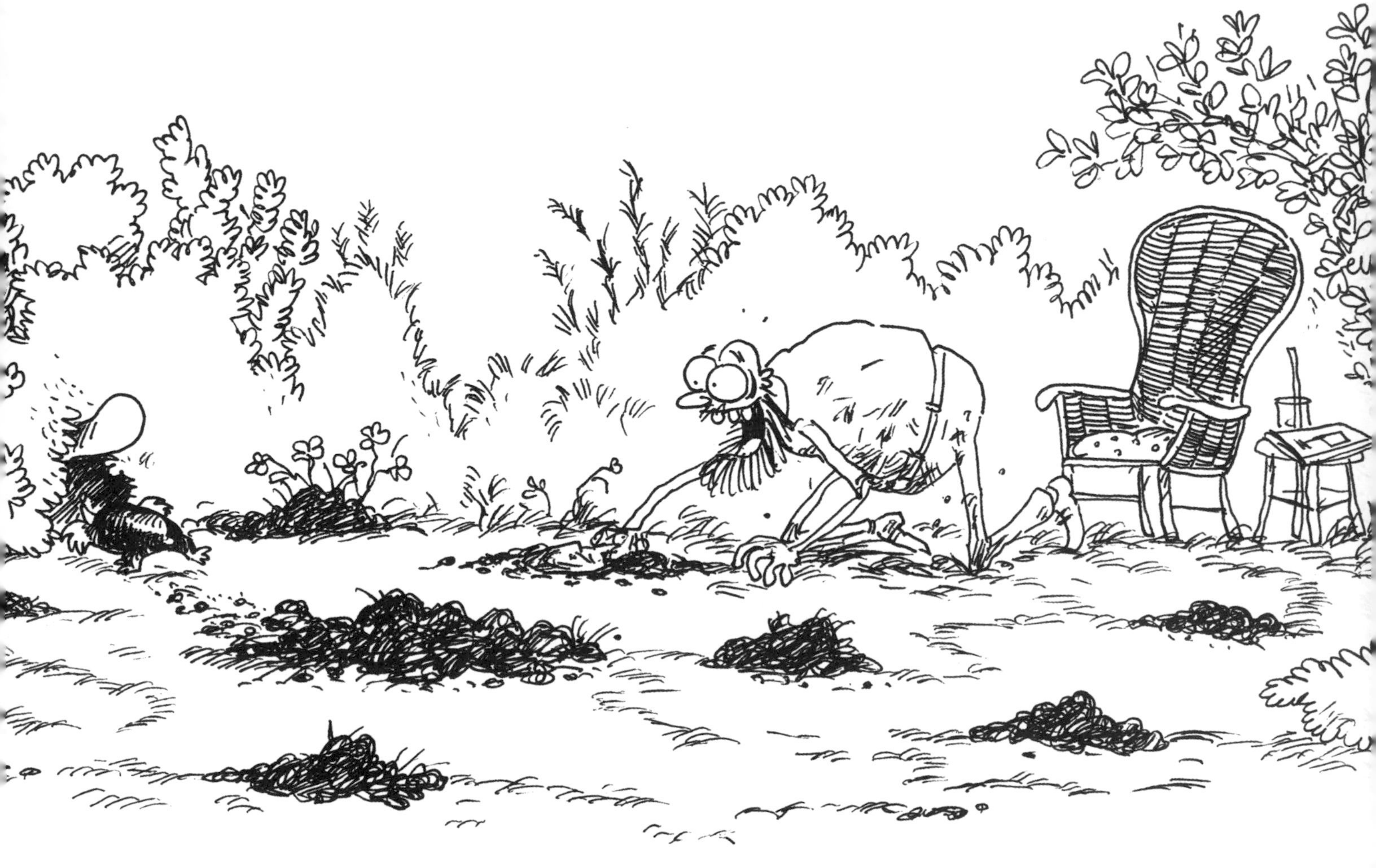

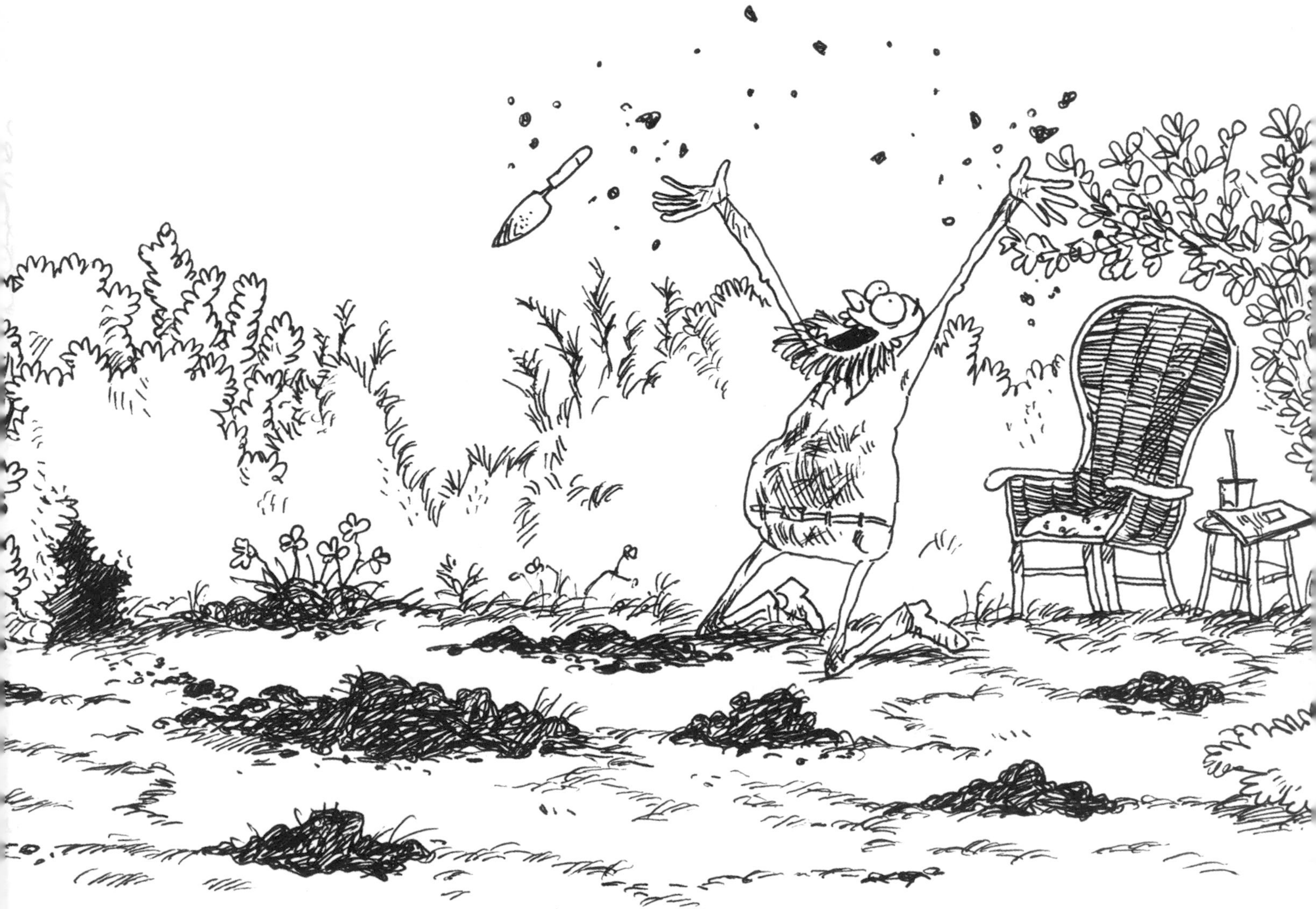

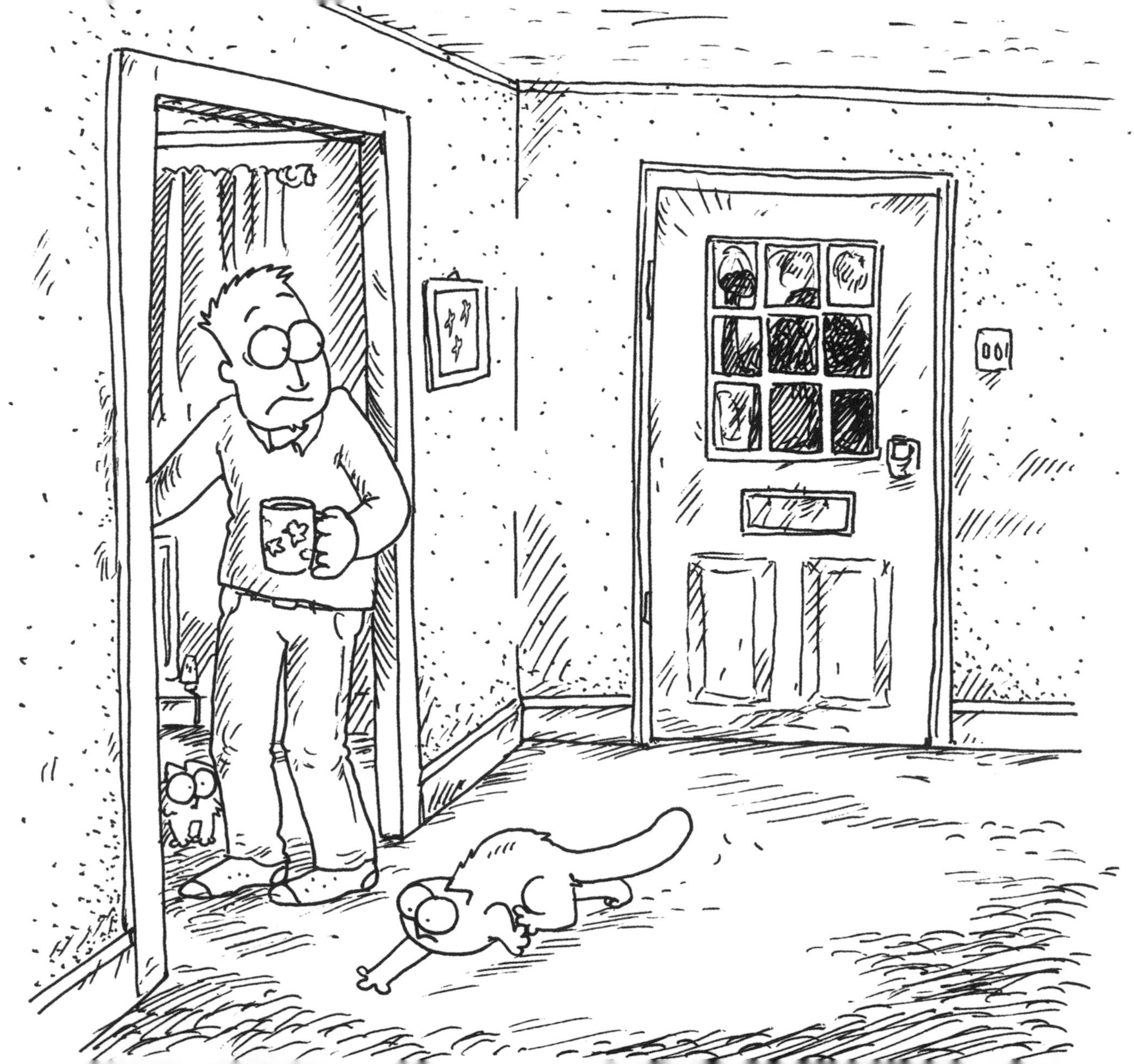

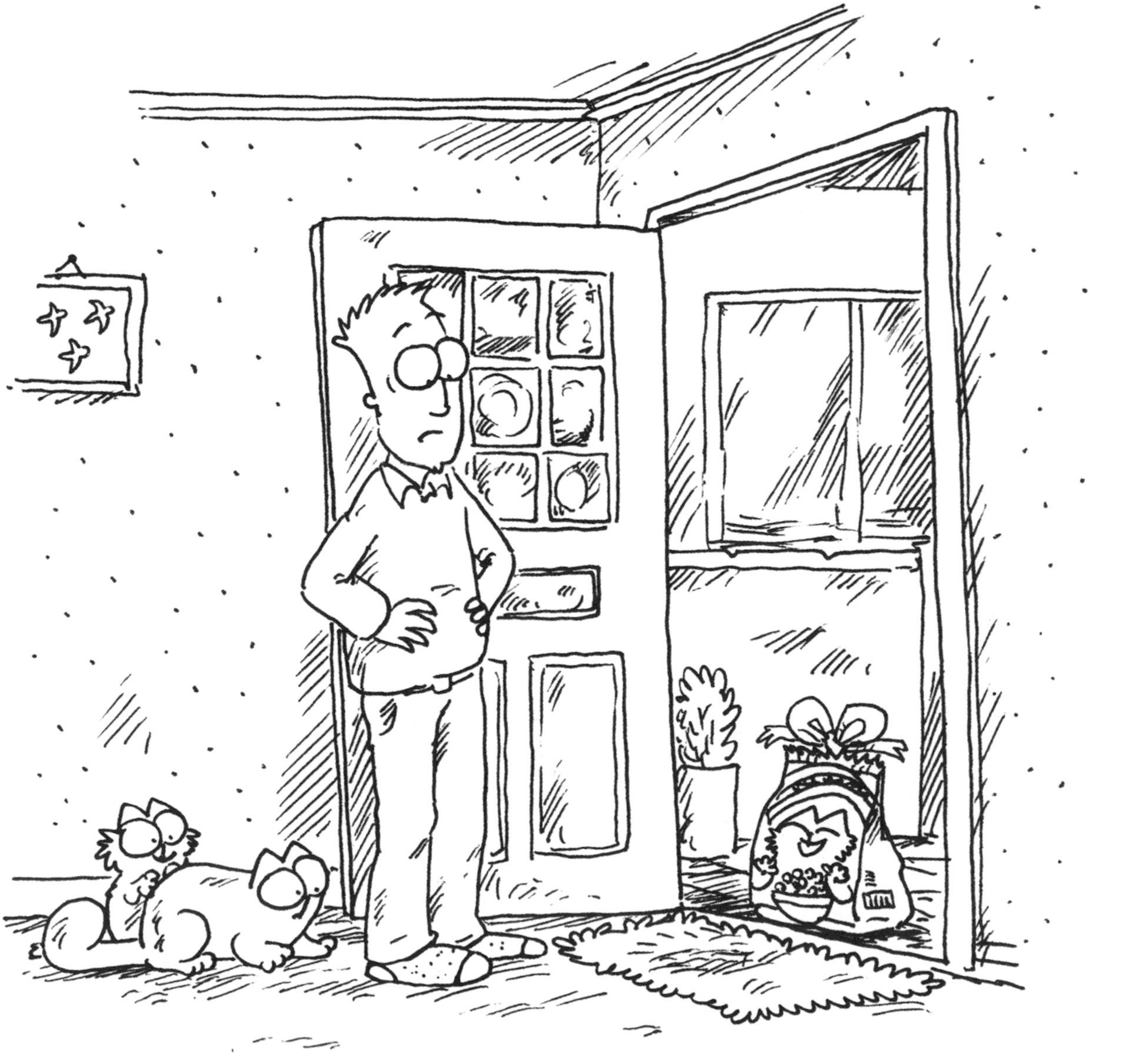

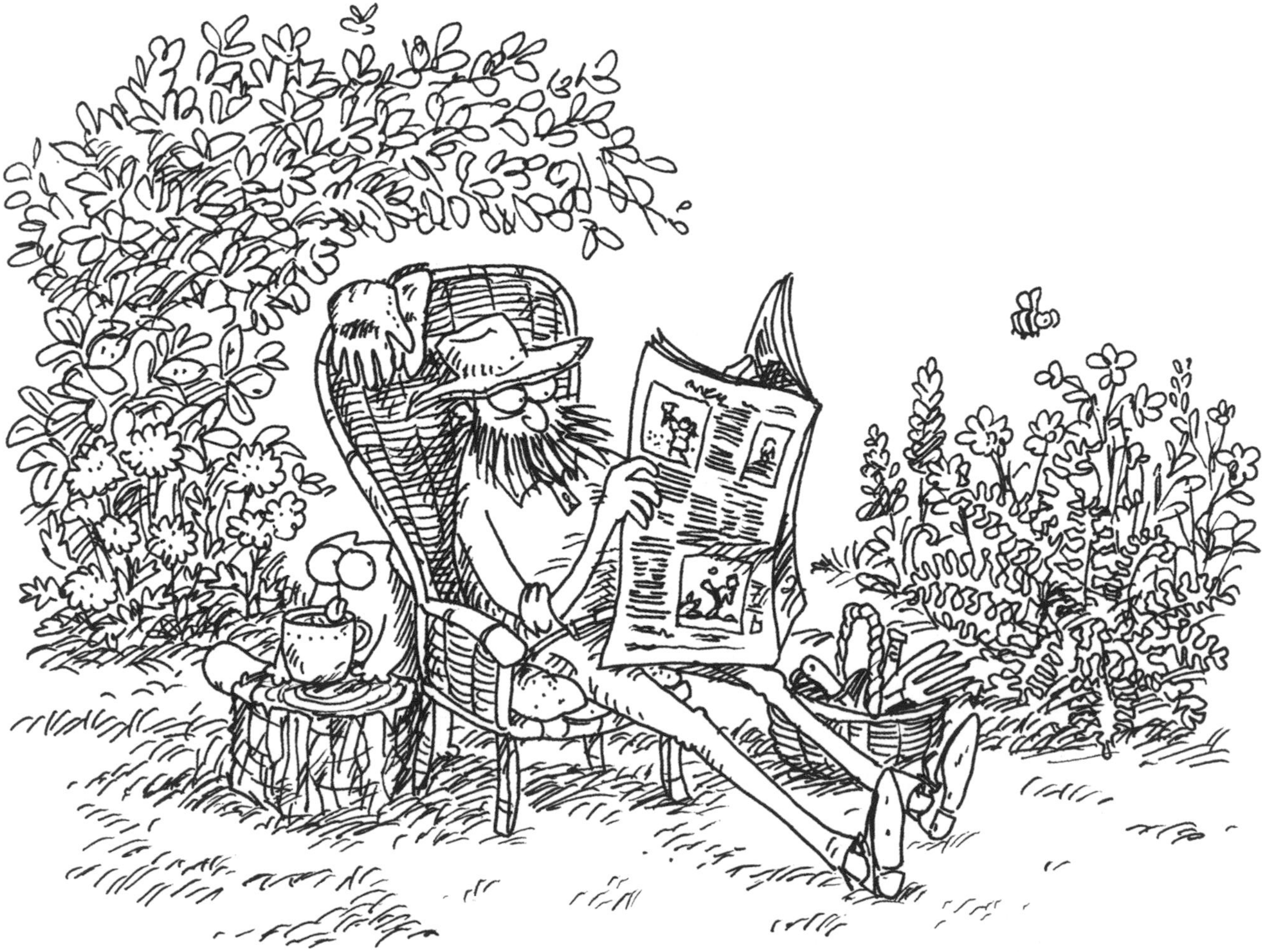

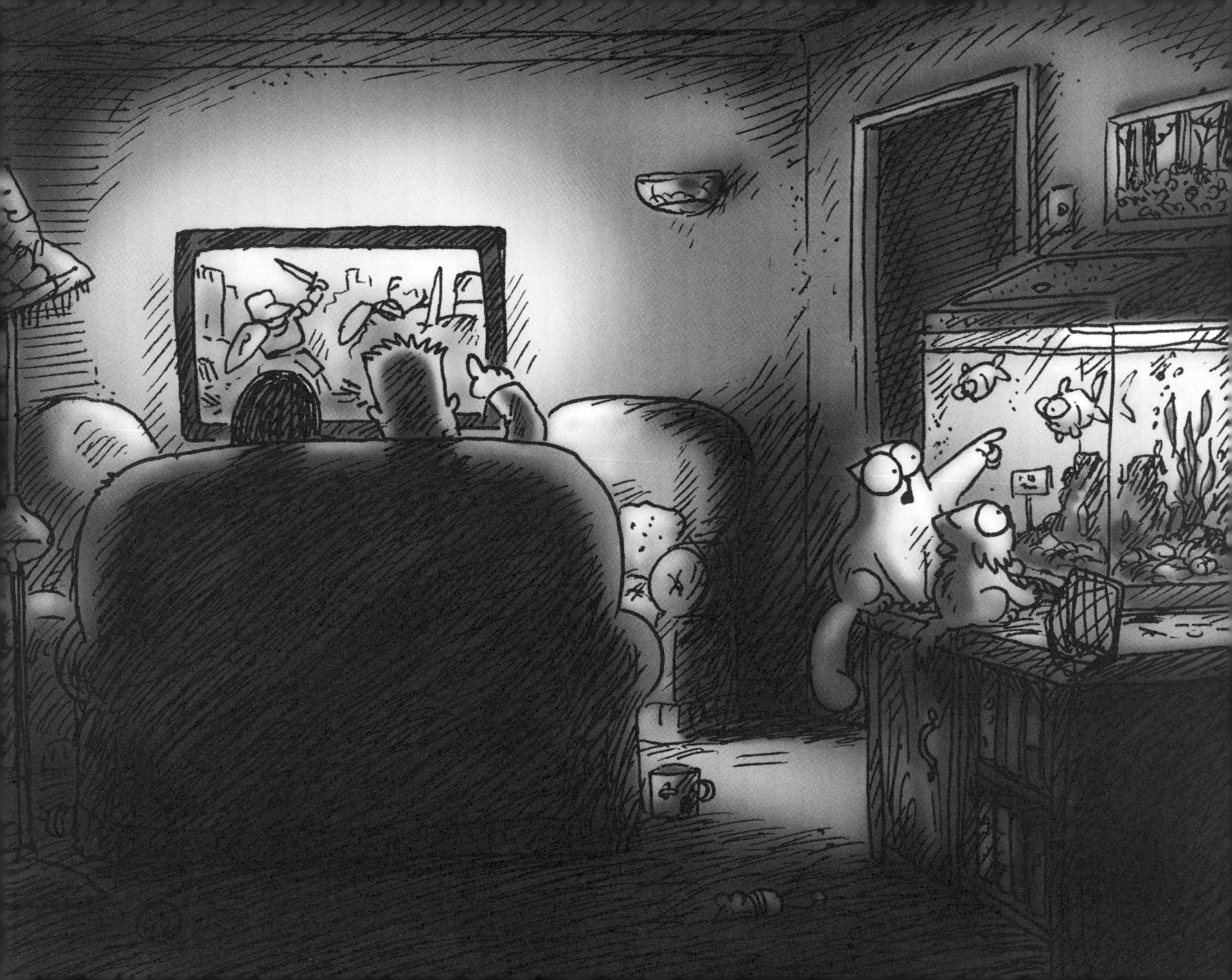

Acknowledgements

Zoë Tofield, Edwin Eckford, Liza Nechaeva,
Christine Dunsby, Louise Brownlow,
Jenny Lord and the Canongate team, Robert Kirby,
Mike Bell, Nigel Pay, Daniel Greaves,
a big thank you to my Simon's Cat crew,
and of course my four moggy muses –
Jess, Maisy, Hugh and Teddy.

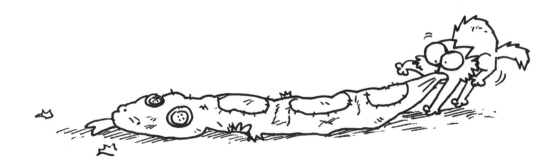

For all your Simon's Cat goodies, check out the webshop
at www.simonscat.com

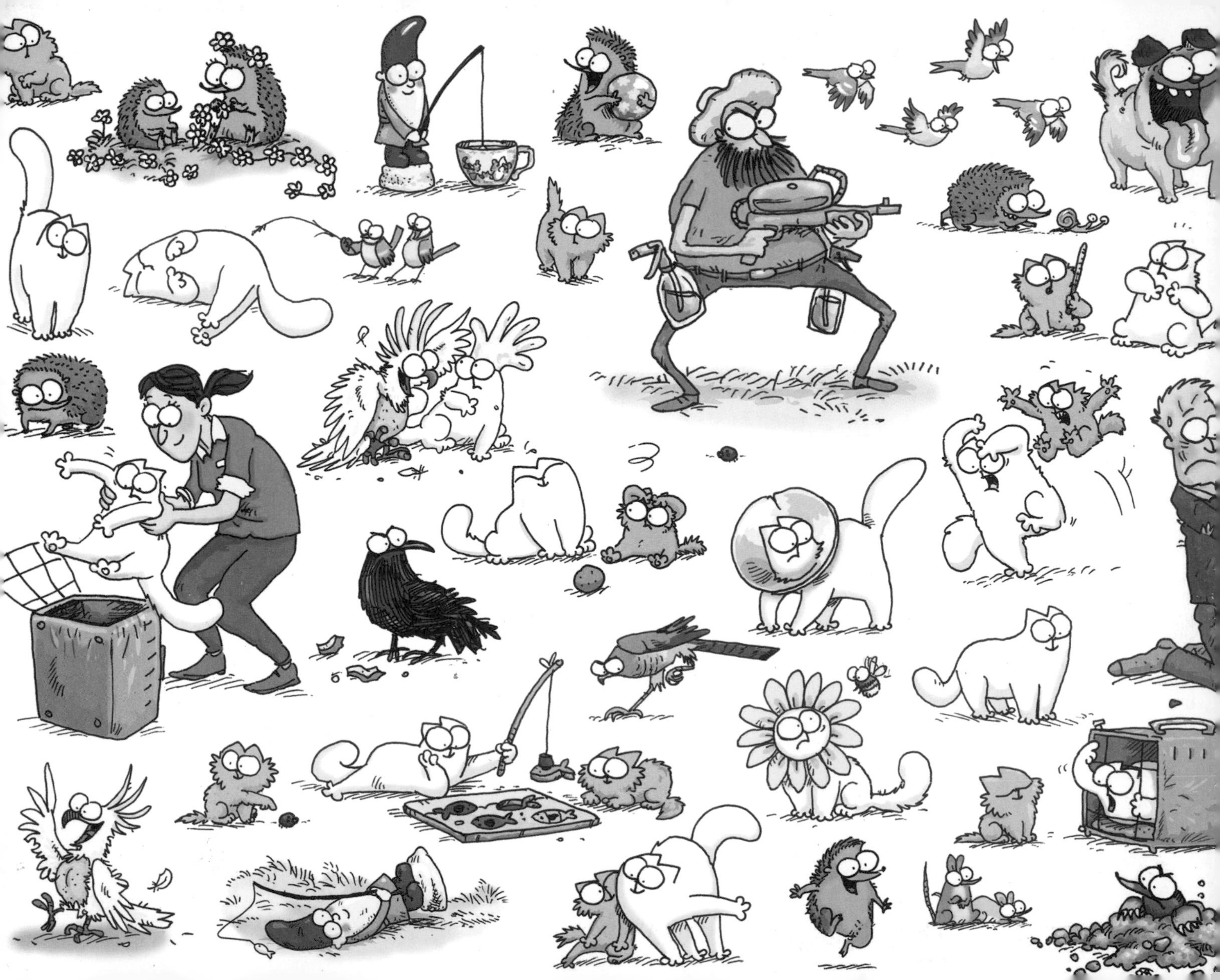